An Economic History of England
Founder Editor: T. S. ASHTON

1870-1939

An Economic History of England
Founder Editor: T. S. ASHTON

In preparation
A. R. Bridbury: THE MEDIEVAL PERIOD
F. J. Fisher: THE 16TH AND 17TH CENTURIES
A. H. John: 1800–1870
M. E. Falkus: 1939–1964

Already published
T. S. Ashton: THE 18TH CENTURY

An Economic History of England 1870-1939

WILLIAM ASHWORTH

*Professor of Economic and Social History
in the University of Bristol*

METHUEN & CO LTD
11 NEW FETTER LANE   LONDON EC4P 4EE

First published 1960, by
Methuen & Co. Ltd, 11 New Fetter Lane, London EC4P 4EE
Reprinted 1963, 1965, 1967 and 1969
SBN 416 57900 0
First published as a University Paperback 1972
SBN 416 57910 8
© *1960 by William Ashworth*
Printed offset in Great Britain by
The Camelot Press Ltd, London and Southampton

Distributed in the USA by
HARPER & ROW PUBLISHERS, INC.
BARNES & NOBLE IMPORT DIVISION

Preface

IN the preface to his volume on the eighteenth century Professor T. S. Ashton, the editor of the series to which this book belongs, made plain the common objectives of the authors and the circumstances in which their work developed. He added that they followed their own individual ways and did not attempt uniformity of treatment. Here it is necessary for me to comment on no more than the ways in which I have slightly deviated from the general plan of the series.

The chief difference is in the area concerned. Though the object of the series is to survey the economic history of England, it is, for recent times, often impracticable and oftener unrealistic to look at England alone. Much of the evidence, especially the statistical evidence, is available only for Britain or the United Kingdom as a whole. In its main outlines the present volume is therefore a British rather than an English economic history. But I have not attempted to discuss the distinctive characteristics given to some economic activities outside England by differences of law or social organization. For instance, I have not been concerned with the important ways in which Scottish agriculture has differed from English because of differences in the law of land and property. I have regarded Ireland as being outside my province, except where it is impracticable to disentangle the Irish constituent of figures relating to the United Kingdom. Wherever there might be doubt, I have tried to make clear in the text whether the information I have used refers to England, England and Wales, Britain or the United Kingdom.

The economic evidence of the years since 1870 is too abundant for any individual to survey more than a select fraction of it, yet it is marked by many gaps and much imprecision. For both reasons it would be impossible for any general economic history of the period to be definitive, even if an author were not bound by his own limitations. The present book claims to do no more than give one man's estimate of the most likely reasons for a course of events in which what is known for certain has to be filled out with his own judgment of probabilities. I have, however, tried to assist the reader, who may seek either greater certainty or a different interpretation, by drawing attention, where it seems appropriate, to the nature of the available evidence and, without attempting a large bibliography, by giving in the footnotes enough documentation to enable him to begin fuller study of any of the major topics I have touched.

One other limitation should be noted. Like other volumes in the series this one is intended to be an economic, rather than an economic and social, history. I have, of course, been at pains to describe and heavily stress some of the ways in which social and political matters altered the course of economic affairs. But the central theme is economic change and its causes. Social history is treated only in relation to that; it is not elaborated for its own sake as an equally central second theme.

A work ranging over as many topics as the present book can be written only because the author has been accumulating debts to others for many years; debts to those who were formally responsible for teaching him, to those from whom he learned when he was nominally teaching them, and to those whose writings preceded his own. More immediately, I am indebted to Professor Ashton and to Professor F. J. Fisher, both of whom have read the whole book in typescript and enabled me to correct some of my errors. I have also had the advantage of discussion with Dr A. H. John, who read part of my book which most closely links with his own projected volume. My debt to Mr H. L. Beales, with whom I had at one time hoped to collaborate in writing this volume, has continued to grow through countless discussions as the years go by. To all these, and to others from whose conversation I have drawn more stimulus than they ever realized, I express my gratitude.

University of Bristol   W. ASHWORTH
January, 1960

Contents

Tables

PART ONE

1870-1914

England's position is not that of a great landed proprietor, with an assured revenue, and only subject to an occasional loss of crops or hostile depredations. It is that of a great merchant, who by immense skill and capital has gained the front rank, and developed an enormous commerce, but has to support an ever-increasing host of dependents. He has to encounter the risks of trade, and to face jealous rivals, and can only depend on continued good judgment and fortune, and the help of God, to maintain himself and his successors in the foremost place among the nations of the world.

DUDLEY BAXTER (1868)

CHAPTER ONE

The Characteristics of the Mid-Victorian Economy

MID-VICTORIAN England is by now far enough distant in time for it to have acquired certain standard descriptions, intended to epitomize its economic character. Unfortunately for those who seek enlightenment some of the descriptions are not, at first glance, easy to reconcile with each other. 'The great Victorian boom', 'the good years', and even more gilded labels have been attached to the third quarter of the nineteenth century. But then even a summary account has to move forward only a very few years, recognize that a falling cost of living was easing the condition of the masses, and yet draw attention to 'the submerged tenth' (or larger fraction) and refer to the hundreds of thousands living 'below the poverty line', i.e. without the means to buy enough necessities to keep themselves physically healthy. It seems a strange kind of good years that had such a state of affairs at the end of the sequence; perhaps 'good' really means 'better' or 'less bad'.

The historian whose task is to try to find truth through (or in spite of) this seeming paradox is nowadays expected to find his most telling information among the economic statistics which, by the last third of the nineteenth century, were becoming more and more voluminous. If he is wise he will draw on them abundantly but will not forget to apply to them that element of scepticism which should be one permanent constituent of his professional character. Some statistics are nearly true, some are approximate guesses disguised as exact knowledge, some are merely the shortest kind of short story; and some in all three categories are meaningless. For the third quarter of the nineteenth century there is excellent quantitative material about population, prices and foreign trade in merchandise, and abundant, though somewhat less exact, information about the occupational distribution of the people. The course of wage-rates in many important occupations is well documented, but there remain so many people about whose precise earnings little is known that quantitative generalizations about the national trend of wages or earnings are bound to rest on more unproved assumptions than should underlie any good index. Plenty of quantitative material also exists on output, investment and income, but attempts to derive series of national figures from it are still less reliable, though not necessarily useless. For some particular activities and particular groups of people the statistical information on these subjects is probably an excellent guide to what was happening. But for the country as a whole there are many gaps. Many things went unrecorded or falsely recorded, sometimes because nobody asked about them at the time, sometimes because those making returns were interested in evading taxation, sometimes because the recording of accurate information appeared too troublesome or genuinely impossible. Consequently, all quantitative statements about the absolute amount and rate of growth of the income, production, and investment of the whole nation at this time are no more than approximations subject to a large margin of error.

This is a little unfortunate because, if they are accurately known, nothing provides a more useful brief guide to the condition of a nation's economy than its output and income. As it happens, however, it seems justifiable to pay serious attention to some of the mid-Victorian statistics on these subjects because they indicate changes so considerable that, even if they have been appreciably exaggerated by the defects of the basic information, they must still have been of fundamental importance.

For the year 1867 the contemporary statistician, Dudley Baxter, who had investigated the subject more thoroughly and carefully than any of his nineteenth-century predecessors, calculated the national income of England and Wales to be £661,929,000, an average of £68 for every person with a separate income (whether earned or unearned) or £32 per head of population. The income of the entire United Kingdom he put at £814,110,000, i.e. £59 for every person with a separate income or £27 per head of population.[1] Since, however, half the total income went to rather less than one-tenth of the income-receivers the great majority of people had incomes far below these general averages. Later investigators have not been able to improve much on Baxter's work. If anything, he probably under-estimated a little both the amount of the national income and the inequality of its distribution, since he failed to allow for the widespread under-statement of income by those paying tax on it. But his enquiries

---

[1] R. Dudley Baxter, *National Income* (1868), pp. 52 and 64.

suggested clearly enough that by this time the nation was producing an amount which, evenly spread, would have provided very modest comfort, and no more, for everyone. Since, however, the distribution of income was what it was, the country was still far from producing enough to give a reasonable, healthy standard of living to the mass of the population.

Other investigators, using information about wage-rates and about the amount of income assessed to income tax, have suggested that in the third quarter of the nineteenth century the growth of income was gathering momentum. The gross amount assessed to income tax in the United Kingdom grew, in fact, as follows:[1]

Year ended 5 April	Income (£mn.)	Increase % over preceding date
1845	264	—
1855	308	17
1865	396	28
1875	571	44

Only for the first decade, when the value of money fell considerably and therefore offset most of the increase in money incomes, did changes in the price level do much to alter the trend of these figures. A general price index, based on 1900, averaged 119·0 for 1844-45, 135·5 for 1854-55, 137·5 for 1864-65, and 132·0 for 1874-75.[2] At the prices of 1874-75 the assessed income would thus be £292 million for 1844-45, £296 million for 1854-55 and £380 million for 1864-65. Imperfect information about wage-rates suggests that by the eighteen-sixties those below the income tax exemption limit were also sharing, though less fully, in the more rapid growth of income: an index of the real wages of those in full work stood, with 1850 as base year, at 95·5 for 1854-55, 117·0 for 1864-65 and 134·0 for 1874-75.[3]

---

[1] L. Levi, 'On the Reconstruction of the Income and Property Tax' in *Journ. of the Stat. Socy.*, XXXVII (1874), 177 and R. Giffen, *Economic Inquiries and Studies* (1901), II, 101. The income for 1845 has been raised by £20 mn. to compensate for the non-application of the income tax to Ireland at this date. The addition of £30 mn. for this purpose, used by Giffen in other papers, seems too large. Irish taxable incomes in 1854-55, the first year of the Irish income tax, totalled £21 mn.

[2] W. T. Layton and G. Crowther, *An Introduction to the Study of Prices* (3rd edn., 1938), p. 237. These are wholesale prices. There is no satisfactory retail price index for the period. A rather rough one, beginning in 1850, shows considerable differences from these figures and is, for instance, appreciably *lower* in 1864-65 than in 1854-55 or 1874-75 (*Ibid.*, p. 273).

[3] *Ibid.*, p. 273.

And the increase of incomes was a good deal more than commensurate with the increase of population: from 1851 to 1861 the population of the United Kingdom grew by 10·2 per cent, that of England and Wales alone by 11·9 per cent; between 1861 and 1871 the figures were 11·9 per cent and 13·2 per cent respectively. Even when the many deficiencies of some of these figures are admitted—when it is recognized, for example, that part of the very rapid growth of taxable income between 1865 and 1875 is probably best explained by a checking of tax evasion[1]—it still seems plausible to look on the period from the Crimean War to the early eighteen-seventies as one of striking economic growth, in contrast with the years immediately preceding it.[2]

It could be, of course, that in the mid-Victorian years relatively more attention than before was being given to activities which would help to expand incomes quickly and relatively less to making economic provision for the more distant future at the expense of a slower immediate growth of income; but this appears unlikely. Figures of accumulated wealth and of the value of additions to capital have sometimes been stated in very precise form, but no sensible person would believe in their exactitude. Nevertheless, there is little doubt that the level of investment in the mid-Victorian years was generally high and that much of the new wealth that was created was likely to yield its full benefits only gradually. Baxter estimated, on the basis of the income tax assessments, that in the ten years up to 1865 the capital of the United Kingdom was increasing in value by an average of £124 million per year,[3] which was probably about one-sixth of the national income. Giffen believed that the same returns implied a rather larger increase of capital than this.[4] Some of the increase may have been an increase in valuation without any

[1] For 1864 the Board of Inland Revenue estimated evasion at 52 per cent of the recorded Schedule D assessments; for 1880 Sir Arthur Bowley put it at 25 per cent of the recorded Schedule D assessments. (C. Clark, *National Income and Outlay* (1937), p. 229.)

[2] Contemporary estimates of national income, analysed by Phyllis Deane ('Contemporary Estimates of National Income in the . . . Nineteenth Century' in *Econ. Hist. Rev.*, 2nd series, VIII (1955-56), 339-54 and IX (1956-57), 451-61) show the contrast less strongly. Miss Deane derives from them a rate of growth of real income per head of 13·4 per cent per decade for 1822-46 and 14·1 per cent per decade for 1841-67. But even these figures show stagnation in the late 'thirties and 'forties and rapid growth in the 'fifties. (*Loc. cit.*, IX, 459-61.)

[3] Baxter, *op. cit.*, p. 97.

[4] R. Giffen, 'The Progress of the Working Classes in the last half century' in his *Essays in Finance* (1886), II, 401.

physical improvement in the assets concerned—in effect, a capitalization of pure economic rent—but most of it represented a net addition
to investment. Indeed, the most rapid increases were in capital assets
whose value was not likely to be much affected by changes of the
former kind. Giffen, attempting to value all types of capital at different
dates, suggested that there was an increase of 40 per cent in the value
of the capital of the United Kingdom between 1865 and 1875.[1] Mr
Douglas, using similar methods but leaving out of account those
items (such as lands and houses) whose value might vary a good deal
independently of new investment in them, estimated that the other
types of capital increased by 51 per cent in the same period.[2] A
glance forward in time strengthens the impression that this was a
most remarkable period of capital formation. Professor Cairncross
points out that, if the figures are accepted, a higher proportion of the
national income was being saved and invested in 1872-74 than at any
subsequent time.[3] That much of the new investment was providing
for the more distant as well as the immediate future is suggested
by the uses to which it was put. Of the £2,400 million added to the
capital of the United Kingdom between 1865 and 1875 nearly a
quarter was placed abroad, mostly in schemes whose economic effect
was likely to increase steadily over the years, a sixth was in houses and
other buildings, and a tenth was in railways at home.[4] The mid-
Victorian generation certainly did not secure its expanding income
through neglecting to provide for its successors.

It is its astonishingly dynamic quality that is the outstanding
economic characteristic of the mid-Victorian period. It was not a
good time in the sense that it brought to most people a reasonable
degree of security and comfort. It was not free from sharp interruptions to trade, production and employment. But if the accumulation
of wealth and its application to further accumulation is taken as the
criterion of economic success then this was a very successful age, and
it is useful to enquire what made its success possible.

[1] R. Giffen, *The Growth of Capital* (1889), p. 43.

[2] P. H. Douglas, 'An estimate of the growth of capital in the United Kingdom,
1865-1909' in *Journ. of Econ. and Business Hist.*, II (1929-30), 675.

[3] A. K. Cairncross, *Home and Foreign Investment 1870-1913* (1953), p. 198.

[4] Giffen, *op. cit.*, p. 43. The estimates of the way in which total wealth was
divided among different types of capital were very rough; in particular Giffen was
not able to distinguish very clearly what investment income was derived from
assets abroad. The most recent estimate of the increase in British foreign investment
in these ten years puts it at £575 mn. (A. H. Imlah, *Economic Elements in the Pax
Britannica* (1958), pp. 72-3.)

Fundamentally, what mattered most was the ability to concentrate on meeting more efficiently a fairly narrow range of universal human needs. The mid-Victorian world was one in which most people, even in Britain, had little to spend except on the basic necessities of food, clothing and shelter, and a country seeking to expand its economic activity could do so to any great extent only if it could provide these things, or the equipment for producing and distributing them, more cheaply and more abundantly; and that is what the British economy mainly relied on for much of the nineteenth century. The number of manufacturing activities in which the methods and efficiency of production were utterly transformed by mechanical innovation before the middle of the century was small, but it included one group—the textiles—and within that group one industry in particular —cotton—for whose products the demand at home and abroad was enormous and ever-increasing. The transfer of more capital and labour to this group of activities, in which Britain excelled all other countries, was one of the key features of the development of the economy. To maintain and augment the supply of other basic necessities whose production was not aided by such sweeping technical changes—food, garments and houses are the obvious examples —required the retention of a high proportion of the rest of the available labour for this purpose. This need, however, was modified in two ways. Though they were less impressive than those in the textile industries, there were in other basic activities, notably agriculture, changes in organization and technique, made effective by additional investment, that made possible some savings in the use of labour, relative to the amount of the output. And, in addition, the growth of exports permitted some increase in the supply of elementary needs from imports instead of home production. Thus a minor but increasing proportion of the food consumed in Britain was raised abroad and much of the material used in building the rapidly increasing number of houses was imported.

Britain's economic activity in the mid-nineteenth century was therefore immediately dependent on three things above all else: the concentration of a high proportion of the nation's efforts on the production of basic necessities; the achievement, through mechanical innovation, investment and new forms of organization, of greatly increased efficiency in the production of some of these; and the expansion of foreign trade. But underlying these characteristics were certain other influences of great importance. One was the expansion and increased efficiency of those industries, especially coal-mining and iron manufacture, whose products were used by the great export and consumer goods industries. The other was the improvement in the means of distribution, among which the changes in transport were outstanding. Without these, industry could never have secured the advantages of local specialization to anything like the extent that was actually realized, the growth of towns must have been retarded and the expansion of foreign trade greatly reduced. Better transport made it worth while to apply productive innovations more fully and at the same time did something to offset the technical stagnation which persisted in many industries. Before 1850, indeed, the contribution made to technological advance by the civil engineer was far more pervasive than that by the mechanical engineer. It was not machines but houses, roads, canals, docks, harbour works and railways, built for the most part with few mechanical aids, that embodied most of the reproducible fixed capital of this early industrial age, and on these to a great extent the industrial and commercial supremacy of Britain rested.

The best available illustrations of the way in which the country set about earning its living are those which may be derived from the occupational distribution of the people and the commodity structure of foreign trade. In England and Wales in 1851, 20·9 per cent of the occupied population was engaged in agriculture, 11·1 per cent in textile manufacture, 10·3 per cent in making articles of clothing, 5·5 per cent in the building trades, and 4·0 per cent in mining. This small number of productive activities thus provided rather more than half the total employment. Manufacturing industries other than textiles and clothing employed 11·3 per cent of the total, i.e. hardly more than the textile industries alone and a smaller proportion than was engaged in domestic service. Among these other manufacturing activities the metallurgical industries, which employed 3·5 per cent of the total, were the largest group. Transport employed 4·1 per cent of the total.[1] In Scotland the distribution of occupations was on the same general lines, but with an even heavier preponderance of a

[1] C. Booth, *Occupations of the People: England, Scotland, Ireland, 1841-81*, (1886), p. 68. Booth tried to maintain a uniform classification of occupations throughout the period with which he was dealing. Since the census authorities repeatedly changed their classification this compelled him to rearrange many of the census figures and also to make various estimates, e.g. of how many were engaged in making and how many in selling certain articles, when the census tables lumped the two together. The percentages cited are therefore slightly different from those which would be calculated direct from the census tables.

few large industries; thus agriculture employed 22·7 per cent, textiles 18·8 per cent, clothing 8·4 per cent, and other manufactures only 9·3 per cent.[1]

It would be illuminating if similar figures of the distribution of capital among different uses at home could be produced, but, in similar detail, that would be possible only in a work of fiction. The most that can be said is that, in terms of market value, land was the largest single item among the nation's capital assets; that the man-made fixed capital consisted mainly of buildings and constructional work, devoted chiefly to residential purposes and to transport and other public utility services; and that most of the capital used in manufacture was circulating capital embodied in stocks of raw material, work in progress and finished goods, and in cash for the payment of wages.[2] It is probable that numbers employed were at this time a reasonable indication of the relative importance of most types of productive activity, but that they failed to show adequately the importance of transport, mining and one or two manufacturing industries, such as iron making, because of the much higher proportion of capital to labour used in these.

A glance at the figures of foreign trade immediately reveals the importance of textiles to the country's economy. In the early eighteen-fifties textiles provided about 60 per cent of the exports of home-produced goods and cotton goods alone provided two-thirds of the textile exports.[3] But it is also clear that even with this great industry dominating foreign markets and with its efforts supplemented by those of other industries of less importance, merchandise was insufficient to pay for all that was wanted from abroad. Professor Imlah's reconstruction of the balance of payments, admittedly a little speculative but as near to the truth as we are likely to get, suggests that between 1851 and 1855 there was an average annual deficit of £27·5 million on merchandise trade and that there had been deficits of similar magnitude since the middle eighteen-thirties and smaller ones for at least twenty years before that. But these deficits were more than offset by 'invisible' exports, of which the chief were the earnings of shipping. For 1851-55 Professor Imlah put shipping earnings at £18·7 million, and by this time they were being usefully supplemented by

---

[1] Booth, *op. cit.*, p. 72.

[2] Giffen, *op. cit.*, p. 43, gives estimates for 1865 which suggest that, of the total national capital, land then represented 30 per cent, houses and other messuages 17 per cent, farm capital 10 per cent and railways 7 per cent.

[3] J. H. Clapham, *An Economic History of Modern Britain* (1926-38), II, 228.

the interest on foreign investments (£11·7 million) and by the profit obtained in the performance of trading and other services abroad (£11·9 million).[1] The significance of these earnings is best appreciated by comparing them with those obtained by the largest exporting industry: in the same years the average annual value of exports of cotton yarn and piece goods was £31·8 million.[2] In return for these exports Britain obtained principally raw materials for its manufactures and building, especially raw cotton and timber, staple tropical foodstuffs, notably sugar and tea, and a gradually increasing proportion of its bread grains, together with a diversity of smaller items.[3]

An economy of the kind indicated by this brief analysis had been established very rapidly in the eighteenth and early nineteenth centuries. Its main features were almost as characteristic of 1830 as of 1850 and many of them persisted, though with some modifications, in the eighteen-seventies. In view of this, it seems a little odd that the mid-Victorian period should have been more expansive and dynamic than the years which preceded it. There is too much evidence for the difference to be dismissed as an illusion. Are, then, the modifications of the 'fifties and 'sixties, slight though they appear at first glance, sufficient to explain the difference? Or was this new industrial economy slow to yield its fruits, by reason either of its own inherent characteristics or of unfavourable external circumstances?

Certainly the British people continued to concentrate the greater part of their efforts on the same basic activities as before, but not to quite the same extent. In 1871, 14·2 per cent of the occupied population of England and Wales was engaged in agriculture, 9·3 per cent in textile manufacture, 8·5 per cent in making articles of clothing, 6·3 per cent in the building trades and 4·5 per cent in mining; these fundamental jobs which twenty years earlier had employed 51·8 per cent of the occupied population now employed only 42·8 per cent. The proportions engaged in manufacturing industries other than textiles and clothing had risen to 13·8 per cent, including 4·1 per cent in the metallurgical industries, and those in transport to 4·9 per

---

[1] Imlah, *op. cit.*, p. 72.

[2] T. Ellison, *The Cotton Trade of Great Britain* (1886), table no. 2.

[3] In the later eighteen-fifties 55 per cent of retained imports (by value) consisted of raw materials and 39 per cent of foodstuffs; rather more than half the imported raw materials were for the textile industries, and of the imported food just over a third consisted of grain and flour and nearly a quarter consisted of sugar and other tropical produce. (W. Schlote, *British Overseas Trade from 1700 to the 1930s* (1952), pp. 53, 58 and 65).

cent.[1] In Scotland the trend of change had been similar; there, in 1871, agriculture employed 17·3 per cent of the occupied population, textiles 14·2 per cent, clothing 6·6 per cent, and other manufacturing industries 13·9 per cent.[2] At the same time, as has already been emphasized, a rapidly increasing amount of capital was being created and used, and its distribution among activities seems to have been changing significantly. While Giffen estimated that the capital of the United Kingdom increased by 40 per cent between 1865 and 1875, the income tax returns showed a rise of only 8 per cent in the value of lands and 8 per cent in the value of farmers' capital, whereas the value of ironworks rose by 314 per cent, of mines by 195 per cent, and of railways by 58 per cent.[3] Moreover, in industry as a whole the proportion of fixed to circulating capital was almost certainly increasing.

The most important among these changes were the decline in the proportion of the nation's resources devoted to food production at home and the slight rise in the proportion devoted to transport and to non-textile manufacturing industries, especially those which were highly capitalized; about half the manufacturing workers outside the textile and clothing trades were employed in the metallurgical, shipbuilding and engineering industries,[4] where capital was rapidly increasing. The relative decline of agriculture had been proceeding at least since the Napoleonic Wars, but about 1860 it began to quicken and the number of people employed, which until then had been rising slowly, began to fall absolutely. That this was not only possible but should appear to have been a national benefit was due to the greater ease with which food supplies could be obtained by import. As the demand for food increased, it became more economical to develop industrial and commercial activities in order to purchase the extra amount abroad than to produce it at home. The growth of exports was an essential accompaniment of those changes in the distribution of productive resources which were making the economy rather less balanced, rather more specialized towards manufacture and finance than it had been. In twenty years from the early eighteen-fifties the value of British exports of home-produced goods rose roughly two and a half times, and whereas the value of these exports represented £3 10s. 2d. per head in 1854 it represented £7 7s. 9d. per head in 1874.[5] At the same time other income from abroad greatly

---

[1] Booth, *op. cit.*, pp. 68-9.　　　[2] *Ibid.*, pp. 72-3.
[3] Giffen, *op. cit.*, p. 43.　　　[4] Booth, *op. cit.*, pp. 68-9, 72-3.
[5] J. S. Jeans, *England's Supremacy* (1885), p. 435.

increased. The net earnings of shipping were estimated to have risen in about the same proportion as merchandise exports, income from foreign investments to have quadrupled, and the profits from trading and other services performed abroad to have nearly trebled. In the years 1871-75 these three items are estimated to have averaged annually £50·8 million, £50·0 million and £32·9 million respectively, while insurance earnings provided another £16·4 million.[1] Thus, at a time when the value of exports of home-produced goods was averaging £239·5 million per year, it was possible for retained imports greatly to exceed this amount, and in fact the deficit on merchandise trade averaged £62·5 million, in spite of a high rate of foreign investment.

The imports obtained in this way were changing in character as the preponderance of industrial raw materials among them declined and the proportion of foodstuffs rose until, by the middle 'seventies, more or less equal amounts were being spent on imports of each.[2] Significantly, the foodstuffs of which the import was growing most rapidly were commodities of common consumption of the same kind as were raised at home: the proportion of grain, flour, butter, cheese and eggs among the imported foods was rising, while that of sugar and other tropical produce and of wines and spirits was falling.[3] From 1854 to 1874 the total value of imports rose by 143 per cent, but that of foodstuffs by 165 per cent (despite the fact that 1854 was a year of exceptionally heavy wheat imports), and the increases in some particular items were far greater: for example, imports of bacon and ham increased sevenfold, those of butter and cheese between four- and fivefold, those of eggs elevenfold. Most of these very large increases occurred in the late 'sixties and early 'seventies.[4]

The greater involvement of economic activity in dealings with foreign countries was the most significant change of all in the mid-Victorian period and goes far to explain its expansiveness. A more rapid growth in the quantity of goods sold abroad was being achieved without export prices being forced down much more quickly than the prices of the imports obtained in return for them, as had been the case earlier, especially in the late 'twenties and the 'thirties. The

---

[1] Imlah, *op. cit.*, p. 73.

[2] Schlote, *op. cit.*, p. 54, shows that the main change took place between 1845 and 1875.

[3] *Ibid.*, p. 65.   [4] S. Bourne, *Trade, Population and Food* (1880), pp. 41-2.

net barter terms of trade, which express the level of export prices as
a percentage of the level of import prices, changed little in the third
quarter of the nineteenth century. Until 1857 they were moving
slowly against the United Kingdom, then they turned a little in its
favour, fluctuated indecisively for a few years and then moved rather
more favourably from 1868 until 1873.[1] In these price conditions the
success in expanding foreign markets was all the more valuable,
because it meant a bigger contribution to the country's income, in
the form of more imported goods or larger credits abroad, or both.
The more striking contribution from foreign trade is well illustrated
by the relationship that is sometimes called the income terms of trade
and sometimes the export gain from trade. This is expressed quantitatively by multiplying the net barter terms of trade by an index of
the volume of exports, and changes in the value of the ratio thus
indicate changes in the real income earned abroad by means of
merchandise exports.[2] On the basis of the best available estimates,
the average level of the export gain from trade for 1846-50 was 130
per cent higher than twenty-five years earlier, in 1821-25, but between 1846-50 and 1871-75 the increase was 229 per cent. In the
second quarter of the century only the last two quinquennia (1841-45
and 1846-50) had an increase of more than 20 per cent in the export
gain from trade over the previous one. In the third quarter there was
only one quinquennium (1861-65) which did not show such an
increase.[3] The importance of such a change in the trading achievement, to a country whose dominant manufacturing industry had no
hope of prospering on sales mainly to the home market, can hardly
be overstressed.

Greater success in foreign trade depended primarily on improved
market conditions, the result of action both at home and abroad.

[1] Imlah, *op. cit.*, pp. 96-7.

[2] The concept of the income terms of trade was first introduced and expounded
in G. S. Dorrance, 'The Income Terms of Trade' in *Review of Economic Studies*,
XVI (1948-49), 50-6.

[3] Calculated from the figures in Imlah, *op. cit.*, pp. 95-7. The amount of the
increase may be exaggerated by the use of five-year averages centred on years
which come in different parts of the business cycle. To eliminate this, alternative
calculations were based on the average value of the export gain from trade for
complete cycles, measured from trough to trough. The results were just as favourable to the later period. From 1819-26 to 1842-48 the increase was 105·8 per cent,
i.e., at the rate of 118 per cent per quarter century; from 1842-48 to 1868-79 the
increase was 249·4 per cent, i.e. at the rate of 219 per cent per quarter century.
Professor Imlah himself no longer makes use of the concept of the export gain from
trade, though he traced it in detail in an earlier study published in *Journ. of Econ
Hist.*, X (1950).

Britain's free trade policy, coming as it did just at the time when the size of the population was compelling the country to retreat further from self-sufficiency, may have helped. One of its effects was to make debtor countries less dependent on one or two lightly taxed commodities, such as raw cotton, in order to earn credits with which to meet obligations in Britain. This in turn made them more ready to incur obligations by buying or borrowing more from Britain and it also meant that a larger number of sound investment opportunities was created.

But the greatest influence was that of better transport. Britain itself in 1850 already had the nucleus of a nation-wide network of railways, with over 6,000 miles in operation, but was only just beginning to feel its effects. In the next twenty years about 9,000 miles of new routes were added to the railways of the United Kingdom and the equipment of the earlier lines was improved. Elsewhere, and above all in the best actual and potential markets, development was still more striking, thanks in part to the investment of British capital. In 1850 the whole of continental Europe had little more railway than Britain, but between 1850 and 1870 some 40,000 miles of additional railways were opened in continental Europe and rather more than that in the United States, while in India the first 5,000 miles of line were completed.[1] At sea, the efficiency of sailing ships increased and the introduction of the compound engine in the eighteen-sixties at last made the steamship a practical proposition for long-distance ocean cargo traffic. In 1870 the greater part of maritime cargo was still carried by sailing ships, but the use of steamships was rapidly increasing.[2] From 1865 onwards the yards of Britain, the largest shipbuilding country, launched every year a greater tonnage of steamships than of sailing ships.

The third quarter of the nineteenth century thus saw the application of power-driven machinery to transport on a very extensive scale for the first time. The effect was to permit the movement of a much greater physical quantity of goods, to lower the real costs of distribution, and to make accessible as markets many districts which

[1] There is a useful table of comparative railway mileages in many countries at different dates in G. D. H. Cole, *Introduction to Economic History 1750-1950* (1952), pp. 194-5.

[2] Changes in the technical equipment of steamships and some of their economic effects are summarized in C. E. Fayle, *A Short History of the World's Shipping Industry* (1933), pp. 240-2. For an account of improvements in the design and operation of sailing ships see G. S. Graham, 'The Ascendancy of the Sailing Ship 1850-85' in *Econ. Hist. Review*, 2nd series, IX (1956-57), 74-86.

previously had been of little commercial importance. At the same time the heavy investment involved in the new railways, ships and docks was a source of extra employment and income and a general stimulus to greater economic activity in the regions where they were situated. There were bigger incomes to be spent and the means of sending more goods, more cheaply than before, on which to spend them.

This condition presented British exporters with great opportunities because, although there was at this time considerable advance in manufacturing in a few other countries, it was as yet hardly comparable with the progress being made in mechanical transport. Almost everywhere at this stage a bigger demand for goods meant a bigger demand for a few consumer necessities and for capital equipment, especially for use in transport, and there was still no other country so well equipped as Britain to supply most classes of these, though by the eighteen-sixties the challenge to British technical supremacy was growing. Even had there been no further improvement in the productive efficiency of British industry, the kind of work which, in the first half of the century, it had fitted itself to perform would almost certainly have 'paid off' better than before. The expanded volume of exports still consisted mainly of the same commodities in much the same proportions as in the second quarter of the century. In 1854-57, 86 per cent of home-produced exports consisted of manufactures, a slightly higher proportion than just after the Napoleonic Wars; by 1867-69 the proportion had risen to 89 per cent, though it was soon to fall slightly again, because of the rapid growth of coal exports. Textiles, which between 1840-42 and 1854-57 had fallen from 78·7 per cent to 67·9 per cent of the exports of manufactures, more than held their own and provided 71·6 per cent in 1867-69.[1] The cotton famine during the American Civil War might have been expected to upset these proportions but in fact had no lasting effect on them. During the War the quantity of cotton goods exported unavoidably declined, but the decline was offset by much higher prices which maintained the value of exports: they averaged £44·1 million a year in 1856-60 and £48·7 million a year in 1861-65. In addition, exports of woollen goods grew quickly, as, on a smaller scale, did those of linens, partly to meet the demand which the cotton industry was temporarily unable to supply.[2] After the War the woollen industry kept its newly-won ground and the

---

[1] Schlote, *op. cit.*, pp. 71, 74 and 125.   [2] Ellison, *op. cit.*, p. 130.

cotton industry made a very rapid recovery and was soon building up its exports to new heights: between 1867 and 1869 they averaged £68·5 million annually, between 1871 and 1875 £75·3 million.[1] Apart from textiles, the biggest item in exports was iron goods which, though far behind textiles, advanced greatly in importance during the eighteen-fifties, when their sale was stimulated by the demand from the new European railways, and, with minor ups and downs, they maintained their relative position thereafter. In 1840-42 iron goods had formed only 6·1 per cent of the exports of home-produced manufactured goods, but they formed 11·8 per cent in 1857-59 and 10·5 per cent in 1867-69.[2]

Though better transport and the higher incomes of their prospective customers were the chief influences on the growing business of Britain's merchants and manufacturers, improvements within industry also made a contribution. More reliable equipment, new techniques of production and better organization made it possible to improve the quality of some commodities and produce others at lower real cost, and thereby attract additional customers. In the biggest manufacturing industry, cotton, the greatest cost reducing innovations had already been generally applied, in spinning during the Napoleonic Wars and the eighteen-twenties, in weaving between 1830 and 1850, when the price of cloth fell by a third while the price of raw cotton fell very little.[3] But further, though less spectacular, reduction was still possible and was achieved. A larger industry, served by better local transport, was able after 1850 to increase specialization, both among localities and among firms.[4] Gradual improvements were made in the speed of operation of machinery and one major new invention in spinning, the ring traveller, which was brought out in the United States in 1844, was introduced, though its use spread slowly and was still by no means general in the early 'eighties.[5] Through these and other changes the real costs of production in the cotton industry fell between 1855 and 1875

---

[1] Ellison, *op. cit.*, table no. 2.

[2] Schlote, *op. cit.*, p. 74. The exports of machinery are not included in these figures.

[3] T. S. Ashton, 'Some Statistics of the Industrial Revolution in Britain' in *Trans. Manchester Stat. Socy.*, 1948, pp. 6-7 and 18; Ellison, *op. cit.*, pp. 30-8 and 59.

[4] A. J. Taylor, 'Concentration and Specialization in the Lancashire Cotton Industry, 1825-1850' in *Econ. Hist. Rev.*, 2nd series, I (1948-49), 122.

[5] P. Dunsheath (ed.), *A Century of Technology* (1951), p. 90; Ellison, *op. cit.* p. 34.

by just over 10 per cent.[1] In the other textile industries, where earlier change had been slower, there was more scope for technological innovations to cause great improvements in efficiency. The woollen industry, for instance, still wove much of its cloth on hand-looms in 1860 but thereafter rapidly increased its use of steam power.

But it was outside the textile industries that the greatest innovations were made. The growing importance of the iron industry in the nation's economy made its technological improvement specially influential. The experiments in the use of the hot gases from the blast furnace led to notable savings. The gradual adoption of the steam hammer, invented in 1842, improved the average quality of wrought iron and freed foundries from using otherwise unsuitable waterside locations. Above all, the inventions, by Bessemer in 1856 and by the Siemens brothers in 1866, of cheap methods of making steel in bulk, though their widespread use still lay in the future, were providing a better material for an immense range of industrial purposes.[2] Even more fundamental, perhaps, were the increases in the productive capacity, the speed and accuracy of equipment, and the variety of the finished products of the mechanical engineering industry. By the eighteen-fifties machine-making had become a more mechanized industry than in the early stages of the Industrial Revolution. Had it not been so, the other manufacturing industries of mid-Victorian Britain could never have obtained the equipment which enabled them to expand output at the rate they did. A wide range of machine tools existed by 1850, though its usefulness was limited by small size, slow speed, inadequate precision, and awkwardness in the movements imposed on the operator. Some of the deficiencies were being steadily lessened, particularly by the work of such men as Whitworth, who in 1855 produced a machine which could measure to one-millionth of an inch, and who standardized screw pitches and made many improvements both in the design of machine tools and in engineering practice. Important changes about this time included the adoption of the turret lathe, the invention in 1862 of the first milling machine, which superseded many difficult and costly manual operations, the introduction of self-hardening tool steel which permitted a 50 per cent increase in the speed of cutting tools, and

[1] C. Clark, *The Conditions of Economic Progress* (2nd edn., 1951), pp. 304-6, summarizing the investigations of G. T. Jones published in his *Increasing Return* (1933).

[2] Dunsheath, *op. cit.*, pp. 13-24.

the development of a grinding machine.[1] As a result of such innovations engineering workshops in the 'seventies could do many things in quantity which, a quarter of a century earlier, they could have done only very slowly and with difficulty.

Progress in engineering was contributing to a gradual change in the equipment and technological basis of industry as a whole. In the early nineteenth century steam power and revolutionary new machines were introduced in only a few industries, though these few included some of the largest. After 1850 not only were the already mechanized industries still growing rapidly but machinery, some of it power-driven, was being devised for industries whose techniques hitherto had remained entirely manual. Even in the eighteen-seventies handicrafts still had a substantial part in British industry, but the range of handicraft activities was shrinking more quickly, though many of the tasks in which the craftsman was being replaced were less important than those in which he had been superseded earlier. Thus the influence of technological innovation was becoming more widely diffused in industry and some modest improvement in output may be attributed to this change. One further important consequence of the trend of technological change was to increase the demand for the three natural resources—coal, iron ore and water—that the country possessed abundantly. A steady expansion in the supply of all these, without a significant rise in cost, was basic to mid-Victorian economic growth and was achieved without radical innovations, since the necessity to develop the scantier and less accessible sources of supply had not yet been reached.

Improvements in productive techniques and in the supply of basic materials enhanced the economic opportunities presented by larger markets and cheaper distribution. That the opportunities were grasped is attributable to the enterprise of countless individuals, the thrifty habits of many of those to whom most of the nation's income accrued, and the flexibility of economic institutions. The factors of production moved more readily than before to activities most favoured by current market conditions. In most branches of industry and commerce it was still practicable for the enterprising individual, with energy and common sense, a very modest education and a little capital, to set up his own business in a small way and gradually

[1] Dunsheath, *op. cit.*, pp. 142-53.

move to bigger things. There was probably no period when more genuine competition prevailed, when established interests put fewer obstacles in the path of the newcomer. The concentration of population in towns and the emergence of a generation that had known none but an industrial way of life provided a larger, more conveniently located pool of workers adapted to the needs of the time; and educational facilities were just about sufficient to ensure a supply of skill adequate to maintain the momentum of the economy, though there was no margin to spare. Those activities (fundamental to every other branch of the economy) which needed capital in large quantities could obtain it more easily than before. This was due to the improvement of the capital market by the extension of limited liability, the widening of the activities of the London and provincial stock exchanges and the growth of financial journalism, and also to the increase in the amounts which the public saved. In mid-Victorian conditions expanding markets meant buoyant profits, and buoyant profits, accruing mainly to families accustomed to modest standards and not confronted by the temptation of a wide variety of consumer goods and services, meant rapid accumulation rather than a spending spree. The labouring masses may have improved their economic position relatively more than the rest of the community, as some contemporaries suggested,[1] but they still received too small a proportion of the national income for their spending habits to have any adverse effect on the growth of the national capital. This was most important as capital requirements were still very heavy in proportion to the national income, partly because of the need to increase capital *pari passu* with the continued rapid increase of population, but mainly because of the need for fuller provision of exceptionally durable forms of capital—railway tunnels and cuttings, and new towns, for example —both here and in other countries which were important markets or sources of supply for Britain.

The rapid accumulation of capital was one major reason why 'invisible' as well as visible exports responded so well to new opportunities. The main sources of invisible earnings, long-term foreign securities and shipping services, both depended directly on heavy investment, and the provision of more short-term capital for the financing of world trade was a stimulus to the growth of other British business services for foreign commerce. Larger savings and better

---

[1] e.g. R. Giffen, 'The Progress of Working Classes in the last half century' *passim*, in his *Essays in Finance*, vol. II.

financial institutions enabled Britain's foreign income to become relatively less dependent on merchandise exports than before. The estimated income from foreign investments and from business services (including insurance and shipping) rendered to foreigners equalled 54 per cent of the value of home-produced merchandise exports in 1851-55, having fallen from the 58 per cent reached in 1821-25. By 1861-65 it had risen to 61 per cent and reached 63 per cent in 1871-75.[1] Had those who spent most of the national income so chosen, they could have greatly increased consumption out of the proceeds of these services which Britain was performing for the rest of the world. In fact, they did not do so. The import surplus did not grow by nearly as much as the income from invisible exports. In 1846-50 the adverse balance of merchandise trade was 18·0 per cent of the total of merchandise exports and net imports (i.e. excluding the figures of the re-export trade): in 1871-75 the proportion had fallen to 11·5 per cent.[2] Instead of being used for the purchase of additional imported goods a large part of the income from invisible exports was saved and invested overseas. Thus provision was made for a bigger income from foreign dividends and at the same time a contribution was made towards the continued expansion of foreign purchasing power, on which British prosperity had come to depend so much.

To save abundantly and invest prudently; to develop foreign markets and to be ready to supply them with the kind of goods they could most plentifully absorb; to concentrate productive resources on the enlargement of capital equipment, on providing the basic necessities of existence while paying little attention to luxuries, and on the development of those business services which the whole trading world required; to improve productive techniques in the main occupations where practicable and, having done so, to specialize on those where the greatest comparative advantage was attained—these were the tasks which the mid-Victorians attempted. They were not essentially different from the tasks confronting the two or three preceding generations but some of them, especially the active promotion of foreign markets and enterprise, the development of business services and the extension of industrial specialization, were carried

---

[1] Calculated from the figures in Imlah, *Economic Elements in the* Pax Britannica pp. 37, 70-3 and 166.
[2] *Ibid.*, p. 166.

a good deal further; and, in a setting where institutions, policies and foreign political and economic conditions were generally more favourable than before, all of them were tackled with greater success.

Nevertheless, the mid-Victorian economy was not perfectly adapted to the conditions and opportunities of its time. It worked as it did, not in accordance with some centrally conceived and directed policy, but in accordance with the choices made by the minority who received and spent most of the national income, in so far as market organization permitted the effective expression of choice. Not all the choices were wise and far-seeing, not all the markets functioned smoothly, though most of them had been improved. The greatest economic weaknesses were probably those indicated by the way in which labour was used and wasted. Superficially at least, it looks as though much of the available labour was applied to not very productive purposes. The immense number of domestic servants, greater than the number of workers in any manufacturing industry, is particularly striking. Domestic service employed 13·3 per cent of the occupied population of England and Wales in 1851 and 15·8 per cent in 1871; in Scotland the proportions at these dates were 10·5 and 10·7 per cent respectively.[1] Plentiful domestic service was perhaps the chief means by which the upper and middle classes used their incomes for the increase of their own immediate comfort. On balance, it may have slightly reduced the rate at which the national income grew, though the immense productive energy and enterprise of so many middle-class men must surely have owed a good deal to home comfort and freedom from domestic chores. Far more serious was the loss of labour power through illness, physical weakness, early death, inadequate training, and a badly organized labour market. The trade union figures of employment, the only continuous series in existence, suggest that unemployment was generally low. From 1856 to 1875 the average rate of unemployment among trade unionists varied between 7·35 per cent in 1858 and 0·95 per cent in 1872, and in thirteen of the twenty years it was less than 4 per cent.[2] But these figures, though they may be a useful guide to fluctuations, are utterly misleading as a measure of the absolute level of unemployment, owing to the small number and specialized character of the

[1] Booth, *op. cit.*, pp. 68-9 and 72-3. To some extent these figures exaggerate the importance of the occupation, because they include a large proportion of girls aged 10 to 19.

[2] W. H. Beveridge, *Full Employment in a Free Society* (1944), p. 312.

occupations they cover.[1] They take no account of the large numbers of casual workers, general labourers, petty hucksters, people of no regular trade, and domestic outworkers. When Baxter was calculating the national income, he wrote:

> None but those who have examined the facts can have any idea of the precariousness of employment in our large cities, and the large proportion of time out of work, and also, I am bound to add, the loss of time in many well-paid trades from drinking habits. Taking all these facts into account, I come to the conclusion, that for loss of work from every cause, and for the non-effectives up to 65 years of age, who are included in the census, *we ought to deduct fully 20 per cent from the nominal full-time wages*.[2]

Other contemporary statisticians thought that his 20 per cent was far too big an allowance,[3] but there can be little doubt that he was much nearer the truth than they. The picture that emerges from contemporary investigations into the lives of the poor in the large towns, the figures of illness and mortality recorded in official reports, and the discussion by informed doctors and statisticians of the conditions and causes underlying them,[4] all provide overwhelming confirmation of the economic waste as well as personal misery that arose from the condition of the lower ranks of the labouring classes. Many people were not physically capable of doing a full day's work regularly; many of these, and others too, had never received the schooling and training that would enable them to do any but the simplest and least disciplined manual jobs; and some of those who were abler and fitter could not, because of the haphazard organization of the labour market, find better jobs which they might have effectively filled.

[1] The people to whom the figures relate throughout were the members of some unions in the metal trades; the bookbinders, printers, carpenters and joiners, coachmakers and furniture makers were brought in at various dates up to 1868. The membership of the unions covered by the figures never reached 100,000 until 1872 (J. Hilton, 'Statistics of Unemployment Derived from the Working of the Unemployment Insurance Acts', in *Journ. of the Royal Stat. Socy.*, LXXXVI (1923), 180).

[2] Baxter, *op. cit.*, pp. 46-7.

[3] Leone Levi, calculating the income of the manual labour class a year earlier, allowed only a 4 per cent deduction. (*Ibid.*, pp. 41-2.) Giffen thought it right to correct Baxter's estimate of national income by applying to it Levi's deduction from manual labour incomes instead of Baxter's own. ('Further notes on the progress of the working classes' in his *Essays in Finance*, II, 459.)

[4] Among much discussion some of the best-informed is to be found in W. Farr, *Vital Statistics* (1885) and J. Simon, *Public Health Reports* (1887).

B

Mid-Victorian England was not under severe economic pressure to improve the quality of its workers and few people considered that an attempt to do this would have much relevance to economic affairs. Labour always appeared plentiful, mainly because of the continued rapid natural increase of the population and greater geographical mobility; and as the degree of skill and responsibility needed in most jobs did not take much effort to acquire, a frequent turnover of labour did not seem costly. To improve the general quality of labour would have required a more rapid increase of expenditure in the unfamiliar fields of public health and popular education than was in fact undertaken, and to many people such expenditure seemed likely to undermine the virtue of self-reliance. Had it been undertaken, the country would after a few years have been producing still more and better goods and services. But economic growth was so impressive even without it that the importance of provision of this kind was overlooked or even denied. Not until technology and social organization became more complex and foreign competition more acute did it become essential to reduce the wastes, as well as to continue the achievements, of the mid-Victorian economy.

CHAPTER TWO

The Environment of Economic Change

THE economic opportunities which presented themselves to the British people in the late nineteenth century changed considerably as a result of changes of which some originated chiefly from non-economic causes and of which many were outside British control. Not only were the opportunities different, but partly because of that very difference and partly because of changes in the structure and aspirations of British society, the ease with which economic activity could be adapted to make the most of them was also affected, in some ways for the better, in others for the worse. Among the influences which gave British economic activity a new setting, three were specially important. These were the acceleration and broadening scope of technological change; the expansive surge of industrialization in several large foreign countries and the commercial development of vast primary producing lands overseas for the first time; and the gradual modification of the wasteful demographic situation at home which had been one of the chief conditioning factors of economic life from the beginning of the Industrial Revolution.

Many of the technological changes were merely the obvious next steps along paths that had been clearly marked out immediately before. The great mid-nineteenth-century development of mechanical transport, for instance, was far from complete in 1870, especially at sea. The compound engine, which in the 'sixties had first made long-distance cargo steamship services practicable, was widely adopted in the 'seventies but rendered obsolete in the next ten or fifteen years by the introduction of triple and quadruple expansion engines that achieved far greater savings of fuel. At the same time operating costs were further reduced by the use of auxiliary steam-engines for working ships' tackle and for driving the loading and unloading equipment of the ports. Steam power steadily superseded sail and manual labour, and enormous reductions in transport costs were achieved. The rate for carrying bulk grain from New York to Liverpool, for example, varied in 1860 between 6d. and 1s. 1½d. per bushel but in

1886 averaged only 2½*d.* per bushel.[1] On land the quality of transport equipment probably improved less swiftly but the efficiency of railway operation was nevertheless increased by countless additions and innovations, many of them individually small but cumulatively significant. Existing tracks were used more intensively, the mechanical equipment of civil engineering was enlarged, and the building of new railways abroad proceeded on a greater scale than ever, especially in two periods of immense activity, in the eighteen-eighties and in the decade immediately preceding the First World War.[2] Many inland districts, previously hard to reach, obtained transport that was cheaper than any previously known on land: the average freight charges of the railways of the United States, for instance, fell from 2·5 cents per ton-mile in 1869 to 1·06 cents in 1887, and in the more thickly settled districts they fell considerably more than that.[3]

Much of the extension of the use of machinery in manufacture and agriculture was also the direct result of innovations developed a few years earlier. Some of it was the fruition of protracted efforts by inventors to overcome problems that had defied them for many years. The relation between economic conditions and innovations in technique is not a constant one. Some inventions, easily within the scope of the knowledge and resources of their time, remained unmade or were made and left unused, simply because there was no economic demand for them. But there were other cases in which, though market conditions were clearly such as to promise large profits for mechanical innovation, the innovations were delayed for many years because attempts to solve the technical problems were unsuccessful. Throughout the first half of the nineteenth century, to take one example, the clothing industries, despite their large market, lagged hopelessly behind the textiles in techniques; yet throughout that period there was scarcely any device to which inventors gave more attention than the sewing-machine. No satisfactory one was designed, however, until the late eighteen-forties and production in large numbers did not come until towards 1860.[4]

---

[1] D. A. Wells, *Recent Economic Changes* (1890), pp. 29-30 and 35-9.

[2] Between 1870 and 1910 over 80,000 miles of new railway were opened in continental Europe (excluding Russia and Turkey), 38,000 miles in Russia, 158,000 miles in the U.S.A. (of which nearly half was opened during the eighteen-eighties), 24,000 miles in Canada, 27,000 miles in India, and over 50,000 miles in Latin America, as well as smaller amounts in Africa and Australia, which had hardly any railway in 1870.

[3] Wells, *op. cit.*, pp. 40-2.

[4] W. H. Doolittle, *Inventions in the Century* (1903), pp. 310-23.

By 1870 the improvement in the equipment of mechanical engineering was making such delays more avoidable. As long as engineering shops were few, small, and incapable of applying very refined
standards of accuracy, the machines they produced could satisfactorily
replace human skill only in the simpler crafts and were not plentiful
or cheap enough to help the smaller industries. The increase in the
number and accuracy of machine-tools, so noticeable by the eighteen-
fifties, the steady growth in the supply of cheap steel from the
eighteen-sixties, and the standardization and mass-production of
universally-used components, such as screws (of which in 1875 two
girls with two machines could turn out 240,000 a day, as compared
with 20,000 a day by twenty men and boys in 1840),[1] changed that
situation. The output of machinery greatly increased, and since
machines were built more accurately from better materials to designs
which provided for finer operational adjustment, they could execute
more complex actions which previously had been beyond their competence. Moreover, each improvement in machine-tools was a step
towards producing still better machine-tools and so it was possible
constantly to increase the complexity of engineering products. By the
early years of the twentieth century there were few handicraft operations for which machinery could not be devised as an alternative and
a growing number of industrial processes had come into existence
which were beyond the reach of human skill without the use of
machines. Consequently, it was in the period from the eighteen-
seventies to the First World War that mechanization became characteristic of industry in general rather than of a few individual industries
only. By the early years of the twentieth century some power-
driven machinery was being regularly used in most manufacturing
industries, though in some (especially the smaller ones) there
were many stages in the productive process that remained un-
mechanized. In agriculture, mining and service occupations the use
of machinery spread more slowly but in these also there was some
increase.

These important changes in technique and equipment resulted
mainly from the piecemeal, cumulative achievements of engineers
and mechanics, repeatedly making new advances from the basis of
previous practical experience. But in this period the technological
setting of economic activity changed still more radically because it
became much more closely associated with the progress of pure and

[1] *Ibid.*, p. 246.

applied science.[1] The 'heroic' inventions of the eighteenth and early
nineteenth centuries—the steam-engine, the textile machines and
the other apparatus of a familiar story—were mostly the work of
practising craftsmen and enthusiastic amateurs with, at best, a very
modest knowledge of scientific theory, though it is worth noting
that the most successful line of advance was the one whose underlying scientific principles had been familiar for the longest time,
thanks to the achievements made in mechanics by Newton and his
contemporaries. In other fields, such as chemistry, purely empirical
experiments, undertaken out of idle curiosity or in response to some
pressing economic difficulty, led to a few very important industrial
innovations. These included new methods of producing sulphuric
acid and alkalis, which were very important for the growth of the
textile industries,[2] and advances in metallurgy, especially that of iron
and steel. But in all fields, except mechanics, technological progress
was retarded because of lack of knowledge of basic scientific principles, without which the relatively small amount of experiment was
bound to be somewhat haphazard and its occasional successes too
heavily dependent on chance coming to the aid of persistence and
shrewd observation. The immense new economic potentialities
which were appearing at the end of the nineteenth century were the
practical outcome of the previous hundred years' achievement in
pure science, particularly in thermodynamics, electro-magnetism,
chemistry and geology.

The synthesis in the eighteen-fifties of recent accumulations of
knowledge in thermodynamics, so that they formed one coherent,
comprehensive body of theory,[3] prepared the way for the invention
of new and better prime movers. A study of thermodynamics became more and more commonly part of the training of the engineer,
and though it contributed little to the further improvement of the
reciprocating steam-engine it both inspired and guided the search
for prime movers which would come nearer to possessing the properties of a perfect heat engine. Besides leading incidentally to the
invention of refrigerators, it soon resulted in the development of new

---

[1] The relations between science and technology and between theory and empiricism in the making of inventions in the nineteenth century are discussed in
J. Jewkes, D. Sawers, and R. Stillerman, *The Sources of Invention* (1958), chap. III.
These writers do not suggest that the relations were much different in the late
nineteenth century from what they were in the early nineteenth or late eighteenth.

[2] S. F. Mason, *A History of the Sciences* (1953), pp. 416-18.

[3] *Ibid.*, pp. 401-2.

types of power unit. By 1860 the first internal combustion engines, operated by gas, were in use, but they remained rare until after the invention of a much improved machine by the German, Otto, in 1876. A petrol-driven engine was brought out by Daimler in 1883 and two years later Priestman produced one driven by heavy oil though it was another ten years before a really satisfactory engine of the latter type was developed, by Diesel.[1] The year 1884 saw the first appearance of another new type of prime mover, the design of which was greatly influenced by thermodynamic theory. This was the steam-turbine, invented by Parsons, which soon showed its superiority to the steam-engine in driving ships and which before long found one of its major uses in driving electrical generators.[2]

Here the applications of two developing sciences were made directly to supplement each other. At the end of the eighteenth century electricity had been an increasingly familiar but puzzling force whose practical application was little more than an amusing bit of mystification. Its gradual rise to industrial importance was entirely dependent on the experiments and theorizing of scientists. Its first significant application was in telegraphy, which became possible after the first electro-magnets had been made in the eighteen-twenties and Daniell, in 1836, had designed a cell which was a more reliable source of a small, constant current than the original Voltaic cell of 1799. By the third quarter of the century these discoveries had already led to a great improvement in the transmission of information, as the overland telegraph was supplemented by the submarine cable. But still more important was the discovery of electro-magnetic induction by Faraday in 1831.[3] It was this which showed the way to the development of electricity as a source of power on a large scale, as well as posing problems of theoretical explanation the solution of which pointed to the possibility of radio transmission and formed a major step towards the re-casting, with revolutionary consequences, of the most fundamental concepts of physics. Some practical use of Faraday's discoveries was made fairly quickly, but it was not until many experiments had been made in the design of generating equipment that they became of general industrial significance. The outstanding innovations were those of the Siemens brothers who in 1866 began to replace permanent magnets by electro-magnets in their dynamos, and one of whom, Sir William, went on in 1880 to

[1] Mason, *op. cit.*, pp. 411-12; Clapham, *op. cit.*, II, 110.
[2] Mason, *op. cit.*, p. 413; Clapham, *op. cit.*, III, 133-5.   [3] Mason, *op. cit.*, pp. 387-9.

produce the much more efficient shunt-wound generator.[1] With this improvement, soon followed by Edison's great practical innovation, the central power station,[2] and by the invention of the steam-turbine, the way was clear for electricity to become a major factor in industrial activity.

In chemistry the influence of pure science on production extended less into detail until near the end of the century.[3] Most of the innovations in technique in the chief established branches of the chemical industry were the work of experienced manufacturers and even the numerous economically important discoveries of the laboratories came mainly from empirical programmes of research without much concern to establish or confirm general principles. But it was empiricism made fruitful by a new, rational conception of the subject. The establishment of the necessity of quantitative methods of investigation and the formulation of several empirical laws concerning the combination of different substances all came in the closing years of the eighteenth century and the first few of the nineteenth, and they led to a great increase in the scope and reliability of chemical analysis. New compounds and previously unknown elements could then be more readily identified by further experiment, and the abundance of new mineral specimens available for analysis, as a result of the current interest in geology, helped to create a much fuller stock of information about the chemical composition and reactions of a great variety of substances.[4] But the creative contribution of chemistry to economic life remained small until the last third of the nineteenth century. Attempts to synthesize new compounds, though sometimes successful, were extremely chancy until a consistent theory of molecular structure and valency was available as a guide. Not until the 'sixties and early 'seventies were the general principles definitively established, after which it was practicable to maintain regular research as the basis of the fine chemicals industry, producing such things as synthetic dyes, perfumes and drugs.[5] The new theoretical knowledge also made it possible to draw up the periodic table of the elements and thus stimulated the search for those elements in

[1] Mason, *op. cit.*, pp. 414-15; W. T. Jeans, *The Creators of the Age of Steel* (1884), pp. 175-7.

[2] J. D. Bernal, *Science and Industry in the Nineteenth Century* (1953), p. 127.

[3] For an account of many of the developments in the industrial applications of chemical knowledge see F. Sherwood Taylor, *A History of Industrial Chemistry* (1957), chaps. XIV *et seq.*

[4] Mason, *op. cit.*, pp. 364-7 and 371.   [5] *Ibid.*, pp. 374-5 and 423-4.

the table which had never been found. Most of them were discovered by the end of the century[1] and eventually proved of commercial value. By the end of the century, too, even those large sections of the chemical industry which had paid little attention to pure science were beginning to be affected by it, as the study of physical chemistry, which indicated the optimum conditions for a chemical reaction to take place, pointed the way to new manufacturing processes superior to those based on rule-of-thumb methods.[2] Improvements in metallurgy were also becoming too complex to be accomplished without a considerable chemical knowledge. The trend of change is well illustrated by the difference between the untheoretical, common-sense approach which led Bessemer to his cheap method of making steel and the careful marshalling of scientific knowledge for the solution of a specific problem which twenty years later enabled Gilchrist Thomas to devise the basic process of producing steel from phosphoric ores.[3]

Just as important for the improvement of the supply of materials, in both quantity and quality, was the development of geology and its associated sciences; and here also much of the advance was through detailed, piecemeal investigation, often aided by chance, but stimulated and guided by a gradually enlarging body of general principles. Geology as a rational science linked to observation took shape in the eighteenth century, at the end of which it was developing rapidly as the expansion of mining and civil engineering brought new material for study.[4] The great controversies about the origins of rock formations, which arose at this time and were resolved only slowly, were a major factor encouraging field investigations for the sake of proving or disproving existing theories, and in the course of these controversies an immense amount of information about the character, distribution and location of mineral deposits (some of it of great value) was gradually accumulated.[5]

The extension of comprehensive geological surveying was one of the major sources of knowledge of additional economic resources in the nineteenth century. Britain was the pioneer in this respect. Its government established in 1835 a Geological Survey, whose original

---

[1] Mason, *op. cit.*, pp. 375-8; Taylor, *op. cit.*, chap. XIX.
[2] Mason, *op. cit.*, pp. 425-6; Taylor, *op. cit.*, chaps. XXIV and XXV.
[3] Bernal, *op. cit.*, pp. 107 and 110.
[4] Mason, *op. cit.*, pp. 323-32; A. M. Bateman, *Economic Mineral Deposits* (1942), pp. 11-12.
[5] Bateman, *op. cit.*, pp. 13 and 16-17.

survey of the solid geology of England and Wales was completed at the beginning of 1884.[1] Much of its earlier work was somewhat sketchy, but it gradually became more detailed and was considered by a committee of enquiry in 1901 to have fully justified itself on purely utilitarian grounds, through its services to mining, agriculture, water-supply and sanitation.[2] It may be, however, that in so well-developed a country the geologists did less than the mining engineers to increase knowledge of workable resources. But the Geological Survey had another importance in serving as a model which was taken up by many other countries about whose natural resources far less was known, and it also provided a training ground for some of the men who took a leading part in the geological surveying of undeveloped parts of the world.[3] By the last quarter of the nineteenth century there was a great deal of reliable information about the association of particular minerals with particular geological ages and types of formation, and a contemporary mining expert could declare that 'the laws which govern geological phenomena . . . serve as sure guides to the skilful miner in his adventurous search'.[4] Within the next few years knowledge of this kind was widened and became more definite[5] and the rapid extension of geological surveying in the world permitted much fuller use to be made of it. Most of the great new mineral discoveries were made by adventurous prospectors who had little or no technical training, or by mining engineers in the vicinity of existing workings. But increasingly they were helped by geology to search in districts likely to be rewarding. Moreover, some minerals of growing importance were very difficult to locate unless the trained geologist was employed as a prospector. This was particularly true of the most abundantly-needed new mineral, petroleum, of the existence of which there are usually few surface expressions,[6] such as had been the guide to the first few discoveries.[7] Increasingly, too, was geological knowledge applied in detail to the examination and development of newly-discovered mineral deposits.[8]

The influence of geology was supplemented by easier means access to remote areas, by extensive field-work, and by improvements

[1] Sir J. S. Flett, *The First Hundred Years of the Geological Survey of Great Britain* (1937), pp. 24-5 and 106.

[2] *Ibid.*, p. 142.   [3] *Ibid.*, p. 78.

[4] R. Hunt, *Ure's Dictionary of Arts, Manufactures and Mines* (7th edn. 1878-79), III, 295-9.

[5] Bateman, *op. cit.*, p. 16.   [6] *Ibid.*, pp. 375-6.

[7] Dunsheath, *op. cit.*, p. 175.   [8] Bateman, *op. cit.*, pp. 392-3.

in boring machinery[1] and other mining equipment; and with this assistance no science did so much in the late nineteenth and early twentieth centuries to acquaint the world with the extent and practical utility of its own wealth. By 1914 most of the earth's surface had been subjected to geological reconnaissance, if not to detailed survey, and it was in the immediately preceding decades that most of the great mineral-bearing districts were discovered, though not all were fully explored and developed.[2]

The simultaneous advances in all these and other sciences interacted with each other and with the practical improvements in the engineering industry. The application of power-driven machinery to former handicrafts often depended on the introduction of new types of prime mover; machinery for new and more difficult processes called for new materials, especially new steel alloys; new materials were forthcoming only through the combined efforts of the metallurgical chemist, the geologist and the mineral prospector. Technological innovation became more pervasive and more frequent. For established productive processes to be rendered obsolescent by such innovation became an almost continuous instead of an occasional feature of industrial life.[3] In this way competition was made more acute for, though it was more expensive for a competitor to establish himself, once he had succeeded in doing so, the more recent design of his equipment was likely to give him an advantage over older producers. Where competition was rooted in technology those competitors were likely to fare best who had access to the results of regular scientific research and to material supplies drawn from all round the world.

The connexion between technological progress and the increase of both competition and trade in the international sphere was thus a close one. The fundamental advances in science were not the monopoly of any one country; men from Britain, France, Germany and the United States all made large contributions to them. Their detailed application to technology often did for a few years confer a definite advantage on the country where the application was first made, but a capacity to apply science to industry was likewise no nation's monopoly. In the mid-nineteenth century, industrial development

---

[1] Detailed accounts of nineteenth-century improvements in boring machinery are given in Hunt, *op. cit.,* IV, 734-71.

[2] C. K. Leith, J. W. Furness and C. Lewis, *World Minerals and World Peace* (1943), p. 86.

[3] *Cf.* Wells, *op. cit.,* chap. II, esp. pp. 27-9, 49-57 and 61-7.

outside Britain had meant, in general, that other industrializing countries had to occupy themselves more with doing the things that Britain had begun rather earlier and to do them in the way they were already done in Britain. But, as new products and processes became more and more numerous and frequent, it was easier for other countries to equal or overtake Britain. Instead of copying where Britain excelled they could become pioneers in fields of growing economic importance which would be as new to Britain as to themselves. Britain was therefore bound to find itself in a more challenging international situation than before, with rival nations taking a more prominent place as manufacturers. Figures of industrial production as a whole were even more approximate in the late nineteenth century than they are today, but their errors of detail scarcely matter in view of the tremendous change they illustrate. British industry did not stagnate; it more than doubled its output between 1870 and 1913. But in the world as a whole there was a fourfold increase, and whereas Britain in 1870 produced nearly a third of the world's output of manufactures, in the closing years of the nineteenth century it produced only about a fifth, and in 1913 only about a seventh. In the early eighteen-eighties its manufacturing output was exceeded by that of the United States, and thereafter the margin between the two went on widening. In the first decade of the twentieth century Germany also passed the British output of manufactures. Other countries, though still not comparable with Britain as manufacturing nations, became much more industrialized than in 1870 and increased their output of manufactures a good deal faster than Britain did. Russia, Italy, Sweden, Canada and Japan all made notable advances, while France, much more industrialized than any of these in 1870, though it developed its industries less quickly than they did, more than kept pace with Britain.[1] If, instead of manufacture as a whole, some of the major industries were considered individually, then the extent to which dominance passed to countries other than Britain would appear even more striking.[2]

But if there was much stronger competition to be faced in industry, there were various compensating features in the changing

[1] League of Nations, *Industrialisation and Foreign Trade* (1945), pp. 13 and 130.

[2] For example, in 1880 Britain produced about as much steel as all the rest of Europe but in 1913 only about one-fifth of the European output; in 1880 it produced more than three times as much coal as Germany and more than twice as much as the United States, but in 1913 its output was only about one and a half times that of Germany and rather more than half that of the United States. (I. Svennilson, *Growth and Stagnation in the European Economy* (1954), pp. 252 and 260).

international scene which made it likely that all the chief competitors could improve their position without inflicting serious mutual injuries. It was possible, for instance, for an industrial nation, particularly for Britain, to concentrate more heavily on those manufacturing activities which it did best; to use fewer of its resources in a relatively costly way to produce basic items such as foodstuffs and to obtain these things from places where they could be produced more cheaply. The railway, the steamship, the prospector, the builder and the settler in the forty years or so preceding the First World War opened to production and trade an immense area that had previously been of little commercial significance. In no other period of its history has the world come into possession so quickly of so huge an increment to its natural wealth. So much good agricultural land came into use for the first time that hundreds of millions more could be fed at perhaps lower real cost than ever before; so many rich new mineral deposits were discovered that the mining of a large proportion of raw materials could be concentrated on those that were most accessible and easily worked. The supply of some of the primary commodities most largely consumed by the industrial areas was completely transformed within a few years. The eighteen-eighties, for instance, saw lands which were producing nothing at the beginning of the decade yield great quantities of wheat for sale before its end: the territory of Dakota raised no wheat for sale up to 1881 but over 62 million bushels in 1887; Russia in the same year exported 112 million bushels, and Argentina, which in 1878 was of no concern to the world's wheat supply, was exporting over 8 million bushels by 1887.[1] In the latter year the surplus of these three regions alone would have been roughly enough to supply all the wheat needed by the population of Britain. Such conditions were specially favourable for increasing industrialization. New and competing demands for new kinds of raw materials and foodstuffs, and for extra quantities of old ones, did not result in a struggle for scarce supplies in which the costs were driven up. They were matched by a new abundance which meant a real saving to industrial communities.

The opening of new areas of supply was also an opening of new markets, most of which had a demand for the industrial goods that had been the foundation of Britain's commercial success a little earlier, while their development as sources of supply to the industrial areas also gave rise to demands for newer types of manufactured

[1] Wells, *op. cit.*, pp. 170-2.

goods. Moreover, increasing political intervention by the great powers attached more and more of such areas to the commercial orbit of the western world and, where they were lacking, introduced such conditions as civil peace, effective administration and the enforceability of legal contracts, which made trade with them far easier to expand. At the same time the new productive powers of the more industrialized regions and the productive employment of hitherto neglected resources created bigger incomes and a demand for a greater range of goods in markets of already-established importance. So, while there were more countries each seeking an outlet for a much bigger production, there were also many more opportunities of selling. International trade did not grow quite as quickly as the output of manufactures but it grew by an immensely greater amount than ever before. From 1880 to the First World War the international trade of the world as a whole was approximately trebled, the increase in its annual value being around £5,500 million, whereas between 1850 and 1880 its increase is estimated to have been about £2,200 million.[1] Foreign countries might try, as most of them did increasingly from about 1880, to reserve to themselves a larger share of this increased trade by means of higher tariffs, open or concealed subsidies to exports, and the direct control of the trade of newly-extended colonial areas.[2] But in practice such measures were no more than a minor limitation of the constantly widening opportunities in world trade.

All these changes in technology and in the economic life of foreign countries were bound to be of the utmost importance to Britain, since it had already tied its fortunes to specialization in what had been the most technologically advanced industries and to supplying international markets. Its improved economic position in the mid-Victorian period had been attributable above all else to the more buoyant demand for a narrow range of manufactures and services which it equipped itself to supply with an efficiency which at that time was seldom approached and hardly ever surpassed elsewhere. When the world began to change much more quickly it was obvious that Britain could not just continue to do much the same things in much the same way and still achieve an almost continuous rapid

[1] League of Nations, *op. cit.*, p. 157; M. G. Mulhall, *The Dictionary of Statistics* (4th edn., 1899), p. 128.

[2] The beginning of this change and its economic effects are discussed in Wells, *op. cit.*, pp. 264-318. For a fuller treatment see P. Ashley, *Modern Tariff History* (3rd edn., 1920).

expansion of income. The increasing manufacturing ability of other countries was bound to trench upon some of the established fields of British economic pre-eminence, and there were times, particularly towards 1900, when foreign competition seemed to be a brooding menace rather than a bracing challenge, and the familiar label, 'Made in Germany' was used as the theme of the grimmest forebodings.[1] In particular, it was bound to be harder to sell the chief British exports, textile goods, in what had been some of their best markets. More countries which had imported such goods from Britain could make many of them for themselves, and some of those that still could not do so were now able to buy them instead from other industrial countries nearer at hand.

At the same time the changes in technology and the increase in the consumption of materials reduced another British advantage. Supremacy in nineteenth-century industry never rested exclusively on an abundant local supply of raw materials; the extraordinary growth of the British cotton industry is a clear indication of that. But it was enormously helpful to Britain to have a large supply of iron ore, from which to build machinery, and of coal and water for the steam-power to drive it. When, however, so much more machinery had to be used and more and more saleable products were made from steel, Britain slipped further and further from self-sufficiency in iron ore. The ultimate exhaustion of Britain's coal reserves had also been a subject of alarmed, if premature, speculation since the early eighteen-sixties, but abundant coal continued to be a great asset, though it was clear that its winning would gradually become more difficult, while newly discovered and more easily worked deposits in other countries were coming into use.[2] The other raw materials which a changing technology was making more important were nearly all scarce or non-existent in Britain. Some of what had been familiar minerals in industry—copper, tin and lead— had been supplied to a useful extent from home ores, but the domestic supply was dwindling as the demand increased.[3] Of the more varied stock of minerals which, though needed usually in much smaller amounts, were becoming essential to an advanced industrial country, only fluorspar, which had an important use as a flux in the

[1] See, in particular, E. E. Williams, *Made in Germany* (1896), which quickly went through several impressions.

[2] For a balanced appraisal of Britain's coal position as it appeared to thoughtful observers in the 'eighties see J. S. Jeans, *England's Supremacy*, pp. 358-73.

[3] Clapham, *op. cit.*, II, 104-5 and III, 169.

basic process of steel-making, was abundant in Britain.[1] The rest of the new demands had to be met from abroad.

These were serious problems, but the new conditions were far from being wholly disadvantageous to Britain. In fact they presented quite a varied set of opportunities for her to expand economic activities which were already well established. Though old textile markets might be lost to new rivals, the simultaneous extension of the international trading area was opening other markets whose demand for manufactured goods was likely at this stage to be concentrated mainly on textiles and other simple consumer goods. Even the industrialization of foreign countries had its direct advantages for many British producers. It meant, among other things, a much increased foreign demand for coal and machinery, which not all industrializing countries could supply for themselves. Whatever might be the ultimate threat to the British coal supply, there was for the time being no other country as well placed to export large amounts of coal, since none had such high-grade coal deposits so close to the tideway.[2] And it was reasonable to hope that some of the mechanical equipment for foreign industry would be supplied by British producers. Much of the machinery that was needed was, of course, very different from what British engineering shops had been making in the mid-nineteenth century, but at least British engineers could draw on an unrivalled experience when they were confronted by the demands of a new age. The immense increase of international trade also presented a wonderful opportunity for Britain to earn much more through invisible exports. In shipping, insurance, agency services and international banking British supremacy was already established by the 'sixties, and the demands on all these grew by leaps and bounds without the appearance of any very serious rival; and even if a nation sought to do more of its own carrying trade it was likely to buy the necessary ships in Britain. In another way, too, the growth of invisible earnings was facilitated. The commercial development of hitherto neglected parts of the world, in response to the needs of industrial areas, provided abundant lucrative investment opportunities. The economic need was urgent; the political environment was favourable; there were few alternative sources of capital; and the resources to be developed were often rich. British investors

---

[1] On the use and sources of fluorspar see Bateman, *op. cit.*, pp. 721-5; on Britain's mineral resources generally *ibid.*, p. 369.

[2] J. E. Spurr (ed.), *Political and Commercial Geology* (1920), pp. 30 and 44-5.

could use their earnings to stimulate the supply of food and raw materials, without which industrialization must have slackened, and create as their reward an ever-increasing inflow of dividends from abroad.

None of these possible lines of economic advance necessarily excluded any of the others and it was also open to British manufacturers, if they thought the effort worthwhile, to take up entirely new types of production instead of leaving these to their rivals abroad. But, whatever course was taken, it would involve a considerable effort by a large proportion of the people to adapt themselves to novel conditions, though the extent of the need for adaptation varied. The course that involved the least upheaval was to continue to concentrate on the familiar staple manufactures, especially those least affected by technological innovation, and to rely for prosperity on finding new markets for them. But this by itself was unlikely to maintain the previous momentum of economic expansion. If Britain was to remain a prosperous country it was almost bound to devote more of its efforts and resources to new and rapidly changing manufacturing industries, or to the larger provision of financial and other commercial services to the rest of the world, or to both. Thus it could not avoid being heavily involved in a way of life characterized by more frequent innovation, more complex methods of production, and more elaborate forms of organization; a way of life in which success depended on trained and experienced judgment, specialized technical skills (including intellectual as well as manual skills), and a high degree of economic mobility which should not be impaired by unthinking fear of the unfamiliar.

All these qualities had been present in the people of mid-Victorian Britain but they were not all as thoroughly diffused among them as became necessary towards the end of the nineteenth century. In particular, only a small proportion of people had the opportunity in the earlier period to acquire highly developed skills, whether mechanical, clerical or executive, and wide experience was relatively rare because of the prevalence of early death. It was not then economically essential for the situation to be different from this, and the grasping of new opportunities of economic progress was facilitated because the labour supply was constantly replenished by new workers who had no deep-rooted attachment to old practices which they must unlearn. The more extensive use and more complex design of machinery, which came subsequently, created a demand for a greater number of skilled mechanics and engineers. It was also a major influence on the increasing size of businesses, which in turn posed new problems of administration that could be dealt with only by better-trained executives and a larger number of clerks. A greater specialization on finance and commercial services also increased the need for people to be trained for clerical and administrative jobs. The greater frequency of innovation made it essential that workers of many different kinds, from the senior administrator to the operative, should have a sufficiently varied knowledge in their own field to be capable of readily changing some of the routine details of their everyday tasks. The need for more training became almost universal, and the more effort and expense were put into training people the more wasteful it was if they found their way to an early grave. Moreover, since every aspect of human activity was becoming more varied and its organization more complicated, the importance of wide experience, as part of the foundation of sound judgment, was increased. For all these reasons a change was necessary in the population if many of the new economic opportunities of the late nineteenth-century world were to be seized and most of its dangers avoided. There had to be an improvement in quality and a lengthening of life, and a mere increase in the numbers of the population was no longer likely to matter so much when adaptability depended on positive training rather than on the replacement of the old guard by new recruits.

There were, of course, other good reasons, political, humanitarian, and self-regarding, why an improvement in the quality and length of human life should have been sought. The change that took place in this respect after 1870 did not arise solely from economic causes, but it is unquestionable that new economic needs greatly influenced the decisions which made it possible and that its economic effect was large. Equally important was the gradual reduction in the rate of increase of the population.

The first appreciable long-term changes in demographic trends during the nineteenth century occurred about 1870, when the death-rate for England and Wales fell a little. At first this might have seemed no more than a slight fluctuation, such as was continually occurring, but it proved to be the beginning of a prolonged decline. In every quinquennium since 1870, except 1891-95, the rate of mortality has been lower than in the preceding quinquennium.[1]

[1] *Report of the Royal Commission on Population* (*Parl. Papers*, 1948-49, XIX), p. 19.

Since the beginning of this decline coincided with a temporary upward movement of the birth-rate, its initial effect was to accelerate the increase of population. The natural increase of population in England and Wales between 1871 and 1881 was 15·1 per cent,[1] which was probably a higher rate than at any time in the previous fifty years. But very soon the falling death-rate was accompanied by a falling birth-rate. Around 1880 this was probably attributable more to the changing age composition of the female population than to anything else, but what may have begun as a temporary fluctuation quickly developed into a protracted decline. Of the immediate sources of this decline one was a tendency for progressively fewer people to marry very young: in 1911 the proportion of people aged 20 to 24 who had been married was nearly one-third lower than it had been in 1881.[2] The other, not entirely independent of the first, was the fact that married couples began to have fewer children; of the married women who survived until 1911, those born between 1841 and 1845, nearly all of whose children must have been born between 1860 and 1885, had an average of 5·71 children each, whereas those born twenty years later had an average of 4·66 children. A generation later still, the women who married between 1900 and 1909 produced an average of 3·37 children each.[3] This reduction in family size was not offset by any permanent decline in infant mortality until the early years of the twentieth century, for signs of an improvement in this respect about 1880 were soon reversed and the number of deaths under one year per 1,000 live births was the same (153) for 1891-1901 as it had been for 1841-51.[4] Consequently, although the general death-rate fell more quickly after 1895, the lower birth-rate prevented this from causing any return to the very high rates of population growth of the eighteen-seventies.

The combined result of these various demographic changes was in general very favourable for economic advance, especially after about 1890. The stimulus of a rapid increase of numbers was not lost. The actual rate of increase of population fell from 14·4 per cent in 1871-81 to 10·9 per cent in 1901-11 but was still quite high.[5] In absolute terms, the increment to the population of England and Wales between 1871 and 1911, which was 13,358,000, was greater than in any other

---

[1] T. H. Marshall, 'The Population of England and Wales from the Industrial Revolution to the World War' in E. M. Carus-Wilson (ed.), *Essays in Economic History* (1954), p. 343.

[2] *Report of the R.C. on Population*, p. 22. [3] *Ibid.*, pp. 24-5.

[4] Marshall, *loc. cit.*, p. 343. [5] *Ibid.*, p. 343.

forty-year period of its history. And it was an increase achieved less wastefully than before. Fewer men died when they should just have been in their full powers; fewer women were worn out by excessive child-bearing; the children on whose rearing money and effort were spent without economic return because they never lived to maturity became a smaller proportion of the total population. Until about 1890 the effect of the high birth-rate of the eighteen-seventies was still being shown in the existence of a large proportion of dependants in the population, but thereafter the survivors of that generation of children passed into the working age groups and the number of new children did not increase proportionately. From the last decade of the nineteenth century England was acquiring a more mature population; more mature, not appreciably more senescent. There was little saving of life among the very young or the elderly. When the death-rate began to fall, the reduction in mortality was at first confined entirely to adults below the age of 35 and was for a time accompanied by rising mortality among those aged 45 or more.[1] By the early years of the twentieth century a larger proportion of the population was in the working age groups than for a very long time past (perhaps a larger proportion than ever before) though this change had then by no means reached its maximum; the percentage of the total population of Britain who were aged 15 to 64 inclusive rose only from 59·8 to 60·1 between 1851 and 1891, but by 1911 it had gone up to 63·9.[2]

Thus, though with some delay, the demographic situation made it easier for the British people to take some of the steps necessary to meet the challenge of novel practices and stronger competition. There were proportionately more people at the peak of their mental and physical powers; individual skill and training and experience were yielding their fruits for a longer period; the task of providing more thorough education and training was made less daunting as the proportion of children declined and, indeed, the disappearance of the superabundance of children made them seem a more precious asset, to be preserved and made the most of by public action as well as private care. All this does not amount to saying that the assential improvement in the quality of the people was achieved, though the reduction in mortality is a clear sign of the better health which was one of the greatest needs. But it does mean that more favourable conditions for the achievement of that improvement came into existence.

[1] Marshall, *loc. cit.*, p. 337.   [2] *Report of the R.C. on Population* p., 88.

If, however, some of the influences underlying the demographic changes are considered, they suggest that these advantages may have been secured in part only at the cost of modifying some other characteristics of society which in the immediate past had been particularly helpful to economic progress. The willingness of those who received most of the national income to save a high proportion of it, and their judgment in investing a large part of their savings in ways which made the most comprehensive contribution to economic expansion, particularly in the provision of new means of transport and the development of motive power, had been one of the major immediate determinants of the course of nineteenth-century economic history. But the changing demographic situation was possible only because of other changes which led to claims for the use of more of the available capital for different purposes and which made it rather more difficult for quite so big a proportion of the national income to be saved as before, though change in this last respect may easily be exaggerated.

In the state of scientific and medical knowledge before the First World War a significant reduction of mortality had to depend mainly upon a higher standard of personal consumption among a large proportion of the people and upon the improvement of the physical environment by such means as the provision of a more abundant and purer piped water supply, the completion of drainage and sewerage systems and the building of sewage disposal works, the paving of streets, the improvement of dwellings in respect of structural soundness and density of lay-out, and the provision of places of recreation. The relation between a dirty environment and the spread of some of the most prevalent killing diseases had been clearly demonstrated in the middle of the nineteenth century and more convincingly explained by the work of Pasteur, who showed that contagious diseases were caused by living organisms and whose views achieved general acceptance by 1880.[1] Knowledge of new cures for the diseases whose causative bacteria were identified, as so many were in the last quarter of the nineteenth century, was slow to develop at this time. Improvement had to be almost entirely through prevention and through the building of healthier bodies which would put up a stronger resistance to disease. Better sanitation, water-supply and

[1] F. Sherwood Taylor, *The Century of Science* (1941), pp. 87-9 and 102-4; among numerous contemporary pioneer works see J. Simon, 'The Sanitary State of the People of England' (1858) in his *Public Health Reports*, I, 428-88.

housing came therefore to be recognized as essential for longer survival as well as desirable in order to make life more comfortable. They required heavy capital expenditure which, in a free market, was not always financially remunerative. This was a major reason for their relative neglect earlier. Inevitably the building of additional houses and of the works necessary for some urban services had been an important part of the nation's capital formation, but it was a part which was not allowed to grow much beyond the inescapable minimum. After 1850 there was sufficient increase of such expenditure to prevent any further general deterioration in the physical environment, but it was only from about 1870 that its scale was raised so far as to bring a decisive improvement.[1]

Higher standards of personal consumption, which were also necessary for healthier and longer life, might be provided out of the general increase in incomes and need not cause a reduction in savings. But in the circumstances underlying the fall in the birth-rate it seems possible to detect symptoms of a declining readiness to forgo opportunities of current enjoyment. The smaller size of families was the result of deliberate choice by parents, at first mainly in the upper and middle classes, the source of nearly all the nation's savings.[2] To some extent it was doubtless influenced by improvements in artificial methods of contraception and the greater publicity given to them, but it could have been achieved earlier or left unachieved had people so wished.[3] No one has ever succeeded in explaining fully why it began when it did and a full explanation would almost certainly be very complex. But one important factor was the greater variety of satisfying things that were available for consumption, the greater number of benefits that could be bestowed on children, if only there were money to pay for them. To reduce the size of the family was one way of making the money go round;[4] another was to reduce the proportion of income which was saved. These might be alternatives, but they were likely to be regarded sometimes as supplementary to each other, especially as other influences reinforced them. Changing attitudes to religion, provoked by new scientific knowledge and

---

[1] Taylor, *op. cit.*, pp. 106-10; *cf.* W. Ashworth, *The Genesis of Modern British Town Planning* (1954), chaps. III and IV.

[2] *Report of the R.C. on Population*, pp. 27-8.   [3] *Ibid.*, pp. 36-7.

[4] On the influence of rising standards of consumption on the reduction in family size see J. A. Banks, *Prosperity and Parenthood* (1954), esp. chap. XII. The evidence which Mr Banks adduces seems strong enough to justify a less cautious statement of his conclusions than he himself gives.

reacting on established ideas of morality, must have influenced the ethic of marital life and also have modified ideas about the nature of personal responsibility, including the axiom that saving is one of its most worthy expressions. The increasing complexity and size of business made it harder for the frugal and enterprising individual to build his own personal monument within it. Comparable satisfactions had to be sought in other ways, and it was becoming easier to find them through conspicuous consumption than through the conspicuous creation of an independent fortune and position to be bequeathed to a numerous progeny.

It was hardly possible to achieve the sort of demographic change that was particularly suited to contemporary economic conditions without there being more general social change, which had further repercussions on what was economically practicable and profitable. In the years between 1870 and the First World War the social framework at home was changing no less profoundly than the state of world markets and the techniques and organization of business. Aspirations which previously were too weak to be important had to be given scope even if they ran counter to what national economic considerations might have suggested was most suitable. The development of British economic life could, even less than before, be determined purely by the operation of market forces. It had to emerge from a continuous process of compromise, in the shaping of which the rewards and the risks of innovation, the shifts of effective home and foreign demand, the rise and decline of new sources of supply, and the incentives to which people could and would respond, all took part. The fact that, if too much of the incentive appeared in the form of a promise of better times to come rather than better living now, many people would not, perhaps could not, fit themselves to supply the sort of work that was economically needed was a limiting factor on the way in which the economy could be adapted to its new environment. Fortunately the most striking characteristic of the changing world was its infinite variety. If people jibbed at following what some perfect economic man would have regarded as the straight road to maximum income there were still many ways left of moving towards greater abundance. Only great folly could miss all of them.

CHAPTER THREE

Agriculture

THE impact of new conditions of supply and demand was felt more quickly and more forcefully by agriculture than by any other branch of economic activity. Though the relative importance of manufacture had been increasing for so long, agriculture in 1870 was still one of the largest groups of industries and was still much the largest sphere in which home producers catered almost exclusively for the basic needs of home consumers. Sir James Caird calculated in 1868 that 80 per cent of the food consumed in the United Kingdom was produced within the country and that for livestock products the proportion was as high as 90 per cent.[1] To some extent the surplus of rural Ireland supplied some of the deficiencies of industrialized England but most of the Englishman's food was raised in England. It seemed, however, that the output of such staple foods as bread and meat could not quickly be increased much more. The future to which landlords and farmers hopefully looked forward was one in which a rising population and standard of living would expand the demand for food and keep up its price, with the supply being shared less unequally between home and foreign producers, to the detriment of neither.[2] Anything which drastically altered either the condition of the home market or the expectations about the cost and volume of foreign supplies was bound to have a substantial effect on the whole national economy.

It would be wrong, however, to regard agriculture as a completely homogeneous industry, exposed throughout to the same economic challenges. Great variety could be observed in the types and methods of farming in different localities and even within quite small districts. Mixed farming, rather than the extremes of specialization, was the general rule but the emphasis on particular products within a mixed farming system varied according to geographical conditions, the state of easily accessible markets, and the persistence of local traditions. In the country as a whole there was a fairly even economic

---

[1] J. Caird, *The Landed Interest and the Supply of Food* (1878), pp. 5-6.
[2] *Ibid.*, pp. 142-6.

balance between the raising of crops and of livestock. According to the best available estimate, crops represented 45 per cent and live-stock products 55 per cent of the value of the gross agricultural output (i.e. the produce sold off farms) of the United Kingdom in 1867-69.[1] No comparable estimates exist for England alone but in this country the proportion of crops must have been rather higher, since it was in the drier, lower lands of east, south-east and south England that there was the greatest concentration on the most valuable crop, wheat.[2] If *production*, rather than *output*, were under consideration the relative importance of crops would be a good deal higher because of the large quantities—e.g. almost the entire production of turnips—which were fed to livestock on the farm on which they were grown and which were never offered for sale. But, even where arable most predominated, farmers usually had a considerable interest in livestock. Sheep, the large numbers of which had for centuries been one of the distinguishing features of English agriculture, were an essential element in the husbandry of England's main cereal-growing districts, and the same districts had a large business in the fattening of cattle, though in general they were less noted for cattle breeding.

For the United Kingdom as a whole in 1867-69 the chief items of output, in terms of estimated annual value of sales, were wheat (£35 million), beef and veal (£35 million), milk (£34 million), mutton and lamb (£26 million), pigmeat (£19 million), barley (£17 million), potatoes (£14 million), oats (£11 million), hay and straw (£10 million), and wool (£7 million).[3] Year by year, as average incomes and urbanization increased, the demand for livestock products expanded. With temporary intermissions, the receipts from selling them had tended to grow, relatively to those from the sale of cereals, all through the nineteenth century.[4] It seems probable that by 1870, in response to this fundamental economic trend, British farmers were already tending to concentrate more on livestock production;[5] but the change was a gradual one, made possible by

---

[1] E. M. Ojala, *Agriculture and Economic Progress* (1952), p. 208.

[2] Caird, *op. cit.*, p. 34.   [3] Ojala, *op. cit.*, p. 208.

[4] On the change since *c.* 1850 see Caird, *op. cit.*, p. 30; on longer-term changes J. Caird, *English Agriculture in 1850-51* (1852), pp. 475 and 485-6.

[5] *Cf.* the estimates of production in 1848-50 and 1872-74 given by A. Sauerbeck in 'Prices of Commodities and the Precious Metals' (*Journ. of the Stat. Society*, XLIX (1886), 616-19). These show increases of over 50 per cent in beef, smaller increases in mutton, pork and wool, a 20 per cent reduction in oats and little change in other cereals.

improved breeding and the greater import of store cattle and not as yet making any serious encroachment on the amount of land devoted to cereal production. On land where cereal growing was traditional, farmers could still make a reasonable living from it and continued to make it the centre of their activity, even when it had become possible that some of them might make a still better living from other systems.

This might imply that farming was not adjusting itself perfectly to changing economic conditions, and certainly there were contemporary critics to suggest that agriculture was missing many of its opportunities. Nevertheless, for twenty years English agriculture had enjoyed a great reputation abroad for its high quality, and it was because, in comparison with other countries, it showed higher returns at less cost that farming appeared to justify by results the unusual agrarian system within which it was conducted.[1]

The essence of this system was the division of the agricultural population into three classes with sharply differentiated functions. Most of the land was owned by large landlords, who farmed very little of it themselves, but divided their estates into holdings which were generally large by the standards of the rest of Western Europe and which were occupied by tenant farmers. In a few districts the latter had leases for a term of years (up to twenty-one years) but most farmers in England (unlike those in Scotland) were tenants-at-will, whose occupation was terminable at six months' notice. Most farms were too large to be worked by the farmers and their families alone and consequently they employed labourers who usually had no land of their own and were entirely dependent on their wages. The landlord was responsible for the provision, maintenance and improvement of all the fixed capital of his estate: buildings, roads, fences and drainage. The farmer provided his own movable capital: stock, seed, implements and machinery; and sometimes he contributed to the provision of drainage as well. Any permanent improvements were the property of the landlord. Even if they were partly due to the expenditure or efforts of the tenant the latter received no compensation for them, except in a few districts where, by local custom, an incoming compensated an outgoing tenant for the value of improvements in the farm. To an appreciable extent landlords controlled the farming practices of their tenants. The terms of the agreement might limit the farmer's freedom in the choice of crops and might impose

[1] Caird, *The Landed Interest*, pp. 68-70.

restrictions in the interest of the preservation of game, but the formal requirements imposed by landlords varied widely.[1]

The most striking feature of these arrangements was the heavy reliance placed on the landlords to keep up and improve the equipment and efficiency of agriculture. In practice this meant that the well-being of one of the nation's greatest industries was in the hands of a minute proportion of its people, for the ownership of land was heavily concentrated. In 1873, 18,546,000 acres of England and Wales—almost exactly half the total area of the country—were owned by only 4,217 persons, each of whom possessed 1,000 acres or more. Among these persons 400 peers and peeresses owned 5,729,000 acres.[2] In the whole United Kingdom in 1879 there were 901 landlords with estates of over 10,000 acres each, of whom 44 owned more than 100,000 acres each.[3] One of the key questions for the well-being of agriculture was whether this small number of large landowners had the capital, the inclination and the ability to ensure that the land was well equipped and to secure the co-operation of their tenants in good farming practices.

Many critics around 1870 suggested that large numbers of both landlords and tenants were unable to perform their functions satisfactorily. They argued that, in the absence of the security conferred by a long lease and in the absence of compensation for improvements, tenants had no incentive to make the most of their farms. Still more strongly they urged that many landlords could not or would not improve their estates; they were too heavily encumbered by debts to be able to invest adequately in them, or they were enmeshed in legal restrictions which hampered administration, or they were more interested in the political influence and sport provided by their estates than in their economic possibilities. Particular objection was taken to the widespread practice among the aristocracy and gentry of subjecting their estates to a strict settlement, under the terms of which the owner became effectively no more than a life-tenant, with restricted powers to incur obligations which would bind his successor, and the succession to the undiminished estate was secured to the life-tenant's eldest son and then to the eldest son of the latter. Settled estates ran the risk of being starved of capital, first, because, however

[1] *Ibid.*, chap. V, for a good, brief account of the tripartite system of landlord, tenant and labourer.

[2] J. Bateman, *The Great Landowners of Great Britain and Ireland* (4th edn., 1883), p. 515.

[3] *Ibid.*, p. 495.

the revenue from them fluctuated, they had to provide fixed incomes for younger children, dowagers and unmarried female relatives; second, because it was difficult for a life-tenant to sell part of the estate and use the proceeds for the improvement of the rest of it; and, third, because a life-tenant could not borrow on mortgage so easily as an owner in fee-simple. But, because of the settlement, an estate might remain in the possession of a family encumbered by debts instead of being available for sale to an owner with ample capital to invest in it.[1]

It is difficult to see that these strictures were fully justified by the economic facts of the time and, in part at least, they appear to have been an attempt to rationalize opposition to the continued political power of the landed aristocracy, which the repeal of the Corn Laws had failed to break. In spite of the large area of land held under settlement, there was a very active land market and the lots offered for sale often ran to many hundreds of acres; and it is doubtful whether so much was invested in agriculture in any other period as in the eighteen-fifties and 'sixties. The largest landlords were usually those with the greatest resources for the development of their estates —the notorious debtors were not the representative case—and many administered them with a high sense of responsibility. The influence of the great landlord can be seen at its best on the estates of the Dukes of Bedford. In the twenty years up to 1875 these invested £142,553 in permanent improvements to the Thorney estate of about 19,000 acres in Lincolnshire. In the same years £203,833 was spent for similar purposes on the estates in Bedfordshire and Buckinghamshire, which were increased during the period from 33,000 to 37,000 acres. The investment in permanent improvements was almost exactly one-fifth of the gross income in the latter case, and only a little less in the former.[2] Doubtless few other landowners treated their estates as well as this; but probably equally few were guilty of all the neglect and errors which were said to be the inevitable consequence of the prevailing land system. Up to the eighteen-seventies, though many deficiencies remained, the condition of agriculture was being steadily improved by the more general adoption of the best farming practices

---

[1] For a clear account of the system of settlement and its effects, with adverse comments, see G. C. Brodrick, *English Land and English Landlords* (1881), pp. 129-51. See also C. W. Hoskyns, 'The Land Laws of England' (in J. W. Probyn (ed.), *Systems of Land Tenure in Various Countries* (3rd edn., 1876)), *passim*, esp. pp. 94-109; and J. Kay, *Free Trade in Land* (5th edn., 1880), pp. 23-63.

[2] Duke of Bedford, *A Great Agricultural Estate* (1897), pp. 222-3 and 234-5.

known thirty years earlier, by the use of reaping machines and an increase in the use of steam-power, and by fixed investment, especially in drainage.[1] It is true, as critics averred, that much land that could have been improved by drainage remained undrained,[2] though there were good judges who cast doubt on the figures which they used.[3] It is true also (the other main point of criticism) that greater investment in the land would have made it possible to produce more food, perhaps to dispense with food imports except from the tropics.[4] But whether extra capital used in this way would have been as productive as in other uses is very doubtful. The decline in agricultural investment in the late eighteen-sixties[5] was probably due to the many attractive alternative outlets for capital that were then appearing, and who would say that the choice made by investors was basically unsound?

The great merit of English agriculture as it was around 1870 was the degree to which it had made commonplaces of the most striking innovations developed over the previous century and a half. It had brought to a higher level of efficiency than had been attained earlier or elsewhere an industry whose chief concerns—products, markets, labour supply and social setting—were still determined by a traditional state of affairs in which rural life predominated and which was rapidly fading in England. Its great weakness was the slowness with which it reacted to changing economic and social conditions, and for this the peculiar agrarian system could take only a small part of the blame. That the prevalence of tenancy-at-will and the rarity of long leases discouraged farmers from taking the initiative in improvements is suggested by the contrasting experience of England and Scotland, where nineteen-year leases were the rule, in this respect.[6] That the members of the English aristocracy, though most of them were anxious to see their properties well run, rarely had any special training in estate management was also an obstacle to the achievement of maximum efficiency, even where very able land agents were

---

[1] Caird, *op. cit.*, pp. 28-9 and 79-88.   [2] Kay, *op. cit.*, p. 53.

[3] Clapham, *op. cit.*, II, 270-1.

[4] W. Fowler, 'The Present Aspect of the Land Question' in *Cobden Club Essays*, 2nd Series (1872), pp. 118-20.

[5] See p. 12 above. The suggestion of a general decline in agricultural investment may be supported by important individual instances. Investment in improvements to the Bedford estate at Thorney was at a high level from 1853 to 1869 and then fell sharply until 1875; there was a similar fall on the Beds. and Bucks. estate after 1868 (Duke of Bedford, *op. cit.*, pp. 223 and 233-5).

[6] Caird, *op. cit.*, pp. 100-1.

employed.[1] But it is unlikely that a different set of landowners would have been any better. Even had they had the incentive to seek it, they would not easily have found much specialized education in agriculture or estate management; this was a lack which was one of the dangers in the agricultural situation.

Apart from this the imperfect adaptability of agriculture can be attributed partly to the conservative outlook bred by the occupation itself and partly to the lack of strong economic pressure. Land values in the country as a whole (though not in every part of it) were rising faster than the amount of new investment in land,[2] and there were more applicants for farms than there were vacant farms. In these circumstances landlords did not need to pursue every possibility of improvement or to give greater freedom and encouragement to the most lively-minded, practical farmers. Farmers themselves could pay gradually rising rents and make a reasonable living without doing anything much more original than show a fair competence in the practices used by their most able neighbours in the previous generation. Except in the most industrialized districts labourers remained available in large numbers for agriculture. Wherever this was so the introduction of the most modern labour-saving equipment needed to be only a very gradual process, nor did farmers need worry overmuch about improving the quality of their workers. So farm labourers remained poorly paid, without perhaps being worth more to their employers than the amount of their wages. Being poorly paid, they could not afford the economic rent of decent cottages and therefore the building of better cottages was the improvement which landlords were least willing to attempt; and the persistence of poor living conditions hampered the achievement of any greater efficiency by the workers. In all these ways the need for maximum enterprise was lessened and farmers and landowners, who, like the rest of mankind, often preferred freedom from drastic change to the possibility of a somewhat higher income, could exercise their preference without any obvious penalty. To some extent, too, the errors of the experts may also have prevented agricultural progress from being as great as it might have been. For instance, the improvement on which most money was spent was drainage and, though it undoubtedly was generally remunerative, the insistence on placing all drains deep was subsequently found to have greatly reduced their effectiveness in many cases. Where surface water was the chief problem

---

[1] Caird, *op. cit.*, pp. 102-4.　　[2] *Ibid.*, pp. 31 and 96-9.

the mid-Victorian drainage work often had to be re-done later.[1]

English agriculture, then, in the eighteen-seventies showed many signs of recent progress and looked well in comparison with that of nearly all other countries. But it had its vulnerable points: undue conservatism, the lack of alternative leadership if landlords should somehow fail in their responsibilities, the wasteful use of inadequately trained workers, the rather small provision for the collection, enlargement and diffusion of technical knowledge. At these points it had not been severely tested for many years and the possible dangers were therefore under-estimated by those most immediately concerned.

Into these conditions change came swiftly and with drastic effect. At first the trouble seemed to be no more than an unusual run of bad luck with the weather. In seven years in the decade of the 'seventies the harvest was below average and was especially bad in 1873, 1875, 1877 and 1879. 1875 was particularly wet in summer and late autumn, and the long disastrous sequence culminated in the harvest year 1878-79. The winter sowing had to be done in an unusually wet season and the summer was very wet, cool and short of sunshine, with the result that 1879 produced the worst harvest of the century.[2] Large numbers of farmers suffered severely from these events, but most people looked on them as no more than a temporary trial which could be expected soon to pass away.[3]

There were, however, many signs that more permanent influences were beginning to operate. In the past, farmers had found themselves more or less compensated for a bad harvest by the higher prices which smaller supplies induced in the following year. Now this no longer happened; prices tended downwards in spite of the series of bad harvests. Contemporaries rightly attributed this new phenomenon to foreign competition but looked on it as largely a matter of luck: North America enjoyed good harvests while Europe had poor ones. They were a little slow to recognize that new conditions were

[1] For discussion of this point, with specific cases, see R. H. Pringle's *Report on the counties of Beds., Hunts., and Northants.*, p. 53, in *R.C. on Agric. Depression, Asst. Commrs. Reports* (P.P. 1895, XVII); A. D. Hall, *A Pilgrimage of British Farming 1910-1912* (1914), p. 418; and J. Orr, *Agriculture in Oxfordshire* (1916), pp. 72 and 114.

[2] *Report of the Royal Commission on Agriculture* (P.P. 1882, XIV), pp. 12-13; *Minutes of Evidence of ibid.*, QQ. 62,645-7; *Appendix to Digest of Evidence of ibid.*, p. 159.

[3] *Report of the R.C. on Agriculture*, pp. 24 and 32.

making it possible for foreign suppliers permanently to undercut many British farmers, whatever the weather; but soon this became obvious. In the late 'seventies the extra grain produce of the United States had been ample to make good the deficiency of the British harvest at prices not very different from what had come to be regarded as normal. The tremendous surge in railway construction in the eighteen-eighties, especially in the United States and to a less extent in Eastern Europe, made accessible much greater supplies at much lower cost. British harvests improved but food imports remained as high as when home harvests were bad, and in the 'nineties the imports were again growing quickly, while prices, especially of grain, tumbled.[1] The gross average annual imports of wheat into the United Kingdom increased from 58,314,000 cwt. in 1875-77 to 99,257,000 cwt. in 1893-95. For barley the increase in these years, from 11,261,000 cwt. to 25,902,000 cwt. was even greater in proportion, but mostly concentrated in the period after 1886. The increase in the imports of oats was much smaller.[2] In 1893-95 imports accounted for 77 per cent of the country's wheat consumption, as compared with 50 per cent twenty years earlier.[3] At the later date 44 per cent of the barley supply and 20 per cent of the oats were imported, but the proportion of imports to home production was fairly steady in the case of oats for the time being.[4] Imports of meat were also rising steadily and practically doubled in quantity between 1876-78 and 1893-95,[5] with a particularly significant rise in the proportion of dead meat to live animals among the imports, a change made possible by new methods of preservation, especially refrigeration, in the 'eighties. But imports did not constitute so large a proportion of the total supply as in the case of cereals. In 1895, 28 per cent of the beef and veal, 31 per cent of the mutton and lamb, and 49 per cent of the pigmeat were imported.[6]

Increasing foreign supplies and falling prices, though causing many difficulties, were not in every respect disadvantageous to British agriculture. The prices of most things, except the important item of labour, were falling considerably, and so farmers' expenses were reduced as well as their receipts, though not always to the same extent. In particular, the lower prices which arable farmers received

---

[1] There are annual estimates of the total volume of different types of food imported in Schlote, *op. cit.*, pp. 140-1.

[2] *Final Report of the Royal Commission on Agricultural Depression (P.P.* 1897, XV), p. 54.

[3] *Ibid.*, p. 55.   [4] *Ibid.*, pp. 60 and 61.   [5] *Ibid.*, p. 64.   [6] *Ibid.*, pp. 65-7.

for their produce were also lower prices which livestock farmers paid for feeding stuffs; and some of the cheaper, more abundant foreign supplies were a similar source of economy. Maize, for example, not much imported before the eighteen-forties, was being largely used by the 'seventies. Imports in the last quarter of the century were running at about 30 million cwt. annually and tended gradually to rise, and the large fall in price was a real help to livestock farmers.[1]

There were also important changes in demand for some foodstuffs which presented new opportunities for farmers. The Duke of Richmond's Commission, which reported in 1882, received plenty of evidence that, despite the previous unfavourable seasons, the districts where grazing predominated had come to little economic harm,[2] but it failed to draw the right conclusion. The truth was that the widening range of imports and the rise of real wages were leading to changes in the dietary habits of the working classes, especially in the towns, which by this time housed the great majority of the population. Fewer people relied, as in the past, on bread and potatoes as the main part of their diet, with only minor additions and variations. The consumption of potatoes per head is estimated to have reached its peak about 1871 and then to have declined by one-third by the end of the century; the consumption of wheat per head, which had been rising steadily between the 'forties and 'seventies, remained fairly stable thereafter, with a very slight downward tendency.[3] Instead of bread and potatoes, people wanted more meat and dairy produce and, to a less extent, more fruit and green vegetables, and a bigger proportion of the population than ever before could afford to buy substantial amounts of these things. By the time of the second great official investigation of the state of agriculture this shift of demand had come to be seen as one of the main influences at work. Sir Robert Giffen, indeed, went so far as to suggest that cereal farming at home was being hit more by the increased supply and consumption of meat than by the increase in foreign supplies of cereals.[4] He probably exaggerated but the essential point of his argument was sound.

The most significant point for British farmers was that there was

[1] *Ibid.*, p. 62.
[2] The evidence is summarized in the *Report of the R.C. on Agriculture* (1882), pp. 9-10.
[3] R. N. Salaman, *The History and Social Influence of the Potato* (1949), pp. 613 and 616-17. The estimates refer to the U.K. but make allowances for differences in dietary habits in the different countries.
[4] *Appendix to the Final Report of the R.C. on Agricultural Depression*, p. 74.

c

little foreign competition in the supply of a few of the items for which demand was growing and that, where strong competition did have to be faced, the foreign suppliers had not such great natural advantages as in the case of cereals. Other minor advantages to British farmers came from industrial and commercial conditions at home. The continued growth of towns and of internal trade meant a steady and rising demand for horses for use in local transport and therefore a demand for fodder. In turn, the towns were able to supply large quantities of manure, which simplified the problems of some of the market gardening areas.[1] The coming of motor transport in the early years of the twentieth century soon began to alter this situation,[2] but the change was not very drastic before the First World War. The one way in which manufacturing and commercial developments proved directly disappointing to farmers was in the collapse of the wool market, which took a declining amount of British produce. This was partly because the textile industries were growing more slowly than before, partly because increasing amounts of wool were obtainable from abroad, and partly because some of the cloths for which common types of English wool were specially suitable went out of fashion.[3]

The way in which these various changes in market conditions, so much more unfavourable to some types of farmer than others, made themselves felt was, of course, through changes in prices. All farmers experienced falling prices until about the end of the nineteenth century and then a recovery. But for some the fall was catastrophic and the subsequent rise quite small, while others had a much milder experience and found prices immediately before the First World War almost as good as their predecessors had known in the eighteen-seventies. The details of the price changes are summarized in Table I.

The lesson of these price movements was obvious to farmers: reduce the cultivation of cereals, especially wheat; raise more livestock where practicable; reduce expenses as far as possible, especially if it was impossible to concentrate on the most remunerative products; purchase feeding stuffs wherever it had become cheaper to do this than to grow them on one's own farm. The agricultural statistics bear witness to the extensive changes that were made in accordance with this prescription, though, as far as changes in land use are

---

[1] Hall, *op. cit.*, pp. 63 and 424.   [2] *Ibid.*, p. 428.
[3] *Final Report of the R.C. on Agricultural Depression*, pp. 73-5; Clapham, *op. cit.*, II, 281.

TABLE I

Sauerbeck's Price Indices for English Agricultural Produce,
1870-1913

(1867-77 = 100)*

Years	Wheat	Barley	Oats	Potatoes	Prime Beef	Prime Mutton	English Wool‡	General Prices
1870-74	101	99	97	98	102	102	110	104
1875-79	88	96	98	112	103	109	82	91
1880-84	78	82	83	84	99	109	60	83
1885-89	58	69	70	69	81	92	53	70
1890-94	54	68	73	63	80	87	50	69
1895-99	51	62	63	61	79	87	51	63
1900-04	50	62	69	68	85	91	39	71
1905-09	58	65	70	63	84	92	56	75
1910-13	59	69	74	69	91	93	54	82

Sources: A. Sauerbeck, 'Prices of Commodities and the Precious Metals' in *Journ. of the Stat. Socy.*, XLIX (1886), 642-6; *idem*, 'Prices of Commodities during the Last Seven Years' in *ibid.*, LVI (1893), 241-2, 245 and 247: *idem*, 'Prices of Commodities in 1899', in *ibid.*, LXIII (1900), 93, 101-2 and 105; and Sir G. Paish, 'Prices of Commodities in 1913', in *ibid.*, LXXVII (1913-14), 556 and 565-6.

* The actual prices in the base period were: wheat 54s. 6d. per qr.; barley 39s. per qr.; oats 26s. per qr.; potatoes 117s. per ton; prime beef 59d. per 8 lb.; prime mutton 63d. per 8 lb.; wool 19¾d. per lb.

‡ Lincoln half hogs. The demand for this type of wool was adversely affected by changes in fashion and the fall in its price was therefore somewhat greater than that for other types.

concerned, the revolution was not quite so great as the force and volume of contemporary comment might suggest. The principal figures are summarized in Table II.

The great changes were the increase in permanent pasture, mainly, though not entirely, in replacement of arable cultivation, and, associated with it, a large increase in the number of cattle. Until the end of the nineteenth century the main source of reduction in the arable area was the abandonment of the cultivation of wheat and, to a less extent, of turnips and swedes which commonly followed it in rotation. Turnips and swedes were less necessary on many arable farms because the reduction of corn growing was accompanied by a decline

TABLE II

England and Wales: Acreage under various types of crops and grass, and numbers of livestock, 1870–1914.

	1870	1880	1890	1900	1910	1914
Total cultivated area (acres)*	25,957,035	27,363,782	27,872,335	27,538,130	27,292,588	27,114,004
Permanent Pasture (acres)	11,107,860	13,267,606	14,792,439	15,320,922	15,972,144	16,115,750
Total Arable Land (acres)	14,849,175	14,096,176	13,079,896	12,217,208	11,320,444	10,998,254
Total Green Crops (acres)	2,890,029	2,779,207	2,647,754	2,554,867	2,390,920	2,403,496
Total Corn Crops (acres)	8,123,780	7,471,815	6,715,920	6,076,759	5,826,063	5,758,651
Wheat (acres)	3,374,901	2,835,462	2,324,363	1,796,210	1,756,057	1,807,498
Barley (acres)	2,127,597	2,203,321	1,895,386	1,750,070	1,537,061	1,504,771
Oats (acres)	1,743,704	1,759,651	1,889,352	2,076,960	2,062,824	1,929,626
Horses‡	1,093,838	1,227,167	1,242,893	1,305,605	1,341,809	1,399,547
Cattle	4,361,883	4,812,760	5,322,756	5,607,084	5,866,568	5,877,944
Sheep	21,646,735	19,546,962	19,910,998	19,277,229	19,958,299	17,259,604
Pigs	2,012,448	1,879,917	2,613,935	2,249,519	2,216,599	2,481,481

Source: W. Page (ed.), *Commerce and Industry: Statistical Tables* (1919), tables 73, 77, 78, 80 and 81. These tables are based on the Board of Agriculture's annual *Agricultural Returns and Statistics*.

in the number of sheep, which had been an integral part of the economy of such farms. The stability of the total number of sheep between 1880 and 1910 conceals two contrary tendencies—a decline in numbers in the arable districts and a steady increase in the more pastoral and hilly areas. Until the end of the nineteenth century the reduction of the arable area was kept in check because many farmers, instead of turning over their land to permanent pasture, simply gave their seeds an extra year or two in the rotation, so that the area under artificial grasses steadily increased. When the deterioration of market conditions came to an end they abandoned this practice, and the main item in the further reduction of the arable area between 1900 and 1914 was the fall in the area under rotation grasses. Other minor changes, not shown in the table, were the increases in the areas devoted to market gardening and fruit growing. The total acreage involved was small but had a disproportionate importance because it was more intensively cultivated than other land.[1]

That the turning away from arable cultivation generally, and from corn growing in particular, was not even greater and more rapid, despite the intense pressure of market conditions, may be attributed partly to the fact that the alternatives had already been adopted by some farmers in the middle of the nineteenth century.[2] But probably more important were the necessity for new capital (which was not generally available) if a change was to be made, and the unsuitability of natural conditions in many districts. A farmer who reduced the crop area and went in for more livestock was likely to find himself with barns that he did not need and a lack of other buildings which his landlord thought it unprofitable to provide. To some extent agriculture suffered because not enough investment had been put into buildings suitable for livestock and dairy farming a little earlier when capital was plentiful and agricultural prospects bright. No reliable figures exist of fixed capital investment in agriculture, but it is extremely probable that from 1880 to 1914 net investment of this kind was negative.[3] Moreover, the adoption of a new system of

---

[1] Detailed statistics for acreages under various minor crops are summarized for selected years in Lord Ernle, *English Farming Past and Present* (5th edn., 1936), pp. 512-14.

[2] Clapham, *op. cit.*, III, 86-7.

[3] Figures given by Giffen (*The Growth of Capital*, p. 43) and P. H. Douglas (*Journ. of Econ. and Business History*, II, 661) suggest that the current value of farmers' capital was almost halved between 1875 and 1914 and that the value of lands fell from £2,007 million to something between £1,155 million and £1,305 million, but these figures are not closely related to the amount and condition of the physical equipment of landed estates and farms.

farming made new demands for working capital and in times of low prices most farmers simply could not accumulate extra capital or provide adequate security on which to borrow it. Investigators found many instances of farmers who would have liked to abandon systems which had become unprofitable but could not do so, for lack of capital.[1]

Conditions of climate and, especially, of soil also restricted the possibilities of change, though not to such an extent as many farmers chose to believe. The very light soils in parts of Lincolnshire and East Anglia which, never having been more than rough sheep walks until the eighteenth century, had become excellent corn growing lands, gave very poor results when experiments were made in laying them down to grass. Some of the heaviest clays also proved unsatisfactory. In some places where attempts were made to develop permanent pasture on such soils, notably in Essex, the land was conquered by weeds and became almost derelict. But even in such cases the change was usually difficult and costly rather than impossible. Some farmers successfully developed dairying on the heavy Essex clays, but the changeover usually demanded time and money before it was commercially rewarding, and many farmers could not afford either to invest or to wait for the fruition of their efforts.[2] In many places it happened that the local men maintained that natural conditions made impracticable any methods of farming other than those to which they were accustomed; but, when their conservatism had led them to ruin, some of them were replaced by immigrants from other districts who, uninhibited by local traditions which had never been their own, managed to accomplish what had been thought to be against nature. Many Scotsmen moved from the grazing districts of their own country to take low-rented arable farms in the Midlands and South-East England, particularly in Essex, and turn them over mainly to grass.[3] Some comparable migration also took place from Devonshire, with similar results.[4] The time-lag before such

---

[1] e.g. Pringle's *Report on Beds., Hunts. and Northants.*, p. 43.

[2] See the summary of evidence in F. A. Channing's dissenting report, printed with *Final Report of the R.C. on Agric. Depression*, pp. 258-9.

[3] e.g. Pringle's *Report on Beds., Hunts. and Northants.*, p. 43; H. Rider Haggard, *Rural England* (1902), II, 99; C. S. Orwin, *A History of English Farming* (1949), pp. 79-80. For a detailed account of the practices adopted by one immigrant Scots farmer in Essex see P. McConnell, *The Diary of a Working Farmer* (1906).

[4] Pringle as above; Haggard, *op. cit.*, I, 195 and 216 and II, 99; Orr, *op. cit.*, p. 5, for the part played by this migration in the development of the milk business on the Chilterns.

movements became worth while helps to explain why much of the re-adjustment of farming practices took place after market conditions had begun to improve instead of during the worst years. But even after 1900 the attempt was still not being made everywhere to adapt the type of agricultural production to the needs of the market; and there were still cases where natural conditions defeated such attempts when they were made.

For all farmers when prices were falling, but especially for those whom ignorance, lack of money and equipment, or the hard facts of nature compelled to go on raising the least remunerative products, some means of cutting costs was essential. Rents and the wage-bill were the most obvious targets for economy. Both were rising in the early eighteen-seventies and both landlords and labourers were likely to resist any attempts to reverse the trend. The former looked to be the more capable of doing this successfully but, in fact, it was impossible for them to do so for very long. In the first years of bad harvests and falling prices rents were generally maintained at the high levels recently reached, but requests for abatements or reductions soon had to be met. By the 'eighties, and still more in the 'nineties, landlords often had to choose between granting a further reduction of rent and having a vacant farm left in hand. Information about the actual level of rents is scanty. The best available summary of it is that embodied by Mr Rhée in his index of the rent of agricultural land in England and Wales. This, taking a rent of 28 shillings per acre as 100, moved thus:[1]

1870-74	101	1885-89	83	1900-04	72
1875-79	104	1890-94	79	1905-09	74
1880-84	94	1895-99	74	1910-14	75

It should be remembered that these are average figures which conceal great local variations. In some purely pastoral districts rents probably fell little, if at all, whereas on some mainly arable farms they were reduced to almost negligible sums. For instance, to take an extreme case, 638 acres at Steeple in Essex paid £760 in rent in 1873, £460 a year from 1883 to 1886 but from 1886 to 1891 only £1 a year, with the tenant bearing £140 tithe rent charge instead of the landlord.[2] In general it appears that in the years of falling prices landlords, after

[1] Central Landowners' Association, *The Rent of Agricultural Land in England and Wales 1870-1946* (1949), pp. 41-2.
[2] *V.C.H. Essex*, II (1907), 327.

some delay, relieved their tenants of an appreciable, but not disproportionate, part of their outgoings, and that when prices began to
rise again landlords increased their demands hardly at all.

The fall in rents was to landlords a direct cut in their incomes and
a loss of revenue for the upkeep of their estates. Some landlords had
other large sources of income, part of which they used to keep their
agricultural properties in good order. Many a farmer had his landlord
to thank for keeping him on a reasonably equipped farm while he
was paying very little rent.[1] But few landlords could maintain such
uncommercial behaviour indefinitely. In the not very long run falling
rents persuaded, in many cases forced, them to reduce their standards
of maintenance and to cease all new investment in their estates. For
the farming community as a whole the relief of paying out less in rent
had to be set against a poorer provision of capital equipment.

A reduction of expenditure on labour was also something for which
a penalty had to be incurred. The commonest immediate cause of the
higher wages of the early eighteen-seventies was the pressure of
Joseph Arch's new trade union, the first to achieve even temporarily
any appreciable success among farm workers.[2] That movement could
be defeated within a few years and some of the concessions made to
it withdrawn, but thereafter further reductions in wages were impracticable. Farmers, particularly if they reduced arable cultivation,
could manage with less labour, but if wages were pressed too far
down then too many workers would simply go off to seek other jobs
in the towns. The pull of alternative employment varied greatly
between different districts, according to the proximity of large towns,
manufactures and mining, but almost everywhere in the countryside
the psychological as well as the physical barriers to movement had
greatly diminished. Farmers had therefore to keep up and gradually
improve the wages of their workers, if they did not wish to lose the
best of them. The failure to achieve any appreciable economy by
cutting wages appears clearly from the figures in Table III.

Minor reductions in labour cost were sometimes achieved by
ignoring the old custom that the master must provide and pay for
a full week's work for his men and substituting only payment for

---

[1] Ernle, *op. cit.*, pp. 380 and 384. Lord Ernle's own experience as chief agent to
the Duke of Bedford, an exceptionally wealthy and enlightened landowner, probably coloured his views on this topic and led him to exaggerate the service which
landlords rendered in this way. *Cf.* his treatment of the same question in his
Whippingham to Westminster (1938), pp. 200-2.

[2] W. Hasbach, *A History of the English Agricultural Labourer* (1908), pp. 277-85.

TABLE III

Weekly cash wages of agricultural labourers in different parts of England, 1867-1914

Date	Div. 1 s. d.		Div. 2 s. d.		Div. 3 s. d.		Div. 4 s. d.		Div. 5 s. d.		Div. 6 s. d.		Div. 7 s. d.	
1867-71	15	1	13	4	11	4	10	6	11	7	11	8	11	0
1879-81	16	2	14	5	13	4	12	4	13	0	13	10	12	6
1892-93	16	5	15	2	12	6	11	8	12	4	12	10	11	10
1898	16	10	16	2	13	10	12	7	13	0	14	10	11	11
1902	18	0	16	9	13	10	13	3	13	7	15	4	12	11
1907	17	3	16	3	14	8	13	8	13	11	15	9	12	10
1914	22	3	16	7	15	3	14	3	15	7	17	4	15	10

Source: C. S. Orwin and B. I. Felton, 'A Century of Wages and Earnings in Agriculture' in *Journ. of the R. Agric. Socy. of England*, XCII (1931), 233 and 247.

Key to divisions: 1. Cumberland, Westmorland, Northumberland, Durham, Yorks., Lancs., Cheshire.
2. Derbyshire, Notts., Lincs., Rutland, Leics.
3. Warwicks., Worcs., Staffs., Salop., Herefordshire, Gloucestershire.
4. Somerset, Cornwall, Devon, Dorset, Wilts.
5. Cambridgeshire, Bedfordshire, Hunts., Northants., Herts., Bucks., Oxon.
6. Hants., Sussex, Kent, Surrey, Middx., Berks.
7. Essex, Suffolk, Norfolk.

N.B. Regular allowances of various kinds raised the actual earnings above these figures of cash wages by amounts varying at different times and places, usually between 2s. and 3s. per week, but sometimes just outside these limits.

days actually worked.[1] Something was saved, too, by ensuring that work was better done and by fitting into the routine of the farm odd jobs that previously had been given to casual workers.[2] But substantial cuts in expenditure on labour could be achieved only by a reduction in the number of hired workers, and this is what happened. Not only was much labour saved by the reduction of the arable acreage but those farmers who continued to be concerned mainly with arable had to learn how to carry on with less hired labour. The number of hired agricultural workers (including foremen and farm bailiffs) on farms in England and Wales fell from 988,824 in 1871 to

[1] Orwin and Felton in *Journ. of the R. Agric. Socy. of England*, XCII, 248-9.
[2] *Ibid.*, XCII, 245.

798,912 in 1891 and to 665,258 in 1911.[1] A little of this loss of labour power might be made good by farmers themselves working harder for longer hours, which was often said to be the secret of the success of Scots farmers in England. A little more might be made good if other members of the family regularly joined in the work of the farm; the census figures do in fact show a large increase in the number of farmers' relatives assisting on farms after 1891, but changes of definition make it impossible to say whether this was anything more than a statistical rearrangement. In general, it seems fairly clear that the input of labour and capital into agriculture declined.

For some farmers this was almost the beginning and the end of the economics of adjustment to harder times: to put less into their business and take less out of it, and hope that on balance their net incomes (helped out by such minor changes as the transfer of liability for tithe rent charge from tenant to owner in 1891, and the remission of half the rates on agricultural land after 1896) would not be cut unduly. For a few who carried to extremes the maxim of farming low, the means of securing an adequate income was to take a larger area of land, a practice which became feasible as rents and land prices fell. But this was not a widespread occurrence. The official statistics, in fact, show a slight decrease in the average size of holdings after the 'eighties, though this may be misleading since two farms operated together by a single farmer were nevertheless reckoned as two separate holdings.[2] Some rearrangement of the size and boundaries of farms took place, but hardly sufficient to have any general importance. Even the obligation imposed on County Councils in 1908 to provide smallholdings made no great difference. By 1914 they had established 14,000 smallholdings, with an average size of 14 acres.[3] Such a provision affected only a negligible proportion of the agricultural land and population.

More significant than either the smallholdings movement or the attempts to operate very large farms was the fact that the general average amount of land per farmer changed little. In the early years of the twentieth century much the same amount of agricultural land was supporting nearly as many farmers as in the eighteen-seventies. The number of people recorded as farmers or graziers in England and Wales was 249,735 in 1871, 223,943 in 1881, 223,610 in 1891,

---

[1] The census figures are summarized in Ernle, *English Farming Past and Present*, p. 507.

[2] Hall. *op. cit.*, pp. 42-3.   [3] Clapham, *op. cit.*, III, 109.

224,299 in 1901, and 208,761 in 1911.[1] The thirty years' stability in numbers was doubtless due in part to many men continuing to farm while they went through a temporary period of falling living standards. But there were good reasons why, despite a reduced input of labour and capital, output was kept high enough to provide satisfactory incomes for farmers. One was that, while the number of far mers changed little, their identity changed much more. A quarter o f a century of falling prices and severe competition was an effective way of getting rid of the most incompetent farmers.[2] Another may have been that changes in cropping made it possible to concentrate the various crops more than before on the soils that were most favourable to their growth.[3] A third was the greater concentration on those products which, in terms of market value, had for years been yielding the greatest output in return for a given input. Partly because of this and partly because of changes in relative prices, the 55 per cent which livestock products contributed to the gross agricultural output of the United Kingdom in 1867-69 had risen to 70 per cent by 1886-93 and was 75 per cent in 1911-13.[4] But the most important factor was that the reduced application of labour and capital was offset by the increased use of purchased supplies, mainly imported,[5] which made it possible to maintain and even improve the high yields secured earlier. Farmers bought more and more feeding stuffs, horses and store animals, and it seems probable that the expenditure so incurred was somewhat less than the cost of growing at home an equivalent amount of fodder crops and breeding and rearing additional animals would have been. In this way, while prices were falling, the diminution in farmers' net incomes was lessened.

It is noticeable that successful adaptation to new economic conditions depended mainly on the changes which farmers made in their own practices. The permanent fall in rents made landowners less able and less willing to continue their traditional leadership in agriculture to its former degree, although the tripartite agrarian system was still retained. More of the responsibility for guiding the fortunes of agriculture and keeping up its standards had therefore to pass into

[1] Ernle, *op. cit.*, p. 507.   [2] Hall, *op. cit.*, p. 150.

[3] See the suggestive, though not altogether conclusive, discussion of this poin in relation to wheat yields by H. D. Vigor, 'The Increased Yield per Acre of Wheat in England Considered in Relation to the Reduction of Area', in *Journ. of the R.Stat.Socy.*, LXXIII (1910), 396-408.

[4] Ojala, *op. cit.*, p. 208.   [5] *Ibid.*, p. 213.

other hands. Only the state or the farmers could undertake the extra responsibility and the state had no inclination to do so. Successive governments had, indeed, hardly anything worth calling an agricultural policy, other than a determination not to give protection by tariffs or subsidies and a half-hearted interest in the settlement of smallholders on the land. Their main direct contribution, and that a small one, was made by way of the collection and dissemination of information and the grant of small sums to assist agricultural education. It was useful, too, that from 1889 the state's concerns with agricultural matters should have been centralized in one department, the new Board of Agriculture. The Board was able gradually to extend its functions and influence but down to the First World War it did not have a great impact on agricultural activity.[1]

What governments did establish, through legislation, was a more liberal situation for tenant farmers, so that they had more freedom and more incentive to use their own capital and ideas to make the best of their holdings. The restrictions in family settlements, which sometimes not only reduced the capacity of the head of the family to invest in his estate but also hampered him in making concessions to his tenants, were gradually limited. After an act of 1882 a life-tenant under a settlement could administer his estate nearly as freely as an owner in fee simple, provided that the receipts from any capital transactions were invested through trustees for the benefit of the succession. Henceforward it made no difference to a tenant farmer whether his landlord was bound by a family settlement or not.[2] More important was the legal force given to the principle that outgoing tenants should be compensated by the landlord for any unexhausted improvements which they had made in their holdings. The Agricultural Holdings Act of 1875, which first recognized this principle, was merely permissive and nearly all landlords contracted out of it; but a second act in 1883 made its application compulsory. Further legislation strengthened the position of tenants still more. The most important new provision came in 1906 when landlords were made liable to compensate tenants for damage done by game, for disturbance if the tenancy were determined for any reason other than bad farming, and for repairs executed by the tenant because of default by the landlord. The same act also freed tenants from practically all restrictions on their course of cropping.[3] With so much freedom and security the additional encouragement of long leases, advocated

[1] Orwin, *op. cit.*, pp. 132 and 144-5.   [2] *Ibid.*, pp. 135-6.   [3] *Ibid.*, pp. 138-9.

by mid-nineteenth-century reformers, hardly mattered any longer. In any case not many tenants had been anxious to commit themselves to a lease while prices were falling and by the beginning of the twentieth century even those districts where the granting of leases had formerly been increasing had reverted in most cases to tenancy-at-will.[1] Tenant farmers by this time could be sure that legal and customary restrictions would very seldom act to deny them the full fruit of their efforts and enterprise. Almost the only remaining arbitrary burdens were the entry fines and dues imposed on those few whose land was still held under some form of copyhold. But the mid-nineteenth-century machinery for the extinction of copyholds by agreement had been slowly reducing this anomalous survival to negligible proportions.

The more favourable situation of tenant farmers was only one of a number of great differences in agricultural matters just before the First World War in comparison with what they had been in the eighteen-seventies. To interpret the agricultural history of the intervening period only in terms of a long depression followed by a recovery would be a great over-simplification. There were some sectors of agriculture which were never very depressed and which did not need to change much because they were serving growing demands with reasonable efficiency. There were others which came under intense economic pressure in the late nineteenth century and which never fully recovered. The big changes were not confined to the years of falling prices; they were permanent, and though they only slightly affected many districts they went deep enough elsewhere to change fundamentally the position of agriculture in the whole national economy.

The depression of the late nineteenth century was very uneven in its incidence. Farm incomes must have fallen nearly everywhere in monetary terms because prices fell so much, but in real terms people engaged in producing milk or meat for nearby urban markets probably suffered no worsening of their economic position. The great hardships, which compelled drastic changes, were in those districts which drew a large part of their income from cereals grown on land that was costly to cultivate. The depression was worst on the heavy soils in southern England, which had been the traditional wheat

---

[1] For examples see Orr, *op. cit.*, p. 116; Hall, *op. cit.*, pp. 368 (for Devon) and 432; Haggard, *op. cit.*, I, 541-2 (for Herts.).

growing districts for centuries and which had continued to concentrate on this crop after the Norfolk innovations of the eighteenth
century had given some of the lighter soils a cost advantage over
them in cereal growing. The counties in which the value of agricultural land fell most heavily in the 'eighties and 'nineties (more than
30 per cent in 15 years) formed a continuous block in the south-east
quarter, made up of Wiltshire, Berkshire, Oxfordshire, Northamp-
tonshire, Huntingdonshire, Cambridgeshire, Norfolk, Suffolk, Essex
and Kent. In more detail, the districts where values fell most in the
whole quarter century after 1870 were the greater part of Essex with
some of the adjoining Suffolk parishes, part of East Wiltshire with the
adjoining parts of Berkshire and Hampshire (around Pewsey and
Hungerford), and a much smaller area in Gloucestershire. On the
other hand, values in 1894 were still higher than they had been in
1870 in most of Cumberland, Westmorland, North Lancashire and
the north-west of the West Riding, in the western half of Wales, in
parts of Devon and Cornwall, in the dairying area of Cheshire, North
Shropshire and North Staffordshire, in an arc around London to the
west and south, and in a few other scattered districts.[1] The contrast
can be broadly explained by differences in soil, cropping and access
to large urban markets.

In districts that showed so little sign of injury from falling prices
there was neither incentive nor need to make much change in agricultural conditions and methods. Cheaper feeding stuffs and the pull
of higher wages in the towns encouraged some substitution of purchased supplies for labour; changes in urban demand led to some
changes in the final product, e.g. rather more farmers selling all their
milk instead of making it into cheese or butter, some replacement of
farms by market gardens; little more than this. But in districts where
the bottom dropped out of the market the reorganization of farming
had to be drastic, and in spite of this the great days of agriculture
were never restored. The general national picture of appreciable
change was the resultant of such contrasted developments.

If agriculture is looked at as one of the nation's great producing
industries, then the changes which it underwent between the
eighteen-seventies and the First World War may be summed up by
saying that as a source of employment and means of livelihood
it greatly declined; that, despite rather greater concentration on

---

[1] *Statement showing the Decrease and Increase in the Rateable Value of Lands*
(*P.P.* 1897, XV), maps A and B.

products to whose growth it was naturally best suited, in terms of net output it was more or less stagnating while most other large industries were still growing; and that consequently its relative contribution to the national economy was much less. Despite all the vicissitudes, the volume of the gross agricultural output of the United Kingdom appears to have risen slightly but persistently with only a minor interruption at the end of the eighteen-seventies. The best available estimates, those of Mr Ojala, show an increase, at constant prices, of just over 12 per cent from 1867-69 to 1911-13.[1] But this was achieved only by the use of more non-agricultural services and purchased supplies. Calculation of the value of these, which must be deducted from the gross output in order to measure net output, is more speculative than the calculation of gross output, but is reliable enough to indicate the general trend. Mr Ojala suggests that the net output, measured in the prices of 1911-13, stood at £153 million per year in 1867-69, fell to a minimum of £143 million in 1894-1903 and averaged £147 million in 1911-13. As a result the contribution of agriculture to the national consumption income (i.e. national income minus net savings) fell, over the whole period, from 17·4 per cent to 6·7 per cent.[2] If Ireland could be excluded the drop would probably be a little greater. The precise figures are questionable, but their general order of magnitude is not. What they illustrate is the ending of agricultural pre-eminence among British industries. And with that transition to a less important status went a change in the condition and activities of all classes connected with the land. The late nineteenth century was the true period of large-scale rural decline in England,[3] the time when the countryman ceased to be a representative figure and the long-standing traditions of village society began to crumble, even though the economic position of those who remained behind was strengthened. It was the time, too, when the position of landowners was first seriously undermined. Even in the early

[1] Ojala, *op. cit.*, p. 209.   [2] *Ibid.*, p. 66.

[3] Fourteen typical rural counties of England and Wales showed a decline of 4·2 per cent in population between 1871 and 1901. (*Statistical Memoranda and Charts relating to Public Health and Social Conditions (P.P.* 1909, CIII), p. 9). Though the decline of rural population was becoming more widespread, the absolute number of people leaving rural areas had passed its peak by 1890. This was probably because the large exodus during the previous fifty years had left the rural areas with a population that included a much smaller proportion of young adults (especially young women) than before and consequently led to a decline in the rate of natural increase. (Cairncross, *Home and Foreign Investment 1870-1913*, pp. 74-7.) For a detailed analysis of rural depopulation and its causes see J. Saville, *Rural Depopulation in England and Wales, 1851-1951* (1957), chaps. 1-3.

twentieth century it was no unpleasant thing to own a large estate, at any rate in the north-western half of England, but the landlord class as a whole had suffered a permanent loss of capital and income. Just before the First World War it was reckoned that they could not in general hope to receive a net income of more than 3 per cent on the reduced capital value of their estates.[1] With the loss of wealth went the diminution of social influence and political power, and an inability to resist policies which ensured that their position would never be restored. Only the tenant farmers came near to maintaining both their numbers and their incomes, and even they had to some extent to change their function in order to do this. They were less exclusively engaged in raising food from the resources of their farms and, to a greater extent than before, used land as standing room yielding meat and dairy produce from animals bred elsewhere and fed on things grown elsewhere.

Most of these changes appear to be symptomatic of decline in some sense, but they can hardly be held to be proof of greater agricultural inefficiency. Rather they were signs of one not unreasonable way of adjustment to a changing economic environment. England still had one of the more productive farming industries of the world, which had maintained its efficiency through the many varied shocks since 1870. But it was no longer a model to the rest of Europe; it had made few technical advances in a period when other industries made many; and it still appeared to neglect many of the opportunities presented by its own home market, opportunities which the Danes, with no great natural advantages, were quick to seize. Comparison with what happened in other countries suggests that the kind of adjustments made in England could have been carried further without any fundamental change of policy and with profit both to those engaged in agriculture and to the nation as a whole. An industry of similar size and character might well have produced rather more than it did. A fundamental change, essential to survival, had been accomplished, yet agriculture was still open to the same criticisms as forty years earlier: more adaptable to economic conditions than it had been but still not adaptable enough; still too content to pay worse wages for worse labour than other industries; still too slow to seek out and apply new knowledge. Its great need was that which its best-informed contemporary critic besought for it—'More light'.[2]

---

[1] Hall, *op. cit.*, pp. 433-4.   [2] *Ibid.*, p. 446.

CHAPTER FOUR

Mining, Manufacture and Building

THE manifold changes in technical knowledge and in market conditions in the world as a whole in the late nineteenth century, together with the dwindling demands which home agriculture was making on available productive resources, could hardly fail to induce considerable changes in British industry. On the face of it, they might have been expected to encourage not only a large absolute increase in industrial activity but also a further relative rise in the contribution of industrial pursuits to the country's economic life, a rise partly dependent on the development of virtually new branches of industry. Only, perhaps, a doubt as to how much more industrialized a country could become than Britain already was in 1870 might modify these expectations a little.

To questions about the extent to which such expectations were, in fact, fulfilled only approximate answers can be given. Part of the difficulty in trying to be more exact lies in the imprecision of the categories that have to be used. Any measure of change in output or income as a whole must be to some extent arbitrary when the nature and quality of its individual components are also changing; and the line between industrial and non-industrial activities cannot be drawn with complete certainty and sharpness. Even with the most abundant and exactly compiled statistics, quantitative statements about the absolute or relative growth of industrialization would have to be in terms of a range of possible variation, though the range might be fairly narrow. But the difficulty is enhanced by the deficiencies of the statistics. No census of production was taken in the United Kingdom until 1907, though the annual production of a number of important commodities was regularly recorded in the late nineteenth century; and direct information about the amount of capital used for industrial activities is very scanty. Thus many reservations have to be borne in mind when attempts are made to present a quantitative account of industrial growth. But, provided the reservations are not forgotten, there is enough reliable material to make possible conclusions of some significance.

Probably the best way to consider the change in the position of industry generally is to see what can be made of the information about the uses to which industrial resources were put, and then to turn to questions of the amount of industrial output. The decennial census of population provides much detailed information about the numbers of people following different occupations. Unfortunately, in 1881, the classification was changed in such a way that while there was more precise information about some of the *occupations*, there was less information about the way in which the numbers in similar occupations were divided among different *industries*. Not until 1911 was an attempt made to classify the population by industry as well as by occupation. Consequently, attempts made to estimate the proportion of workers in individual industries or in broad groups, such as building or manufacture or commerce, involve some arbitrary assumptions, and estimates by different persons do not exactly agree with each other. But the general picture is fairly clear. The proportion of the working population which was engaged in the group of activities that are unquestionably industrial, i.e. those concerned with manufacture, changed little but, if anything, tended to decline. The proportions in mining and in building and contracting, which are often treated as part of 'industry', were both rising, but whereas the increase for mining was unchecked up to 1911, that for building and contracting was more irregular and was sharply reversed between 1901 and 1911. All these general movements appear to be continuations of trends that were clearly established by the eighteen-sixties. Charles Booth, writing in 1886, had already indicated that employment in manufacturing was no longer increasing in relative importance. According to him, the percentage of the occupied population of England and Wales engaged in manufacture fell from its peak of 33·0 per cent in 1861 to 31·6 per cent in 1871 and 30·7 per cent in 1881; while the proportions in mining at the same three dates were 4·5 per cent, 4·5 per cent and 4·8 per cent respectively, and those in building 5·8 per cent, 6·3 per cent and 6·8 per cent.[1] Mr Clark, slightly rearranging some of Booth's categories but keeping as far as possible to the same general scheme, shows a fall in the manufacturing percentage only from 38·6 per cent to 38·3 per cent between 1861 and 1881 but thereafter a much steeper drop to 1901. For 1911, with a somewhat different classification, he put 34·2 per cent in manufacturing, 6·8 per cent in mining and 5·3 per cent in building

---

[1] C. Booth, *Occupations of the People: England, Scotland, Ireland*, pp. 68-9.

and contracting.[1] Other classifications show rather smoother changes. One, which in 1881 allocates 32·6 per cent to manufacture, places 33·5 per cent in this category in 1901 and 33·5 per cent in 1911 also. The same source in 1911 gives 7·1 per cent to mining and 5·2 per cent to building and contracting.[2] This last set of figures refers to Great Britain but, in such a broad grouping, differences between figures relating to all Britain and those for England and Wales alone cannot be very great.

From all this one may reasonably conclude that in the years just before the First World War a little under half of the working population was engaged in industrial occupations, that this proportion had not increased much since the middle of the nineteenth century, and that any increase in it came from the relative growth of mining rather than manufacturing. In one respect, however, the figures are almost certainly a little misleading. In the middle of the nineteenth century many industrial workers were, in fact, employed for part of their time in commerce and transport. Outworkers did most of the fetching and carrying of their raw materials and finished goods, and many producers in small workshops and one-man businesses also spent a good deal of their time in wholesaling or retailing. As outwork declined and economic activities became more specialized, the proportion of industrial employees whose full working time was given to industrial activity must have increased. The greater part of this change was probably accomplished by about 1900, but up to that time there was some real increase in the proportion of the labour force engaged in manufacturing, which is not apparent from the occupational figures of the census.

Even with this modification, however, the increase must have been quite small. Descriptive evidence, particularly that relating to the greater use of power-driven machinery, suggests that an industrial demand for an increasing share of the available economic resources may have shown itself more in the use of capital than of labour, but it is impossible to confirm this from quantitative evidence. No more can be said except that the somewhat hazardous estimates which have been made of the amount and functional distribution of the national capital tend to support this view. Estimates of capital wealth in the United Kingdom, which Giffen derived mainly from the

[1] C. Clark, *The Conditions of Economic Progress* (2nd edn.), p. 408.
[2] Economic Co-operation Administration Mission to the U.K., *Economic Development in the United Kingdom 1850-1950* (n.d.), pp. 20 and 22.

payments under the various schedules of the income tax and which others subsequently continued on the same basis, include two items, 'mines, ironworks, quarries, gasworks, waterworks and canals' and 'other trade capital', which cover most of the capital used in industry and commerce (excluding the railways). These two items together amounted to 15·1 per cent of the estimated total capital of the country in 1875, 19·0 per cent in 1885 and 23·2 per cent in 1905. Alternative estimates made in different ways for 1914 allocated in one case 24·1 per cent and in the other case 26·3 per cent to these two items.[1] The trend appears quite definite, but there is no means of knowing how much of the increase should be attributed to industry and how much to commerce. It is highly improbable that it belonged exclusively to one or the other.[2]

Information about output, unsatisfactory as much of it is, gives a similar impression to that concerning the allocation of capital and labour. The first census of production established that in 1907 the net output of manufacturing, mining and building in the United Kingdom was £712,135,000 for the firms that were investigated.[3] Some addition was necessary in order to cover small firms omitted from the census—the census authorities suggested up to £50 million[4] —and statisticians using the census material subsequently have sometimes found it appropriate to rearrange some of its items. But all would agree that the net output of industry was somewhere about £750 million (exclusive of duties) in a year when the total national income was approximately £2,000 million.[5] In other words, manufacture, mining and building together were directly contributing about 40 per cent, or a little less, of the national income.[6] The situation in 1907 may have been slightly abnormal, because it was a year

[1] Calculated from figures in Giffen, *The Growth of Capital*, p. 43 and Douglas, 'An estimate of the growth of capital in the United Kingdom' in *Journ. of Econ. and Business History*, II, 661.

[2] The rough estimates of A. W. Flux, who was in charge of the Census of Production, suggest that in 1907 at least as much capital was employed in transport and distribution (exclusive of the railways) as in industry. (*Final Report on the First Census of Production* (1907), pp. 35-6.)

[3] *Ibid.*, p. 21. Net output is the value, at the place of production, of total output *less* the value of materials (whether raw or semi-finished) used in production *less* the value of work and parts sub-contracted.

[4] *Ibid.*, p. 10.

[5] *Cf.* A. L. Bowley, 'The Census of Production and the National Dividend' in *Econ. Journ.*, XXIII (1913), 54.

[6] Strictly, this proportion rather over-states the direct contribution of industry to the national income since part of the net output of industry is devoted to making good depreciation and not to the increase of income.

in which some important activities entered a depression, but a relationship of the same general magnitude must be representative of the early years of the twentieth century as a whole.

The proportion is certainly high enough to be characteristic of an industrialized economy, but there is no reason to think that it can have risen much in the previous forty years, though no calculations to support this view can aspire to great precision. Nearly all attempts to measure British industrial growth before the first census of production are derived in part, at first or second hand, from the index of production compiled by Dr Hoffmann. This index, though less unreliable for the late nineteenth century than for earlier years, is not altogether satisfactory; but it is noticeable that between 1870 and 1914 it grows at just about the same rate as the national income (corrected for changes in the price-level). Both the index of production (covering mining and manufacturing) and the real national income of the U.K. were in 1913 from two and a quarter to two and a half times as great as in 1870. The exclusion of mining from the production index very slightly reduces its increase in the period, but the inclusion of building reduces it appreciably—the index for mining, manufacture and building together did not quite double itself between 1870 and 1913.[1] The Hoffmann index, however, is more nearly an index of gross production than one of net output. At least one attempt, from these and other data, to estimate the increase in the net income derived from manufacture has indicated a rate of growth rather less than that of either the Hoffmann index or the total national income.[2] But the assumptions underlying such an estimate are somewhat speculative and there are at least two other relevant considerations. One is that the Hoffmann index (and any derivative from it) probably understates the growth of production after 1870 by failing to allow adequately for the increasing complexity of many of the goods produced.[3] The other is that, in manufacture, the ratio of net output to gross production may have been rising because of a relative decline in the importance of textiles, a group of industries in which the cost of raw materials is an unusually high

[1] Clark, *op. cit.*, p. 63 and W. Hoffmann, *British Industry 1700-1950* (Eng. trans., 1955), table 54 part B. The Hoffmann index was lagging a little behind the growth of national income if the higher estimates of the increase in the latter are accepted.

[2] Clark, *op. cit.*, pp. 269 and 316-17.

[3] e.g. it treats equal additions to the gross tonnage of shipping as equal additions to shipbuilding output, irrespective of complete changes in the design and structure of ships, and ignores comparable changes in other types of transport equipment and of machinery.

proportion of the value of the final product. There is clear evidence of such a change between 1907 and 1930[1] and it must have begun earlier, though it cannot have been so marked before 1907. On balance, then, it seems likely that the relative share of industry in the nation's expanding economic activity was maintained in the period from 1870 to the First World War, and quite possible that it increased, but not by very much.

In all the circumstances the apparent smallness of the change in the degree of industrialization may seem surprising. But it becomes less surprising when it is viewed against the industrial developments of the immediately preceding period and against the broader economic changes of the late nineteenth century. The very mixed economy of the eighteen-forties had become much more industrialized in the next quarter of a century. Henceforward, industrial activity dominated economic life. Its importance continued to increase not so much because of the relative expansion of manufacture as because of the greater expansion which an industrialized economy necessitated in other types of activity. The production of material goods was the main basis of economic activity and the proportion of goods which were the result of industrial processes continued to increase (all the more so if mining is classed as an 'industrial' activity); but, in new technical and market conditions, in order to maintain rising industrial output it was necessary to provide an even bigger increase in transport and distributional services. Thus by 1914 Britain was, in fact, appreciably more industrialized than in 1870, in the sense that more of what it had available for consumption or exchange consisted of industrial goods. The apparent paradox that in the intervening years industry had not grown much in relation to other activities merely reflects the fact that transport and commerce were adding a rather bigger proportion of the ultimate value of those industrial goods than they had done earlier.

Changes in the relative importance of different industries were more obvious, though their extent was not very large. In 1871 textiles and clothing still employed more people than all other manufacturing industries together in England and Wales, though the proportions engaged in other manufactures, especially the metallurgical and engineering industries, were increasing, as were those in building and in coal-mining.[2] Since engineering and the metallurgical industries used more capital than most other industries their

---

[1] Clark, *op. cit*, pp. 252-4.   [2] Booth, *op. cit.*, pp. 68-9.

relative importance was greater than was indicated by the numbers employed. Even so, it seems certain that the output of no other industry was worth so much as that of cotton manufacture, with coal-mining as probably the second most valuable industry. Textile manufacture, the making of articles of clothing (including boots and shoes), the iron and steel industry, the making of machines and tools, coal-mining and the building trades accounted for about four-fifths of all industrial workers at this time. No other industry was of anything like comparable size and value, the most important of the rest being the old staple activity of brewing and two industries which had grown rapidly in the mid-nineteenth century: shipbuilding and railway construction, repair and maintenance (so far as it can be distinguished from engineering and railway operation).

For the early years of the twentieth century the 1907 census of production is the best guide to the contribution made by different industries to the national economy. In that year the largest industries of the United Kingdom, in terms of the value of their net output, were, in order of magnitude: coal-mining (£106 million), engineering (£50 million), cotton (£45 million), building and contracting (£43 million), iron and steel (£30 million), brewing and malting (£28 million), clothing, handkerchief and millinery trades (£27 million), shipbuilding (£21 million), woollen and worsted (£18 million), gas (£17 million), railway construction, repair and maintenance (£17 million), and printing and bookbinding (£15 million).[1] The position in England and Wales, considered separately, was much the same except for a slight reduction in the importance of shipbuilding, because of the unusually large share that Scotland had in this industry.

In general, the major industries of the country just before the First World War were the same as they had been in mid-Victorian times but their relative size had changed. Coal-mining had undergone more than average expansion—output rose from 110 million tons in 1870 to 287 million tons in 1913—and so had some of the more highly capitalized and complex manufacturing industries, notably iron and steel, engineering and shipbuilding. These became more

---

[1] *Final Report of the First Census of Production*, pp. 39, 93, 285, 387, 443, 595, 743 and 831. The figure for cotton excludes the bleaching, dyeing and finishing trades. The figure for brewing has been reduced by £13 million, which was the amount of duty paid. Clothing, etc., omits the boot and shoe, hosiery, glove, hat, laundry and various other small trades; moreover the census failed to cover the many very small businesses in this industry.

important, whereas some of the technically simpler industries, such as textiles, brewing and flour-milling, grew a good deal more slowly and became less important, though in 1907 the textile, clothing, and food, drink and tobacco manufactures still contributed a third of the United Kingdom's net industrial output.[1]

Among the larger industries of the early twentieth century a recent rise to prominence was most striking in the case of gas-making and printing. But there were several examples of rather smaller industries that were growing at abnormally high rates. The rate of increase between 1881 and 1911 in the proportion of the population engaged in different major groups of industrial activities was highest (apart from the public utilities) in the chemical and allied trades,[2] which, however, produced only about 3 per cent of the net output of industry in 1907.[3] Other rapidly expanding industries were paper-making, rubber manufacture, the manufacture of copper and brass products and the manufacture of cocoa, sugar confectionery and preserves.[4] Some of hese, notably paper-making, were very old industries which had been stimulated by new demands and new sources of material. Others were of more recent development; the making of jam and preserves outside the home was of negligible importance before the eighteen-fifties.[5] None of them in 1907 had a net output of much over £5 million and together they provided little more than 2 per cent of the total net industrial output.[6] But to some extent the importance of their recent growth was partly concealed by money valuations, because it had been accompanied by a much more than average fall in prices—this was true of paper, for instance[7]—and all of them were well situated for further notable growth.

A growing industry of a different kind, which was more novel and had still greater possibilities of expansion, was electricity generation. Unless production on little more than an experimental scale is counted, this industry can hardly be said to have existed until the early eighteen-eighties[8] and, though its output at any time before the First World War was small in comparison with what was achieved later, it

[1] Calculated from *Final Report of the First Census of Production*, p. 21.
[2] *Census of England and Wales, 1911*, vol. X, part I, pp. 552-7.
[3] Calculated from *Final Report of the First Census of Production*, p. 21.
[4] *Cf.* the indices in Hoffmann, *op. cit.*, table 54, part B.
[5] H. Cox (ed.), *British Industries under Free Trade* (1903), pp. 178-9.
[6] *Final Report of the First Census of Production*, pp. 595, 653, 239 and 443.
[7] Cox, *op. cit.*, p. 202.
[8] A. Plummer, *New British Industries in the Twentieth Century* (1937), p. 12.

was increasing steadily. In 1907 it was still quite a minor producer among the fuel and power industries but, with a net output worth £5·6 million,[1] it was no longer negligible. It was probably the most notable late-nineteenth-century example of the influence of technology in the creation of new industries. Other examples were provided by the aluminium and rayon industries, which attracted less attention because they still remained so small until after the First World War. Aluminium was first made commercially in England on a very small scale and by a costly process in the early eighteen-sixties, but was never firmly established until the British Aluminium Company was formed in 1894 to exploit the new electrolytic process. From then on production gradually increased, mainly in Scotland where hydro-electric plant was an economic proposition, though the final stages were located in England.[2] Rayon was first used commercially in England in 1885,[3] but here also the secure establishment of the industry awaited the development of new and cheaper processes of production, which came in the 'nineties. The first important rayon factory was operating in 1900 and production was developed (mainly by the leading silk manufacturing firm of Courtaulds) partly in substitution for the silk industry.[4]

This last point is a reminder that, though industry continued to be dominated by the same great staple activities as before, there was a good deal of readjustment on the fringes. The rapid growth of some small industries was offset by the stagnation or dwindling away of others. That mining, for instance, became more important to the British economy in the late nineteenth century was entirely the achievement of the coal industry. Most of the lesser mining industries were simultaneously in decay: tin mining reached its peak about 1870 and after 1890 its output rapidly fell off; copper mining was in continuous decline from the eighteen-fifties and had almost disappeared by the twentieth century; lead mining reduced its output by two-thirds between 1870 and 1900; and though zinc mining was growing until 1900 its output was in no way keeping up with consumption.[5] The minor textile industries were also becoming less important, so that by 1900 'textiles' was for England more nearly synonymous with 'cotton or woollen manufactures' than ever before.

---

[1] *Final Report of the First Census of Production*, p. 831.
[2] Plummer, *op. cit.*, pp. 188-91.   [3] *Ibid.*, p. 210.
[4] Clapham, *op. cit.*, III, 180-1.
[5] G. R. Porter and F. W. Hirst, *The Progress of the Nation* (1912), pp. 226-33.

In the silk industry there was after 1870 a persistent fall in the numbers employed and after 1880 exports, which took a large part of the output, grew little.[1] In England the linen industry was contracting by 1860 and had shrunk to very little by the early years of the twentieth century, though it maintained itself in Ireland and, to a less extent, in Scotland.[2] Jute manufacture, which was virtually new in the second half of the nineteenth century, was a mainly Scottish industry and both the jute and hemp industries, though they grew a little, remained small.

More significant, however, than the rise and fall of relatively small industries were the changes in the products turned out by the great staple industries. The fact that the same industries dominated economic life in 1914 as in 1870 is misleading if it suggests an absence of much change, for between those dates some of the industries had come to concern themselves with the production of an almost entirely new range of commodities. Clearly this is not true of coal-mining, the greatest industry of all, nor was there very drastic change in the products of the building industry. The major textile industries, cotton and wool, also remained essentially of the same character as before, though there was a general tendency in the cotton industry to turn increasingly to the production of finer yarns and cloths.[3] But in one of the lesser industries of the group, hosiery, there were great changes of product. An industry which in the middle of the nineteenth century had been mainly, though not exclusively, concerned, as its name implies, with the manufacture of stockings began to turn out an increasing variety of knitted goods, especially articles of underwear, so that by 1907 stockings formed only half of its output.[4]

But it was above all in the iron and steel and the engineering industries that the continuity of the same name concealed the most sweeping changes in the character of the things produced. In the iron and steel industry the outstanding general change was the decline in the use of puddled iron, which reached its peak of production (2,800,000 tons) in 1882,[5] and the substitution of steel for an ever-widening variety of purposes. In 1870 Britain produced less than 250,000 tons of steel but by 1913, 7,664,000 tons.[6] Steel itself under-

---

[1] Porter and Hirst, *op. cit.*, pp. 350-4.   [2] *Ibid.*, p. 358.

[3] S. J. Chapman, *The Cotton Industry and Trade* (1905), p. 34.

[4] Porter and Hirst, *op. cit.*, pp. 390-4.

[5] Clapham, *op. cit.*, II, 52.   [6] *Ibid.*, II, 57 and III, 150.

went important changes as it came to be made by new processes and from different types of ore. From about 1880 nearly all the increased output was made by the open-hearth process, while Bessemer output, which hitherto had predominated, changed little. Most British steel at this time was acid steel and until 1900 Thomas's basic process was neglected in the country of its origin. But thereafter the proportion of basic in total output rose rapidly.[1] In the nature of the finished and semi-finished products of the industry, too, there were notable changes. The great boom in the iron industry in the early eighteen-seventies was dominated by the demand for rails, but by 1876 it was recognized that the market for iron rails was dead,[2] and though there was a considerable revival of trade in steel rails, other products began to form a bigger proportion of the output. Plates, sheets, bars and angles became still more important and had to be designed for many new purposes; and there were particularly striking increases in the production of plated iron—the output of tinplate soared between 1865 and 1891 and again after 1906.[3]

In engineering there came into existence a whole series of what were virtually new industries within that strikingly heterogeneous industrial group. That by 1907 14 per cent of the output of the rather narrowly defined engineering industry came from electrical engineering[4] was a testimony to the development of a whole new range of products in the preceding quarter of a century; and the mechanization of many former handicrafts gave rise to much greater variety and specialization in the manufacture of machine-tools, while innovations in retailing practice created an outlet for such products as new types of balances and weighing-machines.[5] Other novelties which were helping to transform the engineering industries in this period were cycles and motor-cars. Fundamental changes in the design of cycles in the eighteen-eighties made them easy and acceptable for general use and made possible a tremendous growth of cycle manufacture in the 'nineties; and in the opening decade of the twentieth century the manufacture of motor-cars, in which for a few

---

[1] *Ibid.*, II, 58 and III, 147-8; D. L. Burn, *The Economic History of Steel-Making 1867-1939* (1940), p. 336.

[2] Burn, *op. cit.*, p. 28.

[3] W. E. Minchinton, *The British Tinplate Industry* (1957), pp. 29, 74 and 80.

[4] *Final Report of the First Census of Production*, pp. 125-7.

[5] G. C. Allen, *The Industrial Development of Birmingham and the Black Country 1860-1927* (1929), pp. 302-4 and 306-7.

years England had lagged far behind France, also began to grow quickly.[1] In shipbuilding, the other great industry closely linked to engineering, changes were equally striking. A shipyard was producing something very different in 1900 from what it had done in 1870. The virtual cessation of the building of sailing vessels, the adoption of steel as the main constructional material, a steady increase in average size, repeated improvements in engines, the emergence of entirely new types of specialized vessel, innumerable modifications in the details of design—all these changes made the sea-going vessel of the early twentieth century almost a new commodity.[2]

Industries which began to turn out final products that were very different from those of an earlier day were inevitably involved in new processes and new methods of work. But the adoption of new methods of production was widespread even for the manufacture of goods whose design was little changed. In detail the innovations showed great variety but there was a clear, common trend running through most of them. In most industries which had remained entirely or partially handicrafts until after the middle of the nineteenth century there was much replacement of hand-operated machines and tools by power-driven machinery; and in industries that had been mechanized earlier it was common for machines that were more reliable, more complex and faster in operation than earlier ones to be introduced. A few examples from the major branches of industrial activity illustrate what was happening.

In the great textile and clothing group of industries, cotton and worsted had been fairly fully mechanized by the middle of the nineteenth century and further innovation was very gradual. But in cotton-spinning the hand-mule survived fairly generally until after the cotton famine of 1861-64 and its replacement by the self-actor did not much affect the finer classes of work until the later 'seventies and 'eighties,[3] while the adoption of ring spinning increased most rapidly in the last quarter of the century.[4] The woollen industry lagged behind in technical development but even here most of the replacement of handwork by power-driven machinery was accomplished by the eighteen-seventies,[5] though dwindling numbers of

---

[1] Allen, *op. cit.*, pp. 294-8; Porter and Hirst, *op. cit.*, pp. 267-8.

[2] A brief account of some of these changes is given in A. W. Kirkaldy *British Shipping* (1914), Book I, chaps. IX-XIII.

[3] Clapham, *op. cit.*, II, 81.   [4] Chapman, *op. cit.*, p. 25.

[5] Clapham, *op. cit.*, II, 83.

handlooms still continued in use for special purposes into the twentieth century.[1] But in such important industries as hosiery and in all branches of the clothing trades the widespread adoption of powered machines did not come until the last third of the nineteenth century or later. No satisfactory steam-driven stocking-frames were devised until the eighteen-fifties and their economic advantage in competition with cheap labour on hand-frames was not great, so that handwork still predominated in the mid-seventies.[2] Thereafter the improvement and adoption of hosiery machinery was rapid, though there were stated to be 25,000 outworkers (doubtless many of them part-time) as late as 1907.[3] The clothing industries changed their techniques far less completely, but nevertheless they did change. In the eighteen-fifties the sewing-machine was coming into use, but it was a machine operated by hand or by treadle. Mechanical means of cutting were first devised in 1858 and thereafter small steam-engines and gas-engines came slowly into use to drive equipment for cutting, sewing and pressing. Machinery gradually improved but its scope remained limited for many years. Its use was mainly restricted to the making of suits and coats until the 'nineties, when machinery began to be used to a greater extent in the millinery and dress-making trades, and nearly all the finishing processes in every branch of the trade were done by hand until some time after 1900. Moreover, before the early years of the twentieth century, it was only the poorest qualities of clothing that were made by machinery. Even in 1914 handwork still had a large place in the clothing trades, though the use of machinery had made great advances in the previous forty years.[4] In the boot and shoe industry its victory was more complete. Machines for some processes were coming into use from the eighteen-fifties but for a long time few of them were power-driven. It was mainly between 1895 and 1905 that the industry came to be equipped with powered machinery for high quality work in nearly all of its processes.[5]

Some of the largest and oldest of the food manufacturing industries, as well as the newest, also experienced much technical change. A great transformation came over flour-milling in the

---

[1] J. H. Clapham, *The Woollen and Worsted Industries* (1907), p. 128.

[2] F. A. Wells, *The British Hosiery Trade* (1935), pp. 144-5 and 154.

[3] *Ibid.*, pp. 184 and 188.

[4] Joan Thomas, *A History of the Leeds Clothing Industry* (1955), pp. 9-11 and 37-40; Clapham, *Econ. Hist. of Mod. Brit.*, III, 183-4.

[5] Clapham, *op. cit.*, II, 93-6 and III, 181-3; Cox, *op. cit.*, pp. 236-40.

eighteen-eighties with the adoption of grinding by steel rollers driven by steam-engines, and thereafter the old watermills and wind-mills, grinding by stone, declined rapidly.[1] A transition to the use of steam-power in brewing, with a steady improvement in equipment, had begun in London before 1800, but though it spread a little it was never generalized until the late nineteenth century. Even in a large centre of population such as the Birmingham district it was only after 1870 that the great power-operated breweries developed.[2]

In the growing metallurgical and engineering group of industries the introduction of new techniques and new equipment was perhaps most important of all. The increase in mechanization in many branches was for long a very gradual development but it became much more striking and general towards the end of the nineteenth century. The building of warships, probably the most elaborate industrial products of the age, involved a great amount of handicraft work, much of it conditioned by the habits and equipment of the days of wooden sailing vessels; and not until after 1886, when the equipment of the Royal Dockyards began to be drastically modern-ized, was there fundamental change in this respect.[3] In the civilian shipyards it was around 1900 that the great changes associated with the introduction of pneumatic or electrical equipment for various processes began to be prominent as extensive re-equipment was undertaken.[4] At the other extreme, so far as size and elaboration of product were concerned, were the light engineering trades and those producing small hardware goods, which were so numerous in and around Birmingham. In 1860 nearly all such industries were still handicrafts and, though there was an appreciable increase of mech-anization among them in the next 25 years, it was only towards 1890 that it began to be rapid and fairly general.[5]

The other most important industrial activities, mining and build-ing, showed less technical advance. In the methods of sinking new shafts and in winning coal underground there were piecemeal improvements but no revolutionary changes. Only, perhaps, in the adoption by the twentieth century of new equipment for handling coal at the pit-head can mechanization be said to have fundamentally changed any section of the mining industry between 1870 and

---

[1] Clapham, *op. cit.*, II, 88-9; Cox, *op. cit.*, pp. 257-8.

[2] Allen, *op. cit.*, p. 309.

[3] Lord George Hamilton, *Parliamentary Reminiscences and Reflections* (1917-22), I, 298-9 and II, 81-3.

[4] Clapham, *op. cit.*, III, 159.　　　　[5] Allen, *op. cit.*, pp. 316-22.

1914.[1] Building, of all great industries, was least affected by machinery and even by non-mechanical technical advance. The late nineteenth century saw an increased use of concrete and in the first few years of the twentieth century a steel frame became more and more common for large buildings. But most building on a smaller scale was still done by methods that had long been known. It was in the methods of making some of the universal components of buildings, rather than in building work itself, that machinery was bringing some improvements and economies.[2]

Thus fundamental technical change, though common, was not a universal experience in industrial activities, and even in some large industries where a few important changes took place after 1870 there were signs that innovation was slowing down and that notable developments elsewhere were not being taken up in England. In the cotton industry, for instance, though new types of spinning machinery came into general use, there was little change in the design of looms. By the end of the nineteenth century automatic looms were being introduced in rapidly increasing numbers in the United States, but were almost unknown in England.[3] It might even be that, in the large basic industries as a whole (though with individual exceptions), innovations of a radical kind were becoming rarer by the opening of the twentieth century. Yet, when these qualifications have been made, it remains true that the technical basis of British industry changed profoundly between 1870 and 1914, and that at no time within the period was this type of change halted. Even in those industries where radical innovation seemed to have come to an end (at least for the time being) detailed improvements in processes that remained unchanged in principle had a far from negligible influence. Industries in this situation came to be characterized by a greater speed of work and to depend on a larger power equipment. And even more striking was the fact that by the early years of the twentieth century the use of power-driven machinery was the central feature of almost all types of manufacturing industry, whereas in the eighteen-sixties that had been far from being the case.

The increased amount and more varied use of power equipment was, indeed, one of the most pervasive and significant symptoms of the nature of industrial change at this time. The late nineteenth

---

[1] Clapham, *op. cit.*, III, 162-6.
[2] *Ibid.*, III, 196-200; G. T. Jones, *Increasing Return*, p. 97.
[3] Chapman, *op. cit.*, pp. 28-31.

century saw the industrial dominance of the steam-engine carried to
its peak, though just how much its use increased cannot be precisely
stated. A collection of the very incomplete information suggested
that the capacity of steam-engines used in the United Kingdom for
purposes other than transport increased two and a half times
between 1870 and 1896.[1] In 1907, when comprehensive enquiry
was first made, the total capacity of industry's power equipment was
10,578,000 h.p., of which 9,650,000 h.p., represented the capacity
of steam-engines.[2] In most cases the steam-engines were used
directly to drive industrial machinery, but increasing use was being
made of electrical power. Generating equipment in 1907 had a total
capacity of 1,748,000 kw., and must have required nearly a quarter of
the country's engine power to drive it.[3] But electricity was wanted
chiefly for lighting and only in some sections of the engineering and
shipbuilding industries does electrical power appear to have been
much used. Similarly limited was the use of internal combustion
engines, which at this time were usually driven by gas. It was only
in many of the engineering and small metal goods industries that the
gas-engine was one of the chief sources of power. Even in the most
modern of the power industries there were some signs of backwardness, for in 1907 three-quarters of the electrical generating equipment
was driven by reciprocating steam-engines,[4] although the superiority
of steam-turbines for this purpose was already established. Clearly,
many possibilities of the improvement of power supplies and
equipment were being neglected or, at least, retarded, yet the changes
that were made were wide-ranging in their influence and impressive
in magnitude even when compared with the great innovations earlier
in the nineteenth century. In this combination of missed chances and
great, novel achievements the history of power equipment seems very
typical of the history of the techniques of British industry generally
in this period.

[1] Mulhall, *Dictionary of Statistics* (4th edn.), pp. 545 and 807. The figure for
1896 (2·3 mn. h.p.) appears to be much too low, but it would not be surprising if
the proportionate omissions from the 1870 figure were even greater.

[2] *Final Report of the First Census of Production*, p. 17.

[3] *Ibid.*, p. 18. The figure of 'nearly a quarter' is based on the assumption that
3 kw. is roughly equivalent to 4 h.p. and that there is a 10 per cent loss of energy
in conversion (*cf. ibid.*, p. 107). The figure is in one way misleading, as much of the
electrical generating equipment served the tramways, not industry. Other means of
transport, such as ships and railway locomotives, carried their power units with
them and their capacity, which was in total much greater than that of the power
equipment of industry, was not included in the returns of the census of production.

[4] *Ibid.*, p. 18.

That, in spite of shortcomings, so many technical changes had been adopted was one reason for expecting considerable changes in other features of industry. In new technical conditions it was quite likely that some firms and industries would find their old locations and forms of organization less profitable than they had been, though technique alone was not always a decisive factor, especially in determining location. In fact, changes in the location of industry were probably less sweeping in the forty years preceding the First World War than at any other time from the early days of the Industrial Revolution to the present, and the larger ones that did occur were influenced more by the position of markets and raw material supplies than directly by the adoption of new techniques. The influence of technical change showed itself mainly in small local shifts within the same region. Where an industry which had been a handicraft adopted power-driven machinery (as woollen weaving, hosiery and some of the small metal trades did) it tended to gather in one or two large centres within the district in which it was already settled instead of being scattered among many neighbouring towns and villages. Industries which had been found all over the country began very gradually to become less widespread as they were more mechanized and to settle in the larger centres of the regions in which there had already been incipient localization; the boot-making of Northampton and the clothing industry of Leeds are witnesses to change of this kind. More striking displacements occurred when new techniques were accompanied by drastic changes in the source of material. Flour-milling and steel-making were probably the most important illustrations of this. Large numbers of small flour mills, which had ground the local wheat, disappeared from the main arable regions and were replaced by larger, up-to-date mills in the ports. In steel-making there was less change in location, mainly because a considerable transfer of the iron industry to places nearer the coast had already taken place in the third quarter of the nineteenth century, so that the main producing centres were already fairly well placed to cope with an increased dependence on imported ores.[1] Indeed, there are signs that this seemingly favourable position actually hampered further re-location of iron and steel production to take advantage of new technical possibilities. The large supplies of not very high grade phosphoric ores in the East Midlands (from Lincolnshire to North Oxfordshire) were economically suited (with

[1] Clapham, *op. cit.*, II, 47-9, 515-16 and III, 145-6.

D

some admixture of other ores) to the supply of a large production of basic steel if plants were erected close to the ore. But though there was some increase in steel output from this district, it had, down to the First World War, only a minor place among the steel-making districts of the country.[1]

Apart from these changes affecting manufacturing industries there were inevitable shifts in the extractive industries as old mineral resources approached exhaustion and new ones were exploited, but few even of these were of great national significance. None of the old coalfields went out of production, though output from some of the smaller ones dwindled, and the only new coalfield, in East Kent, was only just being prepared for production in the early years of the twentieth century. The main change came from the extension of mining in existing fields beyond the earlier boundaries of development, as happened conspicuously in Yorkshire.

If it seems surprising, in a period when dependence on coal spread to practically the whole of manufacturing industry, that there were not greater changes in location, two considerations may perhaps make it less so. One is that by 1870 most industry that was not actually on the coalfields was already in easy, not very distant, communication with them by rail or sea. The other is that most of the industries that were new, or that were turning to steam-power for the first time, were producing fairly highly finished goods, the total cost of which was often less affected by local differences in the cost of fuel than was the case for many of the older industries. Often a large supply of skilled labour was specially important to them. The same labour force, sometimes the same firms, could economically develop the manufacture of new types of finished goods without moving from an old industrial area.[2]

In some respects the very absence of drastic industrial re-location was a symptom of changing conditions of industrial development, for it was contrary to recent experience. By about 1880 the powerful pull of industry to the northern half of England (especially, though not exclusively, to the coalfields) was over. Up to that time the northern industrial and commercial towns had been the greatest attractions to population outside them, because in them the greatest number of extra jobs was created. But the movement of the iron and steel industry to Cleveland and the north-east coast and to the coast of Furness and Cumberland in the third quarter of the century was

---

[1] Burn, *op. cit.*, pp. 167-70 and 181-2.　　　[2] Allen, *op. cit.*, pp. 439-40.

the last great instance of this trend. From about 1880 the northern industrial towns lost their exceptional attraction and the balance of population movements began to tilt in favour of the south, though not many important new, or greatly enlarged, manufacturing centres arose in the south at this time.[1] This was a period in which coal and iron had passed the peak of their influence as determinants of profitable industrial location but newer influences, such as the amenities and services of great metropolitan areas and the pull of a very large, locally concentrated market, were still not usually strong enough to outweigh them. Most industries probably had not much to gain or much to lose by moving to a new district and consequently they usually stayed where they were. In a few cases, however, notably in the steel industry, new locations could have reduced transport costs, and refusal to move was a source of loss.

The effect of new conditions on industrial organization was far more drastic. One result of the spread of power-driven machinery to most types of industry was to reduce to small proportions the many variants of the 'domestic system', under which a manufacturer or merchant gave out raw materials or partly finished goods to be worked up by people in their own homes. Such arrangements had still had a large place in British industry in the middle of the nineteenth century, but in 1907 the census of production recorded only 102,147 outworkers in a total labour force of over 7 million.[2] Of these outworkers nearly three-quarters were women and girls and nearly three-quarters were engaged in the clothing trades. Most of the rest were textile workers, principally in the lace and hosiery industries.[3] These figures do not fully indicate the surviving extent of outwork, since some occasional or seasonal workers must have escaped mention, part-time help from other members of an outworker's family probably went unrecorded in most cases, and census schedules were not completed by all small businesses. In a few industries the number of outworkers may, for these reasons, have been appreciably higher than the number recorded, at least if part-time workers are included. But, even so, for industry as a whole, outwork had lost its importance by the early years of the twentieth century. It was economically practicable only in industries where the scope and efficiency of machinery were still very limited and where

[1] Cairncross, *Home and Foreign Investment 1870-1913*, pp. 69-73.
[2] *Final Report of the First Census of Production*, p. 9.
[3] *Ibid.*, pp. 12, 362 and 365.

there was plenty of cheap labour, e.g. in poor districts where many of the men were irregularly employed and there was little factory work available for their wives and daughters. In some such localities, notably in East London, outwork in what had come to be known as 'sweated trades' was a serious social problem. But the clothing industry was the only large one where this was at all common.

Much the same influences that led to a decline in the amount of outwork encouraged an increase in the size of factories and workshops. In some industries which in 1870 were still equipped mainly with hand-machines there was already a tendency to gather more of them into workshops; in Leicester, for instance, in 1860 there were twenty or thirty hosiery workshops each with some thirty-five hand-frames.[1] In this and many other industries the adoption of mechanical power quickly made the trend much more general and often necessitated workshops a good deal larger than this. The cost of an engine and of the more elaborate machines that were coming into use was often too great for them to be installed in a workshop unless it was much bigger than the shops that had formerly been typical of many finished goods industries. As well as in the lesser textile industries, mechanization brought a considerable increase in the size of workshops in most of the finished metal goods and light engineering industries between the eighteen-eighties and the First World War.[2] The development of fairly small gas-engines and, later, of electric motors, helped to make it practicable for workshops to carry on profitably without growing unduly, but even so it was becoming usual for their employees to be counted in tens rather than in ones.

In some of the principal industries of the country, including cotton, iron and steel, heavy engineering, and shipbuilding, a much larger average unit of production had been usual for a long time. But even in these the scale was much less in the mid-nineteenth century than it became in the twentieth. In 1850 a factory or works which employed more than 200 people was outstandingly large and even in 1870, though it had become less remarkable, it was above the average for all but a very few industries. According to the information of the factory inspectors the average number of employees per 'factory' in Britain in 1870-71 was 177 in the cotton industry, 219 in iron-making, and 570 in iron-shipbuilding (private yards). In such important industries as woollen manufacture and machine-making it was still only 70 and 85 respectively. Undoubtedly it was tending to

[1] Wells, *op. cit.*, p. 148.   [2] Allen, *op. cit.*, p. 447.

rise generally and it was noticeable that in some of the relatively large-scale industries, such as iron-making and shipbuilding, the districts of recent development contained a preponderance of the largest establishments.[1] But the great works providing employment for thousands existed only in rare conditions. A few public utility services in the big cities were on this scale and in special circumstances the engineering and shipbuilding industries could develop plants far beyond their average size. Railway companies, for instance, were necessarily among the largest businesses of the mid-nineteenth century and, where they built as well as repaired nearly all their own rolling-stock, their central works were often very large. The Great Eastern Railway, to take one example, already in 1872 had 3,000 employees at its Stratford works, the number having doubled since 1850 and more than doubling again by 1900.[2] The occasional firm which combined with shipbuilding the production of a great variety of engineering goods likewise needed a big establishment. One such firm, the Thames Ironworks at Canning Town, employed 6,000 men at the peak of its activity in the early 'sixties, and, though its shipbuilding business rapidly dwindled thereafter, the number on its roll in the late nineteenth century continued between 1,500 and 3,000.[3] But in shipbuilding, as in the building of railway rolling-stock, it was especially where there existed a large concentrated demand for an exceptionally complex group of products that giant industrial establishments could be maintained. The needs of the Royal Navy created just such conditions and for much of the nineteenth century the Admiralty, which undertook most of its own shipbuilding and repairing, may well have been running the biggest industrial enterprise in Britain. In 1882 the five Royal Dockyards in England and Wales employed 19,349 men. Even the smallest of them, Sheerness, had 1,758 employees and the largest, Portsmouth, had 6,256.[4]

The conditions which encouraged the establishment of plants as big as this were still exceptional in 1914, though less so than they

[1] *Return of Factories and Workshops* (*P.P.* 1871, LXII), p. 105. The return is summarized and discussed in Clapham, *op. cit.*, II, 114-19.

[2] E. G. Howarth and M. Wilson, *West Ham: a study in social and industrial problems* (1907), p. 161. For other examples see Various Authors, *Round the Works of Our Great Railways* (1893).

[3] S. Pollard, 'The Decline of Shipbuilding on the Thames' in *Econ. Hist. Rev.*, 2nd series, III, 85-8; Howarth and Wilson, *op. cit.*, p. 161.

[4] *Return relating to men employed in dockyards at home during 1882-83 to 1886-78* (*P.P.* 1888, LXIX), p. 2.

had been, but over a large part of industry there had by then been a considerable increase in the scale of operations. The increased share of the heavy industries in total industrial production meant that the activities in which a fairly large plant had been least uncommon became relatively more important and therefore more representative of industry generally; and both in these and other industries the necessity for reorganization or re-equipment which could be fully remunerative only with a larger scale of production was a common experience. The speeding up of production, by the use of more power and more reliable equipment, fostered an increased scale of operations even in some industries where the fundamentals of technique did not greatly change; and where this influence was supplemented by the mechanization of nearly all stages of a more sub-divided productive process, the incentive to adopt a bigger scale was usually all the greater. Moreover, while technical factors were probably the most important influence on the rise of larger plants, they were often reinforced by changes in markets and market organization which, at the very least, removed obstacles to the profitable operation of bigger establishments.

Just when or how much the size of industrial establishments increased is hard to say, mainly because figures of numbers employed per works are sporadic and very incomplete—the neglect to elicit any information about this in the first census of production was perhaps the worst deficiency of that enquiry. But there are signs that in the 'seventies and early 'eighties there was no great change.[1] It would appear that, on the whole, manufacturers did not adopt drastic changes in the type of equipment and organization until a good many years of stronger competition, falling prices and a sterner struggle for profits had convinced them that they were inescapable. From then onwards there are many indications of the appearance of more numerous big establishments. By this time the increased use of machinery was making the number of employees, by itself, a rather less satisfactory criterion of size; in many ways the quantity or value of equipment or of capital was becoming a more suitable one. Information on this subject, however, usually relates to individual firms, which may have more than one plant, rather than to individual plants. But it does give some, more or less imperfect, indication of what was happening. It is most useful for such an industry as cotton, where most firms had only one establishment and those which had

[1] Clapham, *op. cit.*, II, 115.

two or more nearly always located them in the same district and might run them almost as a unit. In the Lancashire cotton spinning industry the number of firms exclusively concerned with this activity rose only from 639 to 657 between 1884 and 1911 but the number of their spindles increased from 24,041,000 to 44,712,000.[1] At the earlier date much the commonest size of firm was one with 10,000 to 20,000 spindles and though this size remained common in 1911 there had by then been a remarkable increase in the number with 70,000 to 100,000 spindles.[2] In cotton weaving in Lancashire the trend was similar. In 1884 the commonest size of firm had about 150 looms, but in 1911 the preponderance of this size had lessened and firms with 500 to 600 or 1,000 to 1,100 looms had become increasingly important and not much less representative than the smaller firms.[3] There was an impression that the great increase in the proportion of large firms, at any rate in spinning, was fairly recent and would have been much less noticeable before 1907.[4]

Satisfactory information to illustrate what was happening over a wider area of industry is less fully available, but something may be made of the amount of paid-up capital of public companies. For coal, iron and steel companies the average capital per company was £362,000 in 1885, £376,000 in 1895 and £525,000 in 1915; for breweries the increase was from £501,000 in 1895 to £557,000 in 1915 and for electric supply companies from £232,000 in 1895 to £423,000 in 1915; while the numerous and miscellaneous group of companies classed by the stock exchange as 'commercial and industrial' averaged £129,000 in 1885, £214,000 in 1895 and £340,000 in 1915.[5] Such figures are, of course, not representative of the absolute size of industrial firms, as the smaller firms were not organized as public companies with shares quoted on the London stock exchange. Nor do they reflect only the growth in the size of industrial establishments, for they were undoubtedly influenced by the increasing consolidation of several plants in the ownership of a single company; and there were industries which had a high proportion of small establishments, even though the public companies within them

---

[1] S. J. Chapman and T. S. Ashton, 'The Sizes of Businesses, Mainly in the Textile Industries' in *Journ. of the R. Stat. Socy.*, LXXVII (1913-14), 538.

[2] *Ibid.*, pp. 472-7.　　　　[3] *Ibid.*, p. 486.　　　　[4] *Ibid.*, pp. 551 and 555.

[5] Calculated from figures in J. B. Jefferys, *Trends in Business Organization in Great Britain since 1856* (Univ. of London unpublished Ph.D. thesis, 1938), p. 459. The figures are based on the entries in various editions of *Burdett's Official Intelligence*.

were highly capitalized. Just before the First World War, for instance, a quarter of the collieries in Britain employed fewer than 75 men each.[1] But when all these qualifications have been made, the figures of company capital indicate a clear trend towards larger size between the 'eighties and the First World War.

They probably deserve to be given more weight because during this period the adoption of company organization was one of the most prominent and widespread of all industrial changes. In 1885, with only a very few industries as exceptions, most industrial firms were owned and run by individuals or partnerships; before 1914 company ownership was usual, though private companies were then much more numerous than public ones. By far the most important reason underlying this change, especially before the 'nineties, appears to have been the desirability of operating on a bigger scale, with a consequent need for larger capital outlays, though once the fashion of converting a family business into a company had been set it also tended to be followed merely for the sake of obtaining security through limited liability, which was fast losing the last remnants of disrepute which had clung to it in some business minds.

The distribution of companies among different industries at different times seems clearly to support this interpretation. On the basis of contemporary estimates of the number of firms above the one-man size, not more than 5 to 10 per cent of them (apart from public utilities) can have been organized as limited liability companies by 1885. But 28 per cent of the Lancashire cotton spinning firms and 41 per cent of firms operating blast furnaces had this form, and among the larger firms the proportion of companies was much higher.[2] Moreover, at this time, the great majority of companies were public companies, seeking capital from outside. The private company (which obtained limited liability without making any public issue of shares), though not the subject of legislation until 1907 and not distinctively recognized by the courts before the 'nineties, already existed in practice, but only a small proportion of the little firms made use of it.[3] Subsequently in the industries using much fixed capital a further increase in size made company organization still more usual. The proportion of blast furnaces owned by

---

[1] Chapman and Ashton, *loc. cit.*, p. 548.   [2] Jefferys, *op. cit.*, pp. 105-6.
[3] H. A. Shannon, 'The Limited Companies of 1866-1883' in Carus-Wilson, *Essays in Economic History*, pp. 380, 391-2 and 398.

companies rose from 44 per cent in 1882 to 83 per cent in 1900 and 90 per cent in 1910. In Oldham the proportion of cotton spindles owned by companies rose from 50 per cent to 80 per cent between 1884 and 1893, and between 1900 and 1907 limited companies became completely dominant in the cotton industry. The firms in the new industries of the post-1885 period, such as chemicals, electricity, motor-cars and cycles, were mostly organized as companies from a very early stage of their existence.[1] In the same period it became more and more usual for smaller firms in the older industries to be turned into companies, even though they did not need outside capital. The number of companies in the United Kingdom increased from 9,344 in 1885 to 62,762 in 1914, although there is unlikely to have been much, if any, increase in the number of business firms, and in the latter year 77 per cent of companies were private companies, as compared with 23 to 33 per cent in the early 'nineties, when the definition of a private company was less clear.[2]

The conversion of partnerships into private companies was mainly responsible for a fall in the average capital per company from £59,000 in 1885 to £55,000 in 1895 and £41,000 in 1915,[3] which shows that the trend towards large size was not without exceptions. Since, however, the companies of 1885 were mostly the biggest ten or less per cent of firms, whereas in 1915 they were probably nearer to two-thirds of all firms, this fairly small drop can hardly fail to indicate an appreciable increase in the average size of firms. It is, indeed, very probable that, even among the smaller firms, higher capitalization was one of the influences in many cases of conversion to a private company. The fact that no outside capital was sought at the time of conversion proves that capital needs could still be met by the existing partners, but when they had more at risk the attractions of limited liability became all the greater.

The adoption of company organization at this time was not peculiar to industry; it was prominent also in trade, transport and finance, and any conclusions from the statistics of companies must also be qualified because of the inclusion of many companies operating overseas. But in business at home it was probably in manufacture and mining that the greatest change in organization took place between 1885 and 1914. In transport and finance a much bigger proportion of business was already in the hands of joint-stock companies before 1885 and in

[1] Jefferys, *op. cit.*, pp. 123-4 and 126-7.
[2] *Ibid.*, pp. 104 and 130.   *Ibid.*, p. 131

trade it is probable that in 1914 a bigger proportion still remained in the hands of small unincorporated firms. In building, too, the company in 1914 was still much less important, partly because so much building work, especially repairs, could be done at least as easily by a very small firm as by a large one, and partly because some even of the largest contractors could finance much of their activity from progress payments by their customers.[1]

The transition to company organization in industry was part of an adjustment to gradually changing technical and market conditions. It facilitated an increase in scale which in many cases was economically essential; it helped firms to attain a size and position in which they could better accumulate reserves, either to protect themselves in times of bad trade or to contribute to their further expansion; it encouraged more precise and careful accounting, the advantages of which grew as the complexity of business grew; and it led slowly to a greater separation of ownership from management, and hence made it possible to use managerial ability which otherwise would have been neglected. In the long run, therefore, the development of industrial companies brought with it greater stability among firms, the use of a greater amount of more specialized talent to cope with more complex business methods, and greater impersonality in industrial affairs. None of these results came overnight. The earlier companies could hardly be called a stabilizing influence since, down to the end of the nineteenth century, there was always a substantial minority of the new companies which was the creation of the incompetent or the fraudulent.[2] And the running of sound firms did not change immediately, when incorporation brought no change of ownership, and when management by partners continued as management by the same persons with the title of directors. But in the years just before the First World War, when the formation of fraudulent companies had become more exceptional and when many first-generation company directors were reaching retirement without almost automatically being succeeded by their sons, the long-term

[1] One of the largest Victorian contracting firms, S. Pearson & Son, founded in 1856, was able to finance itself by accumulated profits, bank advances and progress payments and, although at times it had in hand work to the value of over £5 mn., it did not become a limited company until 1897. Even then the change was made only to enable the sole owner to undertake government contracts without thereby becoming technically the holder of an office of profit under the Crown and thus becoming ineligible to continue as a M.P. (J. A. Spender, *Weetman Pearson First Viscount Cowdray* (1930), pp. 22-5).

[2] This point is discussed in some detail for the period to 1883 in Shannon, *loc. cit.*, pp. 384-8 and 392.

results of late Victorian institutional change were becoming clear. By that time the organization of industrial business had been still further changed by various forms of association or fusion among firms that had once been entirely separate, a development in which the adoption of company form was involved both as cause and as effect. The permanent amalgamations which produced large new combines were basically of two different kinds: the vertical integration of specialist firms engaged in successive processes in the same industry or in industries which were linked by sales and purchases to and from each other; and the fusion of firms which had been directly competing with one another by making the same products or buying the same raw materials. In British industry before the First World War vertical integration stemmed chiefly from the iron and steel industry and was unimportant in other manufactures, though there was some sign of it in the chemical and allied industries—just before the First World War the large chemical firm of Brunner, Mond obtained control of two of its important customers among the soap-makers, and the leading soap-makers were purchasing interests in industries which supplied' them with materials, particularly in firms which hardened fats.[1] In the iron industry some integration through the ownership of coal and ironstone mines by iron-making firms was of long standing and continued further along these lines in the last third of the nineteenth century. But the increase of steel-making, in which the savings effected by carrying on many of the higher stages of production immediately after the lower were unusually great, gave an increasing advantage to the more integrated (and therefore larger) firms. Thus, through the ordinary working of competition, a greater share of the industry was in the hands of large, integrated firms by the end of the nineteenth century, and their very size and costliness doubtless made them more anxious to secure greater control over the outlets for their final products. The demand for armour-plate had already taken some steel firms over the boundary of the armament industry, and when new amalgamations began to be formed in order to secure still fuller vertical integration the fusions were mainly of steel-making, shipbuilding and armament firms. Most of the amalgamations in this group of industries took place between 1894 and 1902, the main period of amalgamation in business generally in Britain, but a few came a little later, partly because of the special influence of a continuously expanding re-armament programme, in

[1] C. Wilson, *The History of Unilever* (1954), I, 126-7 and 129-39.

the execution of which a declining share went to government establishments.[1]

Amalgamations among competing firms in the same industry were more widespread but by no means general in industry. The first large example came in 1888 with the formation of the Salt Union, a combination of firms which then controlled 90 per cent of the British salt production.[2] It was followed in 1891 by the even larger United Alkali Company in which were combined all the makers of bleaching powder by the Leblanc process, which was then coming under challenge by other processes and depended for its profitability on the sales of chlorine as a by-product.[3] But most of the great amalgamations did not come until after 1894. Then in the next seven years there came a number of very large amalgamations which transformed the structure of the sewing-cotton, textile dyeing and finishing, cement, wallpaper and tobacco industries, as well as notable but rather less comprehensive amalgamations in the chemical and brewing and one or two other industries.[4] Even in the iron and steel and related industries, where vertical integration was more usual, there was a certain amount of horizontal combination, though usually the firms concerned were complementary to each other in some of their activities, while competitive in others. In this group of industries, as to some extent in the chemical industries, there was also the distinguishing feature that some of the fusions involved arrangements with foreign as well as British firms, e.g. for the operation of joint subsidiaries or the sharing of particular processes and patents.

The explanation of this amalgamation movement, which was by no means peculiar to Britain (it went a good deal further at this time in Germany and the United States) is to be found principally in the influence of the dominant trends of technology, operating in a setting where a prolonged decline of prices made profits more difficult to maintain. In a variety of fields technical conditions were already leading to greater concentration of industry as smaller firms became uneconomic and went out of business. The very reduction in the number of firms made agreement among the rest easier to negotiate,

[1] Clapham, *op. cit.*, III, 259-62; H. W. Macrosty, *The Trust Movement in British Industry* (1907), chap. II and pp. 329-30.

[2] Macrosty, *op. cit.*, pp. 182-7.

[3] *Ibid.*, pp. 187-93; T. C. Barker and J. R. Harris, *A Merseyside Town in the Industrial Revolution: St. Helens 1750-1900* (1954), pp. 440-4.

[4] The whole movement is discussed in detail in Macrosty, *op. cit.*

competition could increasingly (though not always rationally) be blamed for the seemingly irresistible slide of prices, and the success of some of the larger firms in surviving times of difficult trade and inescapable technical reorganization encouraged attempts to emulate or surpass them. It took years of hard experience to weaken old individualist attitudes to the point where a business owner would voluntarily merge his property in that of a larger, impersonal organization, but it is clear[1] that, by the mid-eighties, cherished business ideas had been severely shaken and that a way out from falling prices was the most general demand of manufacturers. It is significant that the main burst of amalgamations came in the later stages of this prolonged and extreme price decline, and that its momentum was greatest from 1894, when money was at its cheapest and extra capital for reorganization most easily obtainable. Even around 1900, when prices were just beginning to rise and amalgamations still proceeding, the statements of some of the firms concerned show that decisions were still being influenced by the mentality which falling prices induced, while in some cases powerful competition from combines recently formed abroad was present to provide an extra stimulus to combination in Britain.

Some of the combines appear to have been run with few ideas beyond the raising of prices through the acquisition of a near-monopoly. Where this was so their price-raising efforts merely provoked new competition and within a few years brought disaster down upon them. Of such a history the Salt Union was the most notorious illustration. Others made amalgamation the occasion for seeking real economies. They reorganized the industry in which they had gained preponderance, by closing the least efficient plants, by unifying and simplifying administration, and by making new marketing arrangements. They did something to justify the name of 'efficiency-combines' which began to be applied to them and thereby established a permanent place for themselves in industry. Provided that combines took trouble with their management, there were indeed strong reasons to expect them to increase in number, size and importance, for the influences which favoured them were not transient and were likely to strengthen with time. That the combination movement slackened from 1902 to 1914, before it had affected more than a small corner of British industry, was the result of more

---

[1] e.g. from the voluminous evidence presented to the *Royal Commission on the Depression in Industry and Trade* (*P.P.* 1886, XXI-XXIII).

temporary influences. Rising prices and easier trading enabled old individualistic ideas to reassert themselves; dearer money made reorganization less attractive; the ill-success of some of the worse-managed combines both in Britain and the United States falsified earlier expectations; and some public suspicion, fostered by the press, damaged the prospects of large combines—in 1906, for instance, it was able to kill the proposed merger of the leading soap manufacturers, though it did not prevent nearly the same result being achieved gradually over the next eight years through the acquisition of other firms by Lever Brothers.[1]

If, however, permanent amalgamation was still rare before 1914, some kind of formal machinery for joint action by otherwise independent firms in the same industry had become fairly common. Associations of producers in the same industry or the same district have been known for a very long time, and despite growing stress on the virtues of unrestricted competition, they were still common in the eighteen-forties.[2] They may well have become less common during the next quarter of a century, though it was not unknown for new associations to be formed, or old ones reconstituted, in order to deal with some specific question of common concern. By the 'eighties such associations were apparently being formed in increasing numbers and thereafter the rate at which they came into existence probably increased. It is difficult to be precise about the course of their history since sometimes they began in a rather informal way and, at least in their earlier years, many of them were very careful to shun publicity. But by 1914 most industries had a trade association. To some extent this development was attributable to the same causes as led to the formation of combines; certainly the influence of the late-nineteenth-century price fall in permanently modifying the business world's taste for competition was important. But it probably had less effect than the parallel growth of trade unions. The one function which was common to nearly all trade associations was the formulation of an agreed policy for dealings with labour. The very existence of such associations, of course, provided an opportunity to discuss prices and the allocation of markets and to consider government policy as it affected the industry concerned. Some of them made explicit provision for dealing with these matters, though adherence to common price lists and an agreed division of markets could not always be

1 Wilson, *op. cit.*, I, 72-88 and 115-24.
2 For some examples see Barker and Harris, *op. cit.*, pp. 246-55.

maintained for more than a few years. But, with conspicuous exceptions in a few industries, such as iron and steel, most trade associations before the First World War did not interfere directly with prices. Well-informed observers concluded that down to this time most of British industry was still conducted under very competitive conditions.[1] A trend towards a different kind of organization was clearly in progress, and over part of the industrial world a much less atomistic structure had already established itself. But, though reorganization had been extensive, oligopoly had not yet superseded competition as the norm.

Changes in scale and the adoption of a more associated form of industrial structure were, along with technical innovation and the introduction of new products, the principal ways in which industrialists sought to maintain or improve their earning capacity in the face of new conditions. But they could hardly be effective without some other consequential changes. In particular, they often forced attention to the need for some reform of managerial methods. The improvement of management, however, seems to have been mainly incidental to other changes and to have been pursued almost entirely on empirical lines. Certain very widespread changes influenced the administration of large numbers of firms in similar ways. The much more general adoption of corporate form and the growing importance of companies' dealings with the inland revenue authorities generalized the use of double-entry bookkeeping, with an associated increase in the influence of professional accountants on the running of businesses;[2] and the effect of certain court decisions may have been to standardize some accounting practices, particularly after 1900, when all registered companies were made subject to compulsory audit.[3]

But management is a wider subject than accounting. By the end of the nineteenth century it was being given increasing attention by a few pioneers who sought to identify problems and propound principles which transcended any one industry or type of firm. Before 1914, however, the practical influence of such efforts appears to have increased only slowly; and American work in

---

[1] Clapham, *op. cit.*, III, 316-18. Clapham had access to much unpublished material obtained by the 1919 Committee on Trusts.

[2] B. S. Yamey, *Introduction* to A. C. Littleton and B. S. Yamey (eds.), *Studies in the History of Accounting* (1956), p. 11.

[3] H. C. Edey and Prot Panitpakdi, 'British Company Accounting and the Law 1844-1900' in *ibid.*, pp. 371-2 and 379.

developing what was termed 'scientific management' had little effect
in Britain.[1] Small firms, the nature of whose business changed little,
were probably run in much the same way as for many years past. In
others, past and present experience, supplemented sometimes by a
knowledge of recent writings on management and some formal
training in accountancy, suggested the lines of managerial adjustment
to changing conditions. The result was probably to widen the range
of efficiency in managerial methods more than ever. One observer
wrote in 1907 that 'rule of thumb is dead in the workshop, the day is
with the engineer and the chemist with their methods of precision; in
the counting-house and boardroom there is no longer a place for the
huckster or gambler, the future is with the commercial statesman
whether in a large individual business or a combination'.[2] He was
right about the direction of change, but at the time his description
was relevant only to what was still a minor part of industry, though
a part of which the importance was growing year by year. Rule of
thumb still had a considerable place in industry, perhaps even more
in its administration than its technique. Knowledge of the most
modern managerial practices was far from universally diffused, and
the variety of conditions to which they were suited had not been
fully demonstrated in practice. A good deal of change had to be
made, but whether it was made in ways that were well suited to
individual conditions depended very much on the native shrewdness
of individual managers and on the chances that had determined the
breadth of their experience.

To recall that the varied characteristics of management were much
influenced by the individual quirks, inborn abilities and particular
experiences of individual owners and managers is a useful safeguard
against the temptation to put forward too simple an explanation of
the course of British industrial development. That so many of the
general features of industry were modified only gradually between
1870 and 1914, while the details in some sections were almost untouched and in others completely transformed, was, immediately, the
cumulative result of decisions by large numbers of men acting within
the limits of their own training, seeking their own sustained profit

[1] Not much detailed work has been done on the history of management. Some of
the points mentioned here are discussed in L. F. Urwick and E. F. L. Brech,
The Making of Scientific Management (1945-48), esp. vol. II, chaps. VI-X.

[2] Macrosty, *op. cit.*, p. 337.

where they judged it likely to be found, often preferring to stay close to what was familiar, sometimes obstinately following the idiosyncrasies of their own curiosities and seemingly irrational aspirations, reconciling these conflicting pulls on them as far and as well as they could. But it is, of course, undeniable that the extent to which industrialists could go their own way with success, or at least without immediate disaster, was continuously controlled and limited by the most pervasive technical, economic and legal features of their environment.

Any attempt to indicate some among these features which had a specially strong influence on industrial history must be speculative and cannot be confined only to a consideration of what was happening in industry. An explanation of industrial change must, for instance, be very incomplete until the history of foreign trade has been considered. It was the opening of vast new markets that made it practicable for textiles to retain such a large share in British industrial activity at a time when they met increasing competition in many old markets and when other leading industrial countries were finding it rewarding to give relatively more attention to other industries. It was the general growth of international trade, too, that was responsible for the relative rise of shipbuilding, with its important repercussions on the engineering and steel industries. And foreign trade was also an important factor in the expansion of the demand for coal which, through its effect on prices, gave such a fillip to British mining. The general price-level was falling from 1873 to 1896 but coal prices never fell much below the level of 1879-80 and began to rise after 1887 (though with a sharp setback in the middle 'nineties),[1] and so encouraged a continued steady growth of output, although the further exploitation of this wasting asset was beginning to involve increasing costs.

If market conditions encouraged the predominance of a few large industries, it was not always mere indolence or inadaptability that kept some of them running in ways that involved the minimum amount of change. It has been suggested of a somewhat later period (and the argument applies at least partly to this) that, in the short run, the textile industry found an economic advantage in persisting with old, well-tried methods. Much of its equipment was old enough for its cost to have been almost completely written off yet was physically in good enough condition to be kept working. So capital charges were

[1] *Journ. of the R. Stat. Socy.*, XLIX (1886), 645 and LXIV (1901), 9.

very low and helped to keep costs down to a level where competition with the output of newer equipment was not difficult.[1] Other industries, however, with smaller markets and sometimes more intense competition, were less comfortably placed. The abundance of comment in the late 'seventies and 'eighties shows a widespread, sad realization in the business world of the difficulty of maintaining profits while keeping to established ways.[2] From that time dates a more rapid adoption of new techniques, new methods of organization, new products.[3] Yet the types of innovation that became at all common were limited in range. Of the many successful novelties in the world's industry some important ones were totally neglected in Britain and many more, though taken up in this country, were not so thoroughly applied as in a few others. Inevitably, one asks why this should have been so.

Many suggestions have been offered, none of them complete in itself, perhaps none conclusively proved. The heavy capital needs of some new processes and new industries may well have been an obstacle to their introduction when so many demands on the impersonal investor were coming from schemes that were more familiar or held promise of greater immediate reward. But heavy investment was far from being a universal pre-requisite of innovation. The difficulties placed in the way of inventors have also been alleged to have acted as a brake on progress. The costs and delays in taking out a patent were a serious matter for the man of small resources and when they were reduced in 1883 the number of patents straightway more than doubled and remained at the higher level;[4] but even then complaints persisted that British patent law remained more discouraging than that of other countries.[5] On the other hand the cost and trouble of taking out a patent were no real obstacles to an established firm which wanted to monopolize a new process or design in order to suppress it; and until 1907 it was open even to a foreign firm to take out a British patent in order to ensure that there would be no production in Britain in direct competition with its factories

[1] F. R. J. Jervis, 'The Handicap of Britain's Early Start' in *The Manchester School*, XV (1947), 121.

[2] H. L. Beales, 'The "Great Depression" in Industry and Trade' in Carus Wilson, *op. cit.*, p. 410.

[3] *Ibid.*, p. 412; for detailed regional illustration Allen, *op. cit.*, Part IV.

[4] J. L. Garvin, *The Life of Joseph Chamberlain*, I (1932), 419-20; *Seventh Report of the Comptroller General of Patents, Designs and Trade Marks* (P.P. 1890, XXXII), Appendices E and F.

[5] A. Shadwell *Industrial Efficiency* (2nd edn., 1909), p. 342

abroad.[1] But more fundamental was the suggestion that Britain was short of the training, the organization and the environment which were likely to encourage a sufficiency of new industrial ideas worth patenting. Complaints of the inadequate provision of technical education had been growing since 1850 and by the 'eighties were being so reinforced by the signs of foreign competition that they were beginning to carry conviction. Thereafter there was more systematic provision, though it was still not very extensive.[2] At the same time there was little continuous, organized research in industry. Few firms had the resources to do more than probe spasmodically into a few specific questions; joint organizations of firms in the same industry rarely, if ever, included industrial research among their duties; and government departments and establishments made little contribution outside a few specialized fields, such as armaments. Since improved industrial techniques were becoming more dependent on the extension and application of knowledge of the natural sciences, this situation was almost certainly a handicap to British industry, though not all other industrialized countries were in much better case. But even so, there still was at the end of the nineteenth century some scope for the innovator whose characteristics were native shrewdness, practical skill and the grasp of a few elementary principles rather than the possession of an advanced technological training.

All of these difficulties had adverse effects in some fields. But none of them can be said without qualification to have been universal barriers to industrial progress. Perhaps all of them together had less responsibility for the gaps among British innovations than had the ability of the British economy as a whole, and of most business men in particular, to get on fairly well without adopting those innovations.

This is a relevant consideration when the question is raised whether British industry in the late Victorian and early twentieth-century years was becoming less efficient. Both by contemporaries and later commentators the question was often framed in such a way as to imply that its answer was 'yes'; and failure to take up new

[1] Clapham, *op. cit.*, III, 435. In 1906, 40 per cent of the new British patents were granted to foreigners and in previous years the proportion was usually higher. At that time foreigners were estimated to hold about 30,000 patents which were still in force. (A. F. Ravenshear, *The Industrial and Commercial Influence of the English Patent System* (1908), pp. 80 and 134.)

[2] For a comparative study of the provision and effect of technical education in Britain, Germany and the U.S.A., see Shadwell, *op. cit.*, chap. XVII. Shadwell, who in general was very critical of Britain's industrial condition, reached conclusions on this point which are by no means unfavourable to Britain.

practices that flourished elsewhere was assumed to be obvious supporting evidence. But this is unrealistic. Any nation that had tried to develop all the manifold innovations that were becoming available would have been guilty of a disastrous dispersal of effort. Industrial efficiency cannot, in any case, be indicated by a consideration of industry alone; what matters, economically, is how effectively industry, in association with other activities, achieves its potentialities for creating income over both short and long periods. And that, in practice, can be only very roughly estimated.

In one sense British industry was certainly becoming less advanced, since in the late nineteenth century it lost its leadership among the nations of the world. But no serious indictment can be made of that, for the transfer of leadership to nations that were both larger and more abundantly endowed by nature was inevitable when they obtained the means to develop their economy. More substantial was the charge that, in some major industries, British producers were becoming much slower in reducing their real costs of production than they had been earlier and that they were unable to produce as cheaply as contemporary foreign competitors. There is a good deal of evidence to suggest that there may be something in this, but it is too incomplete to support the conclusion that there had been a general decline in efficiency. The most thorough investigation of real costs in particular industries, that made by G. T. Jones, revealed very little change in them between 1885 and 1910 in the Lancashire cotton industry and the Cleveland pig iron industry, and a fall of about 10 per cent in the London building industry in the last twenty years of the nineteenth century and no improvement thereafter. By contrast, real costs in the Massachusetts cotton industry fell by 20 per cent between 1885 and 1900, remaining fairly stable in the next decade, and those in the American pig iron industry fell by nearly one-third between 1885 and 1910.[1] Too gloomy a view should not be taken of these comparative figures. Jones recognized, for instance, that there had been increases in efficiency in the Lancashire cotton industry that had been offset by unmeasurable improvements in working conditions, which could not show in his figures.[2] And it is also likely that, in the conditions of the late nineteenth century, Lancashire cotton goods could earn a bigger increase of income from their markets than could other manufactures whose real cost of production could be more easily reduced. The cotton industry and trade was the

[1] Jones, *op. cit.*, pp. 268-9, 274, 278, 289-90 and 296.   [2] *Ibid.*, pp. 118-19.

biggest, but almost certainly not the only, example of this situation. This is a major consideration in the vexed question of British industrial efficiency. With all its technical shortcomings and its retention of many practices that were not the last word in modernity, British industry in the late nineteenth century appears to have been fairly well adapted to current needs and opportunities. Over a large part of the industrial field national as well as industrial advantage was found in quite gradual change rather than drastic innovation, and industry was able to contribute to a rather more rapid growth of national income. There may have been in this achievement a deceptive amount of luck (in the form of exceptionally favourable external conditions) but the achievement was considerable.

It is, however, less certain that what was happening in industry was as well adapted to long-term as to immediate needs. Whatever the present opportunities for developing new markets for the simpler staple products of British industry, it was becoming clear by the end of the nineteenth century that the number of effectively competing countries could more easily be increased in these fields than in any others—recent developments in Japan carried an obvious warning. And the corollary was also emerging that the most rapid increase of opportunities was likely to come to those countries that could make, use and sell rather more elaborate industrial products through the development of more industries in which high capitalization assisted a relatively large output per worker. The 1907 census of production suggested that Britain had not put itself as clearly among this group of countries as it might have done. Output per worker is not by itself a measure of efficiency, but there was some ground for anxiety that so large a proportion of workers should be in industries with a relatively low output per head. In the cotton industry, for instance, which was still so important, the value of net output per worker was more than 20 per cent below the average for industry as a whole, and in nearly all the other textile industries the level was still lower than for cotton.[1] Nevertheless, in the late nineteenth century the general trend of change was in accordance with what seemed the likely balance of future as well as present advantages.[2] But in the first decade of the twentieth century this was no longer so; in 1911 a bigger proportion of the labour force was employed in textiles

---

[1] *Final Report on the First Census of Production*, pp. iii and 13.
[2] For changes in the relative importance of different industries see pp. 76-9 above.

generally, and in the cotton industry in particular, than in 1901.[1] Temporary conditions in foreign trade had so far upset judgment as to produce changes exactly opposite to those likely to yield national or individual advantage in the not very long run.

It is probably at this point that serious weakness was beginning to show itself. Until about the end of the nineteenth century, though British industry had some strikingly backward pockets, its shortcomings in general do not appear to have been more serious than those of any activity whose practitioners' gifts of ability and energy are modified by the inevitable mortal touch of stupidity and indolence. But it was perhaps unfortunate that so much success was possible without a more thorough shaking up than did in fact take place in the last quarter of the century. The idea was fostered that the uncomfortable upheavals which some industries had had to undergo in the years of falling prices were a temporary phenomenon and that a quieter life was usually to be expected, whereas the truth was that ever more restless change was becoming normal. By the decade preceding the First World War the adaptability of British industry, which had been fairly adequate, needed to increase but was apparently not doing so. Contemporary trade figures seemed to justify what was happening, though if there had been regular attention then to the course of national income great doubts must at once have arisen. But even if the trading prosperity had been entirely real, there would still have had to be set against it the future difficulties that were being stored up by failure to keep industry quite up to date. In 1914, however, the leeway had opened too recently for its consequences to have become very serious. They could have been rectified in a very few years, had the opportunity still remained. But the intervention of war postponed the opportunity, magnified the ultimate task, and thus increased the penalty for the relatively small industrial backslidings of the early years of the twentieth century.

[1] *Census of England and Wales, 1911*, vol. X, part I, pp. 552-7.

CHAPTER FIVE

Internal Transport and Trade

BY 1870 the integration of separate local market areas into one nation-wide market had already been carried a long way. Persistent improvements in inland transport throughout the eighteenth and early nineteenth centuries had encouraged more and more of the country to rely less than before on the produce of the immediate vicinity for the maintenance of most of its life; and the growth of industry had necessitated a constant increase in the movement of both materials and finished goods between distant localities. The change was a gradual one, limited by the speed and capacity of the means of transport; but from the eighteen-thirties, and especially after 1850, the operation of railways enabled it to develop far more radically. In the 'fifties and 'sixties railways, supplemented by a better postal service (which they helped to make possible) and by the development of a telegraphic service (in which also they had a notable part), brought up the inter-regional exchange of goods to a level previously undreamt of and established the habit of passenger travel among a much bigger proportion of the community than ever before. Yet by 1870 they had not nearly exhausted the possibilities of expansion. Dependence on imported supplies, paid for by exports, both of which had to be carried between the ports and inland centres of production and consumption, had not reached its maximum. Urbanization, which necessarily involved bringing in supplies from outside, was still increasing. The populace was growing rapidly in both numbers and wealth. Those who had wished to have as little as possible to do with the new-fangled ways brought by the railways were beginning to die off and to be replaced by a generation with more taste for variety and movement, and often more money to indulge it. And there were still many to be familiarized for the first time with the possibility of travel as a regular element of life instead of an occasional joyous adventure. Nevertheless, though the opportunities to enlarge the business of transport might seem boundless, the history of transport from the eighteen-seventies to the First World War is best seen as a great extension of developments already well begun. Only towards the end of the period were there signs of something quite new emerging, and the effect of that was not strongly felt until later.

Perhaps the most striking feature of transport history throughout the late nineteenth century was the immense predominance of the railway among all modes of transport except over very short distances. For most classes of long-distance transport in nearly every district that they had penetrated the railways had already demonstrated their competitive superiority to the rivers, canals and roads, and a serious challenge from motor-lorries and motor-coaches did not emerge until after the First World War. For short hauls, where the advantage of speed could not be made to tell and where the charges for collection and delivery might have to be a disproportionately large part of the total charge, the railways were never so well placed competitively and their share of local was always smaller than that of long-distance traffic. But even for local traffic, in both rural and urban areas, their position was stronger in the late nineteenth century than at any other time. Freight which had to be carried only a few miles between factory or market and dockside, and which at a later date would usually have gone by road, went just as usually by rail at this time.[1] And, before the coming of the motor-bus, steam trains of the main line companies, chugging dirtily through tunnels and over viaducts, provided in the very heart of cities a density and variety of short-distance passenger services both for ordinary daily needs[2] and for special holiday occasions,[3] that have long been forgotten.

An account of inland transport in the late nineteenth century and of the changes that were taking place in it must therefore be centred on the history of railways, with other modes of transport viewed

---

[1] *Usually*, not *always*. Horse-drawn lorries shared in the dock traffic in the late nineteenth century (some docks were without railway connexions) just as the railways still retain some share in purely local dock traffic.

[2] See, e.g., the immense variety of long-abandoned services in inner and outer London described in 'G. A. Sekon', *Locomotion in Victorian London* (1938), pp. 177-98.

[3] See, e.g., the description of the transport of over 37,000 London excursionists to and from Chingford station on Whit Monday, 1888, in W. M. Acworth, *The Railways of England* (5th edn., 1900), p. 429. Twenty years earlier Whit Monday was not a universal holiday, there was no railway to Chingford, and fewer people could afford to travel so far into Epping Forest. Forty years later a large proportion of the excursionists would be going further afield and of those who still went to Chingford a large proportion would go by road. Acworth reported that his description of Chingford Bank-holiday traffic in 1888 was still valid a decade later. (*Ibid.*, p. xii.)

principally in relation to the railways. The railway network itself, though it already served most parts of the country by 1870, had not then reached its maximum extent. The length of the railway routes of the entire United Kingdom was 15,537 miles in 1870, 17,933 miles in 1880, 20,073 miles in 1890, 21,855 miles in 1900, 23,387 miles in 1910, and 23,701 miles in 1914.[1] For England and Wales alone the route mileage was 11,043 in 1870, 12,656 in 1880, 14,119 in 1890, 15,195 in 1900, 16,148 in 1910 and 16,414 in 1914.[2] Thus railway routes extended half as far again on the eve of the First World War as they had done in 1870. It is doubtful, however, whether the building of new railways was economically as significant as the magnitude of these figures might suggest. The only new main routes were the Midland Railway's line between Settle and Carlisle, opened in 1876,[3] which completed a third through route from London to Scotland, and the last line into London, by which the Manchester, Sheffield and Lincolnshire Railway, a purely provincial concern, found its way (under the more impressive name of the Great Central) from Sheffield to Marylebone station in 1899.[4] For the second of these it is improbable that there was ever any economic justification; it merely helped to make a not very flourishing undertaking still less profitable. Perhaps its most useful influence on the railway network was in encouraging the building of a convenient relief route in the Home Counties,[5] which the Great Western could also use as part of a new short cut between London and Birmingham, where there really was the traffic to employ a second direct route. The joint Great Central and Great Western line was opened in 1906 and the rest of the Great Western's cut-off in 1910.[6]

Fairly short stretches of new line to reduce the distance on existing routes between centres of large population and economic activity were, indeed, generally more valuable than belated attempts to establish completely new routes. The Severn Tunnel, opened in 1886, greatly improved the communications of South Wales with Bristol, London and southern England generally, and its advantage was increased in 1903 by the opening of the Badminton cut-off which

---

[1] Page, *Commerce and Industry*, II, 170-1.   [2] *Ibid.*, II, 172.

[3] C. E. R. Sherrington, *Economics of Rail Transport in Great Britain* (1928), I, 99.

[4] *Ibid.*, I, 134.

[5] The Great Central's original route into London involved the use of the tracks of the Metropolitan Railway, which carried considerable local traffic.

[6] Sherrington, *op. cit.*, I, 70-1 and 135.

shortened the journey between the tunnel and Swindon.[1] Others of the great Victorian feats of civil engineering that served a similar purpose were the Tay and Forth Bridges, opened in 1887 and 1890 respectively,[2] which gave Aberdeen and Dundee much easier access to the south. Less spectacular contributions of the same kind were the various cut-offs which the Great Western opened in 1900 and 1906 to shorten the route between London and Plymouth,[3] the link through Brockenhurst which from 1885 gave the London and South-Western more direct access to Bournemouth,[4] and the Upminster cut-off of the London, Tilbury and Southend Railway which, opened in stages during the eighteen-eighties, brought Southend eight miles nearer to London.[5] Apart from links of this kind the most useful additions to the railway network were probably short lines serving the most rapidly expanding coalfields and suburban lines to meet the needs of the great cities as they spread outwards. It is significant that the last new independent railway company which was an undoubted financial success owed its prosperity mainly to the movement of coal, supplemented by suburban and pleasure traffic. This was the Barry Railway in South Wales, which opened its first section of line in 1888 and which, when completed in 1905, had no more than 47 miles of routes.[6]

Short cuts, colliery and suburban lines were far from accounting for all the additions to the railway mileage—and not all of these were justified by the traffic that they subsequently carried. There were localities as distant from one another as parts of Cornwall and Inverness-shire which did not make their first acquaintance with the railway till near the end of the nineteenth century.[7] There were others, already adequately served, that were given an extra line. Few of these additions brought much reward to their promoters and probably the majority of them brought little benefit to the nation's economy. Indeed, though a few new lines of the 1870-1914 period were absolutely invaluable, the most significant enlargement of the means of railway communication came not from the extension of the

---

[1] Sherrington, *op. cit.*, I, 67 and 71.

[2] *Ibid.*, I, 145. The first Tay Bridge was opened in 1878 but collapsed after being in use for less than eighteen months.

[3] *Ibid.*, I, 71.   [4] *Ibid.*, I, 44.

[5] H. D. Welch, *The London, Tilbury and Southend Railway* (1951), pp. 15-16.

[6] Clapham, *Economic History of Modern Britain*, III, 348; Sherrington, *op. cit.*, I, 75-6.

[7] The railway reached Fort William in 1894, Padstow in 1899, Mallaig in 1901.

network, but from measures to increase the capacity of established routes. The quadrupling of tracks on busy stretches, the building of additional sidings, the re-alignment of tracks, the reform of signalling systems to permit the more frequent passage of trains, the removal of the last remnants of odd gauges,[1] the electrificatioñ of a few suburban lines[2]—these and related changes had more relevance than new lines to the problems of keeping transport provision abreast of economic needs.

None of the other modes of transport were enlarged as the railways were. The canals and improved rivers did little more than survive. Except for the Manchester Ship Canal, which was concerned with oversea rather than internal trade, hardly any new canals were built. The old canals remained available, though there were sections of some of them which by the early years of the twentieth century had no traffic. But most of the country's canal business was done by a very few of them. In a large, heavily populated industrial area which did not vary greatly in level the canals would conveniently carry much of the local traffic in bulky goods. Low-lying industrial areas, not too far from the sea, could also still make economical use of canal transport to and from their seaports. The local traffic of Birmingham and the West Midlands and of London and its northern hinterland, the traffic over the plain of South Lancashire and Cheshire to the Mersey and that from the mining and manufacturing districts of the West Riding to the Ouse and the Humber nearly exhausted the tale of inland navigation services which by the early twentieth century really mattered to the country's economy. In these areas there was an incentive to maintain the canals in good condition and two or three, such as the Aire and Calder Navigation, by such measures as the enlargement of locks, the strengthening of banks and the provision of additional basins, equipped themselves to carry extra traffic. But these were the exceptions, not the typical cases.[3]

For long-distance freight traffic only coastal shipping remained as

---

[1] The last broad-gauge train on the Great Western ran in 1892.

[2] Before 1914 there was little electrification except in and around London, Liverpool and Newcastle-on-Tyne and in none of these cities had the majority of the suburban services been electrified; the most important set of electric railways was the underground lines of London. For details (not quite complete) of lines electrified, see Sherrington, *op. cit.*, II, 230-49.

[3] The fullest account of canal history in this period is in the 4th volume of *Reports* by the *Royal Commission on Canals* (*P.P.* 1907, XXXIII, part II); see p. 229 for particulars of the Aire and Calder Navigation. This company jointly with the Sheffield and South Yorkshire, opened 6 miles of new canal in 1905.

an important alternative, or supplement, to the railways. Like passenger traffic, much of the traffic in small, miscellaneous items of freight was lost by coastal vessels very soon after the appearance of long-distance railways, but their position remained far stronger in the carriage of bulky cargoes, especially coal from the mining districts close to the tideway. Even in the last type of trade, it had looked in the 'sixties as though railway competition was gradually crushing them; in this decade the tonnage of railborne coal carried to London first surpassed the seaborne tonnage, which was declining absolutely as well as relatively.[1] But from the early 'seventies this trend was reversed and by 1900, out of a total supply which had trebled in forty years, rather more than half was brought by sea. The coasting trade was also important in the carriage of coal to other consuming centres. It had a key position in the activities of the iron and steel industry, e.g. through its carriage of semi-products, such as steel bars and billets, from Cleveland to South Wales, where they were needed for the making of finished products.[2] And, though its share in the movement of lighter goods must have been much smaller than in the past, there was still a wide variety of goods that were carried by coastal vessel—a situation clearly reflected in many railway rates.[3]

Various factors contributed to the continued importance and expansion of coastal shipping. From the early 'seventies very considerable improvements in the design of steamships were being adopted in the coasting trade,[4] and the disappearance of sailing vessels proceeded steadily. Better harbour works and new loading equipment, needed in any case for foreign trade, increased the efficiency of coastwise shipment also, especially for coal. And there was also a tendency for coastal vessels to let more of the traffic of the small ports pass to the railways, or just dwindle away, and to concentrate a bigger proportion of their activities in a few of the larger ports, notably Bristol, London and Newcastle-upon-Tyne, which could offer better facilities and bigger consignments.[5]

With all these favourable influences and signs of initiative, however,

[1] Clapham, *op. cit.*, II, 301.

[2] Burn, *The Economic History of Steel-making 1867-1939*, p. 179.

[3] Clapham, *op. cit.*, II, 528-9; W. M. Acworth, *The Elements of Railway Economics* (1905), pp. 118, 124, 126, 128-9.

[4] W. S. Lindsay, *History of Merchant Shipping and Ancient Commerce* (1874-76), IV, 547-9.

[5] Clapham, *op. cit.*, II, 523-9, and figures for later years in the annual *Trade and Navigation Returns*.

it seems unlikely that the growth of coastal shipping was keeping pace with that of the railways. The statistics show very considerable increase, especially in the 'seventies. The combined net tonnages of vessels entered and cleared coastwise each year were 36·6 million in 1870, 74·5 million in 1880, 90·1 million in 1890, 110·3 million in 1900, and 130·4 million in 1913.[1] But though much of this increase must have been real, an appreciable part of it was illusory, since the returns of coastwise traffic included the movement of vessels that were really employed in foreign trade but which, having discharged their imported cargo at one British port, went on to another for bunkers or to load cargo.[2] It should also be remembered that traffic between Britain and Ireland was an appreciable part of what was officially classed as coastwise traffic; in 1913 shipping entered and cleared coastwise with cargoes aggregated 69·0 million net tons, of which 24·0 million were engaged in traffic between Britain and Ireland.[3] When such modifying facts are taken into account, the place of coastal shipping in the internal transport system becomes clearer: its rôle was still a substantial one but, though it was quite indispensable for a few purposes, its relative importance was not increasing.

The roads had very quickly lost nearly all their long-distance traffic to the railways and, down to the First World War, the internal combustion engine had done no more than help them to begin recovering a very small proportion of it. In these circumstances hardly any new main roads were made outside the towns; and existing roads underwent little improvement until near the end of the century when the new County Councils began to raise the standard of main road surfaces generally to the level set long before by Telford and Macadam on a part of the system.[4] Only on the eve of the First World War did the growth of motor traffic[5] make it necessary to think about building new main roads, especially to lead out of London,

---

[1] Sir John Glover, 'Tonnage Statistics of the Decade 1891-1900', in *J. R. Stat. Socy.*, LXV (1902), 10; H. W. Macrosty, 'Statistics of British Shipping', in *ibid.* LXXXIX (1926), 496.

[2] Macrosty, *loc. cit.*, p. 497.   [3] *The 'Shipping World' Year Book 1914*, p. 271.

[4] S. and B. Webb, *The Story of the King's Highway* (1913), pp. 248-9. In 1912 the County Councils were responsible for the maintenance of 23,549 miles of roads in England and Wales, but there were still, outside the towns, a further 95,143 miles for which the Rural District Councils were solely responsible. (*Ibid.*, p. 252.)

[5] The number of motor-cars rose from 8,000 in 1903 to 120,000 in 1913, when there were also about 110,000 motor-cycles. (E. J. Broster, *An Economic Study of the Growth of Travel in Great Britain, 1903-33* (unpublished typescript deposited in the library of the London School of Economics), table XI and p. 39.)

and, even for this, plans were not completely formulated until the middle of the war.[1]

But in the towns it was a different story. Road transport was one of the largest urban occupations. In terms of numbers it continued to be a greater source of employment even than the railways, for there were still not only a whole army of carters, draymen and cab-drivers but also large numbers of messengers and porters, doing their jobs on foot and using no capital equipment at all, or nothing more than a hand-cart or wheel-barrow. The growth of cities brought with it a far more than commensurate growth of traffic within them and the late nineteenth century saw a multitude of piecemeal expedients for coping with the new conditions—the building of new streets and bridges and the widening of old ones, the provision of more durable and less irregular road surfaces, such as granite setts or wooden blocks or asphalt.[2] Much of the road traffic was supplementary to rather than competitive with that of the railways. The roads carried goods and passengers and messages between neighbouring districts which no railway connected. They were the channels for collection and delivery services to and from railway stations. But for local passenger traffic, at least, they were beginning to compete directly with the railways, especially after 1900. The main instrument of this competition was the street tramway, the effective history of which began about 1870. Thirty more years were needed before the first thousand miles of British tramways were in operation and in 1900 nearly all of these were still horse-drawn. But in the next seven years the mileage more than doubled and most of it was electrified. Thereafter the growth of the tramway system was very much slower, but from that time onwards there was a spectacular development of motor-bus services, bringing a far more formidable challenge to other modes of transport than ever the old horse-buses had done;[3] and private motoring, though still confined to a small minority, was increasing steadily.

To fill out the picture of the state of communications, attention

---

[1] *Annual Reports of the London Traffic Branch of the Board of Trade*, 1910-15; *Annual Reports of the Road Board*, 1911-14.

[2] The evidence for this has never been gathered together for the country as a whole, but is writ plain in many local histories as well as being implicit in the returns of local authority expenditure.

[3] Figures of tramway mileage are given in the annual *Statistical Abstract for the U.K.* Bus statistics were not collected at this time; some particulars of London motor-bus services were regularly given from 1909 onwards in the *Annual Reports of the London Traffic Branch*.

should also be given to the efforts which the Post Office made to adapt and expand itself to make use of the new technical possibilities and to cater for new needs. Its main business continued to be the carriage of letters and for this service alone the provision of additional post-offices, letter-boxes and staff was an overriding necessity. In 1870 the Post Office carried 862·7 million letters; in the last year before the First World War 3,477·8 million. In the same period the number of newspapers and printed papers carried went up from an average of 125 million a year to 1,380 million, and postcards, which were first brought into use in 1870, totalled 926 million in 1913.[1] But the Post Office by this time was operating a wider range of services. In 1883 a general parcel post was introduced—there had been a book post since 1847[2]—and it carried 79·8 million parcels in 1900 and 138·0 million in 1913.[3] In 1870 the telegraph system, the use of which by newspapers and traders had become well-established in the preceding fifteen years, was taken over by the Post Office. Additional telegraph offices and new lines, distinct from those of the railway companies, were provided and in fifteen years the annual number of telegrams quadrupled. But after that the cost of further improvement of facilities became uneconomically heavy, the telegraph service ran into deficits and after 1902-3, when 84·6 million inland telegrams were sent, its use slowly declined.[4] By that time the telephone was providing a more convenient alternative for a good deal of inland communication. The Post Office had begun to operate a small telephone service in the 'eighties, but far greater lengths of line were operated by companies, most of which were gradually absorbed into the National Telephone Company, while a few municipalities ran their own local services. After 1896 the Post Office owned most of the trunk lines but only a small proportion of the telephones and not until 1912, when it took over the National Telephone Company, did the Post Office acquire nearly a monopoly of the whole system. The telephone was then both a profitable and rapidly growing service. In 1913 the number of Post Office telephones first exceeded three-quarters of a million, with an increase of over 44,000 in the last twelve months—a mere beginning, it is true, yet already a most significant addition to the means of communication, mostly for local

---

[1] H. Robinson, *The British Post Office: a History* (1948), pp. 367-8; *Statistical Abstract for 1913* (P.P. 1914-16, LXXVI), pp. 400-1.

[2] Robinson, *op. cit.*, p. 410.

[3] *Statistical Abstract for 1914* (P.P. 1914-16, LXXVI), p. 378.

[4] *Ibid.*, pp. 367-7; Robinson, *op. cit.*, pp. 406-9; Clapham, *op. cit.*, II, 207-10.

purposes but also carrying nearly 40 million trunk calls a year.[1]

Some of these figures suggest not only the increase in the facilities provided by the Post Office but also the extent to which they were used. For transport generally, though many figures survive, it is possible to indicate the growth of traffic only in a rough-and-ready way. The numbers of passengers and quantities of goods carried by rail are summarized in Table IV.

TABLE IV

Railway Traffic: Annual averages for quinquennia, 1871-1913.

Period	United Kingdom		England and Wales	
	Passengers *(mn.)*	Goods *(mn. tons)*	Passengers *(mn.)*	Goods *(mn. tons)*
1871-75	448	186	395	157
1876-80	564	214	503	182
1881-85	671	257	601	218
1886-90	759	281	670	239
1891-95	885	314	780	266
1896-1900	1,064	390	926	328
1901-05	1,191	442	1,043	372
1906-10	1,270	502	1,130	428
1911-13	1,355	537	1,214	461

Source: Page, *op. cit.*, II, tables 66 and 67.

But these figures are not very satisfactory. It would, for instance, be rash to infer from them that during the forty years preceding the First World War both passenger and freight traffic increased roughly threefold, for the figures give no indication of the distances travelled by either passengers or freight; those much more illuminating concepts, the passenger-mile and the ton-mile, were not introduced into the official statistics until 1919. If a financial measure is used, then the expansion appears rather less: the gross receipts of the railways of England and Wales averaged £47 million per year in 1871-75 and £113 million in 1911-13,[2] an increase of not quite two-and-a-half times. This does not mean that the growth in the number of passengers and weight of goods was being offset by rather

[1] Robinson, *op. cit.*, p. 409; Clapham, *op. cit.*, III, 390-5; *Statistical Abstract for 1914*, pp. 376-7.

[2] Page, *op. cit.*, II, 172.

shorter average journeys. On the contrary, since there is every reason to believe that the expansion of business was achieved mostly by attracting lower grades of traffic—more passengers at third-class, workmen's, excursion and season-ticket rates, more goods carried at special rates well below the published schedules, a bigger proportion of bulky items such as coal (carried at low rates per ton) in the total volume of goods[1]—there is no need to look further for an explanation of the slight lag in the growth of revenue. Indeed, this increased preponderance of cheaper traffic may well have been sufficient to account for a still greater difference. It seems probable that, if distance as well as volume could be taken into account, the increase in railway traffic would be rather more than the trebling indicated by the passenger and freight figures.

Traffic statistics for other modes of transport were even less complete and clear than for the railways. Those of the canals were not regularly gathered together and are suspected of being swollen by a good deal of duplication. Even so they suggest no great expansion in the late nineteenth century.[2] Fortunately, neither their magnitude nor their inaccuracy mattered much, since in the early years of the twentieth century canals were carrying not more than about one-twelfth the amount of goods going by rail and almost certainly carrying it for a shorter average distance. Figures for coastal shipping show only whether cargo was being carried or not; they say nothing about how much or how far. Nevertheless, a trebling in the figures of shipping tonnage cleared coastwise, though it must have been influenced by the increasing inclusion of vessels belonging to foreign trade, seems clear evidence of growth in genuine coastal trade. It would not be surprising if cargo traffic along the coast doubled between 1870 and 1914. On the roads only tramway traffic was regularly recorded. Before 1870 it was negligible; by 1903 the annual number of passenger journeys had risen to 1,712 million and by 1913 to 3,304 million.[3] Since the average length of journey probably changed little, such figures are a fair indication of the growth of traffic. But trams carried only a small part of total road traffic. That the rest grew very considerably is obvious from the growth of employment and the evidence of congestion over wider areas. But how much it grew is a matter for guess-work, not very securely based.

---

[1] Acworth, *Elements of Railway Economics*, pp. 61-5.
[2] *Reports of the R.C. on Canals*, vol. IV, *passim*, esp. pp. 2-3 which summarize the figures.
[3] Broster, *op. cit.*, table IV.

E

How far the growth of traffic was a response to fuller and more efficient service was a matter of dispute at the time. From about 1880 onwards there was a protracted chorus of complaint from traders that they were forced to pay excessively for transport, and the causes they alleged were inefficiency, profiteering and too little competition among transport undertakings. On the other hand, railways complained, especially from the 'nineties on, that they had to operate in conditions which made it increasingly difficult to earn a reasonable profit. One source of disagreement was no doubt the fact that railway charges remained fairly stable, since the comprehensive revision of anything so complex was a major operation. So traders suffered while general prices were falling, as they did until 1896, while the railway companies suffered when they were rising.

But there was more to the movement of transport costs than that. The railways' operating ratio (i.e. working expenses expressed as a percentage of gross receipts) tended to rise even while the general price level was falling, though the ratio rose most sharply in the late 'nineties when the general price fall was reversed. In the 'sixties the operating ratio was usually just below 50. It rose above this figure in 1873 and never returned to it, but remained below 55 until the middle 'nineties. Then from 56 in 1896 it rose quickly to 62 in 1900 and thereafter generally remained around 62 and 63 until the First World War, with a maximum of 65 in 1908.[1] Such a change need not necessarily have been unwelcome, since smaller margins were accompanied by higher turnover. But the difficulty which confronted the railways was that they could not carry the extra traffic which brought higher turnover unless they increased their capital. In fact, not until after 1900 did their net receipts grow faster than their paid-up capital, as may be seen from Table V.

Thus, as a profit-making activity, railway transport tended to weaken rather than improve its position, though most railway companies earned a reliable but not very high return down to 1914. Many of the expenses of a railway company were only partially within its control. A large part of the cost of operation—experts at the beginning of the twentieth century suggested about half[2]— was virtually fixed in the short run, irrespective of fluctuations in the volume of traffic, and two of the biggest items of current

[1] There are figures in the annual *Statistical Abstract*; for summaries see Page. *op. cit.*, II, 170-4.

[2] Acworth, *op. cit.*, p. 50.

TABLE V

Railways of England and Wales: Percentage increases in capital, receipts and expenditure, 1870-1910.

Period	Paid-up capital Inc. %	Gross receipts Inc. %	Working Expenses Inc. %	Net receipts Inc. %
1870-80	37	46	57	27
1880-90	23	22	29	15
1890-1900	31	31	51	7
1900-10	12	19	19	19

Source: Calculated from Page, *op. cit.*, II, table 67.

expenditure, coal and labour, fell much less than the general average of prices in the late nineteenth century. Apart from this, the general conditions of operation changed appreciably from the mid-seventies. On the main routes of most of the larger systems the capacity of the fixed equipment in existence in the early 'fifties was well in excess of the needs of the volume of traffic then forthcoming. For the next twenty years or so, increasing traffic could be carried with only a very modest enlargement of equipment. But in the last quarter of a century, on one main route after another, the point was reached at which extra traffic involved heavy expenditure on the enlargement and improvement of fixed capital. Railway companies were in too vulnerable a position, competitively and politically, for them to risk turning away additional traffic or even to neglect the improvement of services in order to attract it. But for many of them the extra traffic for a time brought more burdens than rewards. More traffic required the rebuilding of some stations on a bigger scale and the running of heavier and more frequent trains; it also involved longer time in loading and unloading at stations and, if there was to be no deterioration of service, this had to be offset by higher running speeds and longer non-stop runs. The latter change necessitated bigger locomotives and, on passenger trains, more restaurant cars, corridor coaches and lavatories, with a consequent increase in tare-weight. Heavier trains often made it necessary to strengthen track and bridges; denser traffic, operating at a greater variety of speeds, required additional tracks and sidings and often the drastic reform of the signalling system. And all this by no means exhausted the catalogue of necessary re-equipment, with its accompanying increase in many items of current expenditure.[1] Such provision was inevitable in a railway system if it was to serve the full range of needs of the whole of an urbanized and industrialized society. It showed itself not only in the rise of the operating ratio but also in the great growth of paid-up capital per route-mile. For England and Wales the figures were:[2]

1854	£39,000	1874	£44,000	1904	£66,000
1864	£40,000	1884	£50,000	1914	£68,000
		1894	£56,000		

It will readily be seen that much of the high capitalization of English railways derives not from reckless waste in promoting and establishing the railways before 1850, which is popularly supposed to be the fount of most of their subsequent financial ills, but from the enlargement of traffic capacity in the last quarter of the nineteenth century. Undoubtedly this enlarged capacity was rather more expensive and, physically, rather less satisfactory than would have been the case if it had not had to be superimposed on something smaller, shaped by different ideas and adapted to more limited needs. Undoubtedly, too, some of the later capital expenditure was wasted on unnecessary routes. But most of it went to the serving of an overwhelming national need.

The chief reasons why the railways, except for a short spell early in the twentieth century, were unable fully to recoup themselves for the cost they incurred in meeting this need were the forces of competition and the restrictions imposed by the government. Railway companies were not monopolies exploiting the public. A high proportion of their rates were limited by competition from water transport, and probably

[1] For a brief discussion of some of these changes, see Acworth, *The Railways of England* (5th edn.), pp. 449-54.

[2] Calculated from Page, *op. cit.*, II, 172. The figures for the U.K. are rather different because capital per mile was slightly lower in Scotland and enormously less in Ireland. Increases in paid-up capital are, of course, only a very rough indication of increases in the capital value of the railways. From 1870 to 1913 inclusive the paid-up capital of U.K. railways rose by £815,231,000; their actual estimated capital expenditure for railway purposes (i.e., excluding such expenditure as that on docks, shipping and canals owned by railway companies) was £516,300,000 (Cairncross, *Home and Foreign Investment*, pp. 135-7). There may, however, be some omissions from the latter figure, which should be regarded as a minimum.

a still higher proportion (especially for goods traffic, which was less deterred by a few extra hours involved in following a somewhat roundabout route) by competition among themselves. Of the big companies, only the North Eastern possessed a territorial monopoly and, after the government in 1872 refused to allow a proposed fusion of the London and North Western with the Lancashire and Yorkshire, there were for more than thirty years very few amalgamations or agreements to disturb the *status quo* in respect of railway competition.[1] Edwardian businessmen who urged public expenditure on new and improved canals in order to give railways the missing spur of competition were altogether wide of the mark. In fact, it appears rather that competition was so strong as to induce waste on the provision of extra refinements of service and unnecessary trains, which increased real costs and detracted from operating efficiency as well as from profits. The damage done by excessive competition was most obvious in the deadly rivalry of the South Eastern and the London, Chatham and Dover, which ended with agreement on uniform fares between all competing points from the beginning of 1895 and a full working union, managed by a joint committee of both companies, from 1899.[2] But other and larger companies were also beginning to recognize that mutual fears prevented them from operating their services to meet the needs of their customers most economically.

The outcome in the first decade of the new century was the establishment of a number of co-operative agreements for the regulation of services and pooling of receipts on competitive routes, an arrangement which helped to stabilize the operating ratio, despite a further rise in prices and unchanged railway fares. The greatest of these arrangements was completed in 1909 and covered the London and North Western, the Midland, and the Lancashire and Yorkshire. An even bigger change was attempted in the same year by the Great Northern, Great Central and Great Eastern, which sought statutory approval for a complete working union. Because of the strength of Parliamentary opposition, the bill for this purpose was withdrawn and the companies did no more than operate a number of co-operative agreements among themselves.[3] But public opinion was clearly

---

[1] W. A. Robertson, *Combination among Railway Companies* (1912), pp. 20-1.

[2] P. S. Bagwell, 'The Rivalry and Working Union of the South Eastern and London, Chatham and Dover Railways' in *Journ. of Transport History*, II (1955-56), 65-79.

[3] Robertson, *op. cit.*, p. 23.

changing. A Departmental Committee in 1911 reported in favour of the extension of agreements and even, in some cases, complete working unions or amalgamations among railway companies.[1] Thus, before the First World War, larger groupings of railways, not immune from competition but less handicapped by its excesses, were already being foreshadowed.

Government restriction of railway companies' charges existed only to a small extent for most of the nineteenth century, mainly through requirements inserted in the original acts under which individual companies were promoted. But, since railways were the one form of enterprise which obviously affected closely the whole of business, they were always the most likely subjects of regulatory legislation. It was the path of prudence for them not to provoke political action by appearing to exploit their position to the disadvantage of the public. In the end, political action came just the same. An act of 1888 required the railway companies to devise a new classification of goods traffic and schedules of maximum rates for each class. These new rates, after approval by the Board of Trade, were subsequently confirmed by Parliament in 1891 and 1892 and ordered to be put into effect from the beginning of 1893. The railway companies, however, had always been accustomed to carry much of their goods traffic at rates well below their published maxima. In 1893, whether out of malice or whether from lack of enough time to revise their special rates in conformity with the new maxima, they applied the maximum rates somewhat indiscriminately. The result was an outcry from traders who, under a scheme which they had expected to help them, found themselves charged more for transport when other prices were falling. The government's reaction was to pass the Railway and Canal Traffic Act of 1894. This provided that henceforward anyone might object to a transport charge higher than that prevailing at the end of 1892 and the onus was then on the railway company concerned to satisfy the Railway and Canal Commission (a supervisory body set up in 1873) that the increase was reasonable; otherwise the old rate must apply.[2] From then on, railway companies were very hesitant about altering their rates, because of the risk that an increase would be successfully challenged. And since prices soon began to rise they were put in a position of some difficulty, from which they received no statutory relief until 1913, when they were empowered to increase

[1] Robertson, *op. cit.*, p. 24.
[2] Acworth, *Elements of Railway Economics*, pp. 134-54.

charges to meet the cost of higher wages.[1] The variation of passenger fares, however, was still within their control, with very little statutory limitation.

If the railways might plead that circumstances prevented them from charging as much as they might reasonably have done, there were still critics to point out that they charged more than many foreign railways and that if, even so, they were not profitable enough, the fault must lie in their own management. International comparisons were certainly not always favourable to British transport. It has been suggested, for instance, that in the 'seventies the British steel industry had an advantage over foreign competitors in the cost of assembling its materials which was reversed in the course of the next thirty years, a change in which the cost of sea as well as rail transport had a part.[2] Plenty of instances of neglect of practicable improvements, both technical and administrative, could be cited in support of the view that railways—and ports—failed to make the most of their opportunities. An acknowledged authority remarked in 1899 that, while twenty years earlier foreign railwaymen had always come to England to look for improvements, they no longer thought that England had anything to teach them and sought their lessons in America instead.[3] But even he did not suggest that England was stagnating in railway matters; only that others had caught up.

There were, in fact, many signs of improvement. After the year 1900, while the amount of goods carried by rail rose quite quickly, the rising trend in the number of goods train-miles became less steep and, for a time, was reversed, which suggests more efficient operation.[4] And, quite apart from the fact that some foreign rail services were publicly subsidized, some of the alleged shortcomings of British services were due as much to the nature of the traffic as to bad management. A greater proportion of small consignments and short hauls, arising partly from geographical conditions and partly because some of the biggest industries (coal, steel and heavy engineering, for instance) were dispersed among numerous districts, was bound to cause higher comparative costs. In many cases the economy of bigger

[1] Clapham, *op. cit.*, III, 360-2.

[2] Burn, *op. cit.*, chap. IX, which analyses the position in some detail. The contention (pp. 151 and 167) that there was little improvement in British transport is true if it refers to improvements specific to the needs of the steel industry, but quite unacceptable if it refers to more general changes, in the indirect benefits of which the steel industry must have shared.

[3] Acworth, *The Railways of England*, pp. 470-1.

[4] C. D. Campbell, *British Railways in Boom and Depression* (1932), p. 31.

wagons and better and more specialized loading machinery had to be forgone because there was no immediate prospect of such equipment being regularly used near full capacity.[1] Some of the questionable practices which hindered the reduction of transport costs were also the direct result of concessions to the convenience of traders—the retention of a system of privately-owned railway wagons, the low charges for demurrage which encouraged traders to keep loaded wagons standing idle for days on end and thus saved them warehousing costs. Extra costs arising in such ways were really more attributable to the businesses of the railway users than to the railways themselves, and it is probable that the former escaped the full burden of them, even if they paid slightly higher rail charges than they might otherwise have done. In fact, whatever the defects of the railways, they were providing in the early years of the twentieth century a range of services adapted to the needs of a far greater variety of persons and activities than forty years earlier. This was in itself a qualitative improvement which necessarily imposed extra costs and which received too little recognition in the controversies of the time. Not every industry received much direct benefit from it, but in the economy of the country generally it was an element in the increase of efficiency just as significant as, though less measurable than, a further reduction in price per unit of traffic would have been. Certainly it was as central a contribution to the growing product of industry and commerce as were innovations in their own technique and organization.

How rapidly the internal commerce of the country was growing cannot be stated from any direct evidence. There are only imperfect figures of the number of distributive businesses in different towns and even these have never been brought together on a national scale;[2] and no general information was kept about the size of their turnover. The records of the growth of traffic, viewed in the light of descriptive evidence about both transport and distribution, are as good a guide as can be found to the development of internal trade. They suggest that internal trade was growing at least as fast as industry, even

[1] For discussion of this point in relation to the steel industry see Burn, *op. cit.* pp. 165-6.

[2] The census of 1911 included for the first time an enquiry into the number of shops. The only series of estimates of retail trade begins in 1900; it is that of A. R. Prest and A. A. Adams in their book *Consumers' Expenditure in the United Kingdom 1900-1919* (1954).

though the net output of the latter was probably a little inflated because industry did not have to pay quite the full cost of the extra transport services which it consumed. It may be that between 1870 and 1914 the income from internal trade grew rather more than the two and a half times roughly indicated by the traffic figures.[1] Trade involves not only the actual transport of goods bought and sold but also a host of varied marketing services—in warehouses, shops and offices and by travelling salesmen; and there are many signs that in the late nineteenth century a greater amount of service was involved in the sale of goods than earlier, if only because a greater variety of goods was being sold in quantity to a more diverse range of consumers. If these indications are reliable, they strengthen the conclusion, already suggested by figures of national income and industrial production, that a rather bigger proportion of the nation's livelihood was coming to be derived from transport and distribution. The deployment of the labour force among different occupations supports the same interpretation. In England and Wales the proportion of the occupied population engaged in transport, which was already increasing in the 'fifties and 'sixties, rose from 5·1 per cent in 1871 to 7·5 per cent in 1891 and 8·0 per cent in 1911; the change in the proportion in commercial occupations was from 8·3 per cent in 1871 to 10·3 per cent in 1891 and 11·0 per cent in 1901.[2] In part this increase is attributable to the growth of external trade, but much of it must have been to meet the needs of transactions at home. It is the sort of change that was to be expected when people had more to spend on goods that could not be produced locally, and when a bigger proportion of the manufactured output consisted of more elaborate goods, the ultimate form of which incorporated a greater variety of materials and semi-finished components, which necessarily had to be brought and carried from a wider range of sources.

To carry out effectively this constantly growing volume of internal trade required changes in the methods and organization of distributive businesses, both wholesale and retail. Over an appreciable part

---

[1] The net receipts of U.K. railways rose two and a quarter times between 1870 and 1913. The net income of canals must have grown much less than this and probably that of coastal shipping a little less. But these were less important forms of transport, whereas road traffic of all kinds must have exceeded that of the railways and its net income may well have grown faster than that of the railways.

[2] Clark, *The Conditions of Economic Progress* (2nd edn.), p. 408. For 1911 no figure can be calculated for commerce and that for transport is not strictly comparable with earlier figures. The figures for 1891 and 1901 relate to Great Britain. The classification differs slightly from that of Booth, used for 1871 on pp. 9-12.

of the field fundamental changes in wholesaling were already well established or in process of accomplishment by 1870. Particularly during the previous twenty years (and to a less extent over a longer period) urbanization, the transfer of production from outwork to factory, growing dependence on imported necessities, railways, cheap postage, and telegraphs had made old channels of distribution impossible or uneconomic and diverted trade to new ones of different length. But though the general nature of the change was apparent, it had still to be carried very much further in the rest of the nineteenth century.[1]

Briefly, and with some over-simplification, there were two opposite tendencies at work. On the one hand, fewer people were living within easy reach of the producers of many of their main articles of consumption, such as fresh foodstuffs. So trades which had consisted to a considerable extent of direct sales from producer to ultimate consumer had to pass more and more through intermediaries, both wholesale and retail. On the other hand, in those trades which had been accustomed to pass through a chain of intermediaries (which might include brokers as well as wholesale merchants and shopkeepers), the greater speed and ease of communication, sometimes aided by an increase in the size of consignments, made it practicable to shorten the chain, often quite considerably. For example, in the earlier woollen textile industry the employers who received back the finished cloth from their outworking weavers were too small to do much of their own marketing. Instead, a merchant in their own district would buy the output of a number of them. But he in his turn was usually too far from the ultimate market to be able to reach the consumer, so either directly or through yet another intermediary he would sell the cloth to a merchant in a consuming area, who would then dispose of it in smaller lots for export or to a tailoring house or to a retailer. In the second half of the century one intermediary between cloth factory and retailer or user became sufficient; sometimes, indeed, when ready-made clothing factories developed, they brought direct from a textile factory and cut out the wholesaler.[2]

Attempts by manufacturers to cut out wholesalers (and annex at

---

[1] For a fuller account with details of some of the specific changes in major trades see Clapham, *op. cit.*, II, 297-312 and III, 238 and 292. In my judgment Clapham exaggerated the extent of the changes before the eighteen-eighties, perhaps because so much of his evidence related to the supply of London, which was not altogether typical. *Cf.* J. B. Jefferys, *Retail Trading in Britain, 1850-1950* (1954), pp. 10-11.

[2] Clapham, *op. cit.*, II, 305-6.

least part of their profits) by selling direct to retailers or, where appropriate, to large commercial consumers were increasing all the time. This was particularly the case among large manufacturers making standardized goods, especially if they were branded. One device was for a manufacturer to appoint a shopkeeper or merchant in as many towns as possible to be agent for his products. Thus the agent could be guaranteed prompt delivery to replace goods sold and could be given an incentive to push the sales of a particular product without having to carry the burden and risk of holding large stocks. But, though some goods were being marketed on a national scale by their manufacturers well before 1914, the practice was still exceptional. Most retail orders for any single product were too small for it to be worth the manufacturer's while to deal with them direct. It was more economical for a wholesaler to supply the retailer in larger consignments composed of a number of different products, and the demand of customers in many trades that each shopkeeper should stock a wider choice of goods tended to strengthen this advantage of the wholesaler.[1] Nor was the agency system free of disadvantages to the producer, since an agent often had insufficient business unless he acted for several competing producers. Even in a branch of distribution where the scale of business was bigger than average—the disposal of iron and steel to users in other industries—this was still true. Most makers had several special agents, most agents had a variety of lines and tended to increase the variety, and no maker could secure through an agent sufficient concentrated selling of one particular line to justify him in risking the installation of a large new plant for its mass production.[2] In the iron and steel trade, where the maker held most of the stocks, such shortcomings of the agency system were an argument for attempting more often to sell direct to users.[3] In consumer goods trades, similar deficiencies were likely to suggest that manufacturers might do better not to maintain their own sales depots, from which to rush supplies to shopkeepers, but instead to sell to wholesalers, who would bear the cost of stock-holding.

On balance, it seems probable that the outcome of the conflicting influences operating throughout the second half of the nineteenth century was to reduce the number of wholesalers but to increase both their size and the number of functions entrusted to them. Mid-Victorian shopkeepers had been accustomed to stock appreciable

---

[1] *Ibid.*, II, 306-7; Jefferys, *op. cit.*, pp. 11-12.
[2] Burn, *op. cit.*, p. 266.   [3] *Ibid.*, pp. 291-5.

quantities of a small number of lines of which they often had personally a detailed knowledge. They had also been used to do for themselves many of the final stages in putting goods into saleable form: they compounded their own medicines, skeined their own silks, blended their own teas, often cured their own hams. By 1900 more and more were finding that to do profitable business they had to carry more variety of lines and therefore smaller quantities of each. They had to concern themselves more exclusively with selling goods as they received them, often, that is, without direct knowledge that would enable them confidently to judge their quality. Consequently someone else had to take much more responsibility for holding adequate stocks, for sorting, blending, packing in convenient retail amounts, and grading according to quality and purpose. In part, these extra functions were carried back to the manufacturers, but at this time they were transferred more generally to the wholesalers who, no doubt because of all these extra opportunities, usually abandoned the retail trade which many of them had earlier combined with wholesale business.[1] But in the last twenty years before the First World War there were signs of an approaching reversal of the growing importance of wholesalers. At this time large-scale retail firms were steadily increasing in numbers and size and they were big enough for direct purchase from producers to be profitable to both sides, especially in the case of those retail firms which concentrated on a large turnover of a fairly limited range of standardized articles.[2] But in 1914 small shops still predominated in most classes of retail trade and, since the absolute expansion in the volume of business had probably been sufficient to offset the recent decline in their relative share of it, the needs of small shops kept the position of wholesalers nearly as strong as ever.

This situation suggests that change in organization and methods in retail trade tended to lag a little behind that in wholesaling. Some important changes in retailing, however, had clearly set in before 1850 and had been carried a long way, though not to their ultimate limit, well before the end of the century. Of these, the most striking was the growing importance and number of fixed shops and the decline of fairs, pedlars and other itinerant retailers. The incomplete statistical evidence available supports the impression conveyed by contemporary descriptions that the number of shops must have been growing faster than the size of the population, at any rate until about

[1] Jefferys, *op. cit.*, pp. 14, 27 and 380-1.   [2] *Ibid.*, pp. 12-13.

1880.[1] Thereafter there may have been no further permanent increase in the number of shops per head, which apparently fluctuated in the same direction as the activity of the residential building industry, which was damped down in the 'eighties, active in the 'nineties, and damped down in the immediate prewar years. The figures of the 1911 census suggest that the districts newly built up after 1880, though they were not badly supplied with shops, usually had rather fewer in proportion to population than older residential districts.

A second obvious change was the adoption of an openly proclaimed, definite price for all goods offered for sale in shops. Higgling had come to be treated as a breach of decorum in shops of the West End of London by the eighteen-fifties,[2] but it probably took another twenty or thirty years for so deep-rooted a habit to be fairly generally abandoned throughout the country. Open prices greatly increased the effectiveness of price competition and encouraged some traders to look for ways of increasing turnover (e.g. by concentrating more on articles of mass demand), reducing overheads (e.g. by keeping smaller stocks, especially of slow-selling lines) and buying more cheaply (e.g. by placing larger, regular orders with suppliers), in order that they might profitably undercut their rivals. The growth of working-class purchasing power, which was spent mainly on larger quantities of basic necessities and very simple luxuries, and the simultaneous development of large-scale importing or production of some of those items directly favoured traders of this type, so that in the last quarter of the nineteenth century shopkeepers were involved in price wars of novel intensity.

Two results followed. In the long run nearly all shopkeepers had to depart from their established ways, widen their appeal and cut their working costs by altering their functions in ways that have already been discussed in relation to their effect on wholesalers. But in addition, from the late 'eighties onwards, attempts were made by retailers to protect themselves by inducing suppliers to co-operate in the introduction of resale price maintenance; i.e. suppliers were asked to make agreements which required retailers to adhere to a fixed minimum selling price and stipulated penalties, including a refusal of further supplies, if they failed to do so. Such attempts at

[1] *Ibid.*, pp. 14-15. *Cf.* G. J. Goschen, 'The Increase of Moderate Incomes' in *Journ. of the Stat. Socy.*, L (1887), 600 and 608.

[2] R. S. Lambert, *The Universal Provider: A Study of William Whiteley* (1938), p. 26.

first brought little response from manufacturers, who generally believed that retail cut prices helped them by increasing the sales of their products; but the practice grew of shopkeepers in particular trades banding together in national or local associations which could coerce suppliers by a threat of collective refusal to stock their products unless they agreed to enforce price maintenance. The makers of goods which had become household words usually resisted this pressure, because they calculated that shopkeepers dared not risk losing the custom of the many who would demand these goods. But in other cases attempts to secure resale price maintenance were increasingly successful by the opening of the twentieth century.[1] Moreover, more manufacturers were being converted to the view that they also stood to gain from the practice. Price-cutting of their products, they began to argue, reduced the margin of the higher cost retailers to the point where most of them could not afford to stock the goods affected and so the number of retail outlets for them was reduced; while if they agreed to price maintenance they gave retailers an incentive to push their products at the expense of non-maintained competing goods on which the retailer's margin was less.[2] Thus the movement gathered strength. It was difficult to apply resale price maintenance except to goods which were patented or branded and these were very much a minority; but they were a rapidly increasing minority, so that although price competition was still the general rule in retail trade in 1914 its effective area had perceptibly narrowed and showed every prospect of soon narrowing much further.

The initiative in price reduction, which had these far-reaching repercussions, came almost invariably from those who either hoped to cut or had cut their costs in some way which involved operating on a bigger scale than had hitherto been usual in retailing, and the beginning of large-scale operating was in some ways the most significant of all organizational changes in shopkeeping in the late nineteenth century. Of the different types of large-scale retailers the consumers' co-operative societies, which grew steadily in numbers and size from the eighteen-forties, were the earliest. The strength of their position was that they concentrated on cash sales of basic necessities (mainly foodstuffs and household goods such as matches, soaps and cleaning materials, with gradually increasing quntities of drapery

---

[1] B. S. Yamey, 'The Origins of Resale Price Maintenance' in *Econ. Journ.*, LXII (1952), 522-45, esp. 540-1 and 544.

[2] Macrosty, *The Trust Movement in British Industry*, pp. 248-9 and 271-3.

and footwear) to working-class members whose custom was assured by regular dividends on purchases and by loyalty to an organization over which they had a real measure of democratic control. Their search for low costs was aided by bulk purchasing and large-scale production of some of their goods, which became possible through the establishment of the two wholesale societies, the English in 1863 and the Scottish in 1868. Their success was such that during the last quarter of the nineteenth century they may well have doubled their share of Britain's total retail sales, which is roughly estimated to have risen further from 6·5 per cent in 1900 to 8·25 per cent in 1915.[1] Despite this, however, there were such large areas that were untouched by the co-operative movement that its importance was more regional than national. It flourished above all in the textile and mining towns of Lancashire and the West Riding, always the most fertile soil for the frugal Victorian virtues. In 1880 eight of the ten largest co-operative societies were in these two counties and, though the movement spread rather more thereafter, they still contained five of the ten largest in 1900.[2]

In the late nineteenth century, however, there was a growing mass demand for fairly standard classes of necessities in many areas where there was little apparent inclination for co-operative organization and in some trades which the co-operative shops had rather neglected. It was mainly to take advantage of this demand that other types of large-scale retail organization began to appear. The chief of these were the multiple shops, selling unmanufactured foodstuffs or standardized factory-made consumer necessities and keeping an identical range of goods in a number of shops in different districts, and expanding by opening new shops in new districts rather than by going in for the sale of additional classes of goods. Before the eighteen-seventies, except for special cases such as the railway station bookstalls of W. H. Smith, multiple shop firms were very rare, but in the next twenty years they gained a firm hold in the footwear, grocery and butchery trades. In the quarter century preceding 1914, multiple shops spread to nearly every type of consumer goods trade, though their chief new fields of activity were in the men's outfitting

---

[1] Jefferys, *op. cit.*, pp. 16-19. The estimated figures of retail sales refer to the U.K. as it subsequently became after the Irish Free State was removed from it. Dr Jefferys does not give his figures as exact quantities, but in the form of a possible range. The figures cited here and in later paragraphs are the mid-points of the ranges which he gives.

[2] G. D. H. Cole, *A Century of Co-operation* (n.d. [1945]), p. 213.

and tailoring, chemists' goods, tobacco, sugar confectionery, news-paper and certain branches (mainly hosiery and knitted goods) of the women's wear trades.[1] It is particularly noticeable that whenever any article of common consumption began to be produced in quantity and in a limited but varied range of standardized forms by factory instead of handicraft methods, its retail sale was immediately taken up by multiple shops. The late-nineteenth-century mechanization of the making of footwear, hosiery, suits and overcoats, and chocolates and sweets had thus a most important influence on the development of retailing. Already by 1915 the multiple shops had obtained one-third of the total footwear trade and it seemed certain that the more types of consumer goods could be attractively and cheaply produced by comparable methods, the greater the importance of multiple shops would become. From a negligible amount in the early 'eighties their share of all retail trade had risen to 3·75 per cent in 1900 and 7·75 per cent in 1915.[2]

Multiple shops spread fairly generally throughout all urbanized areas, but the remaining type of large retail organization, the depart-ment store, was mostly confined to the central districts of the larger towns. Most department stores began as drapery shops and in the course of time (sometimes a very protracted course) began to widen the range of textile goods which they stocked and then added other classes of goods. Other trades sometimes served as a starting point— Harrods, which just before the First World War was probably the biggest British department store business, began as a grocer's in 1849—but in such cases, too, expansion into other fields was very gradual. For this reason it is difficult to suggest a precise date for the first appearance of department stores in Britain. It is probably fair to say that no British shop in 1850 could justifiably be called a depart-ment store, whereas by 1875 several were quite certainly in that class. They included a few which were run as department stores from a very early stage in their existence. Whiteleys, in London, for many years the largest and most famous of them, founded in 1863, had seventeen departments by 1867, though nearly all of them were closely allied to the drapery business.[3] From 1872 its founder, William Whiteley, launched out on his career as a self-styled 'Universal Provider' and within four years his store was also selling furniture, crockery, ironmongery, stationery and refreshments, as well as

---

[1] Jefferys, *op. cit.*, pp. 24-5.   *Ibid.*, p. 28.
[3] Lambert, *op. cit.*, p. 67.

undertaking building, decorating, cleaning and dyeing, and running a house agency.[1]

Many of the department stores of the eighteen-seventies and 'eighties were looking to the same sort of public as the new multiple shops. By savings through bulk buying and quick turnover, and sometimes through operating their own workshops for such departments as tailoring, they sought to undercut existing shops in selling articles of wide, popular demand. A few stuck to this type of business and achieved reasonable success; Lewis's of Liverpool, which had begun in 1856 as a men's outfitting business was the best known and probably the most prosperous among them.[2] But only a few department stores could hope to prosper and grow in that way, and then only if their premises were very close to a large working and lower-middle class population with steady jobs, and only if their management showed prudence in limiting the variety of goods which i offered. Even Lewis's failed when they tried to run a store of this type in Sheffield in the 'eighties, and a similar venture in Birmingham, though it became firmly established, was slow in building up its sales.[3] Not until there was a further increase in the purchasing power and leisure of the lower classes and a still wider range of factory-made consumer goods to attract them could many department stores hope to flourish on their custom. During the late nineteenth century, department stores, because of the variety of amenities as well as goods which most of them needed to provide, could seldom keep down their costs to the level possible for multiple (or even small single) shops in this class of trade.

So, by about 1890, department stores generally had lost their reputation for cheapness and price-cutting, and from that time dates the more rapid development of this type of business. Its success was possible mainly because of the increase in the numbers, spending power and leisure of middle-class women. The aim of department stores came to be to provide amenities, attractive display and wide choice which would draw from many miles around a feminine public for whom shopping could be made a pleasure outing, who wanted goods that were smart and distinctive rather than cheap and standardized, and who were prepared to pay the cost of such a service.

---

[1] *Ibid.*, pp. 72-4.

[2] A. Briggs, *Friends of the People* (1956) recounts the history of this firm; for this period see esp. chap. II.

[3] *Ibid.*, pp. 79-94.

Though everyone's style of dress had gradually adapted itself
to changes of fashion, it was not until late in the nineteenth
century that more than the tiniest minority could bother about
their everyday clothes being several years out of date. The new
middle class towards 1900 could and did bother and was prepared
to spend steadily but could not afford to pay millionaire's prices
or to invade the world of *haute couture*. Retail trade adjusted itself
to this situation. Isador Paquin and his wife, whose house was
founded in 1891, were the pioneers among the top-flight Paris dress
designers in making the sale of designs to department stores and
wholesalers a major part of their business,[1] and in this, as in matters
of fashion, where they led, others quickly followed. Department
stores were the chief beneficiaries of these new conditions. Instead
of trying to compete in the disposal of long runs of factory-made
goods, they based themselves on the skilled buying of moderate
quantities of goods, often made up partly by hand, from a wide
variety of suppliers. Though the largest stores covered nearly every
consumer goods trade, the main business of department stores in
general was the sale of women's and children's clothing and of piece
goods. It was estimated that by 1900 they were undertaking nearly
10 per cent of the sales of women's and children's wear and in 1915
about 15 per cent. They had, however, little share in other trades with
a much higher total turnover, e.g. the food trades, and so in 1915
their share in the total British retail sales was still only about 2·5
per cent.[2]

There is obviously a danger of over-emphasizing the development
of large-scale organization in retail trade. In 1915 about four-fifths
of all retail sales were made by small firms, mostly single-shop
businesses.[3] Much shopkeeping was still very primitive in its
technique—untouched by mechanization or by any notion of system
in administration or bookkeeping. But fifty years earlier the small
businesses had had practically the whole of retail trade, and since
then large numbers of the small shops which survived had found it
necessary to change their functions, their techniques, their equipment and their appearance. Retail trade was one of the most rapidly
expanding types of economic activity—between 1900 and 1915
British retail sales are estimated to have grown from £750 million to
£1,142 million,[4] an increase of more than 50 per cent—and this in

---

[1] P. H. Nystrom, *Economics of Fashion* (1928), p. 208.
[2] Jefferys, *op. cit.*, p. 21.   [3] *Ibid.*, p. 29.   [4] *Ibid.*, p. 453.

itself was an aid to more rapid turnover and accumulation of profits, which often were ploughed back into extra shops or enlargements of existing ones. What business and social conditions favoured, limited liability made still easier, and from the middle 'nineties more and more of the bigger firms in retail trade and in closely-related types of distribution, such as catering and hotel-keeping, turned themselves into limited companies as a stage in a progress towards greater growth combined with greater stability.[1] Trade, and especially internal trade, was showing more novelty than ever before and in nearly all the new developments it was the large firms which, though still very much a minority, were setting the pace and by their challenge and their example sending innovation rippling over a much larger area of shopkeeping. In spite of the survival of much that was traditional, it is not unrealistic to consider shopkeeping in the half century before 1914 as embarking on changes just as extensive as those in manufacture a hundred years earlier and experiencing them even more quickly. To add a 'retailing revolution' to the already swollen stock of revolutions in which rival economic historians have invested their intellectual capital would deserve the invocation of laws against the deposit of litter. But at least one can recognize that, in the late nineteenth century, retailing was belatedly but with speed caught up in the ways of an industrialized society and drastically reshaped, first to serve the needs of which such a society was aware and then to make it aware of new needs which the shops could straightway meet. This was an essential step in the completion of that thoroughgoing economic transformation which had been continuously in process since the late eighteenth century.

[1] Clapham, *op. cit.*, III, 238-9. Of the large catering firms the Aerated Bread Co. was incorporated from its foundation in 1862 but was not principally concerned with catering until the 'eighties or 'nineties, and J. Lyons became a limited company in 1894. (Jefferys, *op. cit.*, p. 211.) Gordon Hotels, the Savoy Hotel, and Frederick Hotels were all limited companies with assets of over £1 million each by the opening years of the twentieth century.

CHAPTER SIX

External Trade

ALTHOUGH the great majority of the goods produced in Britain were consumed at home and most of the goods consumed there were home-produced, foreign trade was throughout the nineteenth century one of the most powerful influences on the state of the British economy. Particularly from about 1840 the country had moved away from self-sufficiency farther and more rapidly than before. A bigger proportion of the fundamental necessities of life and industrial livelihood was brought from abroad; a wider range of the commodities produced at home incorporated, directly or indirectly, a certain amount of irreplaceable imports; and the communities of more and more localities found in their midst some export industry whose fortunes appreciably affected the amount of their sales and incomes. A boom or a slump in exports, through its influence on the varied demands of the increasing numbers of people engaged in production for export, had more than proportionate repercussions on the level of economic activity at home; and nothing contributed more to the air of prosperity in mid-Victorian Britain than the expansive condition of so many export markets. Circumstances were then very favourable to much of British foreign trade and from 1850 to 1875 it seems certain that it remained consistently more than a fifth (at times perhaps more than a quarter) of all international trade.[1] In the last quarter of the nineteenth century, with the emergence of new rivals capable of efficiently producing what had been some of Britain's chief export goods, and with the appearance of new demands and new products, external conditions appeared less friendly. At any rate they changed so considerably that Britain could no longer hope to obtain a prosperous foreign trade in much the same ways as in the immediate past. But the country's economic structure was such that there could be no turning back towards a more insular assortment of activities. External trade

---

[1] This conclusion is based on a comparison of British trade figures with available collections of data on the value of world trade; see, e.g., Mulhall, *Dictionary of Statistics* (4th edn.), p. 129. It is in line with our more reliable knowledge about the distribution of world trade after 1870. See League of Nations, *Industrialisation and Foreign Trade*, pp. 158-67.

had to be maintained and increased, without unremunerative price-cutting, or economic dislocation and decline would ensue. It remained to be seen how successfully the challenge of new conditions could be met.[1]

At a first glance it appears that Britain's foreign traders did not make a very good showing. After 1875 the rate of increase in the value of exports was very much slower than before and not until the end of the century did exports return to a rapidly rising trend comparable to that of the mid-Victorian years. For 1871-75 the average annual value of United Kingdom exports was £297·64 million (including £58·14 million of re-exports). For 1896-1900 the figure was £313·69 million (including £61·01 million of re-exports). Thus in the final quarter of the nineteenth century the value of total exports increased by only 5·4 per cent and the value of exports per head of population actually declined. Within this period there were shorter spells that were even less successful, notably the mid-seventies and the early 'nineties, both of which saw exports fall by about 20 per cent in four years, but which were followed by a recovery of the lost ground. The early years of the twentieth century, however, saw a marked change. For 1911-13 the annual average value of exports was £596·89 million (including £108·03 million of re-exports), an increase of 90·2 per cent over the level of 1896-1900.[2]

But these figures are somewhat misleading because the last quarter of the nineteenth century experienced an exceptionally large fall in prices, whereas in the early twentieth century prices were rising. Thus the near-stagnation in the value of the late-nineteenth-century exports conceals an appreciable increase in the quantity of goods exported and the subsequent rapid expansion has to be somewhat modified when translated from money into real terms. When export values throughout the period are re-calculated at constant prices the resulting figures show an increase in the volume of total exports (including re-exports) of 57·2 per cent between 1871-75 and 1896-1900 and 45·7 per cent during the shorter period between 1896-1900 and 1911-13.[3] These figures show the development of the

---

[1] *Cf.* pp. 33-9 above.

[2] Calculated from Schlote, *British Overseas Trade*, pp. 125-8.

[3] Calculated from *ibid.*, p. 130. Several other attempts have been made to convert the value figures into volumes and they suggest that Schlote's method tended to understate the increase in volumes; see the discussion in Imlah, *Economic Elements in the Pax Britannica*, pp. 199-204. Prof. Imlah's figures show an increase in volume of 65·1 per cent for exports of home produced goods and 62·4 per cent for re-exports between 1871-75 and 1896-1900, and of 62·9 per cent for home produced exports and 31·8 per cent for re-exports between 1896-1900 and 1911-13. (Calculated from *ibid.*, pp. 97-8 and 207.)

export trade in the late nineteenth century in a more favourable light, though they still leave the early twentieth.century with the more rapid rate of growth. But even with this modification it is clear that after 1875 exports were no longer increasing as fast as they had done. The annual value of exports for 1911-13 was almost exactly double that for 1871-75, while the volume in the later period was at least two and a third times what it was in the earlier. In other words, the proportionate increase in exports over the whole forty-year period was not greatly different from that achieved in the previous twenty years.

For much of the period, however, a smaller growth of exports was partly offset by a favourable movement of the terms of trade—a given increase in the quantity of exports provided the means of paying for a more than proportionate increase in the quantity of imports. An index of the net barter terms of trade, with 1880 as base year, moved thus:[1]

1871-75	112·9	1886-90	105·0	1901-05	114·1
1876-80	101·8	1891-95	109·2	1906-10	112·3
1881-85	99·2	1896-1900	112·7	1911-13	113·8

It will be seen that appreciable help from this source did not come until after 1885 and so, with the slower growth of exports, the last quarter of the nineteenth century, taken as a whole, did not fare particularly well in foreign trade. In the twenty-five years from 1871-75 to 1896-1900 the increase in the export gain from trade was only 64·5 per cent, a much poorer showing than that even of the difficult second quarter of the century. During the overlapping quarter century which immediately preceded the First World War the increase was 107·7 per cent,[2] a considerable expansion but still not nearly as great as had been achieved earlier.

The favourable turn of the terms of trade clearly reflected conditions which made it possible for the growth of imports to show less retardation than that of exports. During the late 'eighties and the 'nineties this movement in the terms of trade coincided with just such a trend in imports. There were, however, other influences at work helping to boost imports even while the terms of trade were

[1] Calculated from Imlah, *op. cit.*, pp. 97-8. The high figure for 1871-5 was purely temporary and not representative of earlier experience.

[2] Calculated from *ibid.*, pp. 97-8. *Cf.* pp. 13-14 above, where the concepts of the net barter terms of trade and the export gain from trade are defined and discussed in relation to the course of trade earlier in the century.

moving adversely, and throughout the last quarter of the century imports grew little less rapidly than before. From 1871-75 to 1896-1900 the total value of imports (including goods subsequently re-exported) rose by 31·7 per cent and the volume is estimated to have risen by 99·2 per cent. But thereafter, though imports increased more rapidly in value, their growth lagged behind that of exports, and the increase in their volume became slower than it had been in the late nineteenth century. Between 1896-1900 and 1911-13 imports increased by 54·2 per cent in value and 23·7 per cent in volume.[1] Thus over the whole period from 1870 to the First World War the rate of increase of imports and exports was very similar in terms of value, though changes in prices meant that the volume of imports grew somewhat more than that of exports. But, within the long period, the final lustrum of the nineteenth century inaugurated a clear change of trend which affected exports and imports differently. The years before then were better for imports, the years after for exports; and the differences in the rate of growth of the value of trade between the two sub-periods were very much greater for exports than for imports, while the opposite was true of the growth in the volume of trade.

On a long view, the picture is less gloomy than at first sight for, despite the retardation of its growth, British foreign trade continued to meet current needs fairly successfully. The switch in the economy towards greater involvement in and greater dependence on external transactions was nearly, though not quite, accomplished by the eighteen-seventies. The main need thereafter was for foreign trade to maintain its recently won position in the British economy, while the economy as a whole kept pace with a world steadily becoming richer. Exports did, in fact, grow about as fast as the output of goods—towards the close of the period somewhat faster. There was in the late nineteenth century, however, some further increase in dependence on imports, which was not covered by the growth of exports, but the ground lost in this respect was made up in the next ten years. Save in so far as the economy as a whole, in which it was one major element, might perhaps have expanded a little more than it did, foreign trade was, in the long run, kept up well enough to provide all that was required of it.

[1] Calculated from Schlote, *op. cit.*, pp. 122-3 and 130. Similar calculations from the figures for net imports (i.e. omitting those re-exported) given in Imlah, *op. cit.*, pp. 97-8 show increases in volume of 114·7 per cent between 1871-75 and 1896-1900, and of 33·0 per cent between 1896-1900 and 1911-13.

Such an achievement was not made without an appreciable change in some of the established patterns of trade. One modification was a slight but persistent reduction in the relative contribution of the entrepôt trade and a correspondingly increased reliance on exports of home-produced goods. New shipping routes made possible by the opening of the Suez Canal made it more economical for many European countries to import directly much of the Asian or African produce they needed instead of buying it in London.[1] Increases in the amount of trade between some pairs of countries made it worth while to establish direct sales of particular commodities where previously it had been cheaper to send them to England, the greatest market, there to be stored and re-exported in smaller quantities to a variety of destinations. And the creation, often with the aid of subsidies, of up-to-date mercantile fleets in countries which had lacked them encouraged some direct transactions which might otherwise have been better served by British entrepôt trade. At the same time, the increasing complexity of international trade and the introduction into it of new commodities which in many countries were wanted in only small amounts, or which needed the services of specialists who did not exist in most countries, created opportunities for new lines of entrepôt trade in which London continued to gain a major share.[2] But this was not quite sufficient to offset the other influences, and the proportion of re-exports in total exports fell from 19·5 per cent in 1871-75 to 18·1 per cent in 1911-13, most of the reduction coming in the twentieth century, though the absolute value of re-exports was then rising faster than before.

Among the exports of home produce there were changes both in the commodities sold in large quantities and in the markets which they found, though neither set of changes was as drastic as might perhaps have been expected, in view of the manifold changes in world economic conditions. The distribution of exports among different parts of the world fluctuated appreciably from year to year, but certain long-term trends became evident, of which the chief were the decline in the proportion going to European countries from about 1880 and to North America from about 1890, and the rise in the proportion going to Asia and Australia and, from the 'nineties, to Africa also.

[1] For a discussion of this influence of the Suez Canal see Wells, *Recent Economic Changes*, pp. 31-3.

[2] S. B. Saul, 'Britain and World Trade 1870-1914' in *Econ. Hist. Rev.*, 2nd series, VII (1954-55), 62.

TABLE VI

Percentage Distribution of U.K. Exports by Continents, 1860-1913

Years	Europe & N. Africa	Rest of Africa	Asia	N. America	C. & S. America	Australasia
1860-69	46·5	2·2	20·5	13·9	10·5	6·4
1870-79	48·1	2·8	18·9	13·9	9·7	6·6
1880-89	41·3	3·3	20·9	16·1	9·7	8·7
1890-99	41·4	5·5	20·5	15·1	9·8	7·7
1900-09	39·5	6·9	21·7	14·8	9·7	7·4
1910-13	38·5	6·8	21·3	14·9	10·5	8·0

N.B. Re-exports are included. N. Africa comprises Morocco, Algeria, Tunisia and Tripoli. The Turkish Empire is included in Asia.

Source: Calculated from B. R. Mitchell, *Abstract of British Historical Statistics* (1962), chap. XI, table 12.

In more detail, the chief declines in the relative importance of particular markets were associated with the growing productive and commercial strength of Germany and the United States, two countries which had been among Britain's biggest customers. Both of them not only began to take a smaller share of Britain's exports but also secured for themselves some of the trade with their own neighbours which had formerly been done by Britain. Of the more distant markets, in which Britain was more successful, India was much the most important and became the most vital area of the whole British trading system. But there were notable gains in the Far East also. In the late nineteenth century China and Japan were importing more from Britain than from all the rest of the world and, though this state of affairs was modified a little, the great preponderance of British trade continued down to 1914; and the commercial development of this region brought additional advantages, since Hong Kong and Singapore became important centres of entrepôt trade, which was mainly in the hands of British firms.[1] Parts of the Ottoman Empire in Asia, especially Mesopotamia, also remained large British markets, despite increasing competition from Germany.[2] And, in the twenty years preceding the First World War, South Africa and the British colonies in West Africa were areas of particularly expansive British export trade. In South America which, as a whole, changed little in relative importance among Britain's foreign markets, there was

[1] R. J. S. Hoffman, *Great Britain and the German Trade Rivalry 1875-1941* 1933), pp. 168-91.
[2] *Ibid.*, pp. 140-59.

particularly striking growth of exports to Argentina and useful gains were also made in the smaller markets of Uruguay and Chile,[1] whereas foreign competition, notably from Germany and the United States, was less successfully met in some of the other states, including Brazil, the largest.

The spread of industrialization is reflected in these changes of markets and the same influence showed itself in changes in the commodities of export trade. The types of manufactured goods which had dominated Britain's commerce expanded their sales more slowly or not at all, because so many more countries could make them for themselves and for foreign customers, while the heavy goods that were needed to establish and operate mechanized industry and transport became more important. Thus by 1911-13 manufactured goods formed only three-quarters of Britain's home-produced exports instead of nearly nine-tenths as in the mid-Victorian years, mainly because of the great rise in the exports of coal, which in the early twentieth century were about 9 per cent of the total, as compared with 2·5 per cent fifty years earlier.[2] Among the manufactured exports textile goods remained much the most important but not by such a wide margin as for most of the nineteenth century. Their relative contribution to total exports began to fall appreciably in the eighteen-seventies and by 1911-13 had gone down to 39 per cent,[3] with cotton still by far the largest of the export industries, since cotton exports were roughly double those of all other textile exports together.[4] Of the other main classes of manufactures iron and steel maintained their relative position very steadily at just under 10 per cent of the total exports and there was a considerable advance in the importance of engineering products. Machinery, railway rolling stock, ships' hulls, motor vehicles and electrical engineering goods together constituted 10 per cent of total exports in 1911-13; in 1857-59 the proportion had been not quite 5 per cent.[5]

The changes in the commodities and the destinations of the export trade (and the limited extent of the changes in both cases) were closely connected with each other. That the growth of competition from European industry did not more seriously reduce the importance of European markets to British trade was due mainly to two factors.

---

[1] Hoffman, *op. cit.*, pp. 192-6; H. S. Ferns, 'Investment and Trade between Britain and Argentina in the Nineteenth Century' in *Econ. Hist. Rev.*, 2nd series, III, (1950-51), 207-12.

[2] Schlote, *op. cit.*, pp. 71 and 73.   [3] *Ibid.*, pp. 71 and 74.

[4] *Ibid.*, p. 151.   [5] *Ibid.*, pp. 71 and 74.

First, Britain was able partly to replace its lost sales of older staples, notably textiles, by exports of coal and machinery, which were needed in much larger quantities by an industrializing continent; and second, as Europe grew richer its trade was growing so fast that, even though other countries obtained an increasing share of it, what was left for Britain was absolutely a good deal more than before. That textile goods, despite the emergence of so many manufacturing nations, still remained much the largest British exports was attributable mainly to the growth of non-European markets for them at the same time as it became impossible to hold some of their chief European markets.

On the import side the main change in the 'seventies was the continued increase in the proportion of foodstuffs in the total until they reached equality with raw materials. Thereafter these two classes of goods formed roughly similar proportions, though if retained imports only are considered, foodstuffs began regularly to exceed raw materials, since the latter made a much bigger contribution to the re-export trade, of which throughout the period they consistently formed about two-thirds. In the last quarter of the nineteenth century the most striking change was the rapid growth of imports of manufactured goods (which had been almost negligible before 1860) until by 1900 they were more than one-fifth of the total, a proportion which then ceased to rise until after the First World War.[1] The manifold detailed changes in the commodity composition of British imports were influenced chiefly by the rising material standard of living and by changes in structure and specialization in industry. The first of these influences showed itself partly in the increased imports of manufactures, for until the last few years of the nineteenth century two-thirds or more of these were consumer goods and were becoming more varied.[2] But the most striking manifestation of it was the change in the proportion of different foodstuffs imported. In 1868-70 dairy produce was 11·3 per cent and animal foodstuffs (mostly meat and store cattle) 4·8 per cent of the value of food imports and these proportions each underwent an unbroken rise until in 1909-13 they were 15·4 per cent and 23·1 per cent respectively. In the same period the proportion of tropical food produce (mainly sugar and tea) fell from 27·5 per cent to 15·3 per cent and that of grain and flour from 37·4 per cent to 30·6 per cent,[3] though there were, of course, considerable absolute increases in

[1] *Ibid.*, pp. 53-5 and 59.　　[2] *Ibid.*, p. 67.　　[3] *Ibid.*, p. 65.

the imports of both these classes of produce. The influence of a changing industrial specialization was shown in the changed kinds of raw materials imported, notably the rapid rise in the imports of metals (especially copper), mineral oils and rubber and the reduced proportion of textile materials which, however, were still 42·3 per cent of all raw material imports in 1909-13.[1] It was shown also in the magnitude and changing nature of manufactured imports. The proportion of these which were for direct use in industry rose quickly and consistently and was at least one-third by 1911-13. Iron and steel, specialized machinery, chemicals and paper products were particularly prominent in this expansion.[2]

These changes in imports tended to maintain or increase Britain's dependence for supplies on Europe and North America, which had long been its chief sources of imports, just when these were becoming relatively less important among its export markets. Europe was the chief supplier of manufactures complementary to British production —Britain became Germany's best customer—and was best placed to

TABLE VII

Percentage Distribution of U.K. Imports by Continents, 1860-1913

Years	Europe & N. Africa	Rest of Africa	Asia	N. America	C. & S. America	Australasia
1860-69	38·4	2·4	27·7	16·5	11·3	3·7
1870-79	41·1	2·3	19·7	22·8	8·9	5·2
1880-89	42·0	2·2	17·8	26·2	5·4	6·4
1890-99	44·4	2·1	14·0	27·6	4·8	7·1
1900-09	42·5	2·1	13·6	26·7	8·1	7·0
1910-13	40·6	3·1	16·3	21·7	10·2	8·1

N.B. Regions as in Table VI.   *Source:* Calculated from Mitchell, *op.cit.*, chap. XI, table 12.

supply much of the increasing British demand for meat and dairy produce. The United States, as the most rapidly developing area of new land, could readily supply an increasing proportion of Britain's food and raw materials down to the end of the nineteenth century, and when it then began to need much more of its agricultural output for home consumption Canada developed very quickly and could partly replace it in supplying Britain. Except for Australia and New

[1] Schlote, *op. cit.*, p. 58.   [2] *Ibid.*, p. 67.

Zealand, the new market areas to which more of British export trade was switched did not show comparable development as suppliers of imports, though in the last few years before the First World War there were some signs of change in this respect. Thus British foreign trade as a whole became more characteristic of the conditions of a world-wide, fully multilateral economy, in which export and import markets were less directly matched than before.

The successes, failures and changes of character experienced in British foreign trade did not come automatically but through a multitude of individual and corporate efforts and applied judgments, sound and unsound, sometimes stimulated or hampered by acts of public policy, in many parts of the world as well as at home. But general economic conditions in the world as a whole set limits to the kind of achievement which was possible. The growth and redistribution of the world's population, the development of new territories with great natural advantages, and the industrialization and enrichment of more old countries made it unavoidable that Britain should have a smaller proportionate share in world trade than before, though it is less certain that the reduction, from 19·65 per cent of the world total in 1876-80 to 18·22 per cent in 1891-95 and 14·15 per cent in 1911-13,[1] need have been quite so large as it was. Not only this protracted permanent change but some of the fluctuations experienced while it was happening were controlled by world conditions. The difficult time for exports in the late 'eighties and the 'nineties and the revival thereafter were characteristic of all areas whose exports were mainly industrial, as can be seen from Table VIII, and cannot be explained mainly in terms of peculiarly British lapses and enterprise, though these would appear to count for more after 1900.

The explanation of these changes in world trading conditions is probably to be found mainly in changes in the volume and direction of investment and in the relative prices of different types of goods. In the late 'seventies the spread of industrialization was increasing the demand for imports of primary produce, which was further swollen by a series of bad harvests in Western Europe. At the same time the output of manufactures was rising as a result of the heavy industrial investment at the beginning of the decade. Thus there was an unusually rapid growth of demand for primary products while the prices of these were falling less than those of manufactures. Hence, primary

[1] Calculated from League of Nations, *op. cit.*, pp. 157-9 and 166-7.

TABLE VIII

Quinquennial Increases in Volume of World and British Trade, 1876-1913 (percentages)

Periods compared	World trade in manufactures	World trade in primary products	Total world trade	British exports	British net imports
1876-80:1881-85	24·4	21·8	22·8	27·1	11·8
1881-85:1886-90	12·9	17·1	15·5	12·1	13·2
1886-90:1891-95	1·7	15·5	10·2	-0·8	17·3
1891-95:1896-1900	4·7	17·1	12·9	13·1	21·6
1896-1900:1901-05	31·8	17·6	22·1	10·6	10·0
1901-05:1906-10	23·3	17·4	19·5	20·6	5·7
1906-10:1911-13	22·7	16·7	18·8	14·7	14·3

Source: Calculated from League of Nations, *op. cit.*, p. 157 and Imlah, *op. cit.*, pp. 97-8.

producing countries (still the overwhelming majority and particularly important to British trade) were able greatly to increase their imports of manufactures. In the 'eighties the demand for food imports was no longer swollen by harvest failures, and heavy international investment and migration led to a more abundant supply of primary products, which lowered the prices of such goods relatively to those of manufactures throughout the next twenty years. So primary producing countries could not afford to increase their imports of manufactures as rapidly as before. In the early 'nineties investment in most industrial countries was unusually low, and this damped down activity and adversely affected the demand for raw materials, thus aggravating for primary producers the effect of low prices. Moreover, by this time some industrial countries had become important markets for foreign manufactures, the demand for which was affected by the depression, while the United States had just become able to supply most of its own needs for manufactures. Hence international trade in manufactures grew little. The trend was reversed mainly by the revival of industrial investment in the late 'nineties, which stimulated the demand of industrial countries for imports of both manufactures and primary products. Since investment in the supply of the latter had recently fallen off there was no corresponding acceleration in the growth of their output and the relative deterioration in their prices came to an end, thus assisting primary producing countries to increase their purchases of manufactures. Furthermore, the rapid expansion of trade was maintained in the prewar years by an unprecedentedly high inflow of foreign capital and labour to primary producing areas, with a consequent great boost to their importing capacity, which mainly benefited the industrial exporters.

Acts of policy may also have reinforced the effect of these underlying conditions. Thus the difficulties of international trade in the 'nineties were aggravated by the need to make adjustments to very recent substantial increases in tariffs and by sharp temporary disturbances arising from such episodes as the German-Russian and the Franco-Italian tariff wars.[1] On the other hand, the acquisition of new colonies, protectorates and commercial concessions by western governments in the 'nineties and the opening years of the twentieth century almost certainly assisted, perhaps by its psychological influence more than anything else, the subsequent great boom in investment and trade with primary producing regions.

Given the general underlying conditions of world trade, which British people could have appreciably altered only by a host of different decisions about when, where and how much to invest, British exports fared as well as anyone could reasonably expect until about 1900. After that, though they showed so many signs of revival and even boom, it looks probable that many more opportunities were being let slip than before. The history of foreign trade, just like that of industry, shows signs of generally successful adaptation to new circumstances in the late nineteenth century, followed by a failure to take account of some of the subsequent lines of change.

The successful adaptation was, as has already been indicated, the cumulative achievement of countless individuals and firms directly engaged in trade or providing services ancillary to it. Its sources are perhaps best illustrated by a consideration of some of the chief factors which made possible the development of new markets or the launching of new sales lines in old ones. The growth of the markets of India, the Far East and Australia, for instance, one of the key elements in the adjustment of Britain's trade to the new circumstances, was conditional on the provision of communications as swift, reliable and abundant as those with any other area; and those who from the 'sixties

---

[1] Ashley, *Modern Tariff History*, pp. 71-2, 202-23, 325-7 and 332-5.

onward met this need had a major part in the commercial success. They included telegraph and cable companies, shipping lines, and coal merchants establishing depots in a lengthening chain of ports. Some of them came late to gain a share in a well-established and growing activity, but many were genuine pioneers, looking for their ultimate reward to business which did not exist before them and which they must help to create. Such were the cable companies operating to the East. By 1865 England had telegraphic communication with Calcutta by the Channel cable and overland lines from Calais, but the ownership of the route was divided among many firms and governments, not always either efficient or co-operative; messages at best were several days in transit and the service not much used.[1] The three companies which in 1869 and 1870 established an all-British route by laying cables from Falmouth to Malta, Malta to Alexandria, and Suez to Bombay respectively (a land line already operated between Alexandria and Suez) had thus no sure commercial prospect to guide them, and in 1870 transmitted no more than a few dozen messages. Yet before the end of 1871 three other companies had extended the system with cables from India to Singapore, Singapore via Hong Kong to Shanghai, and Singapore via Java to Port Darwin.[2] Once the service was established it proved itself to be one of the essentials of commerce and by 1895 was carrying two million messages annually at charges reduced by 96 per cent since 1870.[3]

Equally a pioneer was the Ocean Steam Ship Company, formed by Alfred Holt, the Liverpool marine engineer, which in 1866, in the face of many gloomy prognostications, began the first regular steamship service between England and China.[4] Holt had the enterprise to use the dubiously regarded Suez Canal as soon as it was available and later extended his services to Japan and Australia. His success in overcoming the commercial hazards which he faced brought him numerous imitators, awkward rivals to him, but to merchants a welcome augmentation of the services of Far Eastern trade.

Merely to provide such services was not by itself sufficient, for trade did not flow to them automatically. To obtain business in new

---

[1] H. L. Hoskins, *British Routes to India* (1928), p. 383.
[2] *Ibid.*, pp. 389-94.   [3] *Ibid.*, p. 395.
[4] F. E. Hyde, *Blue Funnel: a history of Alfred Holt and Company of Liverpool from 1865 to 1914* (1956), p. 20.

markets, merchants and shipping firms or their agents on the spot
had to go out and look for it. British merchants resident in Far Eastern
ports were active in investigating the opportunities for trade with the
interior, in taking steps to ensure the reliable grading of goods supplied to them in very miscellaneous qualities, and in advising dealers
at home and shipowners about changes of policy necessary for their
success.[1] The history of the Ocean Steam Ship Company, for instance, shows over and over again how much it depended on the
advice and enterprise of its agent, John Swire, in China and other
agents in Malaya,[2] and on its own willingness to follow that advice.
Thus it was experience on the spot that showed that ships calling
regularly at Singapore would not obtain adequate business unless
feeder services were started in the East Indies.[3] The real history,
immediately underlying the statistics of foreign trade, is found in the
day-to-day activities, extended over several decades, of men and
firms like these.

It was on similar enterprise that the development of new business
in old markets depended. When cotton manufacturing firms grew
up in European countries to compete successfully with imported
British cloth they did not necessarily put an end to the prospects
of British textile exporters. Many of these firms could not make for
themselves, or obtain locally, yarns of the quality they needed.
There was business to be had by the British merchant who would
discover what was wanted, undertake to supply it and prove his
reliability in practice. The activities of such merchants as Webb of
Nottingham, who put on record something of his travels in the
'seventies and 'eighties to establish regular sales of yarn in France,
Germany, Austria and Switzerland,[4] were indispensable. Had there
not been many like him British success in export markets could not
have been maintained.

Contemporary, and some later, critics were often less inclined to
publicize the solid success, founded on the commercial virtues that
these men showed, than to stress the growth of competitors' shares in
particular markets and the British shortcomings which, they alleged,
made it possible. British suppliers paid less attention than their rivals
to the need to adapt their goods to the tastes and precise requirements

---

[1] *Ibid.*, pp. 28-36; G. C. Allen and Audrey G. Donnithorne, *Western Enterprise
in Far Eastern Economic Development: China and Japan* (1954), chaps. II-V.

[2] Hyde, *op. cit., passim.*   [3] *Ibid.*, pp. 51-3 and 83-6.

[4] W. F. M. Weston-Webb, *The Autobiography of a British Yarn Merchant* (1929),
pp. 101-2 and 127-37.

F

of particular markets;[1] they sent out their catalogues in the English language, with the goods described in English weights and measures and priced in sterling;[2] they employed fewer commercial travellers than foreign exporters; they allowed their customers less time to pay.[3] The government provided too little commercial information and that little was published too late; and it did nothing to counter the tariffs, subsidies and excessive consular pressure of foreign governments.[4] Some of these allegations were probably not well founded. The Foreign Office's services to commerce were the subject of official enquiry in 1886 and some improvements were made, especially in the collection and diffusion of information, the changes including the start of the *Board of Trade Journal*.[5] No one who has sampled the immense bulk of regularly-published consular reports can fairly accuse the government of neglecting to provide foreign commercial information; there is probably more truth in the counter-suggestion that businessmen often failed to take any notice of what was published for their benefit.[6] As for the lack of reaction to other governments' protective policies, most businessmen were reluctant to see their own government use many political weapons, and it is hard to see that much could have been done with advantage. The 'fair trade' movement of the 'eighties never won the support of more than a small minority. The members of the biggest exporting trade, cotton textiles, remained faithful to the principles of free trade,[7] and only in the early twentieth century, when Joseph Chamberlain was running strongly his campaign for tariff reform and imperial preference, did opposite views make much headway. Then merchants connected with some important export trades, woollens for example,[8] did begin to regard protection as desirable, and from 1905 onwards the Association of British Chambers of Commerce was regularly able to pass resolutions in favour of protection, though usually only with the aid of a high proportion of abstentions.[9]

The shortcomings of exporters themselves may have been more real, but in the nineteenth century probably caused only a small loss of business. After 1900 they were likely to be more costly because

---

[1] W. S. H. Gastrell, *Our Trade in the World in relation to foreign competition, 1885 to 1895* (1897), pp. 31-2 and 37.

[2] *Ibid.*, pp. 40 and 49.   [3] *Ibid.*, p. 53; Hoffman, *op. cit.*, pp. 85-7.

[4] Hoffman, *op. cit.*, pp. 45-53.   [5] *Ibid.*, pp. 61-2.   [6] Gastrell, *op. cit.*, p. 48.

[7] A. Redford, *Manchester Merchants and Foreign Trade*, II (1956), 97-111.

[8] M. W. Beresford, *The Leeds Chambers of Commerce* (1951), pp. 113-19.

[9] Redford, *op. cit.*, II, 104-5.

more of the new selling opportunities were for more elaborate goods, where design and attention to local idiosyncrasies were important, and in places where English was not the language of the local business community or government. But the deficiencies of British foreign trade at this time probably came less from slipshod commercial practices than from the limited range of commodities which were available for export. Too many of the goods which Britain could most plentifully supply were commodities the markets for which were not among the most expansive, though they were still growing, and the supply of which was coming from a steadily increasing number of countries. Since, nevertheless, profitable sales were coming more easily than they had done a few years earlier, there was less incentive to incur extra effort and expense to change this state of affairs. So the growth of British exports lagged further behind that of world trade in manufactures. Adjustment mainly through the capture of bigger non-European markets for familiar goods had been generally adequate in the late nineteenth century. Now it needed to come more through the competitive offer of new types of goods, and though this development had been begun it was proceeding too slowly.

It would be misleading to leave the history of foreign trade simply as one of slower and irregular growth involving a fairly successful adjustment to difficult new conditions, followed by a greater neglect of opportunities as conditions temporarily eased. The export and import of merchandise was only a part of Britain's foreign dealing and one of the significant changes of the last quarter of the nineteenth century was that it became a relatively smaller part. While the value of merchandise exports grew so slowly at this time, that of some 'invisible' exports was built up much more quickly. In 1871-75 the estimated income from foreign investments and business services (including insurance and shipping) was equal to 63 per cent of the f.o.b. value of home-produced exports. The proportion rose to 87 per cent in 1891-95 and though, with the revival of export values after 1900, it was subsequently reduced, it was still as high as 75 per cent in 1911-13. The chief source of this increase was the interest and dividends on British investments abroad; but it was also helped by the earnings of shipping, which grew by an estimated 23 per cent between 1871-75 and 1896-1900, a much higher rate than that for merchandise exports.[1] After 1900 only dividends and interest, of the

---

[1] Calculated from Imlah, *op. cit.*, pp. 73-5 and 166.

invisible items, could approximately keep pace with the growth in the value of merchandise exports.

The exceptional size of Britain's mercantile marine was such that it could and did carry considerably more trade than was represented by British exports and imports alone, large as these were, and enabled the country to gain some profit from the expansion of international trade outside the activities of British traders. Though the world's supply of shipping grew rapidly, from 16·8 million net tons in 1870 to 34·6 million net tons in 1910, the United Kingdom's merchant navy kept pace with it and, in fact, throughout the period remained very consistently round about a third of the total. Until the 'nineties the British position was still stronger because the proportion of steamships was much larger than that of other countries. Thereafter, though the British merchant fleet probably continued to include a more than average proportion of the most modern vessels, its advantage was somewhat lessened as the other chief maritime countries more and more replaced sail by steam.[1]

The profitable use of this vast fleet was not maintained without some difficulty, owing to the combined influences of competition and politics. On the commonly accepted reckoning that the carrying service obtained in a given period from a steamship is equivalent to that from sailing vessels of four times the net tonnage, the world's shipping supply increased over four and a half times between 1870 and 1910, which must have been considerably more than the increase in the amount of cargo available, though there was the offsetting factor that probably a bigger proportion of maritime trade was over long distances. This state of affairs caused intense competition on many routes and, since shipping is an industry in which overheads are a high proportion of total costs, rates were liable to be driven down to very low levels for long periods, as it would have been even more unprofitable to lay up a vessel than to run it for an income which just covered the prime cost of operation. For many foreign competitors this was not a decisive matter, because they were greatly helped by government subsidies to the cost of building or operation or both; the prevalence of subsidies was, in fact, a major cause of the huge increase in the supply of shipping. But British shipowners were not privileged in this way, except that a few lines received generous payment for mail contracts and a fee for keeping one or two specially

[1] Kirkaldy, *British Shipping*, Appendix XVII.

fast vessels that might be useful to the navy in the event of war.[1] So the success of the shipping industry had to depend on technical and administrative improvement and the limitation of competition.

Much was gained by keeping abreast of technical improvements, which lowered both initial and operational costs and facilitated much greater adaptation of ships, in terms of speed, size and design, to different purposes.[2] The business risks were reduced and financial strength increased by the general adoption of corporate form with limited liability and a large increase in the capitalization of shipping firms.[3] But competitive rate-cutting constantly threatened to cancel out these gains. The sequel was the formation of shipping conferences, of which the first, dealing with the trade to Calcutta, came in 1875. All the firms operating liner services on a particular route agreed to a common system of rates, with variations for differences in speed and special facilities, and arranged their sailings so as not to clash with each other. The intrusion of rate-cutting outsiders was discouraged by the offer of rebates to traders who used only conference vessels, the payment of the rebate being deferred for some months, during which the use of a non-conference vessel rendered the trader liable to forfeit it. The system did much to keep freight rates at a remunerative level and also helped to ensure for traders a reasonable standard of service. It was obviously open to abuse but public enquiry suggested that it was not in practice much abused.[4] By the end of the nineteenth century practically all liner services operating east of Suez and a large proportion of those in the southern hemisphere were within the conference system, but the North Atlantic services and those between Britain and Western Europe, with a heavier concentration of trade on the routes of a fairly small area, remained outside it.[5] It seems certain that this reorganization was a necessary part of the

---

[1] Details of government assistance to shipping in all the chief maritime countries are given in R. Meeker, *History of Shipping Subsidies* (1905).

[2] Kirkaldy, *op. cit.*, Book I, Chaps. VII-XIII and Appendix XVIII.

[3] *Ibid.*, Book II, Chaps. I and II; Jefferys, *Trends in Business Organization in Great Britain since 1856*, pp. 62-72.

[4] The fullest account of the history and working of the conferences is in the *Report of the Royal Commission on Shipping Rings* (*P.P.* 1909, XLVII-XLVIII). The main features are summarized in D. H. Macgregor, 'Shipping Conferences' in *Econ. Journ.*, XIX (1909), 503-16. For details of the origin and practices of the conferences in Far Eastern services see also Hyde, *op. cit.*, pp. 53-79 and 86-96.

[5] Macgregor, *loc. cit.*, p. 508. The considerable volume of tramp shipping, which was better able to concentrate wherever, at any particular time, demand was greatest, and which was much more difficult to regulate also remained outside the conferences.

creation of new conditions which made worth while the continued expansion of British shipping to the extent that its earnings could continue to be a leading element in the balance of payments.

The relatively greater contribution of the other large 'invisible' item, interest and dividends, in the late nineteenth century no doubt owed something to the effect of price movements. An appreciable part of the foreign investment was in fixed interest securities, the yield of which was not reduced, like other foreign earnings, by falling prices. But this influence was reversed at the end of the century and was always far less important than the heavy and continued flow of new British capital overseas. It has sometimes been suggested,[1] mainly because additions to foreign investment seldom exceeded the current income from foreign dividends and interest (as they had often recently done), that after the early 'seventies British investors no longer used their earnings so freely to build up capital holdings abroad. But this view is hard to substantiate. The changed ratio of new foreign investment to income from existing foreign investment was mainly due to the fact that interest and dividends had become a bigger proportion of the total income from abroad. It is much more significant to consider what proportion of the total earnings abroad was used for new investment, and, though this proportion fluctuated a great deal, its general level was high enough to indicate the continued importance of long-term investment among the uses made of increased foreign income. Not only in the 'eighties, a time of revival in external business generally, but even in the early 'nineties, when investment and trade were rather slack, a bigger proportion of the income from abroad was devoted to new investment than in either of the periods 1851-55 or 1861-65; and the revival of foreign investment in the years just before the First World War went to heights probably never reached in the most booming years of the nineteenth century. From 1911 to 1913 inclusive, additions to foreign investment have been estimated at 21·5 per cent of the income earned abroad, a figure which may be compared with 16·7 per cent for 1871-75.[2] It is, indeed, probably more reasonable to stress that foreign investment did not become really large and the central feature in the growth of Britain's wealth

---

[1] Notably by L. H. Jenks, *The Migration of British Capital to 1875* (1927), esp. pp. 333-6. Prof. Jenks described the situation in regard to foreign investment after 1875 by the title-phrase of his final chapter, 'the end of the surplus'. *Cf.* also the argument in W. W. Rostow, *British Economy of the Nineteenth Century* (1948), pp. 25-6 and 88-9, where 'the relative cessation of foreign lending' is given as the main influence on the course of economic activity between 1873 and 1896.

[2] Calculated from Imlah, *op. cit.*, pp. 73, 75, 166 and 207.

until after 1870, and to recognize that it was only the exceptional conditions of the period between then and 1914 that made this possible.[1]

The growth of British holdings of capital abroad was the result mainly of the spontaneous response made by the business classes to the newly-unfolding opportunities of developing the hitherto neglected resources of the non-European world. Until about 1870 or a little earlier the majority of British capital exports went to continental Europe and the older centres of the United States. But by then the supply of capital in many of these areas was becoming much more abundant and the opportunities for very profitable British investment correspondingly reduced. Already in the 'sixties India, where a railway system was in process of creation and where the government was prepared to guarantee the dividend on some private railway capital, was receiving more attention from British investors and it continued to be an important area of British investment. But the chief subsequent attractions were the vast areas with rich natural resources which were just being made accessible to white settlement and in which western (in many cases British) methods and standards of government and commercial law were in force. By the very end of the nineteenth century recently acquired colonial territories to which there was little white migration were receiving an increasing proportion of capital exports, but they remained far less attractive than the new areas of white settlement. The American West, Australia and Argentina in the eighteen-eighties, South Africa in the 'nineties, Canada, Argentina and Brazil in the early twentieth century were among the principal areas receiving British capital. Between 1870 and 1885 the proportion of British oversea investment which had gone to the Empire is estimated to have risen from about one-third to about one-half, India and Australia being the chief recipients. In 1914 the proportion in the Empire was much the same but Canada had become the biggest borrower. Canada's borrowings, however, were still appreciably less than those of the United States, in which about 20 per cent of all British foreign investment was located, while another 20 per cent was in Latin America, nearly half of it in Argentina.[2]

In making their investments abroad British investors had much

---

[1] Cairncross, *Home and Foreign Investment 1870-1913*, pp. 2-3.

[2] *Ibid.*, pp. 182-5; Royal Institute of International Affairs, *The Problem of International Investment* (1937), p. 121.

more information about conditions in borrowing countries than they had had earlier. They therefore had less cause to restrict their lending to the only institutions known to them, viz. governments, and could use their judgment to seek a higher return than was offered by foreign government bonds. British investors concentrated more and more on supplying capital for those purposes which were basic to the economy of new countries and likely to share in the proceeds of every sector of their development. Since all these countries had vast distances to conquer, railways were their biggest indispensable need and became the most important form of British foreign investment. In the 'seventies railway securities were only about a fifth of the total British investments abroad, and about half the railway investment was in India.[1] By 1914 railways accounted for at least two-fifths of the enormously expanded total, while banking and financial companies, whose influence and sources of business were equally general, formed about a tenth. Investment in mines, oil companies, plantations and land companies together also amounted to about a tenth of the total, but that in government and municipal securities, once the majority, had declined relatively to little more than a quarter.[2]

The estimated figures of the total value of foreign capital owned by British people at different dates are a measure both of the magnitude of the new opportunities and of the response to them. The latest, and probably the most reliable, estimates suggest a rather greater increase between 1870 and 1914 than earlier writers used to allow for. In 1870 British capital assets abroad were about £700 million; by 1885 they had risen to £1,500 million and reached £2,400 million in 1900 and £4,000 million in 1913.[3] Willingness to go on exporting capital on this scale is evidence that investors considered that the returns they received were good enough to justify it, and there is little reason to think that in general they were mistaken. From their own point of view the essential thing was that they obtained on the average bigger dividends than were yielded by the most nearly comparable classes of investment at home, and though there was a rather higher risk of default it was not so great as to abolish the margin in favour of foreign investment.[4] The advantages of the capital exports were not

[1] Cairncross, *op. cit.*, p. 229.

[2] Royal Institute of International Affairs, *op. cit.*, p. 122.

[3] Imlah, *op. cit.*, pp. 72-5. The figures have been rounded off to the nearest £25 mn., since they cannot hope to be more precise than that.

[4] Cairncross, *op. cit.*, pp. 226-31.

confined to the investors alone but were spread through the British economy. Indirectly they helped the balance of payments through their influence on merchandise trade. There is a good deal of evidence that a period of heavy British investment in a particular country overseas was followed by an expansion of British exports there, though the relationship was a complex one which needs more investigation.[1] Even more powerful was the effect of concentrating investment on the basic equipment of new territories producing food and raw materials; nothing else contributed so much to lowering the cost of British imports from the 'eighties onwards.[2] Most striking and important of all, perhaps, was the direct influence on the balance of payments. In the early 'seventies Britain was already receiving about £50 million a year as interest and dividends from abroad, but for 1911-13 the figure has been estimated to have reached £188 million a year.[3] An item which was supplying not far short of 10 per cent of the national income and more than 20 per cent of all the income obtained from external transactions was clearly of outstanding importance to the economic life of the whole country.

There were other 'invisible' items in the balance of payments which worked less favourably than the growth of capital exports. It is unlikely that earnings from insurance and from trading and banking services grew any faster than those from merchandise exports—more probably they grew less. On the other side of the account, the spread in the habit of foreign travel must have caused some increase in expenditure abroad; and there was some new investment of foreign capital, chiefly American, in Britain. But all these were only minor modifying influences. The net effect of changes in 'invisible' items was to increase British earnings abroad more rapidly than could be achieved by merchandise exports alone. 'Invisible' income thus provided a margin out of which it was possible to increase the consumption of imports even when little more was being earned by exports. In the difficult trading years of the last quarter of the nineteenth century this is just what happened. In the years 1864-73 only 12·1 per cent of the United Kingdom's foreign trade consisted of imports which were paid for by 'invisible' exports, but this proportion went up to 20·3 per cent for 1874-83, 18·2 per cent for 1884-93 and 23·9 per cent for 1894-1903. When, however, the value of exports began to grow more quickly again, the 'invisible' items were less used to pay for imports and the figure went down again to 15·1 per cent for

---

[1] *Ibid.*, pp .232-3. [2] *Ibid.*, p. 233. [3] Imlah, *op. cit.*, pp. 73-5.

1904-13,[1] and was, indeed, as low as 12 per cent for the last three years. The purchasing power derived from existing capital abroad was then being offset by a higher rate of new investment overseas.

It is now possible to sum up the main features of the changing relation between Britain's external transactions and its general economic position. They all suggest that international matters, already of very great influence in the mid-nineteenth century, had become even more important by the early years of the twentieth. On the basis of the first census of production it was estimated that in 1907 roughly one-quarter of the output of goods in the United Kingdom went for export, one-fifth of the goods consumed came directly from imports and, allowing for home produced goods which incorporated other imports, the total retained imports equalled one-third of the total national consumption of goods.[2] Since 1870 the ratio of imports to consumption must have risen appreciably and that of exports to output had probably risen a little, though it may temporarily have been as high in the brief expansion of the 'eighties as it was a quarter of a century later.[3]

Such figures bring out clearly how utterly indispensable a vast external trade had become to the avoidance of unemployment and starvation. Another change had been making the maintenance of that trade still more complicated, for Britain's external dealings came to depend more and more on the supply of capital and services. Beyond its own trade, Britain, as financier, carrier, insurer and commercial agent, had a direct stake in the trade of half the world beside—and more. No country had ever had so great an interest in the world-wide growth of commerce and the maintenance of the free movement and security of capital everywhere. And there was a third major change which made that interest even stronger; the steady decline in the proportion of wants that could be satisfied by goods purchased from areas which were Britain's best customers or biggest remitters of dividends. Before about 1870 a very large proportion of Britain's

---

[1] A. O. Hirschman, *National Power and the Structure of Foreign Trade* (1945) p. 145. Figures for slightly different periods are also given in Imlah, *op. cit.* p. 166.

[2] *Final Report on the First Census of Production of the U.K.*, pp. 22-9. 'Consumption' in this context includes goods used for capital purposes.

[3] *Cf.* Schlote, *op. cit.*, p. 155. Schlote's index of the proportion of industrial production exported was 15 per cent higher in 1913 than in 1870-4, but this rise may be a little too great since the index is based on the Hoffmann index of industrial production, which for this period probably understates the increase in production.

trade with its debtors was bilateral and only quite small surpluses
and deficits were left to be settled through multilateral exchange.
But British import requirements became so vast and varied, the areas
with profitable investment opportunities to attract a flow of British
capital in excess of any reverse flow of dividends became so widespread, and the range of British export goods remained so limited
that there were fewer and fewer countries to which Britain did not
pay out more (reckoning capital and current payments together) than
it received in return.[1] It therefore became more and more necessary
that, in the few countries with which Britain continued to have a
favourable balance of payments, the surplus should be built up to a
very large amount; and that was possible only if those same countries
could secure a large surplus with the rest of the world and use their
net income from any foreign source to make their payments to
Britain. Such a surplus, in turn, could be earned only if the rest
of the world had adequate funds which were acceptable as payment.

In practice the problems posed by this situation were overcome
very successfully, with only occasional and brief periods of difficulty,
mainly because of the growth of British trade in Asia and the ability
of Asiatic countries to sell large amounts of food and raw materials
to industrializing countries other than Britain. In 1880 probably one-
third of Britain's deficits was covered by receipts from India and by
1910 this proportion had risen to something nearer one-half, for India
not only had a large import surplus with Britain but also paid regular
dividends on large past investments, without doing much new
borrowing, and was the source of remittances made by British
administrators and soldiers. Most of the remaining deficit was met,
by 1910, by British surpluses with the other chief Asiatic markets,
China, Japan, and Turkey (none of which was attracting much
British capital) and with Australia, which was making large dividend
payments (and some repayments of principal) on the heavy borrowings of the late nineteenth century and, for the time being, not importing much new capital.[2] It had become possible for receipts
obtained by any country in any part of the world to be used for
the settlement of debts almost anywhere else. Britain was able to
draw most of its supplies from Europe and the Americas and to
contribute heavily to the capital needs of the latter because these
areas needed the produce of India and the Far East, which could earn

---

[1] League of Nations, *The Network of World Trade* (1942), pp. 84-7.
[2] Saul, *loc. cit.*, pp. 59-65.

the extra sums unobtainable by direct British exports, and pay them to Britain in return for supplies of manufactures and capital. In turn, the successful British trade expansion in the East was helped because the industrializing countries which wished to buy more heavily in Asia did not need to achieve a comparable increase of exports there and thus intensify competition with British traders; they could pay for their needs with what they earned in other parts of the world, which, to a great extent, meant the sums obtainable from increased sales in the one great remaining free trade market, Britain itself.

It was an elaborate and delicate system and the area in which there was a British payments surplus, which sealed all gaps and made possible the smooth working of the whole arrangement, was narrowing to an extent that foreshadowed danger. But for forty years it worked extremely well, enabled world trade to grow faster than it could otherwise have done, and brought a great increase in the supply of goods to the British people. Given such circumstances and their generally favourable outcome it is hardly surprising that, in policy and in the creation and methods of working of the institutions of commercial life, international considerations should always have been in the forefront in Britain. To ease the path of trade everywhere and to carry multilateralism to its utmost extent was a condition of health for such an economy as Britain's had become by the late nineteenth century; and, though there were always some to complain that the results were not good enough and that foreigners benefited more than Britain did from Britain's own practices, the fruits of British external activity, in the form of increased consumption and outstanding economic influence in the world, were highly impressive, both to contemporaries and in retrospect.

CHAPTER SEVEN

Money, Banking and Investment

BRITAIN'S fortunes in the international field were almost as much a financial as a commercial matter. The large and growing income earned abroad by investments and financial services and the essential part that these had in assisting the momentum of merchandise trade bear witness to that. It is inconceivable that the vast ramifications of British economic relations with the rest of the world in the late nineteenth century could have developed unless a highly sophisticated financial system had already come into existence; and, since they did develop with such impressive effect, it was to be expected that the financial system itself would become more closely linked with international influences. In many ways the dominant features of financial history in the late nineteenth century were extensions and refinements of developments inaugurated earlier. They may be summed up as a movement towards greater size, stability and cohesion in the financial system as a whole, and a heavier impact of external dealings on its business and on the determination of the policies which guided it.

All through the middle of the nineteenth century the volume of banking business had been growing rapidly—the assets and liabilities of banks in the United Kingdom, other than the Bank of England, were estimated to have trebled between 1850 and 1874[1]—and an increasing proportion of it had passed into the hands of the joint-stock banks, while the small private banks gradually dwindled in absolute numbers. This change meant that a bigger proportion of the cash balances of the country was made available for commercial use and to serve as the basis of a bigger volume of credit. It also meant that banking gradually passed to institutions which, because of their larger resources and wider spread of business, could offer more extensive services to customers and were less liable to overreach

---

[1] J. Dun, 'The Banking Institutions, Bullion Reserves and Non-Legal-Tender Note Circulation of the U.K. Statistically Investigated' in *Journ. of the Stat. Socy.*, XXXIX (1876), 121.

themselves. In the 'seventies the benefits of this situation were fairly recent, for many of the early joint-stock banks had been just as insecure as any private banks and inferior to the best of the latter. But the combined effect of greater resources and greater experience brought much improvement in the last third of the century. Another change produced by the spread of banking was a much increased facility for settling transactions within the United Kingdom by cheque. This caused a corresponding relative decline in the proportion which involved the use of bills of exchange, though the absolute volume of internal bills (i.e. bills employed to finance transactions which were confined to the home country) doubtless went on increasing until late in the nineteenth century. An almost certain corollary of this change was that internal bills were becoming less important among the various forms of credit. Since many banks did not in their statements of assets make any distinction between bills discounted and loans and advances to customers[1] it is impossible fully to substantiate this by direct evidence, but there are many reasons for believing that, from the middle of the nineteenth century, banks accommodated their customers relatively more by loans and overdrafts and relatively less by discounting bills for them.[2] Even so, the combined demand by home trade and industry for all forms of accommodation was evidently growing less quickly than bank deposits after 1850. Thus a situation had arisen in which the banks needed new interest-earning outlets for their deposits and specialist dealers in bills of exchange found the supply from home sources growing too slowly, all the more so because provincial bankers were sending fewer of their discounted bills to be rediscounted in London. Partial relief was found in the expansion of stockbroking, the finance of which depended to some extent on bank loans, but the chief development was that banks increasingly lent money at short notice to the London bill-brokers, who used it more and more to discount international bills of exchange.[3] Thus the outstanding result of the ability to mobilize more of Britain's cash balances was to enable London to finance a bigger proportion of world trade and to reap the profits therefrom.

Finally, it must be noted that the banking changes of the previous

---

[1] Dun, *loc. cit.*, pp. 86-7.

[2] *Cf.* the figures in T. E. Gregory, *The Westminster Bank through a century* (1936), II, 311-13 and 321; also Dun, *loc. cit.*, pp. 116-20.

[3] E. T. Powell, *The Evolution of the Money Market 1385-1915* (1916), pp. 373-80; W. T. C. King, *History of the London Discount Market* (1936), pp. 174-7.

fifty years had had the effect by 1870 of making the Bank of England willy-nilly into a central bank responsible for keeping the reserve of practically the entire banking system, so that it had become both a unifying influence and a point of greater vulnerability. The joint-stock banks kept most of their cash reserve in the form of deposits with the Bank of England; and the bill-brokers existed on short-term money borrowed from the banks, which the banks recalled in order to protect themselves in any period of stringency. Thus the bill-brokers were dependent in all abnormal conditions on their ability to borrow from the Bank of England, as there was nowhere else they could obtain means to meet their immediate commitments. Only the private country bankers were still somewhat variable in the extent to which their reserves were in London and therefore in the extent to which they were ultimately dependent on the Bank of England, but by 1870 they were of minor importance. Essentially the position was that the Bank of England's reserve of notes to meet its liabilities was the sole ultimate legal tender reserve of the whole country and that since 1844 the maximum which this reserve could reach had depended on the amount of gold which the Bank held at any given time.[1] Thus the Bank of England had the responsibility of maintaining a reserve big enough to meet the banking needs of all England (and to a large extent of Scotland) and of keeping that reserve accessible, at a price, to all the institutions of the money market whenever they needed to draw on it. Even in the late 'sixties the Bank of England still denied in public that it had a *duty* to perform this function, though it had come steadily nearer to acceptance of that position in practice. It seems to have been this denial more than anything else that stimulated Bagehot to produce his classic work on *Lombard Street* in 1873, which rammed the lesson home so forcefully and lucidly that it could never again be questioned.[2] Thenceforward, both in theory and practice, no one doubted that England was a country with one single reserve for its whole financial system, a reserve kept by the Bank of England, which made the safety of that reserve the touchstone of its policy, and acted as lender of last resort to the rest of the money market.

In the closing decades of the nineteenth century most of the tendencies that had become apparent by 1870 went a good deal further. Private banks continued to disappear, mostly through absorption by

---

[1] W. Bagehot, *Lombard Street* (1873), chap. II; Dun, *loc. cit.*, p. 125.

[2] Bagehot, *op. cit.*, *passim*, esp. chaps. II, VII and XII.

joint-stock banks. From 1862 to 1902 inclusive 200 private banks were the subject of amalgamation, 130 of them being taken over by joint-stock banks;[1] by 1913 only 40 country banks and 8 London private banks remained, whereas in 1870 there were still 47 private banks in London and 207 in the provinces.[2] This change brought with it an absolute decline in the amount of private banking business, but a simultaneous reduction in the numbers of joint-stock banks, also achieved by amalgamations, reflected only a trend towards a much bigger average size among banking undertakings. Since banking is carried on by means of a large number of similar actions which can readily be assimilated into a standardized routine, it is well fitted to achieve administrative economies of scale and, up to a point, there is a positive advantage in the further spreading of risks which is made possible by increasing size. By the 'eighties these influences were being reinforced by the greater facility with which some banks could raise extra capital to enable them to absorb others. Although limited liability had been permitted to joint-stock banks since 1858, many of them had preferred not to make use of this privilege. But the disastrous demands on the shareholders of the unlimited City of Glasgow Bank, which was brought down by fraud in 1878,[3] produced a change of outlook, and limited liability spread rapidly among banks thereafter, though many deliberately kept a form of reserve liability by providing that part of the nominal value of their shares should remain uncalled except in the event of winding up. The new financial and legal position of joint-stock banks attracted new investors and new depositors and helped to increase their resources for further growth.[4] At the same time many of the smaller banks began to find it less easy to carry on independently, as pressure increased for the retention of higher cash reserves and greater publicity about reserves, and as some of their investments depreciated.[5] Between 1890 and 1902 amalgamation accelerated to such an extent that 51 joint-stock banks and 64 private banks were absorbed by other joint-stock banks and, though the amalgamation

---

[1] J. Sykes, *The Amalgamation Movement in English Banking, 1825-1924* (1926)' p. 97.

[2] Dun, *loc. cit.*, p. 22; Powell, *op. cit.*, pp. 412-14.

[3] The shareholders of the City of Glasgow Bank were called on to meet liabilities about six times the amount of their holding.

[4] Sykes, *op. cit.*, pp. 38-9.

[5] R. S. Sayers, *Lloyds Bank in the History of English Banking* (1957), pp. 189, 252 and 256-7.

movement was a little slower after 1902, it was by no means finished.[1] In 1880, as in 1873, there were 121 English joint-stock banks, the highest number ever recorded; at the end of 1913 there were only 43, of which 30 lost their separate identity within the next ten years, mostly between 1917 and 1920.[2]

Some of the banks which survived had attained very large size and practically all of them had followed a policy of opening more and more branches, on a scale that made the extensions of mid-Victorian times seem comparatively small, despite the deep impression they made on contemporaries. Between 1870 and the First World War the number of bank offices in England and Wales increased approximately fourfold; in 1872 there was one to every 12,766 persons, in 1914 one to every 5,153.[3] In this way it was made easy for the cash and transactions of more and more people to pass through the banking system and thus help to enlarge the foundation available for the extension of credit. Bagehot declared that English banking in his time utilized 'all the petty cash of private persons down nearly to the end of the middle class'.[4] But sheer difficulty of physical access to a bank office must have made that an exaggeration for many rural and suburban places. Even in London in the early 'seventies Camden Town in the north, the Elephant and Castle in the south, Stratford in the east and Notting Hill in the west were the extreme limits beyond which no bank had opened a branch,[5] and elsewhere there were larger gaps. A complete change in this state of affairs, especially after the mid-eighties, must have been an influence on the increase in the number of depositors and the amount of deposits.[6] The exact amount of this increase cannot be stated because, until well after 1870, there were many banks that did not publish a balance-sheet. The majority of careful estimates would suggest that by the middle 'seventies the total bank deposits of the United Kingdom were something over £500 million. Dun, for instance, estimated them at £530 million in December 1874, of which £391 million represented the deposits of English private and joint-stock banks. Until the 'nineties the growth may have been fairly slow, but more reliable figures give

---

[1] Sykes, *op. cit.*, p. 97.   [2] *Ibid.*, pp. 98 and 195; Powell, *op. cit.*, p. 311.

[3] Sykes, *op. cit.*, p. 113.

[4] W. Bagehot, *Economic Studies* (1879, new edn. 1895), p. 81.

[5] Powell, *op. cit.*, p. 431.

[6] *Cf.* Sayers, *op. cit.*, pp. 102-3 and 107-8. Between 1875 and 1914 Lloyds Bank increased the number of its offices from 36 to 879 and of its accounts from 18,292 to 562,434.

the deposits of the English joint-stock and private banks as £560 million at the end of 1896 and £948 million at the end of 1914; by the latter date the total deposits of United Kingdom banks were around £1,200 million.[1]

Thus by the early twentieth century there had come into existence a banking system tapping a bigger proportion of the national cash resources and dominated by a small number of firms whose interests were spread over most of the country. Such a change consolidated the developments that were becoming evident in mid-Victorian times. Size, administrative economy and experience made the larger joint-stock banks practically as safe as the Bank of England. The attraction of a new class of customers encouraged and was assisted by the provision of extra services, such as trustee and executor departments, which began soon after 1900,[2] and it gave the banks new profitable outlets for lending and probably made rather more of the nation's production dependent on the banking system for part of its short-term finance. The great increase in stock exchange business, arising from the rapid spread of incorporation among businesses after 1890, enlarged somewhat another field of lending: much professional speculation, as well as the routine business of brokers and jobbers, made use of bank loans.[3] Other opportunities were provided by the expansion of the commodity exchanges in London, most of whose operators used money borrowed from the banks. Yet despite these bigger outlets at home the increased deposits ensured that ample sums were still available for lending to the bill market, which continued to evolve much as before. With the further consolidation not only of the banks but of business organization generally, the utility of bills of exchange as a means of payment in internal transactions became less and less, and by about 1900 they had almost gone out of use in home trade.[4] So the bill market became more completely international and the province of specialist London houses. The latter borrowed most of their money from the banks, which themselves dealt less in bills; in 1871 the Birmingham and Midland Bank, for

---

[1] Dun, *loc. cit.*, pp. 118-19; Sykes, *op. cit.*, p. 108; Powell, *op. cit.*, p. 674. The figures exclude money lodged with the discount houses. For a general discussion of the growth of deposits and the shortcomings of the published figures see R. P. Higonnet, 'Bank Deposits in the United Kingdom, 1870-1914' in *Quarterly Journal of Economics*, LXXI (1957), 329-67.

[2] W. F. Crick and J. E. Wadsworth, *A Hundred Years of Joint Stock Banking* (1936), pp. 40 and 338; P. W. Matthews and A. W. Tuke, *History of Barclays Bank Limited* (1926), p. 17; Sayers, *op. cit.*, p. 103.

[3] Clapham, *Econ. Hist. of Mod. Brit.*, III, 295.   King, *op. cit.*, pp. 271-5.

instance, had a bill holding four times the amount of its advances, but in 1910 its successor's advances were six times the amount of its bill holding.[1] Probably most of the bills held by the banks by the end of the nineteenth century were what they obtained from the London houses for rediscount.

Nevertheless, the position of the discount houses was becoming a little more difficult. The importance of London as a trading and financial centre was, even in the middle of the nineteenth century, such as to encourage foreign and colonial banks either to appoint agents or establish their own offices there. The great increase of international trade and the eclipse of the rival financial centre of Paris, as a result of the Franco-German War, strengthened this development, and by 1900 the increase in the number of foreign banks and the amount of foreign money desposited in London was having important consequences.[2] One was to facilitate direct written or telegraphic international transfers of credit between different banks without the use of bills of exchange, and this tended to retard the growth in the supply of business available to the discount houses, which in any case were subject to some direct competition from the foreign banks. The introduction in 1877 of a new class of paper, Treasury bills, to meet some of the short-term financial needs of the government, promised to do something to offset the increased competition for international bills, but only in the last decade before 1914 were Treasury bills used at all abundantly.[3] Another influence of the increasing activity of foreign banks in London was to stimulate British joint-stock banks to take a larger direct part in foreign business. From an early stage of their existence many of them had acted as agents for foreign firms and had done some accepting; i.e. they had (in return for a commission) given their guarantee that bills of exchange drawn on their clients would be met when they fell due, thus making the bills more readily discountable. Probably most of their accepting had been done for colonial banks, and it had been only a minor part of the business of English joint-stock banks. In 1905, however, the London City and Midland Bank opened its own foreign exchange department, and others soon followed suit.[4] Before the First World War the share of the British banks in

---

[1] Crick and Wadsworth, *op. cit.*, p. 337.
[2] King, *op. cit.*, pp. 278-9.   [3] *Ibid.*, pp. 276-8.
[4] Crick and Wadsworth, *op. cit.*, p. 39; Powell, *op. cit.*, pp. 388-9; Sayers, *op. cit.*, pp. 60 and 266.

international activity remained small, and the fields on which they were encroaching were mainly those of the London offices of foreign banks and those of the old merchant bankers dealing in foreign exchange and acceptances; but they also constituted the beginning of a threat to the dominance of the London discount houses.[1]

One other result of the attraction of foreign banks to London was further to increase the supply of loanable funds available there; so much so that in one or two years just before the First World War there was even a surplus of foreign money above the advances made on foreign account, helping to swell the amount of credit for home purposes.[2] Such a situation obviously had its dangers, though they were unlikely to be serious as long as London maintained its unquestioned reliability and usefulness as an international financial centre.

The first decade of the twentieth century undoubtedly foreshadowed significant changes in the functions of British banks and in the organization of the money market. But at that time they went no further than a slight modification of the arrangements which had been built up over the preceding half-century. The essence of the system still was that bigger and safer banks went on mobilizing more and more of Britain's cash balances to serve as a credit base, met an increasing part of the demand for short-term finance from trade, building and manufacture at home, and made their remaining loanable funds available to finance not only British foreign trade but a large part of that of other countries, by lending them to the discount market.

At the head of this system stood the Bank of England, its responsibilities greater than ever, since its reserves had to cover not only much larger British deposits but the increased liabilities to foreigners. The Bank having at last recognized its responsibility as guardian of the national reserve and ultimate support of the whole money market, the main economic significance of its subsequent history lay in the means by which it discharged this responsibility and their effectiveness. When Bagehot analysed the position of the Bank of England in 1873 what worried him most, apart from the lack of continuity of direction at the top, was the small size of the reserves in relation to the immensity of British financial commitments.[3] Rather surprisingly,

---

[1] King, *op. cit.*, pp. 280-1.   [2] Clapham, *op. cit.*, III, 293.
[3] Bagehot, *Lombard Street*, chap. XII.

however, especially in view of the great increase in those commitments, a drastic change of policy in this respect never became inescapable. From time to time, especially in the early 'nineties, there was a good deal of discussion of the desirability of bigger reserves, and the great increase thereafter in world gold output, much of which found its way to the London market, made it a simpler matter to increase the amount of the gold reserve in the issue department; whereas the yearly average in 1890 had been under £14 million it was never below £21 million from 1894 to 1914. This in turn facilitated the keeping of a higher average reserve of notes in the banking department.[1] Nevertheless, the Bank continued to operate with much smaller reserves in proportion to its ultimate commitments than was the case with central banks in other countries.

The persistence of this state of affairs was possible because, whatever the absolute size of its reserve, the Bank became much better able to protect it against any prolonged drain. Its chief instrument for this purpose was the variation of Bank rate in order to attract money when required and to influence the supply of credit in the money market as a whole. It was in the 'fifties that there first appeared a policy of frequent changes in the Bank rate in accordance with changing monetary conditions,[2] but for a score of years thereafter such moves were not generally capable of effecting a rapid and decisive change in the state of the market. During the last quarter of the nineteenth century, however, the Bank was able to turn its rate into an effective control over the money market.[3] Various influences contributed to this. The Bank began to adjust its rate more promptly, in anticipation of changing conditions rather than in response to changed market rates, and it was less tempted to delay because, by agreeing to discount for its regular customers at the prevailing market rate and charging the published Bank rate only to the rest of the market, it no longer risked a loss of business by raising Bank rate.[4] Its actions were also more decisive in that, after 1880, with very few exceptions, increases of Bank rate were in steps of one per cent rather than one-half per cent as they had often been before.[5] In addition the Bank helped to make its rate promptly effective by operating on a

---

[1] J. H. Clapham, *The Bank of England: a history* (1944), II, 342-50 and 365-7.

[2] See the complete list of Bank rate changes in *ibid.*, II, 429-32.

[3] King, *op. cit.*, chap. IX.

[4] R. S. Sayers, 'The Development of Central Banking after Bagehot' in *Econ. Hist. Rev.*, 2nd series, IV (1951-2), 114.

[5] Clapham, *Bank of England*, II, 431-2.

larger scale than before in the open market, selling securities or borrowing money against them when it wished to take money off the market in order to support an increased Bank rate in contracting credit. Action of this kind had been used occasionally long before, but it was only from 1873 that it became an established thing.[1] Once the Bank of England had shown itself regularly able to dominate the money market by these means, as it had by the end of the nineteenth century, the maintenance of its leadership and control became easier. The rest of the market came to look on Bank rate as an indicator of the way in which conditions were likely to affect it,[2] and commitments were adjusted more promptly in accordance with changes of Bank rate.

The Bank was able not only to check a drain on its reserves by thus reducing the demand for liquid resources throughout the market, but was also able to reverse it by attracting additional money to London to earn the higher interest that was offered after a rise in Bank rate. Increasingly towards the end of the nineteenth century the extra money to restore the reserves came from abroad.[3] This was the combined result of the increased floating balances that were available in foreign countries as their banking systems grew, of London's dominant position in international finance as a centre where loans were always being raised for transmission overseas and a profitable use could always be found for spare money, and of the safety of deposits in London; there was no danger either of assets proving illiquid when it was necessary to draw on them or of any capital loss through the depreciation of the exchange. By the years just preceding the First World War the restoration of the reserves by the attraction of money from external sources had become almost automatic. A little earlier the process could be, and was, supplemented by other devices, such as direct measures by the Bank to attract gold from the bullion market,[4] or the arrangement of extra loans or deposits from particular customers who had come to recognize that the strengthening of the Bank's position was in the general interest of the money market. Fundamentally, the Bank was learning how to utilize the strength and stability of Britain's position in international trade and finance in order to safeguard both itself and the whole money market through all the foreseeable ups and downs of business. The more

---

[1] Clapham, *Bank of England*, II, 295-7.   [2] Sayers, *loc. cit.*, p. 115.
[3] *Ibid.*, pp. 113-14 and 116.
[4] R. S. Sayers, *Bank of England Operations 1890-1914* (1936) chap. IV.

successful it became in doing so, the less concern needed to be felt about the absolute amount of its reserves.

Even by the 'eighties the question of the Bank's reserves was being replaced in the forefront of financial discussion by concern about the nature of the monetary standard. Since 1816 Britain had been nominally, and since 1821, actually on the gold standard, its silver coins from then on being legal tender only for sums up to £2. Both its principal circulating coinage and the metallic reserves of the Bank of England, on which the whole credit structure was based, consisted of gold. But for much of the nineteenth century many other countries used either silver alone or both silver and gold as standard money. This divergence of practice caused international difficulty only rarely before 1873, as the ratio between the values of gold and silver remained practically constant. After that, however, the monetary demand for gold increased as several countries, led by Germany, adopted the gold standard, while the output of new gold from the world's mines rose only slowly; and for silver the conditions of both demand and supply changed in the opposite direction. Gold rose and silver fell in value and the relation of gold to silver currencies began to change continuously.[1] In Britain this led to much public controversy about whether the gold standard should be replaced by a bimetallic one. Those who favoured the change argued that the rise in the value of gold was the main cause of the persistent fall in commodity prices, which filled businessmen with gloom; that the contrary movement of gold and silver values was hampering trade between gold standard and silver standard countries, so much so that if Britain did not give a lead by monetizing silver all countries would, for convenience, adopt the gold standard and thereby aggravate the existing scarcity and high price of gold; and that India had its importing capacity restricted and its administrative difficulties increased by the necessity to make external payments in gold while its taxes and internal transactions were paid in money based on the less valuable silver.[2] These arguments never went unchallenged. Some contended that the general price fall could be explained simply by the conditions of production and transport of commodities.[3] Others reinforced this by claiming that a scarcity of

---

[1] *Final Report of the R.C. on recent changes in the relative values of the precious metals (P.P.* 1888, XLV), pp. 2 and 6.

[2] The main features of the Indian currency situation before 1893 are summarized in J. M. Keynes, *Indian Currency and Finance* (1913), pp. 1-3.

[3] e.g. Wells, *Recent Economic Changes*, pp. 122-89.

gold did not mean a scarcity and high price of money in gold standard countries, as a larger credit structure was being built on the gold base.[1] Even the effects of Indian conditions were not all certain, for Britain was expanding its exports there.

With so much unproved, a change in the monetary standard was not very likely. The gold standard had worked satisfactorily in Britain for a long time and officials had no wish to replace it except in return for large and certain benefits. The Bank of England, which must have been closely concerned in any change, never paid much attention to the silver question.[2] And a Royal Commission split evenly for and against bimetallism.[3] In such circumstances the controversy was left more or less to settle itself. India's difficulties were met by ceasing the free coinage of silver in 1893 and completing the transition to a gold exchange standard in 1899. By the late 'eighties a small stream of gold was coming from the new South African fields, and ten years later it was a larger stream supplemented by new supplies from Colorado, the Yukon and Australia. The nations of the world one after another adopted a gold standard, as the bimetallists had foretold, but instead of aggravating a scarcity they made use of what might otherwise soon have become an embarrassing flood of gold. With the adherence of Russia and Japan to the gold standard in 1897 it became practically a world-wide system, only China among the larger countries still clinging to a silver standard for nearly forty years more. From the middle 'nineties bimetallism was a dead subject outside the U.S.A.[4]

For roughly a score of years before the First World War, gold was acting as the basis of what was practically a world-wide currency system. Nearly all countries gave their currency the value of a fixed quantity of gold and used gold ultimately as the basis of their credit arrangements. They recognized as their foremost financial duty the

[1] e.g. A. J. Wilson, *Reciprocity, Bimetallism and Land Tenure Reform* (1880), pp. 116-19, and many later writers. The argument may not be strictly true. Though the scarcity of gold was accompanied by falling interest rates, which meant that loanable money was cheaper, not dearer as it should have been if gold shortage was keeping down its supply, this might be explicable by changes in the demand for money. Moreover, for Britain the apparent steady expansion of bank deposits irrespective of the scarcity or otherwise of gold may be a statistical illusion caused by the increased coverage of the published figures towards the end of the nineteenth century. (Higonnet, *loc. cit.*, pp. 329-31.)

[2] Clapham, *Bank of England*, pp. 300 and 312-14.

[3] *Final Report of the R.C. on . . . precious metals*, pp. 83-91 and 94-104.

[4] For a summary account of the spread of the gold standard see J. B. Condliffe, *The Commerce of Nations* (1951), pp. 360-8.

regulation of their currency and credit in such a way that over a period of years they could balance their international payments without their money departing by more than a small fraction from its par value in gold. To the maintenance of this international trading and financial equilibrium on a basis of fixed exchange rates they each contributed in ways that varied in accordance with their economic circumstances and institutional arrangements. But, since most of them effected far more of their international transactions in sterling than in any other foreign currency, the condition of sterling and of the London money market was a major influence on the process. Indeed, it is probably true to say that the market for sterling (including the market for sterling acceptances and discounts) counted for more than the international gold market in the working of the international gold standard. Thus the credit policies of London were of much more than national significance. They were shaped by the impact of world-wide conditions and were world-wide in their repercussions.

Since fiscal methods had little part in the regulation of British trade, the maintenance of equilibrium in London was not primarily the responsibility of the government but of the Bank of England. The direct concern of the Bank was nothing so grand as the preservation of the financial health of Britain in particular and the world in general; it was simply the regulation of the price of credit to the minimum extent necessary to protect its reserve. But ultimately much more was involved. The procedure could be effective only if changes in the price of credit brought about changes in the prices and the volume of sales and purchases of goods and services, until the demand for sterling and the supply of it were equalized. And this chain of causation did not operate just as a matter of course.

The first necessity was for the Bank of England to become capable of imposing its credit policy on the London money market as a whole. This was achieved in the late nineteenth century in ways that have already been discussed, and its influence was supplemented by greater coherence in some of the chief foreign money markets, which made possible a more uniform and predictable response to changes in dealings with London. The second necessity was that a large proportion of business (and especially that directly engaged in international trade or heavily dependent on the use of imported materials) should be carried on with borrowed money and thus forced to reduce its buying orders if interest rates rose and tempted to increase them if interest rates fell. Even in the early twentieth century there were large numbers of British businesses that were financed without recourse to the banks or the discount market, but they must have been a smaller proportion than in the recent past. And, in any case, since imports entered to such an exceptional degree into British consumption, the fact that international trade was conducted on credit was bound to spread the effect of monetary influences throughout business. Importers and exporters depended on continual service from acceptance and discount houses. The prices of many of the chief articles of international trade (especially certain bulk foodstuffs and raw materials) had to be settled mainly on the commodity exchanges of London,[1] where business was transacted almost entirely with money borrowed in the market. Thus, when the price of credit rose it immediately became difficult or impossible for merchants or speculators to carry the same volume of business as before, and to some extent the same situation affected the market for securities and the promotion and underwriting of long-term loans. The third necessity was that changes in the volume of orders should quickly lead to changes in the prices of goods. In this respect there was great variety because of differences in the organization of different trades and industries and in their ability to withstand a spell of reduced earnings. But the markets for many of the largest items of international trade were almost perfectly competitive because of the multiplicity and dispersion of the suppliers and the concentration of a constant flow of telegraphed information about them in one or two centres of exchange. And even in trades where prices were inclined to be sticky, they usually became responsive after a time, because an initial reduction of demand was multiplied by the effect of reduced business activity in reducing the incomes available for spending.

Thus, although Britain was not a perfectly integrated collection of perfect markets, the interconnexions of its business life by 1900 were manifold and close enough, both internally and externally, for the manipulation of credit policy to do its intended work fairly quickly and effectively. Without such conditions the economic influence of the London money market, nationally and internationally, must have been much less, and the combination of order, stability and economic expansion, which came to be regarded as characteristic of the

[1] The development and working of these exchanges are described in S. W. Dowling, *The Exchanges of London* (1929).

pre-1914 international gold standard, could not have been achieved.[1] The system was not without its drawbacks. For many foreign countries it meant that their financial situation was to some extent at the mercy of decisions made in London in which they had no say. But the advantages of being able to use such large and trustworthy international banking services were so great that there were few attempts to break away and create fuller national alternatives to the London market; and the fact that restrictions emanating from London were imposed not by a government but by a private institution, directed by internationally minded merchants and merchant bankers,[2] removed most of the political sting that might have attached to the arrangement. For Britain the chief drawbacks of relying on credit variations within a system of fixed exchange rates to maintain economic equilibrium were the frequency of cost fluctuations and the somewhat indiscriminate contractions of orders (and therefore of employment and incomes) imposed on home business by decisions which were not based solely on home economic conditions. These disadvantages were mitigated because, as the Bank of England became more experienced, it sometimes deliberately shielded home business; thus it did not always seek to correct a slight foreign drain if it could see a probability that this would reverse itself before long, and sometimes it protected itself mainly by operations in the gold market so as to avoid disturbing interest rates at home.[3] Above all, the general long-term expansion of trade was usually working to overcome quickly the discomforts brought by temporary contractions of credit and made it easier to keep fluctuations within quite modest limits. Discomforts there were, and the financial system might have been less unquestioned if most of those who suffered the worst of them had been better informed and politically stronger; but, in general, it seems unlikely that home business conditions were seriously the worse because credit policy was rooted in international considerations.

The advantages to Britain of the international system in which the London money market played so great a part were considerable. Most obvious, of course, were the profits earned internationally by the various types of financial institution in the City of London.

[1] For a fuller, though still simplified, account of the process of maintaining equilibrium see Condliffe, *op. cit.*, chap. XII, esp. pp. 389-400.

[2] Joint-stock and private deposit bankers were not eligible to become directors of the Bank of England.

[3] Sayers, *op. cit.*, pp. 125-7; King, *op. cit.*, p. 315.

Nobody can make more than an approximate guess at the amount of these, but, though a useful, they can never have been more than a minor, element in the balance-of-payments surplus.[1] The great benefit was the indirect one that came from the creation of conditions of confidence and stability in international transactions and from ensuring that, whenever worth while economic opportunities appeared in the international field, finance would be available to make it possible to grasp them. No country stood to gain so much as Britain from these conditions, because of its exceptional dependence on international dealings for a living. And if they had not been created by the activity of the British economy in general and the organization of the London money market in particular they could not have been made nearly so complete or nearly so smooth-working. That is the economic justification for the peculiar international character of Britain's financial system.

Certain links between the state of the money market and of the long-term capital market can readily be traced, as, too, can certain parallels between their respective organizational histories in the late nineteenth century. Both, for instance, grew in scale and scope to such an extent that a far larger proportion of business finance passed through their organized institutions; both were more completely equipped to deal with international than with the full range of home demands. The timing of long-term investment was directly affected by conditions in the money market. A contraction of credit, inducing a contraction of business, was a disincentive to undertake new long-term commitments and, in any case, when high interest could be earned on short-term lending in the money market many types of long-term project were bound to look less attractive. Moreover, issuing houses, underwriters and stockbrokers were all to some extent dependent on borrowed money and therefore liable to contract their business when credit was tightened. But, though all these links affected the magnitude as well as the timing of fluctuations in long-term investment, its general level and direction over a substantial period were dependent mainly on other influences. British banks were seldom willing to reduce their liquidity in the slightest by investing in securities other than those for which a ready and predictable market

---

[1] *Cf.* the estimation of the profits of foreign trade and services, insurance, brokerage and commissions (which include a high proportion of non-financial activities) in Imlah, *Economic Elements in the* Pax Britannica, pp. 70-5.

existed at all times.[1] Consequently, the vast sums mobilized by the money market made only a small direct contribution to the creation of fixed capital. Long-term investment came from other sources and through other channels.

It is a familiar story that much of British industry in the nineteenth century was financed out of the personal savings of those who owned and managed the business, their borrowings from relatives and acquaintances, and the ploughing back of a large proportion of the profits. The formal institutions of an impersonal capital market served only a few businesses before the eighteen-fifties. The London stock exchange was small and dominated by dealings in government securities, though railway shares were rapidly growing in importance in the 'forties; and provincial stock exchanges were only just beginning to appear. Firms which made a business of the public issue of new securities were few in number and knew little of home industry. Chief among them were the merchant bankers in London, such as Rothschilds and Barings, who in the course of their business as acceptors, foreign exchange dealers and financial agents were able to acquire a great knowledge of international financial conditions and the creditworthiness of foreign borrowers, especially governments who were their customers. There was nothing comparable to serve as a regular intermediary between home business and the public. Except for railways, docks, public utilities, banks and insurance companies, few enterprises at home sought capital from the public; and consequently the man who had accumulated considerable savings but had no business of his own usually had only a narrow range of publicized investment opportunities confronting him. Nevertheless, the tiny proportion of firms that sought investment from the public was responsible for a large part of the formation of new fixed capital.

From the eighteen-sixties onwards the facilities of the capital market were rapidly enlarged. The changes in company law between 1855 and 1862 made incorporation with limited liability available to any firm of more than six partners which was willing to comply with a set of not very onerous conditions, and thus removed one of the obstacles to a public issue of shares. The size of the stock markets and the variety of securities publicly dealt in grew steadily; the London stock exchange, which had 1,100 members in 1864 reached

---

[1] It was, however, by no means unknown for banks to make a few long loans to assist customers in the purchase of fixed capital. For some late-nineteenth-century examples see Sayers, *Lloyds Bank*, pp. 95-6.

a peak membership of 5,567 in 1905, when steps were taken to reduce it.[1] The services of more new issue houses were also available. The most notable augmentation came from the increased numbers of merchant bankers who settled in London in the middle of the nineteenth century and many of whom undertook the public flotation of stock and bond issues.[2] Clearly this was a development likely to reinforce the earlier bias of the capital market towards foreign investment, but there were some influences modifying this. Before the end of the century merchant bankers were occasionally undertaking large home issues; Barings, for instance, were responsible for floating Guiness's, the brewers, as a public company in 1886.[3] And from the 'sixties onwards there had been emerging a number of firms and individuals—finance companies and financial agents— whose job it was to arrange for the conversion of existing businesses into companies and for the disposal of their shares, usually by private arrangements. Many, perhaps most, of these firms were ephemeral, but new ones were continually appearing to replace the old, and a few made a sustained contribution to business finance.[4] In another way, too, it was made easier to increase the number of security issues, both foreign and home. This was through the practice of underwriting. Earlier a promoter or issuing house had either acted as a pure intermediary, performing a service for a commission and bearing no loss if the securities could not be sold, or committed his own resources and those of his associates by buying all or part of the loan outright for resale to the public. In the late 'seventies or 'eighties it became much commoner (though not universal) for arrangements to be made in advance for a number of individuals or firms to underwrite an issue; i.e. each would guarantee to take a stated amount of securities if they remained unsold after the public issue. Underwriters, of course, charged a commission for this service, varying widely in accordance with the estimated risk of the issue being a failure. Trust and finance companies, some of the banks and insurance companies, and a variety of financiers all participated in this kind of business.[5] By spreading the risks of security issues so much more widely, issuing houses were in a position to undertake more

---

[1] Clapham, *Econ. Hist. of Mod. Brit.*, II, 325 and III, 295.

[2] For an account of these firms see Jenks, *The Migration of British Capital to 1875*, pp. 267-71.

[3] Clapham, *op. cit.*, III, 210.   [4] *Ibid.*, II, 360-1 and III, 206-7.

[5] *Ibid.*, III, 207-10; Cairncross, *Home and Foreign Investment 1870-1913*, pp. 91-3; F. Lavington, *The English Capital Market* (1921), pp. 183-4.

business than they could have done with comparable resources in earlier conditions.

Not only did it become possible, as a result of these various developments, for a much greater number of firms to seek capital from the general public, but other simultaneous changes were helping to make investment opportunities better known and more attractive to a somewhat larger section of the public than before. Financial journalism was probably better informed, as well as more copious, by the end of the nineteenth century than it had been in its first great burst of expansion in the eighteen-forties. Much more news of financial affairs was provided for the general newspaper reader and from the 'eighties there was the powerful reinforcement of the specialist dailies, the *Financial News* and the *Financial Times*. Publicity was also strengthened by the activities of the advertisement houses who were employed to distribute the prospectuses of many new issues.[1]

Changes were made in the character of shares, partly with the object of attracting different classes of investor. Shares of high nominal amount (£10 or more, often much more) only part paid up, which were usual before 1866, saddled the investor with an emergency liability beyond the amount of his actual investment, and by the 'seventies were being thought by some observers to act as a deterrent to many middle-class investors.[2] In the 'eighties and 'nineties they were abandoned by most companies which had still clung to them and, except in banking and insurance, the fully-paid share of £1 to £5 nominal value was established as normal.[3] Thus the man of only moderate wealth was given certainty that his limited liability really was limited in practice and he found it rather easier to spread his investments among several companies. And for others, both individuals and institutions, to whom a safe and steady return was more desirable than the chance of a high one, there were at the end of the nineteenth century increasing proportions of preference shares and debenture stock among the securities on offer.

Yet it is doubtful whether all these changes did more than modify the capital market without altering its fundamental characteristics. The investing public certainly widened but it remained a very small

[1] Lavington, *op. cit.*, p. 184.
[2] J. B. Jefferys, 'The Denomination and Character of Shares, 1855-1885' in Carus-Wilson, *Essays in Economic History*, pp. 344 and 352.
[3] *Ibid.*, pp. 344 and 354-6.

proportion of the total population.[1] Though the working classes, whose response to exhortations to thrift had caused so much disappointment before 1860, saved much more thereafter, through friendly societies, building societies, industrial assurance companies and savings banks, the total amount involved was too small to have more than negligible influence on the national supply of capital.[2] And even the smaller middle-class capitalists, owning up to £1,000 of property, made little contribution to the market for securities, except indirectly through their payments to insurance companies.[3]

On the other side, despite the growth and elaboration of the institutions of the capital market, a large part of the capital needed for domestic purposes continued to be raised by a variety of means which by-passed those formal institutions. The initial capital for new industrial companies operating in Britain was usually raised from their own directors and their personal acquaintances and business contacts. Only rarely did such companies begin with a public issue to be quoted on a stock exchange and even then it was more often a provincial than a London quotation. Once they had become established they were more likely, by the beginning of the twentieth century, to use a public issue as one means of enlarging their capital, but for most firms it was not the most important means.[4] It has indeed been estimated that in the particularly active period 1911-13 the organized capital market was not raising more than £45 million a year for old and new undertakings in England and Wales (other than public authorities and railways), although the total new issues in London alone averaged £200 million annually.[5] For most home businesses other than the largest the cost of raising capital through an issue of shares to the public was usually higher than they could afford;[6] and it was commonly not very difficult to obtain capital in other ways. Though the capital needs of most types of business were growing, they often did not much outpace the family

---

[1] Cairncross, *op. cit.*, pp. 84-5.

[2] For the development of one of the main forms of working-class saving see H. O. Horne, *A History of Savings Banks* (1947), esp. the figures on pp. 388-9 and 392, which illustrate the more rapid growth from the last third of the nineteenth century.

[3] Cairncross, *op. cit.*, pp. 86-8.   [4] *Ibid.*, pp. 95-7.

[5] *Ibid.*, p. 97; Lavington, *op. cit.*, pp. 194 and 202-5. British railways at this time were raising only £2 mn. a year in London. (*Ibid.*, p. 277.) The proportionate share of home industry in the capital raised by the organized market may not in other years have been quite so small, as 1911-13 was an outstanding boom period in foreign investment.

[6] Cairncross, *op. cit.*, pp. 100-1; Lavington, *op. cit.*, pp. 218-19.

fortunes of their owners before 1914, and informal channels of investment were unlikely to become obsolete as long as wealth was so highly concentrated that any businessman could tell who in his locality were potential investors of substantial amounts.[1] Sometimes, too, the need for capital was reduced by the extension of trade credit; in extreme cases payment for fixed capital, such as machinery or ships, might be spread over several years.[2]

The modifications in the capital market, though less profound than might at first appear, did, however, make a useful contribution to the maintenance of a substantial volume of new investment. The number of people rich enough to be able to save significant amounts was steadily growing, and the proportion of them who had a business or landed estate of their own, in which they could employ their savings, was declining. The changes in the capital market made it much easier for them to find a productive outlet for any savings that they chose to make. Likewise, these changes ensured that the small minority who were convinced that they had an effective use for more capital, which they were unable to raise privately, could always, at a price, gain the notice of the saving public. But changes in the organization of the market could by themselves do no more than prevent the frustration of decisions to save or to invest, which might arise from a lack of suitable channels between savers and long-term borrowers. They could not directly persuade people to increase their savings as their incomes rose, or persuade businessmen to use more capital as trade expanded.

Some earlier estimates, indeed, suggested that the rate at which the national stock of capital increased fell off markedly in the late nineteenth century while these institutional improvements were continuing.[3] Some slowing down there almost certainly was, in comparison with the rapid augmentation made by the mid-Victorians, though it is impossible to say precisely how much, since direct evidence about net additions to capital is very incomplete. Most of the figures are tentative and subject to a considerable margin of error, but

---

[1] Cairncross, *op. cit.*, p. 102.

[2] Practice in regard to credit varied enormously and no one has ever elucidated it in anything like full detail. For some specific examples see Lavington, *op. cit.*, pp. 263-9.

[3] e.g. the figures given by Douglas (*Journ. of Econ. and Business Hist.*, II, 683) show an increase of 48 per cent between 1865 and 1885 in U.K. capital per head of population, but only 28 per cent between 1885 and 1909. The difference arose partly because Mr Douglas excluded housing from his definition of capital and there was a housing boom in the 'nineties.

G

they indicate fairly clearly that the very high proportion of income saved in the years 1870-74 (which reached a peak of nearly 17 per cent in 1872) was never equalled again and seldom approached. But, though a somewhat lower rate of savings was established by the mid-seventies and there were appreciable short-period fluctuations in it, no continuous downward trend emerged thereafter; in fact, in the early years of the twentieth century the opposite was true, and it is estimated that in all but two of the last nine prewar years more than one-eighth of the net national product was used for net capital formation.[1] It is also to be borne in mind that the national income was growing rapidly in the late nineteenth century and so, even though a rather smaller proportion of it was saved, it was possible to go on increasing the absolute amount of new investment. Moreover, when the level of savings fluctuated the associated swings in the volume of investment were much more pronounced in the foreign capital market than they were in domestic capital formation, as may be seen from Table IX.

TABLE IX

U.K. Average Annual Net Investment, 1870-1913, at constant (1912-13) prices

Years	Net domestic capital formation (£ mn.)	Net lending abroad (£ mn.)	Total net investment (£ mn.)
1870-74	81	65	146
1875-79	77	28	105
1880-84	96	63	159
1885-89	85	100	185
1890-94	84	78	162
1895-99	169	54	223
1900-04	174	46	220
1905-09	127	138	265
1910-13	128	202	330

Thus it was possible to maintain a fairly steady growth in the amount of capital used within the United Kingdom. The wealthier people, on whom investment depended, may have been using their

[1] For detailed figures and notes on their sources and methods of compilation see the appendix to this chapter.

wealth rather more for their immediate ease than their fathers had done, but this was no thriftless age. Quite apart from the vast increase in assets abroad, the importance of which in Britain's unique economy has already been emphasized, the amount of domestic capital per occupied person must have been at least half as much again in 1914 as it was in 1870, and probably more. That was in itself a substantial contribution to a transformation of productive methods, a greater efficiency of business, and a more comfortable material condition of society.

Annual Estimates of Investment, 1870-1913

MUCH more is now known about the amount of investment in this period, and about its relation to the size of the national income, than was the case a few years ago. Nevertheless, it is unlikely that any investigator would claim to have achieved more than a reasonable approximation; and there is some doubt whether the best independent estimates of the different constituent items have all been brought together.

The most comprehensive and useful recent estimates are those given in J. B. Jefferys and Dorothy Walters, *National Income and Expenditure of the United Kingdom, 1870-1952* (1956). There are, however, three particular points of doubt about these figures. The most serious concerns the estimates of net lending abroad, which the authors took from Cairncross, *Home and Foreign Investment*, p. 180. Professor Cairncross's estimates do not fit in very well with estimates of the accumulated total of British foreign investments at different dates. A better fit is given by a more recent series, set out in Imlah, *Economic Elements in the* Pax Britannica, pp. 72-5. The latter series, which is consistently higher, also has the merit of being based on the examination of a wider range of relevant items, and seems likely to be more reliable than those hitherto used.

The second point of doubt concerns the figures of net domestic capital formation, but here it is much more difficult to suggest appropriate changes. The figures given in Jefferys and Walters, *op. cit.*, were derived ultimately from estimates in Cairncross, *op. cit.*, which covered only residential building, shipbuilding, railways and local authority expenditure. Dr Jefferys and Miss Walters worked on the assumption that in every year from 1870 to 1913 these partial estimates bore the same relationship to total gross domestic capital formation as they were known to have done in 1907. But this appears rather unlikely. The discussion of industrial changes in Chapter Four above suggests, for example, that industrial plant (one of the excluded items) must have been a lower proportion of the total before the late 'nineties. Furthermore, the estimates make no allowance for changes in agricultural capital, which cannot be calculated with any accuracy. The abundant descriptive evidence, however, suggests some failure (*c.* 1880-1900) to make good all the physical deterioration of reproducible agricultural capital. Thus, unless there is some offsetting factor (as there may be, for instance, in the uncertainty about the appropriate allowance to make for depreciation) it seems probable that the estimates of net domestic capital formation are somewhat too high in the late nineteenth century.

Dr Jefferys and Miss Walters themselves drew attention to the third doubtful point: the discrepancy (particularly noticeable in the earlier years) between their estimates of national income and those of national expenditure. This discrepancy is slightly increased if Professor Imlah's figures of net lending abroad are substituted for those which they used. They suggested (*op. cit.*, p. 10) that the actual figure of net national product was somewhere between the income and the expenditure estimates, probably much nearer the former than the latter.

In view of these doubtful points, and in the absence of any comprehensive reinvestigation of the whole subject of national income and investment, it seemed worth while to consider how the figures given in Jefferys and Walters, *op. cit.*, would appear if they were modified in the directions that seemed most appropriate, on the balance of the evidence. The figures in Table X show the results of such an experiment. Three changes were introduced into the series set out by Dr Jefferys and Miss Walters: (1) Professor Imlah's figures of net lending abroad were substituted for those of Professor Cairncross. (2) The figures for net domestic capital formation were reduced by 2 per cent from 1870 to 1879, 3 per cent from 1880 to 1889, 2 per cent from 1890 to 1894 and 1 per cent from 1895 to 1899: if adjustment in this direction is needed it could hardly be less, unless it is to be regarded as utterly negligible; possibly it should be appreciably more. (3) The figure for net national product was raised (or, in a few years, lowered) by an amount equal to 25 per cent of the difference between the income and expenditure estimates, the latter having been revised in accordance with the altered figures for net investment.

It should be emphasized that no precise validity can be attached to these figures for any particular year. They do not result from any new enquiry into national income and investment; they merely show the results of applying certain probable (or plausible) assumptions to

TABLE X

National Income and Investment, annually at current prices, 1870-1913

Year	Net domestic capital formation (£ mn. at current prices)	Net lending abroad (£ mn. at current prices)	Total net investment (£ mn. at current prices)	Net national product at factor cost (£ mn. at current prices)	Net domestic capital formation as percentage of net national product	Net lending abroad as percentage of net national product	Total net investment as percentage of net national product
1870	69·5	44·1	113·6	987	7·0	4·5	11·5
1871	85·1	71·3	156·4	1,053	8·1	6·8	14·9
1872	90·7	98·0	188·7	1,117	8·0	8·8	16·8
1873	114·0	81·3	195·3	1,202	9·5	6·8	16·3
1874	94·6	70·9	165·5	1,197	7·9	5·9	13·8
1875	61·7	51·3	113·0	1,146	5·4	4·5	9·9
1876	85·4	23·2	108·6	1,147	7·5	2·0	9·5
1877	94·9	13·1	108·0	1,153	8·2	1·1	9·3
1878	80·1	16·9	97·0	1,129	7·1	1·5	8·6
1879	56·2	35·5	91·7	1,072	5·2	3·3	8·5
1880	99·7	35·6	135·3	1,146	8·7	3·1	11·8
1881	97·5	65·7	163·2	1,177	8·3	5·6	13·9
1882	101·0	58·7	159·7	1,218	8·4	4·8	13·2
1883	88·9	48·8	138·7	1,242	7·2	3·9	11·1
1884	47·6	72·3	119·9	1,195	4·0	6·1	10·1
1885	47·1	62·3	109·4	1,173	4·0	5·3	9·3
1886	53·1	78·9	132·0	1,186	4·5	6·7	11·2
1887	60·2	87·7	147·9	1,220	5·0	7·2	12·2
1888	84·2	91·9	176·1	1,295	6·5	7·1	13·6
1889	97·2	80·9	178·1	1,372	7·1	5·9	13·0
1890	89·8	98·5	188·3	1,432	6·3	6·9	13·2
1891	59·8	69·4	129·2	1,424	4·2	4·9	9·1
1892	53·3	59·1	112·4	1,401	3·8	4·2	8·0
1893	48·7	53·0	101·7	1,373	3·5	3·9	7·4
1894	83·7	38·7	122·4	1,415	5·9	2·7	8·6
1895	99·2	40·0	139·2	1,473	6·7	2·7	9·4
1896	94·2	56·8	151·0	1,508	6·2	3·8	10·0
1897	119·7	41·6	161·3	1,557	7·7	2·7	10·4
1898	160·0	22·9	182·9	1,638	9·8	1·4	11·2
1899	174·3	42·4	216·7	1,719	10·1	2·5	12·6
1900	188·4	37·9	226·3	1,817	10·4	2·1	12·5
1901	143·8	33·9	177·7	1,782	8·1	1·9	10·0
1902	159·7	33·3	193·0	1,801	8·9	1·8	10·7
1903	129·2	44·8	174·0	1,769	7·3	2·5	9·8
1904	144·9	51·7	196·6	1,798	8·0	2·9	10·9
1905	158·4	81·5	239·9	1,877	8·4	4·3	12·7
1906	166·5	117·5	284·0	1,993	8·4	5·9	14·3
1907	139·2	154·1	293·3	2,084	6·7	7·4	14·1
1908	32·4	154·7	187·1	1,966	1·6	7·9	9·5
1909	93·1	135·6	228·7	2,016	4·6	6·7	11·3
1910	107·3	167·3	274·6	2,111	5·1	8·0	13·1
1911	108·6	196·9	305·5	2,192	5·0	9·0	14·0
1912	137·8	197·1	334·9	2,321	5·9	8·5	14·4
1913	147·9	224·3	372·2	2,425	6·1	9·2	15·3

data already familiarized by use. If they are averaged out over periods of several years they ought to give a reasonable quantitative picture of the most probable state of affairs. Such averages have been set out in Table IX on p. 184. The investment figures there have been reduced to a constant price-level by means of the capital-goods price index in Jefferys and Walters, *op. cit.*, p. 39, and the totals are directly comparable with those in *ibid.*, Table VI.

The figures given here do not present a fundamentally different account of the course of investment from that in other recent studies, but they do suggest some slight modifications. In particular, they indicate that in late Victorian times rather more of the national income was invested than was formerly thought to be the case and they also emphasize more than ever the importance of investment abroad. If the higher estimates of saving and investment are wrong it seems probable that this must be due to the over-estimate of domestic investment.

For further information and comparison see Jefferys and Walters, *op. cit.*, E. H. Phelps Brown and S. J. Handfield-Jones, 'The Climacteric of the 1890s' in *Oxford Economic Papers* (New Series), IV (1952), and E. H. Phelps Brown and B. Weber, 'Accumulation, Productivity and Distribution in the British Economy, 1870-1938' in *Econ. Journ.*, LXIII (1953).

CHAPTER EIGHT

Labour

THE background of population changes, which are the strongest immediate determinant of the total supply of labour, has already been sketched.[1] There were downward trends in the rates of general mortality from about 1870, of births from about 1880, and of infant mortality from about 1900. The combined result of these trends was to slow down the natural increase of the population after 1880, while still keeping it high enough to cause a large absolute expansion of numbers, and to begin, about 1890, a gradual increase in the proportion of people in the most economically productive age groups. These were conditions which could be expected to provide plentiful labour for an expanding economy and, in the last twenty years before 1914, opportunities either to expand more rapidly or to give more attention to increasing the comfort and amenity of life.

Two influences in particular modified the changes in total labour supply which demographic factors made possible. One was the increase in the opportunities of migration. Improvements in transport, the opening up of vast areas overseas with a capacity for absorbing huge numbers of extra workers, and the general stimulus of Britain's great involvement in international and imperial affairs, all helped to make emigration a practical attraction for hundreds of thousands of Britons, even while their condition at home was a good deal better than desperate. The United States in the 'eighties and Canada in the early years of the twentieth century presented specially great attractions. Just how much effect this had on Britain's labour supply is uncertain because emigration statistics, which in any case have many imperfections, refer to the United Kingdom as a whole and are thus heavily weighted by the Irish exodus. It is clear that emigration from the British Isles reached a new peak (estimated at 256,000 people a year) in the 'eighties, declined in the next decade, returned after 1900 to its previous absolute maximum (though not to

---

[1] See Chap. Two, pp. 40-2 above.

as high a level in proportion to population), and was highest of all in the last three years of peace, when the average was 464,000 a year.[1] It is also fairly certain that, except during the recession of the 'nineties, the proportion of Irish in this movement, though still high, was appreciably less than it had been earlier.[2] In the whole period 1870-1914 Britain must have been losing more by emigration than before, not only absolutely but, at least until about 1890, proportionately to its total population; and there is much evidence to suggest that in this period the loss was qualitatively reinforced by an increase in the proportion of young adults among the emigrants.[3]

Large as the outflow was, it was not such as to make a crucial difference to labour supply. For one thing, part of it was offset by immigration to the United Kingdom. The biggest element in this latter movement probably consisted of former emigrants who had decided to come back home,[4] but from the 'eighties onwards there was an increased influx from Europe, especially of Polish and some other Jews, afflicted by the revival of anti-Semitism. This made an appreciable difference to the labour market and social life of a few districts in London, Manchester and Leeds, though it was insufficient to have much more general economic influence.[5] On balance, however, the immigration was only a minor item to set against the emigration, and between 1871 and 1911 Great Britain experienced a net loss of 1,950,000 persons by migration. What reduced this to no more than a modifying influence was the fact that natural increase in the same period was about nine times this figure. For England alone the importance of emigration was less than for Britain as a whole, since it is highly probable that a smaller proportion of the English moved overseas than of the Welsh and Scots, and certain that England had a net inflow of population from Wales and Scotland.[6] Even the preponderance of young adults among emigrants was not unduly serious, as this group was in any case becoming relatively more numerous at home. Perhaps in the long run the most influential feature of the emigration was the disproportionately large number of men who departed, which, by upsetting the sex ratio in the population

---

[1] B. Thomas, *Migration and Economic Growth* (1954), p. 57.

[2] *Ibid.*, pp. 64-7 and 75. [3] *Ibid.*, pp. 56-8.

[4] *Report of the R.C. on Population* (1949), p. 16.

[5] Clapham, *Econ. Hist. of Mod. Brit.*, III, 449-51; V. D. Lipman, *Social Histor of the Jews in England 1850-1950* (1954), chap. V.

[6] *Report of the R.C. on Population*, p. 16.

at home, reduced women's chances of marriage, contributed to a long-term decline in the rate of population growth, and stimulated demands for new types of female employment.[1]

Apart from migration, the other chief modifying influence on labour supply was in the extent to which it was found necessary for all members of families, other than mere infants, to seek employment. The late nineteenth century was marked by several influences promoting change in this respect. The increasing complexity of social, economic and political life, with its demands for rather more training, made it appropriate to keep children longer at school, and such a development was backed up by changes in the law. And a widespread rise in the level of personal incomes made it easier for more families to keep their children off the labour market up to a higher age and, to a less extent, reduced the proportion of married women who found it essential to work for a wage.[2] It was mainly for these reasons that the increased proportion of people in what have now come to be conventionally regarded as the working age groups (15 to 64) was not accompanied by an increase in the occupied proportion of the total population. Of the persons aged 10 and upwards in England and Wales 57·8 per cent were engaged in occupations in 1881 and also in 1891, 56·6 per cent in 1901 and 57·1 per cent in 1911.[3] The first use made of more favourable demographic conditions was to provide the country with a less uneducated populace and a little more leisure rather than to increase the proportion of workers.

The outcome of these various influences was that the occupied population of England and Wales increased from 10·3 million in 1871 to 16·3 million in 1911.[4] Whether such figures represent in even approximate measure the increase in labour power depends on many factors, among which one of the most important is the extent to which workers were kept fully occupied. The available statistics do not indicate any clear change in this respect. The trade union figures of the percentage of members unemployed had a somewhat higher average in the late 'seventies and the 'eighties than in the third quarter of the century, and the 'corrected' percentage for 1879

[1] *Report of the R.C. on Population*, pp. 16-17 and 23.

[2] The proportion of females in the occupied population of Britain fell from 31·8 per cent in 1871 to 29·2 per cent in 1901 and was 29·6 per cent in 1911.

[3] *Census of England and Wales*, 1911, vol. X, part I, p. 552.

[4] The corresponding increase for Britain as a whole was from 12·1 mn. to 18·4 mn.

(10·70) was the highest for any year before 1914,[1] but the difference was not great and the average for the quarter-century preceding 1914 was no higher than for that preceding 1875.[2] It is not easy to interpret these figures, because the range of activities that they covered was gradually increasing and making them less unrepresentative than they had been. But there are good reasons for thinking that irregularity of employment diminished in many of the fields not covered by the trade union figures. Outwork in overstocked or declining handicrafts was reduced to small proportions; itinerant petty traders lost much ground to fixed shops; casual labour was less used in farming; and even in the manifold unskilled services of the great cities casual labour, though remaining very common, was probably a diminishing proportion of the total. These were all types of activity in which chronic under-employment had been usual. If the trade union figures (which relate for the most part to occupations that were regularly rather than casually manned) showed no deterioration as more occupations came within that description, then the probability is that the available labour force was becoming more fully utilized,[3] within the limits of the hours which people were prepared to devote to work.

The gains from more regular work may, however, have been offset by an increase in voluntary leisure. Textile hours, which since 1850 had been limited by law to 60 per week, came down to 56½ in 1874 and 55½ in 1901; and in the 'seventies most skilled trades reduced their working week to 54 or 54½ hours, which was at least an hour a day less than had prevailed in the first half of the century. Skilled men in a few places secured no further reduction before 1914, but this was exceptional, and early in the twentieth century 52 and 50 hour working weeks were common and shorter ones by no means unknown. Coal-miners' shifts were restricted to eight hours by a law of 1908 and this meant a reduction in many areas, though there were some in which shorter hours were already in operation. Not all trades underwent much reduction of hours. The legal maximum working week in shops in 1914 was still 74 hours, including meal-times, and

---

[1] For the difference between the 'corrected' and 'uncorrected' unemployment rates see Beveridge, *Full Employment in a Free Society*, p. 41. The uncorrected figures show 1858 as the worst year for unemployment (11·9 per cent), but on the corrected figures 1879, 1885, 1886 and 1893 were all worse than 1858.

[2] Rostow, *British Economy of the Nineteenth Century*, pp. 48-50. Professor Rostow uses the uncorrected figures.

[3] *Cf.* the discussion of this point in Clapham, *op. cit.*, II, 455-6.

even that limit applied only if young persons were employed; and in 1911 there was a strike of London carters with the object of securing a reduction of hours to 75 per week. Nevertheless, reductions of hours, probably not offset by increased overtime except in occasional short spells of pressure, were widespread, and Clapham's guess that for the labour force as a whole there was an average reduction of from 2·5 to 5 per cent between 1886 and 1914 seems plausible.[1]

Quantitatively, then, the change in labour resources between 1870 and the First World War was an increase of some 60 per cent in numbers, enhanced both by a slight rise in the proportion of adult males and by a better organization of employment in many activities, and possibly reduced a little by the prevalence of a shorter working day, though it is unlikely that most people's output was reduced in the same proportion as their hours. But without appreciable qualitative changes there might have been little economic advantage in such a quantitative increase. New jobs were rising to importance and many old jobs had to be done by new methods in a new environment.[2] While industrial occupations remained about the same proportion of the whole, there were substantial changes in the relative labour needs of different industries,[3] and almost a new situation in non-industrial occupations. In 1871 agriculture employed 14·6 per cent of the working population of England and Wales, but in 1911 only 7·6 per cent. On the other hand, though domestic service was slowly declining in relative importance after 1881, distribution and a variety of other services occupied a growing share of the available labour. Thus, for example, 5·1 per cent of the occupied persons were engaged in transport in 1871 and 8·0 per cent in 1911, and the proportion in the armed forces and public administration (mainly the latter) rose from 2·3 per cent to 4·4 per cent.[4] Within manufacturing industries different grades of labour were needed in changing proportions. The process, already evident before 1850, whereby technical

---

[1] Clapham, *op. cit.*, II, 448-9 and III, 477-9; L. T. Hobhouse, *The Labour Movement* (3rd edn., 1912), pp. 22-3.

[2] *Cf.* pp. 39-40 above.   [3] *Cf.* pp. 72-3 above.

[4] Clark, *The Conditions of Economic Progress* (2nd edn.), p. 408. Changes of classification prevent these figures being exactly comparable but they give a near enough indication of the change. For some important categories, e.g. commerce, comparison is even more difficult; the change in the proportion between 1871 and 1911 was from about 8 per cent probably to about 12 per cent, but the later figure is very approximate. *Cf.* p. 127 above.

For Britain as a whole, recent revised estimates of the percentage in government service (central and local, including the armed forces and teachers in local authority schools) are 3·6 in 1891, 5·8 in 1901 and 6·9 in 1911 (M. Abramovitz and Vera F. Eliasberg, *The Growth of Public Employment in Great Britain* (1957), p. 25).

advance gave rise to new skills faster than it made old ones obsolete continued throughout the nineteenth century. By about 1900 the more varied scope and increasing refinement of machinery were beginning to reduce the need for an ever-increasing proportion of skilled workers, but they were making it necessary for the large numbers of craftsmen who survived to exercise a higher average degree of skill, and they were also leaving less for the completely unskilled to do. Moreover, these same technical changes, together with simultaneous changes in organization, were requiring a growing proportion of those employed in manufacturing industry to be engaged in administrative, clerical and supervisory work. Before the First World War this last trend of change was a long way from its maximum development, but it was already quite plain.[1]

All this implies that the economic life of the time was becoming dependent on the acquisition of fuller knowledge and more specialized skill and the development of latent qualities of judgment and responsibility among a large part of the populace. This could hardly come about unless there were a more varied and stimulating social environment and some fairly systematic provision of education for all. Such a situation was new. In 1866 Sir James Kay Shuttleworth, the most eminent educationist of the day, remarked:

The inventive power, the practical sagacity, the enterprise, the courage, and the indomitable perseverance of our race, have made all the vast conquests of our commerce, with little aid from general literary or scientific cultivation. But the future of the nation requires the light and guidance of a generally cultivated and refined mental power.[2]

In general he was right. It was not that education previously had had no important economic influence. But it had been possible for the vast economic changes of the preceding hundred years to be carried through by a people the mass of whom were educated mainly by the discipline of circumstances and the empirical experience of social life and daily work, and only to a very restricted extent by formal schooling. As long as there were some facilities, however unorganized, for diffusing a little more of specialized knowledge and general

[1] G. D. H. Cole, *Studies in Class Structure* (1955), pp. 33-5, 53-4 and 85-6.
[2] Sir J. Kay Shuttleworth, 'The Administration of Educational Endowments' in *Transactions of the National Society for the Promotion of Social Science*, 1866, p. 347.

culture, and an appreciable minority prepared to use them, and as long as a privileged very few had the chance to imbibe the habit of learning and judging as they grew to maturity, and a still smaller number was free to pursue studies at the highest level, this was adequate for *economic* needs, whatever its other deficiencies. But it was becoming less adequate every year.

In the eighteen-sixties a substantial part of the child population was still left untouched in a state of dirt, ignorance and savagery, exempt from all order and discipline save that imposed by the need to come to terms with brute violence among family and neighbours.[1] Few children growing up in such conditions could become anything better than casual, unskilled workers. More fully mechanized factories, needing semi-skilled workers who could conform to a regular routine, could not be manned from such a source. At a slightly higher level, for children who had been to school, the opportunities to progress beyond the three Rs, though more numerous than is often realized, were insufficient in quantity and had to be sought out through a good deal of personal effort. Yet on them the supply of clerks and minor supervisors depended. Even at the upper levels, in the grammar schools and universities, access to knowledge bearing directly on the dominant activities, organization and techniques of the contemporary world was very limited, though improvements were gradually taking place, particularly under the influence of the wide examination curricula of the University of London, whose degree examinations were in 1858 opened to men candidates wherever they had studied, as its matriculation examination had been since 1839.[2]

At every level the period from 1870 to 1914 saw great changes in educational provision. The greatest were probably those that sprang from the Education Act of 1870, which first provided for the creation of a national system of elementary education for children between the ages of 5 and 13 inclusive. From 1880 school attendance was nominally compulsory (with certain partial exemptions for children over 10), from 1891 it was free and by the middle 'nineties, except in a few very rapidly growing localities, a school place was actually available for every child.[3] The schooling provided was crude and

[1] There is abundant evidence of this in many contemporary descriptions and official enquiries. *Cf.* G. A. N. Lowndes, *The Silent Social Revolution* (1935), pp. 15-16.

[2] F. G. Brook, *The University of London 1820-1860* (Univ. of London unpublished Ph.D. thesis, 1958), typescript pp. 258-71 and 367-70.

[3] Lowndes, *op. cit.*, pp. 4 and 26-8; J. W. Adamson, *English Education 1789-1902* (1930), pp. 356-8.

simple but before the end of the century it had become possible to ensure that very few children grew up in a state of complete savagery, and that almost all of them were introduced to habits of discipline and order and to simple ideas of magnitude and meaning. Though it may have been seldom that they were taught to care and not to care, they were at least taught to sit still, a lesson not without benefits for industry and society. By the 'nineties, too, there was the beginning of a rather fuller education for the masses, as provision was made for teaching a greater variety of subjects, including a few vocational ones, in the elementary schools,[1] and there was then also a considerable increase of special provisions for those children whose parents kept them at school for a year or two after their fourteenth birthday. Moreover, in endowed and proprietary secondary schools there was almost certainly a rapid growth in the number of pupils, though no reliable figures exist. In 1895 such schools probably had no more than 110,000 pupils (of whom perhaps less than half received an education of more than elementary content), but this may have been six or seven times as many as they had had thirty years earlier.[2] After 1902, when the whole administrative system was reorganized, great efforts were made to provide more secondary schools, financed from public funds, and to establish an easier path to them from the elementary schools. In 1914 there were 187,000 children in grant-aided secondary schools (besides an unknown number in unassisted schools) and 5·6 per cent of the children aged between 10 and 11 were passing into secondary schools[3]—still too small a number for economic and social needs, but a very different state of affairs from that which existed twenty-five years earlier.

More strictly vocational training was also increased, though mainly at the lowest level. With financial assistance from the government and, for a time, from the City of London Livery Companies, most of the larger towns provided schools or classes in elementary science and certain industrial techniques for working men or their children, who studied for examinations conducted by the Science and Art Department or the City and Guilds of London Institute. In the

---

[1] Changes in the subjects which must or might be provided are summarized in J. R. Hughes and L. R. Klemm, *Progress of Education in the Century* (1907), pp. 42-3.

[2] Lowndes, *op. cit.*, pp. 50 and 52-4. In 32 years down to 1870, 6,976 students passed the London matriculation examination; in the next 30 years, 33,571 did so (Brook, *op. cit.*, p. 372.)

[3] Lowndes, *op. cit.*, pp. 101 and 113.

'nineties, when local authorities had extra money for the purpose, both from the rates and from the government, there was more rapid expansion of technical education, followed, however, by slower progress after 1902, when local authorities were preoccupied with the establishment of a system of more general secondary education. The previous gains were not lost, but little was done to lessen the gaps which had been left untouched earlier, especially the lack of provision for commercial studies and for any kind of technical education for managers and senior industrial staff.[1] At the highest level progress was less interrupted. The period from the eighteen-seventies to the First World War was notable for the foundation of numerous new universities and colleges and the transformation of old ones, for the removal of barriers of religion and sex to university entrance, and for a widening of the range of university studies.[2] It is noteworthy, for instance, that in the first eleven years of its existence, down to 1870, only 105 people obtained the London B.Sc. degree, whereas in the next thirty years another 1,496 did so.[3] Such figures illustrate both the striking trend of change and the still limited extent of what was being achieved.

All these changes in education must have made considerable difference to the kind of jobs which large numbers of people were fitted to perform and to the ease with which they could change from one method of working to another. More people were equipped with the more specialized knowledge that was desirable in order to cope with the more elaborate and specialized organization and activities of government, society and business. Less was done directly to enhance the capabilities of those who would undertake smaller scale manager-ial and minor executive tasks, but the general educational changes helped to enlarge the field of recruitment to such jobs. Perhaps most important of all, for the first time the greater part of the population was familiarized with habits of concentration and with the effort of discovering how to solve unfamiliar problems, however simple. There were hundreds of thousands for whom sordid and unpleasant living conditions and untreated physical weaknesses destroyed the effects of those lessons. But there still remained a far larger number than ever before who had discovered, many at the very simplest and some at a rather more advanced stage, how to learn something new

---

[1] A. Abbott, *Education for Industry and Commerce in England* (1933), pp. 24-43, 122-4 and 156-8.

[2] Adamson, *op. cit.*, chap. XV.   [3] Brook, *op. cit.*, p. 372.

and not to be scared of it, and how to stick at a task until it was done. This was one of the most essential of all achievements for the success of a more rapidly changing economy and society. Moreover, the newly literate population was given rather more opportunity of gaining knowledge outside the formal education system. Before 1870, for instance, only 35 local authorities provided a public library, but in the next twenty years another 118 and in the twenty years after that another 369 did so.[1] 'Self-education' was always an important influence on the quality of part of the Victorian labour force, and there can be little doubt that towards the end of the period more people could and did equip themselves with new knowledge and skills in this way.

The wide spread of such capabilities was all the more important because, on the whole, workers were probably thrown more completely than ever on their own resources while they were learnin 'on the job'. The army of unskilled had, of course, always had t carry out their odd jobs as best they could, with no one formally responsible for showing them how. As more of them were needed for work as semi-skilled machine operatives the same situation was repeated in jobs the technique of which was initially a little more difficult. In skilled trades formal apprenticeship, which had been fairly general before the nineteenth century, came to be less and less used, mainly because the increased mobility of labour and the expansion of employment made it impossible to preserve the practice of a particular craft as a privilege confined to those who had undergone the sacrifices of serving an apprenticeship. At the end of the nineteenth century it was estimated that trade unions which effecttively restricted their trade to men who had been apprenticed had only 90,000 members, and shipbuilding was the only large industry where apprenticeship was still common, though there were other large trades where an effort had been made to retain it until well into the second half of the century. In some of these, notably printing, it continued nominally to operate, but was, in practice, ignored in the greater part of the industry.[2] Even where, as in shipbuilding, apprenticeship persisted, it often lacked much of the training and supervision formerly associated with it and the apprentice had to pick up his trade without much assistance.[3] By the early years of the

[1] W. A. Munford, *Penny Rate: Aspects of British Public Library History 1850-1950* (1951), pp. 33-4.
[2] S. and B. Webb, *Industrial Democracy* (new edn., 1902), pp. 456-74.
[3] *Ibid.*, pp. 479-80.

twentieth century there was a growing feeling that something valuable in industrial training had been lost and there were attempts, on educational, not restrictive, grounds, to revive apprenticeship in some trades where it no longer existed, but they achieved little.[1] Apprenticeship did not die out in the early twentieth century, but in the trades where it remained it was usually only one method of entry among several and the apprentice, as distinct from other young workers in his trade, often received part-time training in a technical school, instead of relying solely on what he picked up at work.[2] There can be little doubt that the efficient conduct of economic life had become more dependent on a greater aptitude for learning by most workers of all types than on any formal steps which business firms took to ensure a labour supply satisfactory in quality as well as quantity.

It was essential, however, that employers and, to a less extent, the state should provide the sort of incentives that would induce enough people to use the greater opportunities of improving themselves and to apply their abilities conscientiously. The most important of these incentives was an increase in monetary rewards, together with a plentiful supply of the necessities and simple comforts of life that were the chief things which most wage earners wanted more abundantly. In fact the great majority of workers experienced rising wages in the late nineteenth century when the prices of most common articles, except house-room, were falling rapidly. Before 1880 wage statistics were hardly sufficient to be very reliable when reduced to general averages, but it is probable that most wage-rates were rather higher in 1880 than in 1870, despite widespread cuts in the late 'seventies. Between 1880 and 1900, for the industrial worker who stayed in the same occupation, money wage-rates increased on the average by 15 to 20 per cent, while retail prices fell by about 15 per cent, a state of affairs which must have done much to reconcile the mass of the people to current changes in living and working conditions. After 1900 average money wage-rates changed little for a decade and in 1914 were only about 8 per cent higher than in 1900, an increase more than offset by the rise in retail prices.[3] Throughout the period, however, the average position was rather better than these figures

[1] Olive J. Dunlop, *English Apprenticeship and Child Labour: a history* (1912), pp. 326-32.

[2] See the details of methods of entry and promotion in various trades given by Lord Askwith, *Industrial Problems and Disputes* (1920), pp. 44-65.

[3] A. L. Bowley, *Wages and Income since 1860* (1937), pp. 6, 10 and 30.

suggest, because an increasing proportion of the workers was moving into higher paid occupations. In general, the more rapidly growing industries of the time needed a higher proportion of highly skilled workers than the other large industries, and skill was attracted and rewarded by the maintenance of a large wage differential between skilled and unskilled. There is, indeed, some evidence to suggest that the differential was increasing, at least in the period 1886 to 1906, at the end of which skilled rates in manufacturing industries were on the average nearly double those of unskilled.[1] This trend probably did not show itself in all important trades,[2] but there were none in which the differentials did not remain wide. So the occupational upgrading of a large part of the population brought about a bigger increase in wages. It was estimated that, but for this cause, the 80 per cent rise in average real wages in the second half of the nineteenth century would have been no more than 50 per cent.[3] For a later period, 1880-1910, of which it is possible to write with a little less uncertainty, the upgrading of occupations added some 12 per cent to the increase in average wages.[4] Altogether, when allowance is made for this redistribution, average real wages in 1914 may be estimated as from 70 to 100 per cent higher than in 1860, and, more certainly, as about 45 per cent higher than in 1880, the level in 1914, however, being only the same as in 1896.[5]

Rising wages alone were not sufficient to spread contentment and co-operativeness among workers. It was important also that wages should be paid at short, regular intervals and in cash, so that workers were not forced into debt or made to accept inferior and overpriced goods. Truck, which had been one of the most hated features of nineteenth-century working-class life, had shrunk to small proportions by 1870[6] and thereafter became even less important. 'Long pays', which were often though not invariably associated with truck, survived to a greater extent, though they were much less common than they had been. Arrangements like those at the Wanlockhead

---

[1] *Ibid.*, p. 42. The modal industrial wage, which was dominated by the wages of unskilled labourers, was 22s. 8d. per week in 1886 and 23s. 10d. in 1906, but the average wage rose from 24s. 11d. to 30s. 6d.

[2] e.g. Cole, *op. cit.*, p. 58, suggests that in the engineering trades a skilled man got about twice as much as a labourer in 1867 but only about 1½ times the labourer's wage in 1914.

[3] G. H. Wood, 'Real Wages and the Standard of Comfort since 1850' in *J. R. Stat. Socy.*, LXXII (1909), 99.

[4] Bowley, *op. cit.*, p. 6.   [5] *Ibid.*, pp. 30-5.

[6] *Report of the R.C. on the Truck System* (*P.P.* 1871, XXXVI), p. iv.

lead mines, where otherwise beneficent employers paid their men once a year (and always kept twelve months' wages in hand), were freaks.[1] But pay-days at variable or regular intervals of 3 to 12 weeks, such as prevailed in the iron industry in South Wales,[2] were less remarkable. During the next twenty years, however, such surviving impositions were removed. At the end of the century the Webbs could quite naturally refer to the working classes generally as 'men dependent on weekly wages', though recognizing that a few were, in fact, still paid only fortnightly.[3]

One other element which affected both the efficiency and the contentment of workers was the method by which wages were reckoned. Employers wanted a wage system which ensured that their employees could not be rewarded for idleness or scamped work, and workers wanted arrangements which did not force them to accept overdriving in order to secure adequate payment and which did not hand to the employer all the benefits of an improvement in their own performance. The methods of remuneration were not, in fact, drastically altered in the late nineteenth century. Most workers continued to be paid on a time basis.[4] But in those trades where the unions were strong by the end of the nineteenth century (mostly those where appreciable skill was needed) the influence of the workers was more often exerted to secure the prevalence of piece-rates than of time-rates.[5] A minority of employers tried various experiments with bonus schemes and around 1890 there was a temporary uprush of interest in profit-sharing schemes,[6] but all this affected relatively few. Perhaps the one significant change was the declining prestige and use of the sub-contract system, under which an employee of a factory, workshop or mine engaged his own assistants and paid them out of his own wages. This system was still much used in many types of business in the 'nineties, but its association with small 'sweat-shops', where workers were occupied for long hours in return for a pittance, brought it into disrepute,[7] and, in any case, the increasing size of firms and greater attention to managerial questions were making it less and less appropriate. The general position in the early twentieth century was that the great majority of workers were

---

[1] *Report of the R.C. on the Truck System*, pp. xxxix-xl.
[2] *Ibid.*, pp. v-vi.   [3] Webb, *op. cit.*, p. 431.
[4] D. F. Schloss, *Methods of Industrial Remuneration* (3rd edn, 1898), p. 43.
[5] Webb, *op. cit.*, pp. 283-8.
[6] Schloss, *op. cit.*, p. 262.   [7] *Ibid.*, chaps. XIV and XV.

engaged by the firm on whose premises they worked and were paid
a fixed time-rate or, less often, a piece-rate, and adjustment to
changes in conditions had to come through the fixing of new rates.

Wage questions were not the only ones which affected the willingness and ability of workers to fit themselves for the type of job that
was needed. There were other desirable benefits less tangible but not
less real than more money. Leisure was attractive for its own sake
and, in addition, rather more of it was probably, for an increasing
proportion of workers, a necessary condition of efficiency in their
jobs. The more extensive use of machinery meant that for many
people work became noisier, faster and more monotonous, with
fewer interruptions to provide relief, a state of affairs that made it
more difficult to maintain full attention for long periods. The reductions in the working week were as relevant to the contentment and
reliability of workers as to the total supply of effort. The machines
themselves also often did something to offset the strains they caused,
since they lightened the muscular effort involved in many tasks,
though they did not affect everyone in the same way. In some industries the mechanization of most processes left a few still to be
done by hand in conditions that were more arduous than ever because
of the mechanization of the remainder.[1]

A removal of some of the conflicts between working conditions
and the maintenance of health and safety was another contribution
to the creation of a more satisfactory labour force and its best use.
New types of equipment and methods of work and more attention
to the details of management and of workshop planning were making
it more practicable to do something about this, and, after the Factory
and Workshops Act of 1891 had been passed, the enforcement of
higher and rising standards in these matters was applied to a wide
range of industry.[2] The Workmen's Compensation Act of 1897, which
first put liability for industrial injury squarely on employers,[3] was
another contribution to the same end and also lessened one element
in the sense of insecurity which a more mechanized, complicated and

[1] For a detailed description of changes in the methods and arduousness of different jobs in one major industry see Helen Gintz, *Effects of technological change on
labour in the iron and steel industries, 1901-1939* (Univ. of London, unpublished
Ph.D. thesis, 1954), chap. IV. Protracted exceptions to the generally beneficial
effects of such changes are described in furnace filling (pp. 115-16), casting pit
work (p. 128), and puddling (p. 136), and it is suggested that in Britain in the first
decade of the twentieth century 'manual handling was in its last and most strenuous
stage' (p. 564).

[2] Clapham, *op. cit.*, III, 430-1.   [3] *Ibid.*, III,

impersonal economic and social life was likely to sharpen in the majority of people.

Changes in wages, hours and physical conditions of work, changes in individual rewards and terms of employment, and also changes in social organization and benefits and in the law were all of them important influences on the economic efficiency and the co-operativeness of the labour force and on the character of industrial relations. They could come about only through an immensely complicated and often haphazard series of discussions, actions and social contacts. But there were many signs that in the late nineteenth century the consideration and settlement of such matters was gradually becoming more systematic and organized, though with many interruptions to this development.

For a large part of the nineteenth century the overwhelming majority of jobs came before workers on a take-it-or-leave-it basis. Employers regarded the determination of pay and conditions as their own sole prerogative and were guided in these matters mainly by the state of the local labour market, by their own estimate of what they could afford and by prevailing conventional ideas of what was reasonable. Individual workmen who possessed new, specialized skills which were in growing demand were often the subject of strong competition among employers and could make excellent bargains for themselves, though they usually had to limit their chance of further improvement for a time by accepting a long-term contract. But most others were less fortunately placed and could hope for little direct influence on the determination of their conditions unless they could stand together to ensure that employers would not get enough satisfactory labour without conforming to certain minimum standards. In many well-established crafts, especially those where it was possible to regulate the number of entrants and the occupation was fairly narrowly localized, it is probable that workers were regularly able to influence their pay and conditions of employment. But in the many less skilled, more scattered and more mobile occupations, attempts at united organization and action, though they were common and gained numerous local and temporary concessions, had little permanent effect on industrial conditions until some time after the middle of the nineteenth century.

In the third quarter of the century many small unions of skilled men continued to act much as before and in some other occupations where local concentration was characteristic (coal-mining, for example) trade unions obtained greater strength through the adherence of greater numbers. But the growth of trade unionism in occupations which were new or where it had hitherto had no lasting success was mainly confined to a minority of skilled trades. Circumstances, as much as outlook, determined the policy of many unions in these trades as one of preoccupation with mutual insurance and the strengthening of their own finances and administration, with the strike as a weapon kept in the background, though not to be neglected in an extremity. In the eighteen-fifties hardly any employer would have contemplated formal discussions and agreement with a trade union and there was no prospect of inducing the government to extend very much its regulation of working hours and conditions, or to interfere with wages. It was therefore a practical matter for the unions, where they had the means, to try to preserve their members from those conditions of desperate need which might drive them to undercut each other. At the same time they also wanted to build up both their strength and a store of public goodwill so as ultimately to induce employers to take them into regular consultation and to bargain with them, and perhaps to induce the government to legislate in their favour.

By the eighteen-seventies some modifications of the organization of the labour market had resulted. New legislation from 1870 to 1876 gave to trade unions (so it seemed until many years later) an unassailable position of legal security, which encouraged their growth, and freed workmen from all possibility of criminal prosecution in cases of alleged breach of contract. Moreover, collective bargaining between representatives of unions and employers had been regularly established in a few trades. Pressure for the establishment of regular negotiating machinery, often with provision for arbitration in disputes, had been a feature of union policy[1] and, in a time of generally expanding trade, some employers in the 'sixties saw advantage in responding to such repeated overtures of peace. Though there had been short-lived experiments much earlier, the establishment of a board of conciliation, equally representative of employers and employed, in the Nottinghamshire hosiery industry in 1860[2] probably marks the effective beginning of permanent industrial negotiating machinery. Over the next fifteen years comparable

[1] S. and B. Webb, *The History of Trade Unionism* (new edn., 1920), pp. 337-9.
[2] H. Crompton, *Industrial Conciliation* (1876), pp. 33-40; W. H. G. Armytage, *A. J. Mundella 1825-1897* (1951), pp. 32-4.

arrangements were made in a number of other important industries, including the coarser section of the hosiery industry centred in Leicester, iron manufacture in all the important districts in which it was carried on, and coal-mining in many of the principal fields,[1] but they still remained uncommon, though not unknown, in trades that were not fairly well localized.[2] The bodies that came into existence were usually described as boards of conciliation or arbitration, but these terms were used loosely, and it is more realistic to regard them simply as formal arrangements for collective bargaining, with some contingent provisions for the resolution of cases of complete disagreement. The success of such arrangements in settling disputed questions without strikes or lock-outs was a sign of acceptance of the idea that employers and employed had many interests in common and were likely to lose less by mutual concessions than by mutual hostility. Another symptom of the same spirit was the acceptance by a growing number of workmen that it was right for their own rewards to vary with those of their employers, a view embodied in agreements that wages should be on a sliding scale, varying with the price of the product. Many sliding-scale agreements were made in the iron industry from the mid-century onwards and in the later 'seventies and the 'eighties they spread rapidly in many of the coalfields.[3] It was events such as these which encouraged the view that the growth of trade unionism was leading to the emergence of a more rational and more peaceful labour market. A distinguished foreign observer in 1890 went so far as to sum up the development in the concise claim 'that England is preparing the way for the reign of industrial peace, and that she seems to be nearest her goal in those industries in which the organization of the workers is most complete'.[4]

But by then new forces were coming to the fore in trade unionism and other attitudes which had long existed were gaining greater potency. By the early 'seventies there were probably a million British trade unionists and, though the numbers dwindled in the ensuing years of trade depression, they had returned to this level by 1885.[5] Among them a majority were in unions which had never known the opportunity of permanent co-operation with employers in the settlement of matters in dispute. And beyond these was a far larger

---

[1] Crompton, *op. cit.*, p. 44 and chaps. IV and V.   [2] *Ibid.*, p. 96.

[3] Webb, *op. cit.*, pp. 734-6; R. Page Arnot, *The Miners*, I (1949), 59-61, 64-7. and 71-5.

[4] G. von Schulze-Gaevernitz, *Social Peace* (Eng. trans. 1893), p. 244

[5] Webb, *op. cit.*, pp. 748-9.

number of unorganized workers in whom successful trade unions had taken little interest and who lacked the means to improve their position through the union practices that had gained the greatest repute. The circumstances of the time enhanced the influence of these sections of the working class.

The disappearance of long-term contracts and the removal of breach of contract by workmen from the list of criminal offences,[1] as well as the new legal immunities of trade unions, made it less risky for organized labour to follow policies of opportunism rather than be tied to permanent formulae for the regulation of industrial matters. The effect of cyclical unemployment (which was most severe in some of the trades in which unionism was strongest) and of falling prices on the decisions of conciliation and arbitration boards and on the working of sliding-scale agreements brought growing dissatisfaction and, by the 'nineties, the abandonment of much of the earlier conciliation machinery.[2] The spread of literacy and the improvements in communication, both physical and mental, assisted the introduction of trade unionism among workers hitherto unaffected by it, many of whom could not afford the subscriptions necessary for successful friendly benefit schemes, and also provided an audience for some of the small but growing volume of socialist utterances which advocated new remedies for existing ills. Even among workers to whom Marxian doctrines were unknown or unattractive, there was increasing awareness that many of their conditions of work and life seemed to be derived less from the immediate variations of nature and the arbitrary decisions of personal employers and more from the operations of an impersonal 'economic system'. This awareness, in turn, encouraged the belief that safeguards against common insecurities should be provided by the government. Trade unions could then use their full resources in redressing those ills that could be attributed directly to the weakness of their members *vis-à-vis* their employers.

The result of these influences was, by the late 'eighties and 'nineties, the development of a larger trade union movement with a changing outlook and an emphasis on new objectives and methods. The most sensational signs of change were the successful strikes for higher pay by groups of unskilled workers hitherto unorganized,

---

[1] For emphasis on the importance which this change had for industrial relations see Crompton, *op. cit.*, pp. 13-14.

[2] Clapham, *op. cit.*, II, 175-6 and III, 341.

notably the London dockers in 1889.[1] It was proved by experience that it was possible to establish effective trade unions including workers of different grades in activities where unions had never flourished before. It was even found possible to maintain unions recruited from that general mass of unskilled men who were not permanently associated with any one industry but who were potential competitors in several. The ultimate significance of these practical achievements was considerable, but most of it was delayed. Trade union membership among the unskilled fell away in the depressed years of the early 'nineties and among the general unions there was no recovery until after 1910,[2] though some of the unions specific to one occupation or industry were able to increase again their intake of lower-paid workers earlier than that. The continued growth of the trade union movement down to 1900, when its membership approached two million,[3] was mainly among the skilled and semi-skilled, especially in those industries where old-established unions had a firm foothold. In the early 'eighties a substantial majority of trade unionists came from only four large groups of trades: engineering, shipbuilding and metal-working; the building trades; cotton manufacture; and coal-mining. Their preponderance was not much different at the end of the century.[4] Changed outlooks and policies among these people consequently had for the moment greater influence than the spread of unionism elsewhere.

That important changes were occurring among these groups was attested by many signs. There was the drive to secure greater strength through a more complete membership and also, in many of the miners' unions, for instance, the inclusion of a greater variety of grades of worker. There was the abandonment of old agreements: the Miners' Federation, which was formed in 1889 and to which were affiliated unions from all the coalfields except Northumberland and Durham, was to a considerable extent held together by a common opposition to sliding-scales of wages and by uncompromising hostility to the employers.[5] There was a growing interest in independent political pressure for the assumption of new functions by the government. There was the greater militancy shown not so much by a

---

[1] The change in trade union ideas and policies at this time is discussed at length in Webb, *op. cit.*, pp. 374 *et seq.*

[2] E. J. Hobsbawm, 'General Labour Unions in Britain, 1889-1914', in *Econ. Hist. Rev.*, 2nd series, I (1948-9), 124.

[3] Webb, *op. cit.*, p. 750.   [4] Clapham, *op. cit.*, III, 321.

[5] Webb, *op. cit.*, pp. 391-4; Arnot, *op. cit.*, I, chap. III.

readier resort to strikes as by an effort to increase the scale of strikes once they had been decided on.

All this, however, made less difference to the conduct of industrial relations than might have been expected. Stronger unions, in trades where unions had long been powerful enough to secure a hearing, could and did negotiate more effectively. Since by this time they often had permanent, salaried officials who built up a vast amount of experience and since they also usually left a great deal of scope for local arrangements, most questions of wages, hours and conditions could be settled by joint committees or discussion between individual representatives as they arose, and the absence of formal boards of arbitration or conciliation was no great loss. There may have been only a few trades in which the negotiating arrangements were up to this high standard, but they included some of the biggest and also a fair proportion of the whole body of trade unionists.[1] When, occasionally, there were widely differing estimates of what was right and practicable, then the resulting dispute was often more damaging than in the past. But even then the dispute was only rarely ended by a decisive victory of one side and surrender of the other. More commonly there was a return to discussion between the contestants and sometimes acceptance of *ad hoc* arrangements for outside conciliation or arbitration.[2] From 1896, when a new Conciliation Act was passed, there was also the opportunity to invite conciliation by the Board of Trade and there was a steady, if small, use of this opportunity, which had, on the whole, very successful results.[3]

At the beginning of the twentieth century, however, the situation was changing in two important ways. First, the immunity of trade unions to actions for damages was whittled away by a series of decisions in the courts, which culminated in 1901 when the Taff Vale Railway Company won an action against the Amalgamated Society of Railway Servants for losses caused by a strike.[4] The effect of this, until the immunity was restored by the Trade Disputes Act in 1906, was to weaken the sanctions that might back up any trade union demand and therefore to discourage the admission of trade unions to regular consultation and negotiation in a wider area of industry.

The other change was an increase of trade union membership in

[1] Webb, *Industrial Democracy*, pp. 204-6.   [2] Clapham, *op. cit.*, III, 342-4.
[3] *Ibid.*, III, 343; Askwith, *op. cit.*, chap. VIII.
[4] Webb, *History of Trade Unionism*, pp. 597-603.

industries where employers had never recognized the right of employees' representatives to bargain with them. Since, on the whole, public opinion outside the wage-earning classes was becoming less favourable to trade unions,[1] recognition was not readily given to new and growing unions by the employers concerned, and the result was the emergence of a number of fairly strong unions that were allowed only very limited opportunities to achieve improvements for their members through peaceful discussion. There was, for instance, a rapid growth of union membership among railwaymen in the 'nineties and again a few years later, but before the first national railway strike in 1911 the companies never recognized the unions as regular negotiating bodies.[2] And from 1910 the great increase in trade union membership (a rise from 2·4 million to 4·0 million in three years) was particularly marked among other transport workers and among not very highly skilled workers in a variety of trades without any tradition of collective negotiation. As this was happening at a time when the majority of workers had experienced no gain in purchasing power for several years and when more violent industrial doctrines were being learned from the leaders of working-class movements in some other European countries, it is hardly surprising that over a substantial part of economic life industrial relations developed into a crude trial of strength. The last four years preceding the First World War saw a great outburst of strikes, widely spread both geographically and occupationally, often accompanied by unusual bitterness and sometimes by violence. It was a time when organized labour gained many concessions without being able to demonstrate any clear predominance over employers; a time, too, when the Board of Trade's capacity for mediation (especially in the person of Askwith, its outstandingly able representative) was tried out as never before and proved extremely valuable.[3]

It is clear that in the quarter-century preceding the First World

---

[1] Webb, *Industrial Democracy*, pp. xxvi-xxvii.

[2] G. W. Alcock, *Fifty Years of Railway Trade Unionism* (1922), pp. 280-1, 295 and 426-33.

[3] For a detailed account of industrial relations at this time by one who had a close and varied experience of them, see Askwith, *op. cit.*, esp. chaps. XV-XXV and XXXIII. An elaborate secondary summary is contained in G. Dangerfield, *The Strange Death of Liberal England* (1936), Part II, chap. IV and Part III, chap. IV. An account from a more revolutionary standpoint is given by M. Beer, *History of British Socialism* (new edn., 1929), II, 354-63. The most recent and most balanced account is E. H. Phelps Brown, *The Growth of British Industrial Relations: a study from the standpoint of 1906-14* (1959), chap. VI. The development of industrial relations in the immediately preceding period is fully discussed in *ibid.*, chap. III.

War organized labour became an effective influence on the determination of wages and conditions of work over a much wider section of economic life than ever before. Yet the conduct of industrial relations remained rather haphazard. There were trades in which well-organized groups of both employers and workers continually met to settle their economic concerns through mutually-accepted procedures; there were others in which they met occasionally, in an atmosphere of mutual hostility. There were yet others in which organization was so recent that it was scarcely considered as more than a means for the achievement of the aims of the moment and had no place as an element in permanent arrangements for the regular modification of labour conditions. In others again workers remained without any permanent organization and had to make what bargains they could as competing individuals or as groups which occasionally and temporarily tried to stand together. And over all the government had little more than a watching brief, with limited powers to help the making of peace if the contestants went to war and grew sick of it.

Where labour was effectively organized its influence was usually exerted on settlements applying only in one locality and restricted to a specific trade or industry, rather than on anything nationwide in its application or more general in scope. Most trade unions were still small and localized, and though the few large, national unions contained a disproportionate share of the total number of trade unionists, even these unions proceeded mainly by the negotiation of district agreements and left most of the detailed discussion to their local officials. This persistence of small-scale activity was by no means completely unrealistic and anachronistic. For one thing, the universal hostility of employers to national agreements meant that much quicker progress could be made through local negotiations. And, in any case, many important trades were fairly narrowly localized, while among those that were more widely dispersed there were real differences in conditions in different districts. Nevertheless, it seems doubtful whether trade union organization was adequately adjusted to deal with the effect of more general influences on the labour market. The growing importance of semi-skilled work, the effects of universal elementary education, the rapid increase in the young adult population and the facilities for easy movement were all contributing by the opening of the twentieth century to a situation in which districts and jobs once fairly distinct were becoming competitive with each other. While the growth of general unions was in part a response to this situation, the limited extent to which more narrowly-based unions forged national policies or acted in concert meant that they modified the competitiveness of the labour market rather less than their size and numbers might suggest.

It was not that more comprehensive labour organizations were lacking, but rather that those which did exist had very restricted functions. In most of the larger towns there was a trades council to which local branches of different unions might be affiliated, but in practice the trades councils never obtained the affiliation of a majority of trade union members, and in many cases their effective action was confined to municipal politics.[1] At the national level there was, from 1868, the Trades Union Congress to which unions including the majority of trade unionists were affiliated. The T.U.C. was an important institution for the ventilation and formation of working-class opinion and for the exercise of political pressure, and it had a growing influence in obtaining legislation in the interest of the workers. But, though it helped sometimes to settle inter-union disputes, it had no real co-ordinating function in industrial matters.[2] Some people hoped that such a function would be performed by the General Federation of Trade Unions, which was established in 1899 on the initiative of the T.U.C., but their hopes were not universally shared within the Trade Union movement and were never realized.[3] A little more significant was the tendency, increasingly evident from the late 'eighties onward, for trade unions in the same or closely-related occupations to form national federations. For many years, however, these federations usually limited their attention to such matters as the settlement of demarcation disputes among their constituent unions and the arrangement of mutual financial help during disputes. Not until the second decade of the twentieth century was there a clear trend towards action by federations on behalf of the workers of a whole industry.[4] Such developments, together with attempts by large unions or federations in different industries to

[1] Clapham, *op. cit.*, III, 344-5.

[2] For a summing up of the functions and achievements of the T.U.C. in this period see B. C. Roberts, *The Trades Union Congress 1868-1921* (1958), chap. X.

[3] The G.F.T.U. never gained the affiliation and the support of all the larger unions, among which the Miners' Federation became extremely hostile to it. In practice the G.F.T.U. found its activities largely confined to running a mutual fund, on which its affiliates could draw for the payment of strike benefit, and to the representation of the T.U. movement on international bodies. (*Ibid.*, pp. 163-4, 245, 262-5, 296-303 and 329-30.)

[4] Webb, *History of Trade Unionism*, pp. 552-3.

co-ordinate their policies, as the miners, the railwaymen and the transport workers undertook to do when they formed their 'triple alliance' in 1913,[1] foreshadowed a much more complete departure from individualistic competition. But down to the time of the First World War it was only a foreshadowing, and the labour market, though no longer the scene of millions of pygmies joining in a free-for-all, had not become an arena for giants.

To some extent, however, the pursuit of improved conditions had been transferred to the sphere of mass action through the devising of new political programmes and instruments for their realization. In the early 'seventies the main political concern of organized labour had been to secure legislation that would permit trade unions to carry on their activities without the risk of legal action being taken against them. When that aim had been achieved, few trade union leaders had any wish to extend the policies of governments further than was being gradually done by the existing political parties, and for the most part they contentedly followed the Liberals.[2] But in the 'nineties this began to change. The Liberals alienated much support by the persistent refusal of the constituencies to adopt working men as Parliamentary candidates.[3] The increasing consolidation of employers in some industries appeared to be leaving purely industrial action by workers less chance of success, and the increase of adverse legal decisions in trade union cases also implied the inadequacy of such action. Moreover, a growing number of workers, who had never had the chance to improve their position much through trade union or friendly society activity, was becoming articulate.[4] It was in such circumstances that a substantial minority of trade unionists was able in 1899 to induce the T.U.C. to call in the following year a conference of interested bodies which created the Labour Representation Committee.[5] This was the effective beginning of what became six years later the Labour Party. The events of the next few years, especially the Taff Vale case and the tendency of price rises to start outstripping those of wages, spread the desire for distinctive working-class political activity much more widely. The financial difficulty created by the decision in the Osborne case in 1908, that trade unions were not entitled to make a levy on their members for political purposes, probably only strengthened support. It did, indeed,

---

[1] *Ibid.*, p. 516.   [2] *Ibid.*, pp. 358-74.
[3] H. Pelling, *The Origins of the Labour Party, 1880-1900* (1954), pp. 235-7.
[4] *Ibid.*, pp. 207-13.   [5] *Ibid.*, pp. 218-20.

create a new clearly-defined political aim, the right to make a political levy, which was achieved when a law for this purpose was enacted in 1913.

Thus from the beginning of the twentieth century there was a distinct and rapidly strengthening organization of working-class political activity, seeking to enlarge the functions of government in such a way as to make it the instrument for conveying to workers benefits and reliefs which previously they had been able to obtain. if at all, only through individual provision or mutual insurance, There was no general agreement about the methods to be used to bring about this change. The persons and institutions that had done most to advocate the need for a separate political organization of labour had nearly all been socialistic, but the Labour Party was not, until 1918, pledged to socialism. Lack of concentration on a single line of approach, however, did not preclude it from exerting more effective pressure on governments than had been possible before it existed. Legislation in the early twentieth century which extended provision for workmen's compensation, set up trade boards that would regulate wages in 'sweated trades', and started a national system of old age pensions and insurance against sickness and unemployment for lower-paid workers was, in part, a response to the pressure of better organization and more articulate demands. To some working-class leaders these changes appeared as important benefits testifying to the soundness of their present political measures; to others they were mere sops that distracted the workers from pursuing the greater power, justice and rewards which, they maintained, would come from the establishment of socialism.[1] Whatever view prevailed, the immediate practical consequences for industrial life were evident. The majority of workers could set out to strengthen their own position with a lessened degree of insecurity to deter them, with more confidence in their collective power to influence the body politic, and with a greater opportunity to vary the nature of their efforts according to the nature of their immediate aims. The activities of a mutual insurance society, an organization for bargaining about wages and hours, and a political pressure group no longer need compete detrimentally with each other. Such a situation was bound to influence greatly the way in which industrial relations were conducted. Less and less could the determination of the rewards and conditions of work be interpreted exclusively in terms of the competition,

---

[1] Beer, *op. cit.*, II, 377-9.

methods of organization and financial strength of employers and workpeople, important as these were. Nothing, in fact, shows more clearly the economic significance of the political environment, for as this changed, so, too, did the range of what was desirable and what was attainable through non-political action.

CHAPTER NINE

The Economic Influence of Government

I T is tempting to look on the repeated invocations of extended governmental action in economic matters in the early years of the twentieth century as symptoms of the emergence of a new relationship between politics and economics, to be contrasted with a conveniently labelled state of *laissez-faire*, prevailing at least until the eighteen-seventies. Both the recentness of much economic and social legislation and the abundance of mid-Victorian advocacy of minimal government lend point to the contrast; and it is undeniable that there had been a change that was both real and significant. Yet a consideration of the impact of central government and local authorities on economic affairs in the 'seventies, or a little earlier, suggests that it was much more substantial than the phrase '*laissez-faire*' implies and that for a generation past it had been increasing in new ways even as it receded in some old ones.

The functions that were unanimously considered appropriate for the central government in the mid-nineteenth century probably did not extend far beyond the conduct of foreign relations, provision for external defence, internal security and the administration of justice, and the preservation of the essential organs of the constitution. Economically, as free trade ideas spread more widely and the piece-meal extension of their practice justified itself by results, the proper rôle of government, in the eyes of a large body of influential people, was to establish conditions in which free and equal competition could prevail and could lead to a fair distribution of rewards. In addition, the government should take measures to redress the competitive inequality of those who were characterized by some unavoidable disability and it must, of course, be carefully concerned with the financing of its own needs. Local authorities, of which there was a curious miscellany, were responsible for a few services of mainly local interest, which could not conveniently be performed by individuals and which companies were rarely able and willing to take on—poor relief, the maintenance of highways and bridges, street lighting, police duties, and a few services the need for which varied from one locality to another—and with raising the necessary money. These functions were more obviously related to economic affairs, but they were very few and small in comparison with the magnitude of private business.

Limitation of government functions mainly to non-economic matters and the drawing of definite boundaries to the small range of economic duties that were added to them were, however, only imperfectly achieved. The practical exigencies of administering existing services compelled a few steps, however small and halting, into new fields; and accumulating experience of the social dangers and deficiencies arising in an increasingly urbanized environment and in more mechanized workplaces led to public as well as private attempts to deal with them. Early and mid-Victorian Britain, indeed, saw public administration reaching out tentatively and empirically to serve new purposes and employ new forms of organization.[1] The whole process was rather haphazard and on a small scale, but it set a precedent for much more extensive activity in late Victorian and Edwardian times, and it was sufficient to cause a steady rise in expenditure. Central government expenditure on civil services rose from £5·3 million in 1840-41 to £12·0 million in 1870-71, whereas the proportionate increase in total expenditure was rather less than one-third,[2] and the sums raised by local authorities in the United Kingdom, though not perfectly known at the earlier date, are estimated to have rather more than doubled during this period.[3]

Quite apart from changes of this kind, there were other political developments that affected the relations between government and the economy. It is, in fact, misleading to divide government functions into 'economic' and 'non-economic'. What is relevant is the economic effect of all the main functions, whatever their immediate purpose, for they all have an economic aspect. In the mid-nineteenth century much the largest absolute increase in government expenditure was for the armed services, but to leave this out of consideration as a non-economic item would be unrealistic. It had obvious repercussions on

[1] 'The régime of *laissez-faire* had in fact been very brief: the pressure of the State on the individual, hardly felt in 1830, was beginning to be sensible in 1870.' (G. M. Young, *Last Essays* (1950), p. 192.) *Cf.* also G. M. Young, *Victorian England: Portrait of an Age* (1936), pp. 37-42. 'The English administration was made by administrators throwing out their lines until they met and formed a system.' (*Ibid.*, p. 39.)

[2] S. Buxton, *Finance and Politics; an historical study, 1783-1885* (1888), II, 346, 367 and 369.

[3] R.C. on Local Taxation, *Memoranda chiefly relating to the classification and incidence of imperial and local taxes* (P.P. 1899, XXXVI), p. 30.

the level of taxation and was therefore a target for the advocates of cheap government. It was an important influence on employment in certain localities and it was a means of extending public enterprise before the indignant eyes of a generation devoted to the belief that production and trade are bound to suffer if not directed by competing individuals. The concentration of small arms production in the government establishment at Enfield in the 'fifties and the reorganization of the Royal Dockyards in the 'sixties produced debate which, in part, would not be unfamiliar to disputants about the nationalization of industry a century later. And it is unlikely that expenditure on defence and on diplomacy had no effect on the growth of markets (especially in Asia) and therefore on the fortunes of private business.

That the growth of 'non-economic' activities had important economic consequences was not novel and was familiar enough to contemporaries. But, in conjunction with the beginning of new civil functions and with a reform of the system of taxation, it was contributing to a general change in the rôle of government as a national economic institution. In the first half of the nineteenth century the outstanding financial task continuously performed by the government had been to redistribute a small proportion of the national income from the poor to the rich. The greater part of its revenue had come from indirect taxes on articles of common consumption and more than half of its expenditure had been absorbed by the payment of interest on and the cost of managing the national debt. A small reduction of debt charges and a growth of other services meant that by 1870 a slightly bigger proportion of government expenditure was for purposes which directly served the majority of the people; and the use of the income tax meant that a rather less proportion of taxation fell on the poor, though customs and excise duties on a few generally-used articles were still the largest source of government revenue. As local authority expenditure (financed very largely by the levy of rates on property) grew faster than that of the central government, this modest redistribution of the burdens and benefits of public activities was carried a little further.

Since new services had been begun despite a fairly general belief in the importance of keeping public expenditure as low as possible, and since those services were still on a small scale and had to operate in a rapidly growing community, it was almost inevitable that the tendency for the economic influence of government to increase should continue. In 1870, however, there seemed little likelihood that it would markedly accelerate. The inauguration of a national system of elementary schooling in that year, partly financed from local rates as well as by the central government, certainly enlarged one field of public expenditure but nobody realized what this would lead to. Gladstone, the supreme apostle of governmental parsimony, was in office as Prime Minister, and his leading financial ideas were by this time firmly impressed on both political parties.

In fact, there were no further marked changes in the scope of government economic influence before the 'eighties and not until about 1900 was there a rapid increase in the proportion of the national income which was spent by central and local government.[1] But well before then new forces were emerging to change the situation, though most of them needed time to accumulate effective strength. There were more people who were able, and eventually more who were willing, to exert political pressure on the government to extend public action for national or sectional interests. The Reform Acts of 1867 and 1884 gave the vote to millions whose interests had never before been directly represented in Parliament. At first, most of their articulate spokesmen were satisfied to have achieved political recognition and freedom to organize themselves industrially and had no new positive functions of government to propose. But before the end of the century there was growing pressure from below for public action to improve the economic position of those who lacked the resources to achieve greater security for themselves. By this time, too, many who had had political representation much longer were being encouraged by events to think that the limits of public action might, with advantage, be enlarged. Sharper international rivalries, both economic and political, the increasing commercial restrictions imposed by most foreign governments, and the belief (fostered by a prolonged price-fall) that the economy had become permanently depressed made it seem less likely that individual virtue and enterprise would attain their just reward unless the government did more to help them.

Even those who clung to earlier views of the proper limits of governmental action had to interpret some of them in a wider sense. The greater size of cities, the more complex organization of business and society, the continued technical innovations—all demonstrated

---

[1] Ursula K. Hicks, *British Public Finances: their structure and development, 1880-1952* (1954), pp. 11-13. Buxton, *op. cit.*, I, xi, described 1881 as 'the last year of what, by any stretch of imagination, can be considered moderate expenditure'.

more clearly both the utility and inadequacy of many of the regulations and services already in existence. These had to be extended because the demands on them were greater and could not readily be met in any other way. To those who had accepted the need for measures to protect people who, unavoidably, could not protect their own interests in the competition of the market it became apparent that there were far more cases in this category than had been touched by mid-Victorian legislation. And the increasing size of many economic institutions, with its tendency to make market competition less complete, enlarged the category still further. What experience made more evident, changing doctrines re-interpreted in a way that made greater changes easier to justify. By 1880 T. H. Green, whose words must have been heard by many of the legislators of the next generation, was presenting the relation of state intervention to economic freedom in a new light. When he wrote that government must not only uphold the sanctity of contracts but must also prevent contracts being made which, because one of the parties to them was helpless, were instruments of oppression,[1] he was only echoing the ideas of earlier liberals. But when he declared that the value of freedom of contract was only that it was a means to the liberation of the powers of all men equally for contribution to a common good, and added that 'no one has a right to do what he will with his own in such a way as to contravene this end',[2] then he was putting a case for much more state intervention than had been attempted before. His was neither a lone nor an extreme view.

One other important influence was change in the organization of government itself. The reforms in recruitment to the civil service between 1855 and 1870, the more rational rearrangement of duties within a number of departments, and the institution of more effective means whereby the Treasury and Parliament could control departmental spending[3] reduced the grounds for distrusting the increase of governmental activity. Much reorganization of administration and accounting remained to be done after 1870 and it was many years before independent auditing and Treasury control were completely applied to all departments—the service departments, the heaviest

---

[1] T. H. Green, *Liberal Legislation and Freedom of Contract* (1881), p. 19.

[2] *Ibid.*, p. 11.

[3] D. L. Keir, *The Constitutional History of Modern Britain 1485-1937* (1938), pp. 416-19. On the whole question of the development of financial control over government administration at this time and later see B. Chubb, *The Control of Public Expenditure* (1952).

spenders, put up considerable resistance to this.[1] But if there were a case for the exercise of new functions, it was no longer possible to dispose of it by suggesting that a government department was too inefficient and irresponsible to be entrusted with the extra funds needed. In local government the improvement in administration had probably not been carried so far. But by the 'seventies some of the larger municipalities were being much more efficiently run, and the great changes in the whole system of local government between 1872 and 1894 assisted the spread of higher standards throughout the country.

Efficient organs of public administration also tended directly to encourage the enlargement of the field of policy. Even if one denies that 'empire-building' is the occupational disease of administrators, there is no doubt that practical experience of operating a specific branch of policy revealed deficiencies and the best way to overcome them, as well as fruitful opportunities for positive action. In education, factory and mines regulation, and public health the experience of inspectors and administrators was probably the most potent of all influences on the development of policy, and its strength increased as the number of those professionally concerned increased. Local authorities, too, were more attracted to new activities when they had good enough administrative machinery to be able to run them. The very increase in the number of costly services which they had to provide encouraged them to try to offset some of the expense by undertaking trading services where there were good prospects of profit.[2] But their own improved quality of administration was one of the essential pre-requisites of their ability to make profits.

The combined result of all these influences was gradually to create a new attitude towards public economic and social action. It did not come into existence overnight. Some events took years before they produced a decisive reaction. Not only did the first enfranchised generation of urban workers think of hardly any new object for which to cast their votes, but such phenomena as more intense international rivalries could be treated as passing worries until they had continued for a dozen or more years with no sign of an end. Some of the

[1] R.C. on the Civil and Professional Administration of the Naval and Military Depts., *Preliminary and further reports* (*P.P.* 1890, XIX), pp. 2 and 13-16; Chubb, *op. cit.*, pp. 50-2.

[2] *Cf.* Chamberlain's remark to the Birmingham City Council in 1873: 'The acquisition of the Gas Works concerns the profits of the town and its financial resources, . . . matters of absolute public necessity.' (N. Murrell Marris, *Joseph Chamberlain: The Man and The Statesman* (1900), p. 112.)

strongest influences, too, did not come until very late in the nineteenth century. The revival of foreign government restrictions on
commerce was a phenomenon of the 'eighties, not earlier, and so too
was the renewal, on more exact lines, of the mammoth investigations
of urban social life at home, which made evident the shortcomings of
previous policy. So, for a good many years, a readiness to give public
authorities larger scope showed itself only in a piecemeal and inter-
mittent way. But by the 'nineties the new attitude was becoming
clear and, if there were any tendency to go back on the intention to use
public organization more comprehensively for the creation of positive
social advantages, it was stopped by the South African War. The
experience of diplomatic isolation, temporary but humiliating military
reverses, an alarmingly heavy rejection of would-be recruits because
they were physically unfit, and some sorry scandals in the conduct of
the war encouraged the belief that stronger government was needed
and helped to set off a new round of enquiries into practical social
improvements which it might achieve.

In this setting of new attitudes, new institutions and new rivalries
the response of government can be seen in a variety of ways—in a
greatly extended regulation of private economic and social activities,
in an increase in the number and scale of services publicly provided,
and in heavier expenditure of money and resources on purposes not
directly economic, notably defence. Among these the increased
control over private actions was the most striking of all. Here the
changes were instigated by the central government, though the
detailed administration of many of them, especially those concerned
with housing and public health, was entrusted to the local authorities.

In the 'seventies and early 'eighties the changes were mostly extensions and consolidations of policies well established: more detail
of regulation in matters already touched by it, the generalizing of
powers previously exercised only under local acts, the conversion of
permissive powers into obligatory duties of local authorities. It was in
control over sanitary and housing conditions[1] and in regulation of
hours and safety in factories and workshops[2] that change was most
prominent at this time. But there were some signs of readiness to
interfere in subjects previously left entirely to those who were
contractually concerned—for instance, the state began to interfere in

[1] See W. M. Frazer, *A History of English Public Health, 1834-1939* (1950) for
a full account of the development of policy.

[2] For details of the legislation see B. L. Hutchins and A. Harrison, *The History
of Factory Legislation* (3rd edn., 1926).

the relations between landowners and tenant farmers[1]—and from the late 'eighties onward this tendency to enlarge the subjects of control became very marked. More classes of business were subjected to a greater variety of restrictions which directly affected their costs and, less often, their returns. Agriculture was not greatly affected, though numerous small inroads were made in the freedom of landowners. But railway companies after 1893 were no longer able to fix their own charges for goods traffic[2] and the whole scope of industrial legislation widened. Regulations of the kind which had improved conditions in factories and workshops began to be extended and adapted to the conditions of other kinds of workplace. From 1886 onwards a series of laws gradually increased control over the hours worked in shops and there were other measures to deal with laundries. Factory legislation proper, which had been predominantly concerned with limiting the hours of children, young persons, and women and with reducing the risk of personal injury, developed into a far more elaborate code affecting most aspects of working conditions and seeking to limit the incidence of occupational diseases. The two comprehensive Factory Acts of 1891 and 1901 took long steps into this new territory and were notable also for their recognition of the need to let practical experience decide the detailed methods of control. Both of them enabled the Home Office to make future large changes in regulation by administrative order without further legislation.[3] Such delegation of powers to the executive was increasing enormously at the beginning of the twentieth century and may well have been the greatest single source of the closer regulation of private activity. Parliamentary legislation, however, continued to spread public control into other industrial matters. To protect outworkers from exploitation it created in 1909 several trade boards, with the duty of prescribing minimum wages, and, having thus departed in an exceptional case from Victorian orthodoxy, it went on in 1912 to apply minimum wage legislation to the much less exceptional case of coal-mining and in 1914 to several other industries.

Nor was it only in industrial and labour affairs that an old nucleus of regulation was extended over several contiguous areas. The same was true of public health. Not only was the closeness of control in such matters as the prevention of nuisances much increased, but legally prescribed minimum standards of housing began to be adopted fairly generally, there was more widespread control of the

---

[1] See p. 66 above.   [2] See p. 124 above.   [3] Clapham, *op. cit.*, III, 429-32.

siting of offensive trades, and there grew up a whole new body of law relating to the preparation and sale of many classes of foodstuffs. There was also a great increase in the number of regulations primarily concerned to preserve and improve the well-being of children. The obligation, under acts of 1889 and 1899, to notify the local authority of cases of certain infectious diseases; the obligation, from 1907 onwards, to submit schoolchildren to medical examination; and the introduction, by an act of 1902 which came into force in 1910, of a system of compulsory registration and minimum qualifications for midwives were among the most important of such measures.[1] But there was also a tendency to interpret well-being in a wider and wider sense and to introduce many new provisions, which went far beyond the regulation of physical conditions. The change is well illustrated by the Children's Act of 1908, a vast measure which codified a good deal of legislation of the preceding thirty years, and considerably enlarged it.[2] Only a small proportion of this act was directly concerned with physical health, though indirectly its provisions were bound to affect it. The main sections of the act were concerned respectively with infant life protection (i.e. the regulation of baby-farming), the prevention of cruelty, juvenile smoking, reformatory and industrial schools, and juvenile offenders. There was also a 'miscellaneous and general' section, the subject-matter of which ranged from restrictions on the giving of evidence in open court by child witnesses in some cases to the exclusion of children under 14 from licensed bars. A similar tendency to extend control outwards from sanitary affairs, rather narrowly defined, was showing itself more generally. Perhaps the best illustration of this was the passing of the first town planning act in 1909, even though in practice it accomplished little. This act, which could be applied to new suburban districts in the course of development, was in many ways the direct successor of the sanitary and housing acts of the nineteenth century, but permitted a far wider degree of control over building and lay-out, in which sanitary objectives were combined with those of economy, comfort and aesthetics.[3]

To set limits to the freedom of individual action in such multifarious ways and to make them reasonably effective required an

[1] Janet E. Lane-Claypon, *The Child Welfare Movement* (1920), pp. 126-30 and 208-9.

[2] The act is summarized and its significance discussed in M. K. Inglis, *The Children's Charter* (1909).

[3] Ashworth, *The Genesis of Modern British Town Planning*, chap. VII.

increase in inspection and a steady growth of administrative and clerical staff, with provision for their accommodation. Inevitably it cost more money but, since it merely narrowed the limits of individual choice without to any significant extent destroying its operation, it did not lead to a vast bureaucratic expenditure. Where, however, increased public activity took the form of providing additional or enlarged services, the need of public bodies for money and employees grew much more. Since the operation of new services was, until just before the First World War, left much more exclusively to local authorities of one kind or another than was the enforcement of additional regulations on private activities, the relative share of local authorities in the work of government went on steadily increasing. By 1905 they were responsible for 55 per cent of total public expenditure, whereas in 1890 the proportion had been only 45 per cent.[1]

The increased services provided by local authorities were of two kinds. There were additions to the activities which were essentially of a communal or collective kind and there was a development of a small number of trading services which were supplied, for the most part, to individual customers. The most familiar communal services were those concerned with poor relief, highways and sanitation. The essentials of all these were fairly generally established by the eighteen-seventies, though they were not everywhere very efficient. From then onwards the main change in them was an improvement of quality and an enlargement of their capacity. But in some respects they were adapted to serve slightly wider purposes. The poor law authorities, for example, had been forced by circumstances to establish some subsidiary services for particular classes of paupers. One of the striking developments of the late nineteenth century was the provision in the larger towns of poor law hospitals, which came to be regularly used by many who were not paupers, because there were no other public hospitals. More significant, however, was the exercise of entirely new functions. Since 1851 local authorities had had powers to build houses for the working classes but had almost entirely ignored them. After 1890, when these powers were re-enacted in the Housing of the Working Classes Act, a small but growing number of local authorities began to make use of them, and there was also then and earlier a little slum clearance, powers for which originated in acts passed in 1868 and 1875. This entry of local

[1] Hicks, *op. cit.*, p. 108.

authorities into the provision of housing was of great significance in the long run, but before 1913 it accounted for only a minute fraction of their expenditure. Far more immediate in its effect was the use of local authorities after 1870 to provide education, which had previously been almost entirely a private service receiving financial assistance from the central government. Nothing else increased its demands so quickly. The number of children grew, some of the voluntary bodies contracted their effort, the quality of schooling had to be improved, and local authorities were given the tasks of providing more technical education after 1889 and more secondary education after 1902. Consequently education, which had cost them hardly anything before 1870, quickly became much the most expensive of their services. From 1890 to the First World War more than half the total United Kingdom expenditure on social services was for education, and, although a good deal of financial assistance was given by the central government, education absorbed 32 per cent of the total expenditure out of rates in England and Wales in 1913.[1]

Of the other services operated by local authorities, water supply and harbour management were the largest in mid-Victorian times and both underwent appreciable expansion afterwards. In part, especially as far as harbours were concerned, this was the result of the expansion of existing undertakings, but there were many transfers of waterworks from private to municipal ownership. There was an even more rapid increase in the municipal operation of gasworks, electricity supply and electric tramways. The last two of these were new services in which municipalities played a large part from the beginning, though the nucleus of many local transport systems was a company-owned horse tramway which was compulsorily purchased by the local authority as soon as electrification was practicable. Gas supply until about 1880 was chiefly for street lighting but during the next thirty years it became a usual service for most houses, and, as the business began to grow, many local authorities took it over from companies. The increase in local indebtedness for trading purposes illustrates the growth of such enterprise. For England and Wales it stood in 1885 at £79 million, of which £30 million was for waterworks and £29 million for harbours, docks and canals. In 1906 it totalled £208 million, which included £71 million and £44 million respectively for those two purposes, and also £24 million for gasworks, £27 million for electricity supply and £28 million for tram-

1 Hicks, *op. cit.*, pp. 31 and 114.

ways.[1] Other trading services, though they existed in a few places, were on a much smaller scale, the commonest (and most ancient) being the running of a market. Even in the small number of trading services where they were well established the local authorities were not unchallenged masters of the field. They were undertaking most of the water supply by the beginning of the twentieth century, but though the majority of municipalities supplied themselves with gas the exceptions included some of the largest, so that the number of consumers supplied by companies grew much faster than the number supplied by local authorities, as was also the case with electricity supply.[2] Nevertheless, the absolute increase in the number and size of local authority undertakings was, as indicated by the growth of their debt, very striking.

The contribution of the central government to this growth of public enterprise was mainly by compelling or encouraging local authorities to do more, by exercising some control over the way they did it, by giving local authorities special facilities for borrowing,[3] and, above all, by greatly increasing its grants towards the expenses of local authorities. For much of the nineteenth century the central government had repaid local authorities part of the cost of various small services. Such payments rose appreciably after 1870 until in 1888 many of them were replaced by the allocation of the proceeds of certain national taxes for local purposes, no longer usually in a definite proportion to the cost of specified services.[4] But specific contributions also continued to be made, notably for education, and grew very rapidly in the early years of the twentieth century. In 1900 exchequer grants to local authorities in England and Wales were equal to only 9 per cent of the expenditure out of local rates, but by 1905 they had risen to 21 per cent, and by 1913 to 23 per cent.[5]

For many years the central government did only a little to increase the number of services which it provided directly. The additional facilities provided by the Post Office and the taking over of the

[1] Local Govt. Bd., *Statistical Memoranda and Charts relating to Public Health and Social Conditions* (*P.P.* 1909, CIII), p. 91.

[2] Clapham, *op. cit.*, III, 441-3.

[3] e.g. through the Public Works Loans Commissioners. In 10 years after 1870 the latter loaned just about as much as in all the preceding period since their formation in 1817. In the 'seventies their loans were chiefly for building new schools and they were the main source of finance for municipal housing.

[4] E. Cannan, *The History of Local Rates in England* (2nd edn., 1912), chap. VI.

[5] Hicks, *op. cit.*, p. 119.

telegraph and an increasing proportion of the telephone services were the principal changes.[1] But early in the twentieth century, when various new services were introduced to add to the security of part of the working population, their operation remained a matter for central, not local, government. The first of these new services was a non-contributory scheme of old age pensions introduced in 1908. This provided a pension of five shillings a week at the age of 70 for persons whose income was not more than £21 a year, and smaller sums for those with incomes up to £31. The second was an attempt to diminish unemployment and casual work by improving the organization of the labour market through a system of labour exchanges. Attempts had been made, with little success, to introduce this system in London in 1902 and more generally in 1905.[2] But these attempts had been only incidental to experiments in the relief of exceptional unemployment. In 1909 a new act provided for the establishment of labour exchanges as a permanent part of the machinery of the labour market, and the first of the new exchanges opened in February 1910. By 1914 the labour exchanges were filling over a million vacant jobs annually.[3] The remaining services were the schemes introduced by the National Insurance Act of 1911, the provisions of which came into force in the following year. One dealt with compulsory insurance against sickness and applied to all workers below a prescribed level of wage or salary, the other dealt with compulsory insurance against unemployment in only seven industries at first. In 1913-14, 2,326,000 workers were insured against unemployment.[4] Both schemes were financed jointly by contributions from employers, workpeople and the exchequer, and the central government was responsible for their administration, though most of the detailed operation of health insurance was left to the voluntary friendly societies. Except for health insurance, these new services affected only a small minority of the population before the First World War, but since they were preventing many of the cases of most extreme poverty which previously had been dealt with locally by the Poor Law, their retention by the central government marked the end of the growing preponderance

---

[1] See pp. 117-18 above.

[2] S. and B. Webb, *English Poor Law History. The Last Hundred Years* (1929), p. 660.

[3] For an account and discussion of the early years of the labour exchanges see J. L. Cohen, *Insurance against Unemployment* (1921), pp. 166-96.

[4] *Ibid.*, pp. 200-17 for a summary of the working of the unemployment insurance scheme.

of the local authorities in public service. As the new schemes had immense potentialities of expansion (which were just beginning to show themselves by 1914), the trend towards centralization was bound to become more and more marked.[1]

Until these new social services were begun, the non-military services of the central government, rather surprisingly, grew very little, though its expenditure on services administered locally, notably education, steadily increased.[2] Only small changes took place in direct response to the demands for more government assistance in securing new markets and countering the commercial policies of foreign governments. Neither the 'fair trade' agitation of the early 'eighties nor Chamberlain's 'tariff reform' campaign at the beginning of the twentieth century achieved the restoration of a protective trade policy. More influential were the increased assistance given to trade by the foreign and colonial services and the addition of vast areas, with some immediate potentialities for trade, to the Colonial empire. But the amount of money and manpower needed to run these services and to administer the new colonies was small. The expenditure on the foreign and colonial services grew faster than that on other central departments but it remained a very small proportion of total government expenditure.

The main expansion of central government outlay until about 1910 was for naval and military purposes, especially the former. In part this reflected mounting international political rivalry, but it was mainly the result of rapid technical developments. Efficient defence equipment became more elaborate and costly and had to be replaced more frequently because of the speed of technical change. Since the technical revolution was at this time more complete and continuous in warships than in military *matériel*, and since British defence was bound to be predominantly naval, the effect on British government finance was large. Until Gladstone's second ministry ended in 1885 the rise in defence expenditure was restricted, even though it left Britain with a dangerously obsolescent navy. But thereafter a marked change took place. Between 1888 and 1913 defence expenditure rose by 138 per cent.[3] In 1880, 33 per cent of central government outlay

---

[1] Hicks, *op. cit.*, pp. 17 and 108.

[2] Expenditure on civil services other than education was falling in the late nineteenth century (as prices also fell); the expenditure in 1887-88 was not reached again (if special grants for needs arising from the S. African War are excluded) until 1907-8. (B. Mallet, *British Budgets 1887-1913* (1913), p. 508.)

[3] *Ibid.*, p. 466.

went on defence and this proportion reached 41 per cent in 1905; in 1913 it was 38 per cent, a slightly lower proportion only because expenditure on social services had recently grown so rapidly.[1]

What had for long been the other large item of public expenditure, interest and management of the national debt, was becoming not only relatively but absolutely less. Except during the South African War, debt redemption persistently exceeded new borrowing, so that the total debt in 1913 was some £75 million less than in 1870. Moreover, advantage was taken of the low interest rates in the late nineteenth century to carry out a large conversion scheme in 1889, under which the interest on much of the funded debt was reduced immediately from 3 per cent to $2\frac{3}{4}$ per cent, and to $2\frac{1}{2}$ per cent from 1902. As a result of these various changes the annual charge for debt interest and management fell from £24 million in 1870 to £17 million in 1912 and by 1910 it had become less than 10 per cent of the annual revenue, a complete contrast with the position in the mid-nineteenth century.[2] It is to be noted, however, that this one example of a large saving in government expenditure merely reduced the annual transfer of purchasing power from one section of the community to another. It did not significantly alter the real cost of government, in the sense of reducing the government's use of productive resources.

In every other important respect government was gradually becoming more expensive, and most of the purposes for which more money was spent involved the use of more labour and capital and materials. Total annual public outlay, central and local together, which in the years around 1870 was of the order of £100 million, was of the order of £300 million in the years just before the First World War, when the general price level was not very different. It had thus grown much faster than population and somewhat faster than the national income, the divergence being most evident in the decade 1895-1904. Until then public outlay had for many years been from 10 to 12 per cent of the national income. After that, until the First World War, it remained at 15 or 16 per cent.[3]

Inevitably such a change presented new problems in the raising of adequate revenue. Though the yield of most of the chief sources of public revenue could be expected to rise more or less *pari passu* with

[1] Hicks, *op. cit.*, p. 14.
[2] Buxton, *op. cit.*, II, 363 and 366; Mallet, *op. cit.*, pp. 494-7.
[3] *Cf.* the chart in Hicks, *op. cit.*, p. 11.

the increase in national income, something more than this was needed. The imposition of new taxes or increases in existing taxes and charges could not be indiscriminate, since it was necessary to take account of the way in which different charges might affect thrift, enterprise and trade, and also to keep the distribution of taxes approximately fair in the eyes of the electorate, the composition of which underwent great changes.

By 1870 the main items of the public revenue had become few in number and, though some anomalies survived and there were many complexities in the details of administration, the essential structure of the tax system was very simple. Local authority revenue came mainly from rates levied on all immovable property.[1] This was supplemented to a small extent by grants from the central government and, for some authorities, rather more substantially by income from tolls and dues charged for particular services or for the use of property owned by the authority.[2] Central government revenue, despite the abolition of hundreds of duties since 1842, still came mainly from customs and excise duties on a few items of food and drink, with stamp duties and income tax as the chief of the direct taxes which provided about one-third of the total tax revenue. There was also appreciable gross income from government business and property, chiefly from the Post Office, but this was mostly offset by expenditure on the same items.[3]

Both the central and local tax systems could be made to yield a steadily increasing revenue without administrative difficulty. The extraordinary miscellany of local rates levied for different purposes by overlapping authorities, which had formerly been in great confusion, had already been put in order as practically all rates (except the sewers rates)[4] had come to be assessed on the same basis as the poor rate and most of them were collected with the poor rate.[5] Moreover, since the passing of the Union Assessment Act in 1862,

---

[1] Woods and mines, other than coal-mines, did not become rateable until 1874. (Cannan, *op. cit.*, p. 101.)

[2] In 1872-73 local authorities in the U.K. received £22·8 mn. from rates, £5·4 mn. from tolls and dues, £2·4 mn. from the central govt. (R.C. on Local Taxation, *op. cit.*, p. 30.)

[3] In 1872-73 the central government raised £46·8 mn. from customs and excise duties and £19·8 mn. from other taxes (including £9·2 mn. from stamp duties and £7·5 mn. from income tax) and had £10·0 mn. revenue in addition to taxes. (Buxton, *op. cit.*, II, 348 and 365.)

[4] The sewers rates were for the services of land drainage and flood protection, performed until 1930 by local Commissioners of Sewers. They usually had nothing to do with street and house drainage and sewage disposal.

[5] Cannan, *op. cit.*, chap. V.

the valuation of property for rating, which had usually been well under the true value, had become much more realistic,[1] though there was still no uniformity in the method of valuation throughout the country. Of the central government taxes those on income and capital could obviously be made more productive with hardly any administrative effort. The machinery for their collection was fully established but the taxes were at very low rates. Income tax, levied on all incomes of more than £100 a year, came down to 4*d*. in the £ in 1870 and, after a temporary rise, reached its lowest point at 2*d*. in the £ in 1874 and 1875;[2] and only in the unimportant case of property passing to non-relatives, when legacy or succession duty was payable at the rate of 10 per cent, was the levy on capital at all substantial.[3] To raise the level of indirect taxes generally, though administratively simple, was likely to be less useful, since so much of the total yield came from duties on alcoholic drinks, the consumption of which was apt to be limited both by higher taxes and by changing social habits. To increase other duties selectively, or to add new ones, was bound to raise the criticism that it would restrict trade and would distribute the burden of taxation unfairly. One aspect of the free trade movement had been the attempt to shift more taxation on to property, especially real property, and to take it off consumers and manufacturers. In the 'seventies and later there were still many, led and organized by the Financial Reform Association in Liverpool,[4] who thought that this change had not gone far enough. Real property, they maintained, was still under-taxed, and the reforms of the previous generation had freed luxuries from tax, while still continuing a levy on articles of mass consumption.[5] The Financial Reform Association went so far as to demand the replacement of all indirect by direct taxation. On the other hand, nobody could prove conclusively who bore the ultimate burden of any particular tax, and property owners argued that, if local and national taxation were considered together, it would appear that they were contributing at least their full share, because of their payment of local rates. Indeed,

---

[1] R. D. Baxter, *Local Government and Taxation and Mr. Goschen's Report* (1874), pp. 17-18.

[2] Buxton, *op. cit.*, II, 378.

[3] W. M. J. Williams, *The King's Revenue* (1908), pp. 117-20.

[4] For an account of the Financial Reform Association's activities and doctrines see its jubilee volume, *The Financial Reform Association 1848-1898* (1898).

[5] J. Noble, *The Queen's Taxes* (1870), pp. 226-7. Noble was an official of the Financial Reform Association.

as the amount raised in rates went up, the argument gathered strength that in order to relieve property of excessive charges more local needs ought to be financed out of national revenue.[1]

The changes in the sources of public revenue in the late nineteenth and early twentieth centuries were very much what might have been expected in the light of these considerations. Revenue from local rates not only increased absolutely but grew faster than that from national taxes. This development was particularly marked in the 'nineties, when the new county and district councils were getting down to work,[2] but thereafter the pressure to transfer more charges from the ratepayer to the taxpayer met with a much fuller response. Nevertheless, the relative contribution of rates to total public revenue remained higher than before 1870 because of the continued need to raise large sums for education. As a contemporary historian put it in 1912, 'since 1870 the ratepayers as a whole have lost by the imposition of this new service more than all they have gained by relief in other directions since 1835'.[3] In England and Wales the amount raised in rates rose from £17·6 million in 1871-72 to £71·2 million in 1913-14.[4]

Central government revenue was drawn increasingly from direct taxes, especially income tax and death duties, and as more was required of these taxes they were modified in order to fall more heavily on the rich and not to press too much on those of very modest wealth. Income tax climbed persistently after 1875 until it reached 8d. in the £ in 1885. It never rose above this figure until the South African War, when it touched 1s. 3d., but in the subsequent years of peace it was below 1s. for only one year and in the last four years down to 1914 it stood at 1s. 2d.[5] Except for a few years during and just after the Crimean War all income-tax payers had been charged at the same rate. But from 1863 onwards some attempt had been made to modify the regressive effect of this arrangement by granting certain abatements to the poorer taxpayers. Thus in 1870 the position was that all incomes over £100 were subject to tax but those with incomes under £200 were exempt from tax on the first £60. As the tax rose it was modified by raising the level at which incomes became

[1] Cannan, *op. cit.*, p. 132.   [2] Hicks, *op. cit.*, p. 75.

[3] Cannan, *op. cit.*, p. 156.

[4] R.C. on Local Taxation, *Final Report* (*England and Wales*). *Appendix* (*P.P.* 1902, XXXIX), p. 75; Ministry of Health, *Statement showing the Amount of the Local Rates for the Financial Years 1913-14, etc.* (*P.P.* 1921, XXIX), p. xiv.

[5] Buxton, *op. cit.*, II, 378; Mallet, *op. cit.*, p. 484.

subject to tax, to £150 in 1877 and to £160 in 1894, and by extending the abatements. From 1898 there were four different abatements for incomes in different ranges up to £700 a year. Thus an approximation to a progressive rate of tax was being gradually achieved, and in 1907 the abatements were supplemented by a reduction of 3*d.* on the standard rate for incomes up to £2,000 a year. The attempt to make income tax more progressive was continued in 1909 when an intermediate rate of tax, 2*d.* below the standard rate, was introduced for incomes between £2,000 and £3,000, a small relief on account of each child under 16 years old was allowed to taxpayers with incomes up to £500, and a super-tax was imposed on all incomes of over £5,000 at the rate of 6*d.* on every pound by which they exceeded £3,000.[1]

Death duties, which were the one form of tax on capital, remained without any element of progression as long as they were light, and down to the 'nineties they were very light, especially for large landed estates. Probate duty, which was payable before the estate was distributed, was levied until 1881 in accordance with a scale of charges which were proportionately much less for large than for small estates. The legacy and succession duties, payable by the beneficiaries, were charged at percentage rates which varied according to the relationship between the testator and the beneficiary but were unaffected by the amount of the bequest. In 1881 Gladstone reduced one anomaly by making the probate duty on estates of more than £1,000 a flat 3 per cent and there were several additions to the death duties during the 'eighties. But comprehensive change came only in Harcourt's budget of 1894. Legacy and succession duties on personal and on real property respectively were retained at the previous rates, though with the value of successions reckoned in a more onerous way, but for the other death duties was substituted an estate duty, applicable to both personal and real property, and graduated progressively in accordance with the size of the estate. The maximum rate was 8 per cent, which applied to estates of £1,000,000 or more. In 1907 the scale was lengthened and steepened for estates of £150,000 and over, the new maximum, which applied to estates of £3,000,000 or more, being 10 per cent on the first £1,000,000 and 15 per cent on the remainder.[2]

[1] Buxton, *op. cit.*, II, 378; Mallet, *op. cit.*, pp. 484-6.

[2] Buxton, *op. cit.*, II, 292-8; Williams, *op. cit.*, pp. 118-24. From 1894 settled estates, irrespective of size, had to pay a supplementary duty of 1 per cent in addition to the ordinary estate duty.

These various changes gave income and capital taxes a new place in the national finances by the beginning of the twentieth century. In 1913-14 income tax, super-tax and death duties produced £74·6 million, which was almost exactly the same as the gross revenue from all sources in 1871-72. For the last three years of peace the yield of these taxes approximately equalled that from customs and excise duties, which thus still retained a very important rôle in the raising of revenue, though their produce had grown less quickly than that of the other chief taxes.[1] Few new duties were added, though the sugar duty, abolished in 1874, was revived in 1901. Alcoholic drinks continued to yield more than half the total customs and excise revenue, though duties on them were not among the most resilient. But tobacco, of which the consumption per head rose by one-third in twenty years after 1888, was becoming gradually more important among the chief sources of revenue.[2] As a whole, over a long period, the proportion of indirect to direct taxation gradually declined and from 1905 more than half the national tax revenue came regularly from direct taxes.[3] If national and local taxes are considered together and local rates are grouped with customs and excise duties as taxes on outlay—the case for regarding rates in this way is strong though it could be challenged—then the rise in the proportion of income and capital taxes in total taxation is more striking still. From only 13 per cent of the total in 1880 they increased to 24 per cent in 1890, 30 per cent in 1905 and 35 per cent in 1913.[4]

It is now possible to try to sum up some of the principal changes in the way in which government affected economic life in the late nineteenth and early twentieth centuries. One change, quite obviously, was that the government was in multitudinous ways limiting the complete individualism of market competition. It was doing so sometimes in the interest of groups who were unable, without help, to defend their own interests fully, and sometimes to try to preserve or secure social benefits which could not be measured by market price. But, though limits were imposed at innumerable points, few of them were very drastic in the sense that the extra expense or loss of profit which they caused to individuals or corporate bodies seriously hampered them; and there is little to suggest that the burden of the restrictions was very unequally spread among potential

[1] Mallet, *op. cit.*, pp. 474-5.   *Ibid.*, pp. 478-81.   [3] *Ibid.*, p. 493.
[4] Hicks, *op. cit.*, p. 75.

rivals of similar enterprise and honesty. The boundaries of free competition were reduced a little all round, but within them a high degree of competition—and freedom to arrange private limitations of competition—remained untouched.

The other equally obvious change was that the government was being used much more as an instrument providing positive services of which many were for the whole people, and of which those benefiting only one section were nearly all for people with fairly small incomes. The clearest illustrations of this were provided by the growth of social services—education, sanitary services, pensions, social insurance—and the relative decline of what had been a major item of cost, the service of the national debt. But in some ways the growth of other activities provides equally good illustrations. The increase in defence expenditure, for instance, involved a much bigger call on the productive resources of the country than did the social services, and it, too, was something undertaken to serve the interests of the whole people. More than any other service it caused the government, as employer, manufacturer, and customer, to have a direct impact on industrial activity: in 1897 a rough estimate, perhaps exaggerated, suggested that the navy, naval shipbuilding and the manufacture of the supplies which they needed gave employment to a million men.[1] Certainly there were several substantial towns whose economy was dominated by the industrial needs of defence and after 1900, when defence orders were more widely spread among private manufacturers,[2] the government must in this way have been exerting, half unconsciously, an appreciable and immediate influence on the general level of economic activity.

Indirectly, too, some of the defence expenditure, in conjunction with increased activity by the colonial service, may have helped to stimulate foreign trade through the extension of the colonial empire. It is easy to show that, though Britain's imperial trade was growing,

[1] A. J. Marder, British Naval Policy 1880-1905: the Anatomy of British Sea Power (1940), p. 31.

[2] In the nineteenth century the government undertook most of its own ship-building and repairing and manufactured many of the armaments it needed. For example, in Gladstone's first ministry a plan was adopted for a normal shipbuilding programme of 19,500 tons a year, of which 13,000 to 15,000 tons would be built in the Royal Dockyards (S. Childers, The Life and Correspondence of the right hon. Hugh C. E. Childers 1827-1896 (1901), I, 221-2). As late as 1884-85, out of a total expenditure of £3·8 mn. on building and repairing warships, £3·1 mn. was expended in the Royal Dockyards (Navy. Dockyard Expense Account 1884-85 (P.P. 1886, XLII), pp. 66-9). From 1889 and especially after 1905, as needs increased, a bigger and bigger proportion of work was placed by contract with private firms. (Marder, op. cit., pp. 38-42.)

only a minor part of the increase was in trade with recently acquired colonies and to argue that, in fact, colonial commerce quite failed to repay the effort and expense put into the expansion of empire.[1] But it is probable that the indirect gain from bringing new areas with new products into a world-wide system of multilateral trade more than offset the smallness in the volume of the direct trade of many new colonies. That small volume often contained an element that had a vital part in some complex interchange of other types of goods in other parts of the world. Since Britain, more than any other country, lived by foreign trade it is unlikely that its imperial expenditure harmed its economy, though the gain may have been modest.

When account is taken of the appreciable direct investment, as well as manufacture, which the government undertook in carrying out its defence policy it appears that there may have been more budgetary influence on the movement of the late Victorian economy than is usually recognized. But there was no attempt to use either the budget as a whole or defence expenditure, which was its largest industrial constituent, as a means of regulating variations in general economic activity. In so far as some limitation of these was attempted, it was through the credit policy of the Bank of England. The budget was usually a compromise between political needs and a desire to keep public expenditure as low as practicable. Normally it was devised in such a way as to cover expenditure without a deficit, but with no more than a small surplus. If the yield of existing taxes increased, so as to promise a larger surplus, the normal reaction was to avoid this by reducing the rates of some indirect taxes, thus stimulating consumption, irrespective of the general movement of economic conditions. It was not an excuse for seeking out new objects of expenditure, nor was there any attempt to vary the size of the surplus. Expenditure and investment for purposes of defence were determined by political and strategic considerations rather than by the state of the home economy. Thus the influence of the budget on the variation of general economic activity, though real, was incidental to other matters, and, in a sense, fortuitous.[2]

The deliberate, substantial influence of government action on economic affairs was concerned with long-term objectives and more with the creation of new opportunities for private individuals and

---

[1] This case is argued at length, for all countries with colonial empires, in G. Clark, *The Balance Sheets of Imperialism* (1936).

[2] *Cf.* Hicks, *op. cit.*, pp. 141-5.

institutions than with encroaching on their preserves. It was in equipping people with the knowledge and physical fitness needed to do better jobs; in providing collectively for many the comfort, amenity and security which only a few could purchase individually; and in spreading familiar laws and stronger administration in new territories which were thereby better fitted to participate in international trade that the achievement of public services was most evident. In more complex technical and social conditions more had to be done by public action if private enterprise was to remain capable of using new economic opportunities as they arose. A large part of the task of government service was new, whereas the much more varied rôle of private enterprise was in essentials unaltered. And it proved possible to begin the expansion of government activities without damaging the incentives of private individuals in their own business. The greater wealth of the country provided some margin out of which to finance new government services, and circumstances helped to keep down the cost of many of them. An appreciable increase in the security of the very poor did not cost an enormous amount. New colonies could be acquired and governed fairly cheaply while communication of western ideas and techniques among most of their inhabitants was difficult and slow. Even the increasing cost of armaments and defence forces was partly offset by some economies of scale and by the opportunity to effect a greater concentration of forces. So the public did not have to be taxed very much more heavily. Trade continued to bear few fiscal burdens and, despite preliminary apprehensions, heavier and graduated taxes on income and capital were still apparently well below the level where they might discourage private saving and investment and a readiness to seize business opportunities, on which the continued growth of the economy depended. The nation received new and real benefits from government service and got them at a cost which left its economic powers unimpaired.

CHAPTER TEN

The Course and Outcome of Economic Change

THE full significance of the changes in the various branches of economic life is apparent only if by some means their combined influence on the whole national economy can be estimated and if it is possible to judge how that influence was exerted. In recent years much attention has been given to matters of this kind and a good deal has been done to define and delimit the main economic trends and fluctuations in the nineteenth century. Several investigators have agreed that there appear to have been long trend periods of about fifty years, in one half of which economic activity was marked by rising prices, more rapidly expanding production and trade, and general prosperity, and in the other half by falling prices, slower expansion, and greater difficulty in maintaining general prosperity.[1] In the late nineteenth century a downward trend of this kind, by no means peculiar to Britain, is commonly taken to have begun about 1873, though some people would date its onset from the end of the American Civil War.[2] Some time in the late 'nineties the trend appears to have been reversed and the ensuing upswing lasted until the First World War.

But any mention of changing economic trends inevitably poses the question: trends of what? Attempts have been made to analyse quantitatively the course of many different economic series and fit them all into the same trend pattern.[3] Prices, interest rates, exports, imports, the terms of trade, industrial production generally and the output of a few important commodities in particular, and real wages

[1] This idea was developed in a systematic way in N. D. Kondratieff, 'The Long Waves in Economic Life' in *Review of Economic Statistics*, XVII (1935), 105-15. For a general presentation of British economic trends see Rostow, *British Economy of the Nineteenth Century*, chap. I. 'General prosperity' refers to business rather than to wages, since the most rapid rises in real wages were associated with long-term downswings, not upswings.

[2] e.g. E. H. Phelps Brown and S. A. Ozga, 'Economic Growth and the Price Level' in *Econ. Journ.*, LXV (1955), 1.

[3] The most elaborate analysis, which tries to relate the long trend movements systematically to shorter cycles of various kinds is J. A. Schumpeter, *Business Cycles* (1939).

have all been pressed into service in this way. Analyses which try to incorporate all these have not, so far, been very convincing, partly because they have to put more weight on some very defective statistics than these are fit to bear, and partly because, even where the figures are acceptable, the various series do not all show either the same turning-points or turning-points that differ from each other in a regular, uniform way. The truth seems to be that the trend periods commonly used are defined primarily by the movement of prices and interest rates, and that, while these are related to variations in production, trade, wages and incomes, the relationships are so complex and shifting that the more general analyses and explanations of economic trends are over-simplified to the point of being sometimes misleading.

If one takes the view that the purpose of economic activity is consumption, both present and future, then it appears more significant if economic periods can be defined in terms of income than in terms of price movements. In practice, the analysis of long-term economic trends, though it has tried to take account systematically of changes in real wages, has not paid so much attention to the growth of the national income,[1] partly because of the obvious deficiencies of the nineteenth-century data. But the more abundant material on this subject from about 1870 suggests that the growth of national income fitted approximately into the pattern of long-term movements defined by prices, though the fit was one of periodicity, not of direction. It also indicates something of more fundamental importance, i.e. a permanent tendency, apart from long-term swings, for national income to grow faster than before. Some estimates would suggest that real income per head in the United Kingdom was growing at the rate of about 25 per cent per decade for most of the last third of the nineteenth century.[2] Others, rather less optimistic and probably rather more accurate, would confirm that rate only for the 'eighties and early 'nineties, but would indicate high rates of about 17 per cent per decade immediately before and after.[3] There seems no doubt, whatever the imperfections of earlier data, that real incomes were growing at a rate that had never been sustained for an appreciable period before, and although there was a marked

[1] *Cf.* Rostow, *op. cit.*, pp. 9-10.
[2] P. Deane, 'Contemporary Estimates of National Income in the Second Half of the Nineteenth Century' in *Econ. Hist. Rev.*, 2nd series, IX, 461.
[3] Jefferys and Walters, *National Income and Expenditure of the U.K., 1870-1952*, p. 14.

change in the early years of the twentieth century, subsequent experience indicated that more rapid growth than had prevailed until the eighteen-sixties could be regarded as normal.

This happy development, which did so much to set the character of late Victorian England, may at first sight seem surprising. The whole final quarter of the nineteenth century has often been named 'The Great Depression'; the export trade and home agriculture were certainly growing more slowly than before and industrial production may have ceased to accelerate; and some suggestions have been made that leaders of business and technology were less ingenious and adaptable than either their fathers or their foreign contemporaries. But this last suggestion is a very doubtful one and the other points do not really indicate a general economic decline. There were spells of several years of bad trade, but the impression that the quarter-century as a whole was depressed is an illusion.[1] Continually falling prices provided a continual theme for complaining businessmen, and new competitors and new techniques compelled unwelcome and often costly reorganization, or sometimes caused firms to be squeezed out of existence. Things were harder for many individual businesses but the economy as a whole flourished. If agriculture and manufacture no longer bounded ahead as fast as before, distribution, finance and other services grew more than ever, and the income derived from dealings of all kinds with the outside world did likewise.

That incomes could grow more quickly was a sign that the most difficult conditions of the transition to an industrial and urban way of life were coming to an end. Until the late nineteenth century a large part of the fruits of economic advance was absorbed by provision for a rapidly increasing population and by heavy investment in what might be considered the basic equipment of an industrial society—railways, docks, towns, and their equipment and services. Much of this investment was of a kind which, in proportion to its cost, could yield only a small increase in current output until it was associated with many other provisions which could come only slowly, though it could go on yielding that increase for a very long time. By the last quarter of the century the burden of providing for a great increase in population had scarcely eased, though it began to do so from about 1890, but the most onerous stage of investment in industrialization was over. The railway system, the docks and harbour works, and the towns had

[1] See the discussion of this point in Beales, 'The "Great Depression" in Industry and Trade' in Carus-Wilson (ed.), *Essays in Economic History*, pp. 406-15.

for the most part been built. Much more capital expenditure, often not immediately very productive, had to be incurred on their enlargement and improvement, but this was not comparable with the tasks that had already been accomplished. Moreover, the world-wide spread of mechanical transport and communications and the speeding up of manufacturing processes probably meant that another large form of investment—stocks of materials and finished goods— could be reduced in proportion to turnover. Thus, by about 1880, conditions had been established in which investment at home could usually be more immediately productive than before. This was probably the most important permanent change in the factors governing the growth of income.

It is sometimes suggested that in the last quarter of the nineteenth century the increase of real wages and incomes was further helped because a smaller proportion of British investment was going abroad, into projects which took a long time to yield their full benefits, while the delayed fruits of earlier foreign investment were being received for the first time.[1] But this appears to be only very partially true. British foreign investment remained quite high, especially in the 'eighties,[2] and much of it was in forms (notably railways) which in the past had often taken a long time to be fully remunerative. The significant thing was not a falling off in foreign investment but a change in conditions which helped foreign as well as home investment to contribute more quickly than before to a bigger flow of goods. This was partly because it was accompanied by an increased migration of labour: British investment in railways and other enterprises in the American West in the 'eighties, for instance, led to a large flow of cheap imports much more quickly than comparable investment in the 'fifties and 'sixties. It was also partly because the opening of the world by mechanical transport made it possible to concentrate a good deal of investment on the development of resources with a high physical yield, often without the need to spend much on the provision of less remunerative capital for wider social purposes in the vicinity. This favourable state of affairs persisted until after the end of the nineteenth century but was less permanent than the change affecting the conditions of home investment.

One other factor that should be taken into account is the great change in the scale of organization of many businesses, both in Britain and other industrial countries, towards 1900. There are

---

[1] Rostow, *op. cit.*, pp. 25-6, 64-7 and 88-9.   [2] *Cf.* p. 188 above.

indications that economies of scale, bringing more efficient production, may have been achieved to an unusual extent within a short
span of years. Since change of this kind is bound to be discontinuous,
it may be that the impossibility of repeating it for the time being was
one reason why things ceased to go on improving so quickly in the
early twentieth century.

But it can be no more than one reason among many, since there
was so much to be explained. The more favourable conditions for
home investment remained and the burden of providing for a rapidly
increasing dependent population was easing, yet the growth of incomes fell away sharply in the early years of the new century—
and similar changes were taking place in other countries.[1] The average
real income per head in the United Kingdom in 1905-14 has been
estimated at less than 7 per cent above the average for the immediately
preceding decade, which is in very sharp contrast with late Victorian
conditions.[2] It is possible that the figures exaggerate the contrast
because methods of measuring real income are inadequate. The
economic improvement of the time, probably to a greater degree than
before, showed itself in the supply of more varied and more convenient goods and not just in increased quantities of basic commodities, which can be more easily measured.[3] There was also a
significant increase in the benefits obtained through collective
services, which likewise are probably not fully represented in
measurements of national income. Nevertheless, when every allowance of this kind is made, there can be no doubt that real income per
head was no longer growing as quickly as before.

The most important immediate causes of the change appear to have
been in the type of investment and the conditions in which it was
made. All the industrial countries, including Britain, were using
rather more of their resources for non-productive purposes, notably
armaments and war,[4] and it is doubtful whether British industrial

---

[1] E. H. Phelps Brown and Sheila V. Hopkins, 'The Course of Wage-Rates in
Five Countries, 1860-1939' in *Oxford Economic Papers* (New Series), II (1950),
226-96.

[2] Jefferys and Walters, *op. cit.*, p. 14.

[3] Phelps Brown and Hopkins, *loc. cit.*, p. 239.

[4] A. C. Pigou, 'Prices and Wages from 1896 to 1914' in *Econ. Journ.*, XXXIII
(1923), 167; Rostow, *op. cit.*, p. 26. Increased expenditure on armaments has often
had a multiplier effect, calling unemployed resources into use, and thereby accel-
erating the growth of national income. But in the early years of the twentieth
century it seems likely that any effect of this kind was offset by other influences.
Greater investment in defence involved a change in the direction of investment
rather than a net addition to its total. Some at least, of these changes in the use
of capital meant a transfer from more to less productive uses.

investment at home was directed as fully as it might have been towards expanding the output of the sort of goods that could bring in the biggest returns. Moreover, in the last ten years before the First World War, British investment, and to some extent that of other industrial countries, increasingly went abroad at a time when the benefits of investment in new areas of primary production needed rather more time and expense for their gathering. The growth of industrial production in the world was apparently at a maximum in the 'nineties and fell off only a little in the first few years of the twentieth century.[1] Consequently the world demand for primary products began to run ahead of their supply, prices rose in consequence and there was an incentive to open new sources of supply.[2] But it seems probable that in many cases this meant developing resources that were slightly less accessible or slightly less easily worked than those brought into production a little earlier. Since this disadvantage was not offset by an appreciable improvement in productive techniques, investment for this purpose brought, for the time being, a lower real return than before.

The situation may be summarized as one in which the British economy at the beginning of the twentieth century passed from its remarkable late Victorian growth to a condition, by no means stagnant or declining, but showing slower progress. And the main reasons for the change were a failure to exploit favourable economic conditions at home and even greater concentration than before on dealings with the outside world in circumstances in which the advantages from so doing could not go on increasing so easily as they had done a little earlier.

Despite the qualifications that must be made about its later years the impression of the whole period from 1870 to 1914 is one of great economic advance. There remain, however, several questions to be asked about the character of the advance: in particular, were its benefits generally diffused through the community, and was their value lessened because they came too irregularly? Irregularity in the course of economic activity, not merely as shown in long-term trends but also in the form of quite brief fluctuations, has always been normal. The cyclical fluctuations which occurred in the late nineteenth century were not new, but in some ways they differed a little from those earlier. The most prominent of them averaged about nine

---

[1] League of Nations, *Industrialisation and Foreign Trade*, p. 130.
[2] Phelps Brown and Ozga, *loc. cit.*, pp. 10-13.

years in duration. Peaks of activity appear to have been reached in 1873, 1883, 1890, 1900, 1907 and 1913, with corresponding troughs in 1879, 1886, 1894, 1904, 1908 and 1914, though there is usually room for dispute about the precise turning-points.[1] The movements of prices, production, foreign trade and employment are all relevant, but not all of them are perfectly known and they do not all follow precisely the same course. Some important sections of economic activity do not fit well into the pattern at all. For instance, trade in some of the chief export commodities shows a much shorter cyclical fluctuation, but one of the differences from the early nineteenth century was that these short cycles no longer made a decisive mark on the course of activity generally. Some other economic series, notably building activity and the number of emigrants, fluctuated over a much longer period, about twenty years,[2] and attempts have been made to show that such longer cycles had a more general incidence. Some economists have suggested that the growth, not only of building, but of manufacturing output, has fluctuated in cycles of about twenty years.[3] It may be that in some important respects the more familiar cycles of about nine years alternated within a more fundamental cycle lasting about eighteen to twenty years. But, on the whole, it was the incidence of the nine-year cycle which most obviously and immediately affected business and the workers: the twenty-year rhythm is often not immediately apparent in the year-to-year sequence of economic events and can be fully displayed only in a series of moving averages, from which shorter fluctuations have been partially smoothed out.

When attention is concentrated on the shorter cycles, the chief distinctive characteristics that can be noted in the late nineteenth century (apart from the obliteration of short fluctuations lasting three or four years) are their more general incidence on the different branches of economic life and their more regular progression through phases of expansion and recession that were roughly equal in

---

[1] Rostow, *op. cit.*, p. 33.

[2] Thomas, *Migration and Economic Growth*, chap. VII, argues the case for the twenty-year cycle with much statistical illustration, and tries to establish that its downswing in Britain approximately coincided with its upswing in the U.S.A., a phenomenon associated with variations in the transatlantic migration of labour and capital. It is, in fact, difficult to fit all the series used into a common pattern, but for Britain, the peaks of the building cycle appear approximately in 1877 and 1899 and the troughs in 1871, 1892 and 1912. The turning points of other series differ by several years.

[3] Hoffmann, *British Industry 1700-1950*, Part C, esp. pp. 130-6.

duration. These characteristics were symptomatic of the emergence of a more integrated economy, served by more reliable institutions. Earlier in the nineteenth century, business conditions often varied widely not only from one occupation to another but also from region to region. As time went on, however, a diminishing proportion of people had their business prospects dominated by the state of a localized market and local banking arrangements. The creation of a national and then an international system of rapid transport and communication, matched by the establishment of similarly comprehensive financial arrangements, broke down many remnants of local self-containment and directly exposed most economic activities to the unifying influence of national or global market conditions. As more and more of Britain's livelihood became associated with foreign trade, some domestic sources of economic fluctuation were almost eliminated. Variations in the abundance of the British harvest, for instance, had formerly had far-reaching effects on prices and purchasing-power, which contributed to sudden recessions or expansions of trade.[1] But by the 'seventies a short harvest at home had little general effect since it could always be made good by increased imports from whatever part of the world had fared better. Some of the institutional changes also affected the regularity of fluctuations. Thus a stronger banking system got rid of the financial panics which for more than half the nineteenth century often helped to bring business booms to a sudden end, with a rapid drop to the bottom of a depression. And a quicker and more abundant flow of both information and goods made it easier to avoid those accumulations of unsold stocks, which used temporarily to choke trade after two or three years of expansion. On the other hand, the growth of most, rather than only some, activities became very closely dependent on the use of more fixed capital. Consequently, the level of activity in the capital goods industries had an increasingly powerful effect on the whole economy; and, since decisions to order more or fewer capital goods often took an appreciable time to carry out completely, the transition between the top and the bottom of the business cycle tended to be more gradual.[2]

Thus, whereas in the earlier nineteenth century many activities fluctuated with a rhythm of their own, determined in many cases partly by fortuitous circumstances, after 1870 most followed roughly the same sort of pattern; and, whereas a common experience for

---

[1] Rostow, *op. cit.*, pp. 50-2 and 109-14.   [2] *Ibid.*, pp. 41-3.

those which earlier followed a regular course was expansion in most years, interrupted by drops which were sudden, sharp and usually (but not always) brief, the common later experience was one of fairly well-matched alternations of rise and fall. Inevitably, from the 'seventies on, there were more years of recession in economic activity than there had been earlier. But this does not necessarily mean that the average level of prosperity fell. Despite assumptions of the contrary, there is no clear evidence that depressions became deeper, and many years of recession were also years of very active business, though a little below the peak.[1]

It seems improbable that such changes as took place in the characteristics of business fluctuations had any general deleterious influence. That more people were directly affected by the trade cycle, even though the effects included some cyclical unemployment, was on balance advantageous since it involved the release of more people from exposure to haphazard fluctuations and from that widespread lack of economic organization which showed itself in chronic under-employment rather than in occasional and limited unemployment. For a small minority of workers there may have been increased hardship because, in occupations where the amplitude of the cycle was greatest, the more gradual recessions brought the risk that a small number might be unemployed for a long spell rather than larger numbers for a shorter period. This apart, however, the changes in cyclical fluctuations did nothing to detract from the benefits which, in terms of welfare and living-standards, the long-term changes made possible. The jerky nature of economic growth certainly involved some waste, through a failure to make full use of productive resources, but in the period from 1870 to 1914 such waste must have been less, not more, than before.

When the outcome of the long-term changes, too, is considered in relation to the improvement of the welfare of the whole community, it appears that, though a minority may have been adversely affected, the benefits of a great increase in the national income were widely diffused. When incomes were growing fastest, down to the late 'nineties, real wages were on the average growing rather faster still— or so the incomplete information on the subject would suggest. Some of this gain was subsequently lost, however, because, while total income continued to grow more slowly, average wage-rates

[1] *Ibid.*, pp. 45-50; W. W. Rostow, *The Process of Economic Growth* (1953), pp. 138-40.

I

changed very little in real terms.[1] But all the time an increasing proportion of the people was moving out of the wage-earning class into occupations which, for the most part, were rather better paid.[2] By this means also the increased national income was spread a little more widely. There were critics in the early twentieth century who thought that the inequality of incomes in Britain was so extreme as to be scandalous.[3] Perhaps it was, but almost certainly it was just a little less extreme than it had been forty years earlier. Chiozza Money estimated that in 1908, 12 per cent of the income-receivers of the United Kingdom had half the national income, and that among this 12 per cent the wealthiest group, who formed less than one-thirtieth of the total, enjoyed a little over one-third of the national income.[4] His estimate of the total income (£1,844 million) was almost certainly rather too low, so that the incomes of the wealthier (i.e. the income-tax paying) classes were a slightly lower proportion of the total than he claimed. Even so, his picture was broadly true. But Baxter's estimates for 1867 suggested that half the national income went to rather less than 10 per cent of the income-receivers, including a tiny group of very rich, less than one two-hundredth of the total, who received 25 per cent of the national income.

In absolute terms there can be little doubt that the biggest share of the great increase in national income went to only an appreciable minority, though within the minority it was an enlarged middle class, rather than the aristocracy, which was the main beneficiary. The aristocracy as a whole may, indeed, have been one important group that suffered an absolute diminution of income, mainly as a consequence of the decline in agricultural rents and land values after 1880. By the late 'eighties a distinguished Chancellor of the Exchequer, looking at the evidence of various taxes, insurance payments and small savings, had picked out 'the increase of moderate incomes' as one of the outstanding changes of the time[5] and the same tendency continued and probably became even more marked after 1900, when taxable incomes were growing and those not subject to

---

[1] Phelps Brown and Hopkins, *loc. cit.*, p. 276.

[2] Changes in the ratio of wages to total incomes and some of the reasons for them are discussed in *ibid.*, pp. 246-51.

[3] This was the theme of one of the best-selling economic works of the Edwardian period, L. G. Chiozza Money's *Riches and Poverty* (1905). References here are to the revised edition published in 1911.

[4] *Ibid.*, pp. 44-9.

[5] G. J. Goschen, 'The Increase of Moderate Incomes' in *J.R. Stat. Socy.*, L (1887), 593 *et seq.*

tax were barely keeping up with the rise in the numbers of non-taxpayers.[1]

Nevertheless, the benefits of an enlarged national income were by no means confined to the middle classes. Relatively to their incomes before 1870 the mass of the wage-earners improved their position even more than the middle classes, and this relative improvement went on slowly but almost continuously except during the first decade of the twentieth century. Moreover, the less tangible factors, which are difficult to measure but which are essential elements in the standard of living, nearly all indicate improvements that were specially advantageous to the wage-earners. The greater variety of goods and services available for consumption, many of them quite cheap, was a fairly general benefit, but the increase in number and improvement in quality of collective services (which continued and, indeed, speeded up even while the personal incomes of most wage-earners ceased to grow) meant rather less to the wealthier people than to the rest. Such services brought a less unpleasant and less uncomfortable environment, with, as a result, a better chance of good health and long life, to millions who, unlike the wealthy minority, had had little chance to buy these things out of their individual incomes. By the early years of the twentieth century, too, collective services were giving a little more economic security to some of those who needed it most, as well as providing increased educational opportunities which brought a wider and more lucrative choice of jobs to the children of many quite poor people. And, because of changes in taxation, the cost of these benefits was borne increasingly by the upper and middle classes rather than by those who received most of them. Changes in taxation and in the objects of government expenditure did, in fact, do something to carry a little further the reduction of economic inequality, though still leaving scope for much, much more to be done than had yet been accomplished.[2]

Thus, although there were still wide gaps between the economic conditions of different sections of the community, the half century preceding the First World War had brought remarkable improvements for the wage-earning classes as a whole, improvements which compared favourably with those gained by any other section of society. In spite of all the manifestations of discontent in the two or three years before 1914 it is improbable that there had ever been a

[1] *Cf.* Money, *op. cit.*, pp. 49-50 and 106-13.   [2] *Cf.* pp. 235-6 above.

time when, materially, things had been so good for most of the population.[1]

Yet this period of great advance was also one in which the existence of widespread poverty, to an extent not hitherto generally realized, was precisely documented and forced upon the attention of a shocked public. Moreover, whatever the average or general improvement might be, there were suspicions that in some important respects the problems of the very poor were becoming no easier. Charles Booth's survey of living conditions in London, carried out between 1887 and 1892, did more than anything else to arouse the public.[2] Not only were its conclusions startling, but they were based on more comprehensive investigation and on a more objective measurement of poverty than anything previously attempted. Before the effect of Booth's revelations could wear off or they could be dismissed as totally unrepresentative, they were reinforced by the large number of rejections of would-be recruits for the war in South Africa, which seemed to reflect the results of life among the poor, and by the results of an even more thorough survey of York, made in 1899 by Seebohm Rowntree. The latter found that 9·91 per cent of the people of York were living in what he called 'primary poverty'; i.e. they belonged to families whose total earnings were insufficient to obtain the minimum necessaries for the maintenance of merely physical efficiency. He also estimated that a further 17·93 per cent, whose earnings would have been sufficient for this minimum purpose had not part of them been absorbed by other expenditure, were in fact living in poverty.[3] Booth's distinctions between different classes of poverty were not of quite the same kind, nor did he define his terms quite so carefully. But he and Rowntree agreed that his estimate of 30·7 per cent of the total population of London living in poverty was comparable with the 27·84 per cent in the two categories of poverty in York.[4]

Such results seem so difficult to reconcile with the evidence of rapidly improving working-class living standards, even when one

---

[1] This might not be true of much of the first decade of the twentieth century but by 1912-13 real wages were rising again. *Cf.* Clapham, *Econ. Hist. of Mod. Brit.*, III, 468-9 and 506-7.

[2] Preliminary results and material were published while the survey was in progress. Booth published the entire work under the title *Life and Labour of the People in London: an economic and industrial survey* (9 vols., 1889-97). A revised edn., with the addition of 7 vols. on religious influences and a final vol. of comparisons, notes, conclusions and summary, appeared in 1902-3.

[3] B. S. Rowntree, *Poverty. A Study of Town Life* (2nd edn., 1902), chap. IV.

[4] *Ibid.*, pp. 298-300. For the London statistics see Booth, *op. cit.*, *Poverty Series*, II, 21.

remembers that some of this evidence comes from the years immediately after Booth's investigations, that one is bound to ask whether these great surveys can have been to some extent misleading. In so far as they were able to apply objective standards, however, they appear to have been soundly based. When Rowntree tried to calculate minimum dietary needs there was certainly not a full scientific knowledge available to him; the existence and functions of vitamins and the necessity of certain other mineral salts, for instance, were still undiscovered. But fuller knowledge would not have revealed a cheaper minimum diet. And if the number of calories which he took as a minimum standard seems a little high, that is appropriate because most of the poor had no means of earning a living other than by physical exertion.[1] Later investigators, with the advantage of a knowledge of more recent discoveries in nutrition, would confirm the validity of Rowntree's demonstration that there were many poor who could not or did not obtain an adequate diet. The most eminent of them even asserted that 'the opening of the twentieth century saw malnutrition more rife in England than it had been since the great dearths of medieval and Tudor times'.[2] Be that as it may, there is no escaping the conclusion that one-tenth of the population of York was too poor to buy the minimum necessaries for continued physical well-being. There is less certainty about the numbers of the others who were living in poverty and about Booth's figure for London, because rather more depended on the subjective impressions of the investigators and because there is some possibility of bias in the sample of cases which Booth investigated.[3] While there can be no doubt that Rowntree's 'primary poverty' was far from covering all who fell below the poverty line which marks the minimum standard for a healthy existence, the total in this condition may have been appreciably below Booth's 30 per cent. It certainly seems much more likely to have been below that figure than above it. Nor is it safe to assume, as has so often been done (with the support of Rowntree himself),[4] that the results obtained in London and York were thoroughly representative of British urban life. The metropolis had

[1] Rowntree, *op. cit.*, p. 97.

[2] J. C. Drummond and Anne Wilbraham, *The Englishman's Food* (rev. ed., 1958), p. 403.

[3] In E. London Booth investigated all the working-class families with children of school age (about half the total) and no others, and assumed that his results were representative for all. But the need to support several schoolchildren was one factor helping to keep some families in poverty.

[4] Rowntree, *op. cit.*, p. 301.

many economic and social characteristics that were all its own and by its sheer size, diversity and prestige had an attraction for large numbers with no regular trade at their command; and York was not a very typical provincial town. Both London and York were short of factories and large workshops, which in so many towns were the most reliable sources of a steady job at a comfortable and rising wage for a high proportion of the working class.

Thus these surveys cannot be reliably used to build up a generally black picture of working-class living standards at the beginning of the twentieth century, with the suggestion that any evidence of recent improvement merely shows what inhuman depths were touched earlier. They do, however, make it necessary to add to the recognition of a wide diffusion of modest comfort an awareness that there was a substantial minority that had not shared in recent improvements. Indeed, it is likely that the submerged tenth (or whatever the proportion should be), far from providing a surviving illustration of what had been general conditions earlier, had undergone some decline in their average material standards. There can have been few times when the lot of the very poor was more miserable than in the early years of the twentieth century. These were the people who had to devote practically all their income to the basic necessities of food, shelter and warmth. But when all other prices were falling, most urban rents were rising, and the price of coal began to rise several years earlier than that of most other commodities. Such differential price movements were hardest for the poorest, and they were matched by changes in relative food prices. The poorest have always had to buy the cheapest foodstuffs and by 1900 much of the lowest-priced food was less nutritious than that of earlier times, though this was not generally realized: bread which had lost most of its vitamin content through new methods of milling, margarine which lacked the vitamins found in butter, factory-made jam with a very low fruit content, tinned condensed milk from which much of the fat had been removed.[1] Though the prices of more nutritious foods such as meat, butter and eggs had fallen absolutely, the gap between these prices and those of bread and potatoes had been widening for a century or more, so that the very poor bought little meat and dairy produce,[2]

[1] *Cf.* Drummond and Wilbraham, *op. cit.*, pp. 388-90 and 405-9.

[2] A sample investigation of working-class expenditure in 1904 showed that whereas the consumption of bread, flour and potatoes by the poorest families (incomes under 25s. per week) was only a little less than that of the highest paid (incomes over 40s. per week), the foodstuffs of which the latter families consumed

and their nutrition suffered in consequence. It was conditions such as these which made extreme poverty and its results so frightful, and until the last few years before 1914 measures of public social policy were concerned almost exclusively with other matters.

So the very poor lived in squalor, misery and insecurity, worse fed than ever. It was the greatest failure of the age. But the very poor, though still distressingly numerous, were almost certainly a smaller proportion of the population than at any earlier time. The rest experienced a substantial enrichment of their daily lives, both in the variety of the supplies and experiences that were opened to them and in the general comfort of their home and environment. They lived rather longer than their parents and grandparents and, despite the reduction in the nutritional value of some common foods, they probably fed rather better.[1] Their material circumstances provide a not inconsiderable testimonial to the strength and success of the late Victorian British economy.

A final assessment of the British economic position must take account not only of the current spread of improved material well-being but also of the extent to which existing arrangements facilitated the continuation of similar improvements in the future. The world was constantly changing and was certain to go on changing rapidly, partly in ways that were foreseeable. Britain's economic success, like that of any other country, depended on the ability to keep on adapting economic life to changes in resources, knowledge and market conditions in such a way as to grasp profitable opportunities as they emerged, instead of being overtaken by events and having nothing with which to replace familiar activities when they were rendered less rewarding.

more than twice as much as the former included fresh milk, butter, eggs, vegetables and fruit. (*Report of Enquiry by the Board of Trade into Working Class Rents, Housing and Retail Prices* (*P.P.* 1908, CVII), p. xxvi).

[1] Not only were there increases in the consumption per head of such valuable foods as meat and dairy produce but there was also a great improvement in the purity of most of the commoner foodstuffs. In the mid-nineteenth century large quantities of food were not what they purported to be (and were less nutritious than they should have been) because of the widespread practices of deliberate adulteration. After the 'fifties there was a marked improvement and from the 'seventies onwards the extent of adulteration was fairly small. For accounts of changes in the quality of food see Drummond and Wilbraham, *op. cit.*, chap. XVII and, with much more detail and explanation, J. Burnett, *The History of Food Adulteration in Great Britain in the Nineteenth Century* (Univ. of London unpublished Ph.D. thesis, 1958).

Such considerations provide additional criteria by which to judge the main economic changes between 1870 and 1914. Of the changes which permeated the whole character of the economy perhaps the most striking was the greater involvement in international dealings. Not only did a somewhat larger proportion of the goods produced or consumed in Britain pass through the channels of international trade, but the great increase in the accumulation of foreign investments converted large newly-productive areas partially into extensions of the British economy. Closely associated with this change was the relatively as well as absolutely greater share which the provision of distributive, financial and other services had among British economic activities. The growth of financial services, in particular, helped to foster the expansion and prosperity of a worldwide, multilateral trading system, on which Britain's livelihood had come to depend, and to give Britain a central position of outstanding strength and influence within it. Other notable changes were in the relative importance of different types of commodities produced and exported, especially the greater dependence on sales of coal and engineering products. And bound up with all these other changes was the development of a more complex organization of economic and social life, in which it was both possible and necessary to make fuller use of the skill and ability of the people, as well as to rely on their greater adaptability and willingness to co-operate in the introduction of new techniques and new types of working arrangements.

There can be little doubt that in the late nineteenth century every one of these major changes was in a direction which helped the British people to take advantage of new conditions in their economic environment as they emerged, or sometimes to change those conditions in ways that benefited themselves—and not themselves alone. The extension of British-financed enterprise far beyond the boundaries of the United Kingdom brought great rewards because it contributed particularly to the production of widely used commodities in conditions where, relatively to the expenditure incurred, a large physical output was possible. It brought direct savings to Britain through imports which were cheaper than comparable home-produced supplies would have been and through the development of new markets which made established lines of home production remunerative to a greater extent and for a longer time than would otherwise have been the case, and which also helped to ensure that the gain from cheap imported supplies was not significantly offset by failure to employ the resources displaced at home.[1] The rise of coal and engineering among the British industries and export trades showed an ability to profit from the rapid spread of industrialization among other countries rather than to let it cause a competitive check. At a time when the steam engine was the power unit of nearly all the world's rapidly growing manufactures, and when goods were being carried in larger quantities over longer distances by mechanical means, the universal demand for coal and machinery among industrializing countries (some of which were far from being self-sufficient in these goods) presented a golden opportunity to a few others, of which Britain took considerable, if not the maximum, advantage. The rise of finance and other commercial services, besides contributing indispensably to the organization of the world economy in the way that suited British needs, was a profitable response to a need that was being increasingly felt all over the world and which hardly any other country could fully meet for itself. And the fact that these adaptations were achieved was a demonstration that the necessary reserves of human skill were being developed and applied, and that the abandonment of some obstructive habits of thought and working methods was taking place, though not without friction.

There was the evidence of results, in the form of much greater wealth, to demonstrate that the British economy had been adapted very successfully to changing conditions. But on the eve of the First World War it was not only the recent slower growth of income that made it seem uncertain whether the type of economy which had emerged would continue much longer to be well suited to its environment. A slower growth of income might be only a temporary phase while the effects of recent investment were coming to maturity, but, since trade and finance were growing without at the same time yielding such evident benefits as before, it was possible that they were no longer turned in the most advantageous directions. There were many signs that competitive and technical conditions were changing, fewer signs that British economic activity was finding new lines to follow.

In the years just before 1914 businessmen appeared to be intensifying some of the earlier changes in the British economy, on the assumption that they would continue to be very profitable. Most

---

[1] *Cf.* Cairncross, *Home and Foreign Investment 1870-1913*, chap. IX, esp. pp. 233-5.

striking of all was the renewed concentration on the expansion of external dealings, both commercial and financial, and it has often been asked whether this showed wise judgment. In a general way, the assumptions underlying it were probably reasonable, but it is doubtful whether enough supplementary economic changes were being made for them to remain reasonable much longer. The advantages from the kind of heavy foreign investment which had been so fruitful in the late nineteenth century were passing their maximum, though they were unlikely to disappear. So many of the previously neglected productive resources of the world had recently begun to be used that further development of a similar kind was bound eventually to involve the penetration of rather less accessible areas, the exploitation of rather less rich resources, more concern with conserving the yield of resources over a long period. Thus the benefits of foreign investment were likely to depend even more than before on the application of increased technical ingenuity and rather less on the bounty of nature. As that happened, the possibility increased that more could be gained by concentrating on the improvement of productive efficiency at home some of the effort that had been going into enlarging the sources of cheap supplies from abroad. It is, however, by no means certain that this point had been reached before 1914. Much of the foreign investment of the early twentieth century still went to areas that were being effectively developed for the first time and which were probably little more costly of access than those opened up thirty years earlier; and the increased supplies of primary produce after the First World War were in part a testimony to the physical effectiveness of the investment.

But even before 1914 it was becoming doubtful whether Britain could advantageously continue to increase its *relative* dependence on dealings with the outside world. Though there might still be great potentialities in a heavy export of capital for familiar purposes, it needed to be matched by a comparable increase in the effectiveness with which home resources were used. Otherwise Britain might not have the means either to utilize or to pay for the supplies which it was helping to create overseas. Britain's livelihood depended on international trade and the performance of international services. There was no possibility of altering that, though some difficulties were being foreshadowed, especially because of the great reliance on earnings from services and investments. Although international trade could be expected to go on growing, and the world's need for finance, transport and commercial services to grow with it, Britain's position in the provision of such things was bound to meet increasing competition as other countries became wealthier and earned larger foreign surpluses. Moreover, Britain's dominant position in the supply of financial services and capital to the outside world depended on its own international earning power. By the early twentieth century, though its current surplus remained large and its security unquestionable, the area from which it earned a surplus had shrunk to narrow proportions and a dangerously large part of the earnings in that area came from the sale of cotton textiles, which were imminently threatened by competition from rising producers elsewhere. It was evident that a healthy economy would soon need new sources of earning power, which it might be profitable to individual investors, as well as to the nation, to prepare forthwith. But one of the remarkable features of the early twentieth century was that the cotton industry, so vulnerable in all but the very short run, grew faster than industry generally: surely an example of short-sighted investment. And increased reliance continued to be placed on the expansion of the output and export of coal—a continuation of a profitable past trend which the contemporary development of new fuels and prime movers showed was unlikely to remain profitable much longer. On the other hand the late Victorian increase in the relative importance of engineering products was something which was leading to better prospects than ever, but there was no consequential acceleration of the change. New products, with specially good market prospects, were being developed in Britain in the early twentieth century, but such progress was less prominent than in two or three other industrial countries.

Thus, although Britain's fortunes were inextricably tied to those of a world economy, it appeared that in some important ways British business was becoming dilatory in taking account of fundamental changes in world economic conditions. No serious damage had yet resulted and no economic mistakes had gone so far that they could not quickly be retrieved. But in the background were things which justified more serious concern. One was the increasing international political tension. Rivalries that cut right across the essential links of the economy were showing themselves ever more sharply and there appeared to be few people anywhere who did not wildly underestimate the destruction and disintegration that would almost certainly happen if those rivalries were carried to the point of war among the great powers.[1] To the British economy such an outcome was bound to bring far greater difficulties than any that were threatened by recent errors of business judgment.

The other things which were particularly worrying were the signs of increasing political and social cleavage at home. The greater complexity of industrial techniques and products and the more elaborate organization of economic activity had already made prosperity more dependent on the continuous co-operation of many different groups of people and more vulnerable to the opposition or unwillingness to join in new ways which any one of them might show. The changes that were becoming necessary in order to keep the British economy up to date could only carry that state of affairs still further. Yet in one field after another, in the last four years of peace, mutual antagonisms were subjected to less restraint than for many years past, with little regard for the probable consequences. Rarely have government and opposition attacked each other, inside and outside Parliament, with such virulence. The opposition was apparently prepared to encourage civil war in Ireland and went to the verge of inciting the army to disaffection. The government failed to assert itself sufficiently to counter the threat of lawlessness or to provide an awareness of common ground for most of those concerned. At the same time, the adoption of novel methods of violence and defiance by the militant women's suffrage movement did much to make the government appear ridiculous, even though it made the suffragists themselves often seem extravagantly foolish. And in industrial relations the minority who wished to change the whole organization of the state showed greater influence and activity, and there was a more widespread readiness to abandon old agreements and new negotiations in favour of bitter strikes and lock-outs, sometimes supplemented by attacks on persons and property.[2]

It may be that these snarling conflicts were symptoms of a permanent threat to the making and implementing of rational decisions about political, economic and social questions, and therefore to the achievement of orderly social improvement.[3] It may be rather that

[1] Thus in 1905 a Royal Commission on the supply of food in time of war failed to appreciate fully the economic difficulties involved in the question and was satisfied that a strong navy was an adequate guarantee of food supplies in wartime.

[2] The history of these various conflicts is treated at length in Dangerfield, *The Strange Death of Liberal England*, esp. Part II.

[3] *Cf.* the comments of Beatrice Webb in December 1913: 'the whole of the thinking British public is today the arena of a battle of words, of thoughts and of temperaments. The issue is twofold: are men to be governed by emotion or by

they were evidence of a new uprush of energy which was not only straining valuable institutions and principles, but was also sweeping away habits, conventions and practices that had outlived their usefulness and was bringing into existence new institutions that had become necessary and had been too long resisted.[1] It is certain, too, that not all the important changes of the time exacerbated conflict. For instance, the quiet progress of official conciliation in many of the tense industrial disputes and the introduction of new collective services, through government action, in order to lessen, for the first time, some of the most serious insecurities of working-class life were likely in the long run to establish greater unity and mutual confidence within society. But even if the least alarmist view is taken of the events just before 1914 it can hardly be doubted that, for the time being, they made economic progress more difficult to maintain. In the long run, it was still possible that British institutions were sufficiently flexible and accommodating and were directed by people with enough creative power for a successful adjustment to be made to the new conditions; but, for the moment, new problems were emerging and some of them were being either ignored or mistakenly tackled in a social and political environment that was not helpful to clear judgment.

So a review of the outcome of economic change between 1870 and 1914 must convey a general impression of prosperity and exceptional material improvement, widely diffused, and yet it must end on a questioning note. Other historians, narrowing their view to the figures of rates of growth of commodity production and trade (some of them very dubious figures) have suggested that the British economic achievement was already falling off by the eighteen-seventies. Others again, ranging as widely as possible over the whole field of social actions, have concluded that the late Victorians were less equal

reason? Are they to be governed in harmony with the desires of the bulk of the citizens or according to the fervent aspirations of a militant minority in defiance of the will of the majority? Two quite separate questions but each of them raising the same issue: the validity of democratic government.' (Margaret I. Cole (ed.), *Beatrice Webb's Diaries 1912-1924* (1952), p. 15.)

[1] This is the interpretation of Dangerfield, *op. cit.*, which argues, on the constructive side, 'that only through the putting forth of an unparalleled, an inarticulate, an irrational energy did the principle of Trade Unionism and the principle of the Minimum Wage pass so swiftly from the realm of formula into the realm of fact' (pp. 296-7); and, on the destructive side, that Liberalism had become in the early twentieth century a venerable burden, which was too slow, too restrictive of behaviour and generally too inconvenient, and that between 1910 and 1913 the nation got rid of it (pp. vii-viii and 7-8.)

to the principal tasks which they encountered than their fathers had been.[1]

Yet if one considers economic activities by themselves and as a whole, and considers also the immense difference wrought by them in the living conditions and variety of experience of most of the nation, without neglect of investment for the future, then it seems doubtful whether any generation tackled its problems more successfully than the late Victorian. No doubt the tasks were lightened because preceding generations had carried the heavy burdens of creating an industrialized society. No doubt there were many problems left unsolved and many miseries unrelieved. Possibly, too, there were some offsetting failures in political and social affairs which did little immediate damage but had a cumulative effect helping to cloud judgment on economic as well as other matters at a later stage. The restriction of democracy, as soon as it emerged, by the development of much more tightly disciplined party organizations; the timidity which hesitated to turn more efficient means of public administration to new collective purposes; the delay in extending secondary and commercial education; the development of a more clamorous press to lead or mislead a more numerous, literate public: all these might be regarded as changes which made future political, social and economic mistakes more likely. But it would be possible to draw up just as impressive a list of things which were likely to have the opposite effect; and the magnitude of the late Victorian economic achievement, in the face of competitive, technical and social changes as great as any ever encountered, is plain to see. It is improbable that this was just a matter of luck and that it did not owe a great deal to the enterprise, adaptability and generally sound judgment of the majority of those with any significant influence on business. Change in this respect appears to have come after 1900 rather than earlier,

---

[1] *Cf.* G. M. Young, *Victorian England: Portrait of an Age*, pp. 186-7: 'the function of the nineteenth century was to disengage the disinterested intelligence . . . and to set it operating over the whole range of human life and circumstance. In England we see this spirit issuing from, and often at war with, a society most stoutly tenacious of old ways and forms, and yet most deeply immersed in its new business of acquisition. In such a warfare there is no victory, only victories, as something is won and held against ignorance or convention or prejudice or greed; and in such victories our earlier and mid-Victorian time is rich. Not so the later. . . . Fundamentally, what failed in the late Victorian age, and its flash Edwardian epilogue, was the Victorian public, once so alert, so masculine and so responsible. Compared with their fathers, the men of that time were ceasing to be a ruling or a reasoning stock; the English mind sank towards that easily excited, easily satisfied state of barbarism and childhood which press and politics for their own ends fostered, and on which in turn they fed.'

though some of its roots may have been in earlier conditions. Had it come less late, Britain's economic state on the eve of the First World War could not have been so strong. As it was, the check to economic progress which most countries had experienced had probably been made a little more serious in Britain by more widespread lack of foresight and of attempts at mutual understanding in business and politics. But the country still maintained an immensely powerful and enviable economic position in the world and had the means to continue doing so.

Yet in the background there was room for doubt. Small problems had latterly been neglected, regardless of the fact that neglect could be the means to turn them into great ones. A worldwide war was imminent which must bring great problems in crowds—economic problems among the rest. Would these provide the stimulus for a renewed effort to keep up with the economic changes of the world and to profit from them, or would the neglect of small difficulties prove to be a symptom of inability to cope with great ones? No one carefully surveying the contemporary scene in 1914 could have been very sure of the answer.

PART TWO

The First World War

Some of us thought that economic disaster would make itself felt more quickly after the outbreak of war; that it would rapidly become so acute as to bring war to an end. In that we were wrong, but we were wrong only in our estimate of the time and manner in which economic disaster would make itself felt. . . . The longer the war went on the greater the magnitude of the economic disaster was sure to be, and the more prolonged and enduring would be the effects of it. Those who had the worst forebodings of what war would mean did not over-estimate the human suffering or the economic distress that it has actually caused.

VISCOUNT GREY OF FALLODON (1925)

CHAPTER ELEVEN

War Economy

WHEN war broke out in 1914 few people suspected how complex were the economic demands it must make and the economic changes it would bring. Previous experience was not a helpful guide. Since 1815 Europe's wars had been small and brief, and the effects of the revolution in armaments which had taken place since 1870 had not been demonstrated in a major conflict of great powers. Peacetime experience had shown that defence was more costly than ever before and it was obvious that in a large war its cost must be multiplied many times. The one economic fact generally recognized as certain was that war between great powers must be very expensive, especially to Britain, which would doubtless have to give financial help to its allies, and the expense might be matched by increases in taxation so great that some suspected that they would spell ruin. There were also prophets, not universally disregarded, who had foretold that the new armaments would bring death and destruction on a scale that would be beyond endurance, in terms both of economic loss and human misery.[1] Even to those who suspected that such prophecies were exaggerated it seemed likely that another major economic task in war would be to develop extra effort to make good as quickly as possible the losses caused by physical destruction. Much of this, however, might perhaps be postponed until hostilities had ended. It had not the same imminence and urgency as the budgetary task which, in the eyes of most influential people, was the essential economic problem posed by war.

Budgetary measures were, indeed, of great importance but it eventually became clear that they were only part of a more comprehensive set of economic tasks, and from the very beginning the performance of these tasks was conditioned by changes in a wider environment. The first economic alarm created by the war, showing

---

[1] The most comprehensive analysis on these lines was I. S. Bloch, *Modern Weapons and Modern War* (1900), a work published in several countries. Bloch argued that the destructiveness of armaments had made wars impossible.

itself even a few days before the opening of hostilities, was not a matter of taxes or the loss of productive resources, but a financial crisis. Though it was caused partly by expectations of a heavy public demand for cash, which led the banks to reduce their loans to the stock and discount markets, this crisis was also associated with the difficulty of maintaining liquidity in London's foreign commitments. Britain's whole livelihood was bound up with the working of an international economy, many of the interconnexions of which were inevitably disrupted when the one economic world was split into two opposed groups. Loss of confidence first caused international lending along some familiar channels suddenly to dwindle. Then both capital and current transactions became impossible between countries which were militarily on opposite sides. In London, acceptors were left with unexpectedly heavy liabilities; discounters and rediscounters were saddled with bills on which they could not obtain payment at the expected time; and the stock exchange was jeopardized both by inability to collect debts from some foreign clients and by difficulty in renewing some of the loans with which its business was carried on.

The expected shortage of cash was met by provision for the issue of £1 and 10s. currency notes by the Treasury. Although the cash shortage did not, in fact occur, these notes very soon began to replace, rather than supplement, gold coins in the circulation and, in effect, they provided the government with an additional and inflationary means of borrowing.[1] Other emergency measures just after the outbreak of war included temporary moratoria on the settlement of certain classes of debts, exceptional rediscounting facilities provided by the Bank of England (with a government guarantee against loss), and special assistance by way of loans to accepting houses and stock exchange firms. By these various means the financial crisis was resolved before the end of 1914.[2]

But the international economy, to which the British economy was so closely attuned, was not restored to anything like its former state. There were many signs of this. One was the absence, in practice, of a common worldwide monetary standard. Some countries, Britain among them, remained nominally on the gold standard. Even the new currency notes were legally convertible into gold (though most

[1] E. V. Morgan, *Studies in British Financial Policy 1914-1925* (1952), pp. 13-14 and 166-9.

[2] *Ibid.*, chap. I. Informed contemporary reaction and criticism is perhaps most clearly and concisely illustrated in the two articles of J. M. Keynes in *Econ. Journ.*, XXIV (1914).

people using them were probably unaware of this), and there was nothing illegal in the use of gold for external payments. But the physical difficulty of moving gold in wartime and the impracticability of arranging transfers of its ownership without the assistance of the Bank of England or the Treasury (given only in special cases) meant that the old arrangements were effectively suspended. Another symptom of change was the failure of the acceptance and discount houses in London, despite the maintenance of their solvency and the restoration of their credit, ever to recover their former volume of business. A third was the drying up of the recent immense stream of long-term commercial investment flowing abroad from Britain. Yet another was the change in the direction and gradual shrinkage in the volume of British foreign trade.

The disruption of international trade and investment made it necessary for Britain to find new ways of meeting its economic needs just when these were being changed by military demands. Some of the many essential supplies which had regularly been imported were from sources that were no longer available. Some of the markets in which the means of paying for those essentials had regularly been earned were in enemy territory. And the closing of established channels of trade took away the income that Britain had obtained by providing finance and services for the business that had flowed through them. Not all was loss, however. Though some invisible exports could no longer be made because of the contraction of merchandise trade, the special wartime difficulties under which much of the remaining trade was conducted provided rich opportunities in the market for other services, such as shipping and insurance, in which Britain excelled. Lost sources of supply could be replaced by others that were still accessible, even though the need for supplies was in some cases greatly swollen by military requirements. While some foreign markets were closed there were others which could no longer be reached by enemy countries that had dominated them in peacetime. More of Germany's best markets were in enemy territory than was the case for Britain. There were parts of the world in which a commercial vacuum was thus created and the naval superiority of Britain and its allies gave them some chance of filling it. Some manufacturers were prompt in trying to seize such opportunities and in so doing they had every reason to feel that they were contributing to national as well as personal interest. Mr Churchill's popular slogan, 'Business as usual', which summed up so much of the prevailing economic outlook of the earlier part of the war, reflected a national consciousness of the need to maintain financial strength so as to be able to apply it to warlike purposes.[1]

But, in fact, business never could be quite as usual and moved steadily further from normality. Though lost sources of supply were replaced, the new supplies were often costlier than the old; that was why they had not been used in peacetime. And transport difficulties added further to their cost. The new foreign markets, too, which might have compensated for those no longer open, could often not be served because the resources needed to make the goods which they wanted were either too expensive or pre-empted for other urgent purposes. On balance, there is no doubt that Britain's foreign business was seriously weakened and all its economic problems were thereby made more difficult.

Essentially, what had to be done was to divert a great deal of economic activity to meet vastly increased military needs without making civilian life impossible, and to do this when circumstances were making external dealings more costly and less remunerative, but not less indispensable. Productive workers were absorbed by the army, and large quantities of labour, capital equipment and materials had to be applied to the production of munitions. Only the reduced economic resources that remained were available to supply civilian needs, but they had to be made to yield enough to ensure that neither the physical consumption nor the morale of civilians fell dangerously low. Readjustment and lowered standards of consumption were inescapable. The situation may most clearly be put in terms of national income and its use, though such an analysis was unfamiliar to contemporaries. In the last three years of peace the national income averaged about £2,300 million annually, of which some £1,950 million was devoted to consumption and not quite £350 million saved; and well over half the savings were invested abroad.[2] When war imposed new demands on scarce resources this high level of savings could be turned into a means of meeting the cost of some of those demands. But it could not be entirely used in this way. For instance, there had still to be some foreign investment, in the form of loans to military allies. In any case, the new demands of war were greater than could be paid for simply by the use of what, in peace-

[1] S. J. Hurwitz, *State Intervention in Great Britain: a study of economic control and social response, 1914-1919* (1949), pp. 62-3.
[2] *Cf.* p. 188 above.

time, would have been saved.[1] The rest of the military needs could be supplied only by producing more in total (through greater efficiency, if possible,[2] and through the use of previously unemployed resources) and by spending less (in real terms) on the satisfaction of civilian demand. The main themes of wartime economic history were bound to be the way in which these changes were accomplished and the effects which they had.

Initially the means used to adjust economic activity to wartime needs were almost entirely financial. The government required extra goods for the prosecution of the war and it had to go out into the market and buy them and place orders for their increased production. Even if it had preferred some other method (which it did not) it lacked the administrative machinery to do otherwise in most cases.[3] To obtain the means for these purchases and to deal with some of their repercussions it relied, in conformity with long-established tradition, on changes in the budget and on borrowing. Such changes, in their turn, would (it was assumed) leave the public with less to spend and would presumably, therefore, induce a contraction of inessential activities. In fact, things did not work out much like that. The government failed to obtain, through the uncontrolled market, anything near all that it needed for the prosecution of the war, and the cuts in civilian supplies and activities fell somewhat indiscriminately on essentials and inessentials. So financial measures soon had to be supplemented by other more direct forms of control over particular economic activities. But financial inducements continued to be one means of adjusting the economy to wartime needs, and the involuntary consequences of government expenditure were the greatest single influence on its stability. When, for instance, the government went into the market on an unprecedented scale it was in the position of an enormously wealthy but hard-pressed consumer bidding for scarce supplies. Nothing was more certain to drive up prices and increase incomes without a comparable increase in output. Nothing, that is, was more certain than the government's situation as a purchaser to generate inflation, which only the government itself

---

[1] Government borrowing in the first $2\frac{3}{4}$ years of war was at more than three times the immediate prewar rate of savings. (Morgan, *op. cit.*, pp. 41-2.)

[2] As the previous discussion indicates, the returns to effort in external activities tended to be reduced for reasons over which there was no control and there could be no general increase in efficiency unless productivity in internal activities increased more than enough to offset this.

[3] W. K. Hancock and Margaret M. Gowing, *British War Economy* (1949), p. 11.

could modify. In spite of the growth of direct measures of economic control, it is therefore worth while to single out war finance for special attention and to look at its operation over the whole period of the war.

The story of financial policy is not impressive. To obtain the necessary revenue the government relied mainly on borrowing, and, despite the changed circumstances, offered what was, by peacetime standards, a good commercial return on the loans. There were also considerable increases in taxation, though not all of those which looked large in terms of money imposed correspondingly large burdens in real terms. But from 1914 to 1919 taxes covered not quite 30 per cent of government expenditure, a far smaller proportion than in the Napoleonic Wars.[1] In these five years the total budgetary deficits amounted, on the official figures, to £6,860 million, and though this sum is swollen by payments made abroad, the internal deficit has been estimated as high as £5,284 million,[2] an amount equivalent to more than a quarter of a century's government expenditure at the highest peacetime rates.

During the first year of the war, when Lloyd George was Chancellor of the Exchequer, attempts to match taxation to the new needs of expenditure were feeble. In the first war budget, that of November 1914, income tax was doubled (to 2s. 6d. in the £) for the last four months of the financial year and so was super-tax; the duty on beer went up by 1d. per glass and that on tea from 5d. to 8d. per lb.; but no new taxes were imposed. In the next budget there was virtually no change, except a heavy increase in the duties on alcoholic drinks (intended to cut consumption rather than raise revenue) and Lloyd George left to his successor, McKenna, a situation in which estimated revenue for the year was only £272 million to set against expenditure estimates of £1,590 million.[3] In a supplementary budget, in September 1915, McKenna did something to improve this state of affairs when he made the most drastic changes in the tax system that were introduced during the war. Income tax was raised by 40 per cent, with lower exemption limits and abatements, super-tax was increased on incomes above £8,000, and postal charges and existing indirect taxes were increased. Of two innovations one was the imposition of new customs duties (on cars and motor-cycles, cinematograph films, clocks, watches and musical instruments), the

---

[1] Hancock and Gowing, *op. cit.*, pp. 4-5.
[2] Morgan, *op. cit.*, pp. 98 and 100-3.   [3] *Ibid.*, pp. 90-1.

first significant reversal of free trade policy, nominally intended to save shipping space and foreign exchange more than to protect home industry. The other was the introduction of an excess profits duty. A levy of this type had recently been imposed on certain munition establishments and now all firms were taxed at 50 per cent on profits that were more than £200 above a standard amount based either on prewar earnings or on a formula related to capital employed at the outbreak of war. In his 1916 budget McKenna increased the excess profits duty to 60 per cent and income tax to a maximum of 5s. in the £ on earned incomes over £2,500 or unearned over £2,000. Some duties were also further increased and a few new ones added, including one on entertainments. But, although all this made up a more rigorous policy than before, McKenna set definite limits to what he would attempt. He was satisfied that taxation was adequate if it was sufficient to cover the interest and sinking fund on all the borrowing necessary to make up the budgetary deficit.[1] This unduly modest aim was not improved on by Bonar Law, who was at the Exchequer for the rest of the war. There were, indeed, no more drastic budgetary changes. Existing taxes yielded a good deal more as personal and corporate incomes and expenditure increased, and there were some minor increases in the levels of taxation: excess profits duty went up to 80 per cent in 1917, and in 1918 there were small increases in income tax, super-tax, postal charges and a few indirect taxes.[2] But essentially the tax structure was what McKenna had made it, stronger than before, but inadequate for current needs.

Taxation failed to provide the means of financing most of the needs of war and, as economic activity and incomes expanded under the stimulus of government demand, it also failed to absorb most of the increased purchasing power which resulted and to prevent it from intensifying the demand for inevitably dwindling supplies of civilian goods and services. Loans were the alternative means of achieving both these purposes, but while they did all that was necessary for the first, they were only very partially successful in securing the second object. Until early in 1917 the government relied mainly on a series of three very large long-term loans and met its heavy immediate needs for cash, while the proceeds of these loans were coming in, by Ways and Means advances from the Bank of England and by enormously

---

[1] *Ibid.*, pp. 91-3; S. McKenna, *Reginald McKenna 1863-1943* (1948), pp. 239-44 and 269-71.

[2] Morgan, *op. cit.*, 93-4.

increased sales of Treasury bills to the market. From the end of 1915 there were also some medium-term bonds continuously on sale to help to fill in the gaps. There were two chief weaknesses in this programme of borrowing. The first was that it was exceedingly and unnecessarily expensive. The rates of interest offered were generally considered high by city opinion and as time went on they became higher. This was partly because the government and the Bank of England were striving to keep up short-term rates in the belief that otherwise it would be impossible to attract much money from abroad and that the external value of the pound would slide out of control. Events showed that this last fear was much exaggerated. Even if this line of argument had been both true and decisive it could not have justified another practice that made borrowing still more costly. This was the option given to the subscribers to many of the earlier loans to convert their holdings into later issues which carried higher rates of interest. The second weakness was that much of the money subscribed to government loans did not come out of genuine savings. When the government borrowed from the Bank of England or sold bills to the money market it provided means for the expansion of bank credit, and when it made payments out of the proceeds of this borrowing it enabled the recipients to increase their bank deposits and so contribute to a still further growth of the credit base. Since the great war loans were treated as demonstrations of the strength and prestige of the City of London, every care was taken to ensure that they were, in terms of the amount subscribed, an obvious 'success'. Ample use was made of the opportunities to expand bank credit and part of the government's borrowing was really no more than a taking back of very recently created credit.

From the latter half of 1916 the weaknesses in the government's borrowing policy diminished. Attempts were made to tap the genuine savings of all sections of the public through the activities of the National Savings Committee and the continuous offer for sale of a greater variety of securities, including war savings certificates for the small saver. The third war loan, at the beginning of 1917, was the last long-term issue during the war. Thereafter short and medium-term securities, 'on tap', produced all that was needed. Interest rates remained high, but the previously rising trend was reversed and the wish to attract foreign funds was served by offering higher rates on foreign than on domestic balances. To an increasing extent government loans were subscribed by the banks. But now, much more than before, the deposits which were lent in this way represented genuine savings from current income. It would seem probable that greater direct control over civilian economic activities had lessened the opportunity and the inducement to try to use extra money income to secure business and personal advantages. As national expenditure rose, most of it went to expand bank deposits, and the banks, for lack of other adequate outlets, had to invest more and more in government securities. Thus in the last eighteen months of the war, public reluctance to save enough was overcome, increased purchasing power was absorbed more completely than before and inflation went on much more slowly and under closer control. But, before then, war finance had been highly inflationary and had permitted such a fall in the value of money as had never been known before. By 1919 its purchasing power was only about one-third what it had been just before the war.[1]

In domestic finance, then, all that was necessary for the conduct of the war was forthcoming in one way or another, but only at the expense of storing up difficulties for the future. Despite the unavoidable trading difficulties from the very beginning of the war, much the same was true of external finance, though there was not the same degree of clumsiness in its management. The only serious immediate difficulty arose from the increased dependence on the United States, not only for special war supplies but also, because of the closing of other channels of trade, for ordinary imports. The need for dollars to settle current trading debts grew rapidly and was augmented by the need to have dollars available to purchase sterling, in order to maintain the value of sterling on this outstandingly important exchange.[2] To help meet these needs, private owners of dollar securities were invited in December 1915 to sell or lend them to the Treasury, and in 1916 a penal tax was imposed on the income from eligible securities which had not been offered to the Treasury. Despite these measures there was real difficulty in finding enough dollars for current needs in late 1916 and early 1917,[3] and in January 1917 the government took powers to requisition some classes of securities. After the entry of the United States into the war the difficulty was much reduced by large

[1] For details of government borrowing and the banks' contribution to it see *ibid.*, pp. 106-15 and 238-47. The techniques involved and their effects are considered in Hicks, *British Public Finances . . . 1800 to 1952*, pp. 181-4. See also Hancock and Gowing, *op. cit.*, pp. 9-12.

[2] Morgan, *op. cit.*, pp. 356-7.

[3] R. H. Brand, *War and National Finance* (1921), pp. viii-x and 284-7.

loans from the American government and many of the securities never had to be used. Of £623 million of securities requisitioned, £332 million were ultimately returned to their owners.[1]

Except for temporary dollar shortages there was never a very serious foreign exchange problem during the war. Britain's prewar external surplus was so large that even in the shrunken trading conditions of wartime the margin was not easily eaten away. It is likely that on current account Britain still had a favourable balance of payments down to the end of 1917 and even the heavy adverse balance of 1918 probably did little more than offset the surplus of the earlier war years.[2] There was, however, the special burden of providing financial help to Dominion and European allies. From the beginning of the war to the end of 1919 such loans by the British government totalled £1,825 million.[3] Since there was no adequate current surplus to finance loans on this scale, this task involved the depletion of some of the permanent sources of British financial strength. Sales of foreign securities, the raising of loans abroad, chiefly in the United States and Canada and to a much less extent in Japan, Argentina and Norway,[4] and the running down of the short-term credits extended by London were necessary. Of these methods of providing adequate foreign exchange for allied needs the last created particularly difficult problems for the future. Short-term credits were the essential means by which London acted as the chief financial centre for international trade. In its wartime financial efforts it wiped out its large net credit balance of 1913 and may have ended the war as a net debtor on short-term account.[5] That was part of the price for being able to cope successfully with wartime international financial needs. But it was not a ruinous or irrevocable price, since, despite the restrictions of the time, Britain remained in the forefront of international trade and sterling retained its international value with little need for artificial support except on the dollar exchange.[6]

The influence of the government on war economy came increasingly to be exerted by more varied means than those only of financial policy. By undertaking the production and distribution of goods previously left to private manufacturers and dealers, and by imposing detailed regulations on more and more of the economic activities

[1] Morgan, *op. cit.*, pp. 327-31.   [2] *Ibid.*, pp. 303-17.

[3] *Ibid.*, pp. 317 and 340-1.   [4] *Ibid.*, pp. 320-1.   [5] *Ibid.*, pp. 331-4.

[6] For monthly figures of the exchange value of sterling in terms of the chief foreign currencies see *ibid.*, pp. 345-8.

left in private hands, the government obtained more direct control over the economy. But this change came about gradually and in a wholly empirical way.[1]

Before, and at the beginning of, the war the government manufactured many of the munitions which it needed, but the proportion bought from private contractors had been increasing and there were at first no great plans for the extension and multiplication of government factories. Nor was there much control over private activity other than that exerted by hasty bidding for supplies that were urgently needed. Almost the only economic enterprise subject to government control from the beginning of the war was the railway system and this was for purely military, not economic reasons. In order to ensure full control over the transport of troops and their supplies, powers had been taken in the Regulation of the Forces Act, 1871, to requisition any railway and its plant during a war, with provision for the payment of full compensation.[2] The application of these powers in August 1914 meant that, although the detailed management of the railways was left to the existing companies, the remuneration of the owners was fixed by the government, which could secure whatever priorities it required for different classes of traffic, a facility which, in the event, had economic as well as military significance. Very early in the war the government took large powers of requisitioning and control by decree, mainly through the Defence of the Realm Act, which was frequently amended so as to make it more comprehensive. But for many months little use was made of these powers, so far as concerned industry and trade.[3] Interference came only in specific cases where it was found impossible to obtain in the normal way commodities of which there was a desperate need, as happened early in 1915 in the case of sandbags. All available second-hand stocks were then requisitioned, as was the output of sacking from the Dundee jute mills, and the prices were fixed by the War Office in relation to prewar prices for second-hand sacks and to raw material and conversion costs for new ones. Once direct control had touched any stage in the production of a commodity it tended to

---

[1] For a detailed account of this field as a whole see E. M. H. Lloyd, *Experiments n State Control* (1924). There are shorter summaries in Morgan, *op. cit.*, chap. II and Hancock and Gowing, *op. cit.*, pp. 14-29.

[2] E. A. Pratt, *The Rise of Rail-Power in War and Conquest 1833-1914* (1915), pp. 176-7.

[3] Morgan, *op. cit.*, pp. 38 and 43-4; D. Lloyd George, *War Memoirs* (new edn., 1938), pp. 106, 155 and 160.

spread over more and more stages. Thus, when the War Office had begun to regulate the production and prices of sacking, it soon found that it must extend its control to jute spinners, since its own expenses were being swollen by the rising prices which they charged. And some eighteen months after first being drawn into the business it had reached the point of buying its own raw jute and having all the manufacturing processes done on a commission basis.[1]

But the deepening of control in this way, so long as it started from only a few small commodities, was bound to be slow in having any fundamental effect on the economy. More influential were the revelations that shortages of munitions were hampering military operations. These shortages were the result less of a failure of the market to supply what was being demanded than of a failure of the War Office to attempt to manufacture or to buy nearly as much as the military commanders found necessary.[2] By the spring of 1915 the shortage of shell was the subject of a newspaper campaign and of dissension within the government. It contributed to a replacement of the Liberal by a Coalition government and led directly to the creation of a Ministry of Munitions. Thenceforward, in the field of munitions, old methods of supply were transformed. A new administrative machine to make this possible was built up as quickly as possible and its capacity for effective control forged by experience and a sense of urgency. Existing stocks of goods and raw materials were requisitioned. Orders for the full output of existing productive capacity were placed at prices determined by the Ministry in relation to cost in various ways—there were several different types of contract. Where existing capacity was insufficient—which was the case with most kinds of munitions—steps were taken to increase it. Some manufacturers were helped to produce goods which they had not made before. Others were provided with extensions to their plant at government expense or, in some cases, with a complete new factory to be run under their management. Yet again, other new factories, such as the National Shell Factories, were built for direct operation by the Ministry of Munitions. Where particular materials or components used in munition production were specially scarce or subject to steep rises in price, the Ministry of Munitions found it increasingly necessary to step in to undertake their purchase and establish priorities in their use. Throughout the whole field of munition production and the supply of the chief raw materials there

---

[1] Morgan, *op. cit.*, pp. 38-9.   [2] George, *op. cit.*, chaps. V and VI.

were powers, more and more fully applied, to regulate production, prices and the distribution of supplies.[1]

It took time for the activities of the Ministry of Munitions to be fully organized but even by the end of 1915 there was a marked difference in the working of the military sector of the economy. But there was still nothing like a totally controlled economy. What was done to expand and give priority to munition production necessarily curtailed civilian activity, but within the limits thus set there was little interference with producers and dealers. Modification of this state of affairs came about gradually, in part through efforts to regulate the use of some of the chief resources and services that were common to both munition and civilian production, and in part through the establishment of direct controls over much of civilian industry and trade.

Of these two classes of control the former was rather more developed than the latter in the first two years of war, though both were very incomplete. The supplies whose direct control was likely to have the widest influence were transport, fuel, food, capital and labour. Very little was done about food supply except for the creation, in August 1914, of a Royal Commission on Sugar Supplies with power to buy, sell and regulate supplies, and except also for a small amount of secret purchasing of reserves of some other foods, including wheat, by the government.[2] Nor was there much detailed interference with coal supplies, but exports to neutrals were made subject to licence from May 1915, in an attempt to ensure enough for home and allied needs, and in the summer of 1915 maximum prices were introduced.[3] More was attempted in relation to transport, capital and labour. Shipping was assisted from the beginning of the war by a war risks insurance scheme which required premiums at only about one-fourth of current market rates, and government insurance was extended to cargoes early in 1915. Shipping supply was distorted from the outset by the requisitioning of vessels for the transport of troops and their supplies, and this resulted in a shortage of shipping space for other purposes, with soaring profits and freight rates. In turn this led to government-sponsored attempts to secure

---

[1] A useful, though selective, account of the organization and achievements of the Ministry of Munitions is in *ibid.*, chaps. IX and XIX. Very great detail is available in the official *History of the Ministry of Munitions* (8 vols., 1918-22. 4 additional vols., written in the same period, became open to public consultation after the Second World War).

[2] Hurwitz, *op. cit.*, pp. 72 and 210.   [3] *Ibid.*, pp. 171-3.

voluntary regulation, but by November 1915 there was power to requisition shipping for the carriage of foodstuffs and other articles of commerce and a system of licensing had been introduced, though licences were still granted without much discrimination.[1] Control over the raising of new capital from the public soon became fairly stringent. Treasury approval for any new issues was required from January 1915 onwards and the control became very tight by the summer. But except for the licensing of building work, there was no direct control over the investment of capital obtained in ways other than by public issue of securities, though the practical obstacles to capital expenditure for private, civil purposes steadily increased; and until 1916 there was no prohibition even of the export of capital.[2]

Regulation of the use and price of labour was potentially the most powerful influence of all and measures in this field were more varied than in any other. The problems were to secure a satisfactory division of manpower between the forces and industry, to secure a redistribution of labour among different industries, and to ensure that output was maximized and not held up by indiscipline, restrictive practices, or a failure to match productive methods to the level of skill available. At first, when temporary dislocation and loss of markets were causing unemployment and when patriotic feeling led to a rush of recruits for the forces, things were left to take care of themselves. But soon there were problems of labour shortage, and indiscriminate recruitment was found to have caused special difficulties in keeping enough skilled men in some of the key industries. The service ministers began to issue badges to mark particular workers as not available for enlistment, and arrangements of this kind were extended and made more systematic. But, on the other hand, in 1915 voluntary recruitment began to leave the services short of men, so that military conscription was introduced in March 1916.[3] Meantime, there had been numerous other measures to deal with labour questions. The practical difficulties were eased because the government was able to negotiate with the Parliamentary Committee of the Trades Union Congress, a representative body of level-headed men accustomed to dealing with public affairs, and because the bulk of opinion among organized workers favoured full participation in the war effort. At the beginning of the war the Parliamentary Committee had urged every union to try during the war to secure an amicable settlement of

[1] Hurwitz, *op. cit.*, pp. 69-72 and 185-7.
[2] Morgan, *op. cit.*, pp. 48 and 263-5.   [3] Hurwitz, *op. cit.*, pp. 83-8 and 103-4.

all disputes without strikes.[1] In March 1915 the government met 36 of the leading trade unions and reached an agreement with 35 of them (the miners would not agree) under which they promised not to strike during the war and to refer unsettled disputes to arbitration. They also agreed to suspend their restrictive practices and rules preventing the employment of unskilled workers on tasks traditionally reserved for skilled men, subject to safeguards about the postwar position and the maintenance of skilled wages.[2] These provisions were given compulsory force in the Munitions of War Act (passed only two months later), as far as munition industries were concerned, and there was power to apply them by proclamation to other industries. The same act also tried to control the mobility of labour by forbidding anyone to employ a person who, within the previous six weeks, had been employed in any industry scheduled by the Minister of Munitions, unless he could produce a leaving certificate from his previous employer.[3]

On paper, there was by this time a great deal of negative control over labour, but not much positive direction. Industrial conscription was considered and rejected. But even the negative controls were less complete in practice than in theory. The application of general principles to specific cases took time. Dilution of labour, though accepted in principle, had to be the subject of detailed negotiation in each district and sometimes each factory. Trade union members, enjoying a secure position, irritated by rising prices and profits, and often stirred up by a militant minority of whom many obtained increasing influence as shop stewards, did not always support the decisions and agreements of their leaders. Strikes were sometimes averted by the arbitration provisions, but they increased considerably in the middle of the war, often in defiance of the government, and they were often bought off by concessions.[4]

Direct interference with supplies in which the services and munition industries were uninterested came seldom in the early stages of the war. Only a special emergency could overcome reluctance to take

---

[1] Roberts, *The Trades Union Congress 1868-1921*, p. 272.   [2] *Ibid.*, pp. 276-7.

[3] *Ibid.*, pp. 278-9; Hancock and Gowing, *op. cit.*, pp. 26-7; George, *op. cit.*, pp. 181-2.

[4] For comments on some of the discontents among workers, their resistance to agreed changes, and cleavages between leaders and the rank and file in some trade unions see Hurwitz, *op. cit.*, chaps. XV and XVI, and Roberts, *op. cit.*, pp. 275 and 287. Fuller detail of relations between government and trade unions and of the major industrial disputes is given at first hand in Askwith, *Industrial Problems and Disputes*, chaps. XXXIV-XL.

K

action of this sort, but occasionally it did come. Indeed, what proved to be the most tenacious of all wartime controls—though no one would have forecast this—was in this category. This was the introduction in 1915 of statutory restrictions on increases of rents for certain classes of dwellings, a sequel to attempts to exploit the shortage of house-room which shifts of population and restrictions on building aggravated and which had led to some violence in Glasgow.[1]

In the second half of the war, however, direct control, by government operation or regulation, spread more extensively over most branches of economic activity. This was partly due to changes of personnel and outlook when, in December 1916, Asquith's government was pushed out and replaced by a new one under Lloyd George, who persuaded more of the leading Labour politicians to come into the coalition. Ministries of Labour, Food and Shipping were set up in the same month, and among other organizational changes soon afterwards were the creation of Ministries of National Service and Reconstruction and of a Controllership of Coal.[2] The new government departments undertook more extensive and detailed responsibilities and supplied fuller information to a more compact and centralized supreme policy-making body in the War Cabinet and its committees, aided by an improved secretariat. There were the means of formulating a co-ordinated policy of direct economic control and the machinery for carrying it out, and there was also an attempt to apply similar co-ordination to some of the essential supplies of all the allied powers.[3]

Changes of personnel, however, were not the sole cause of these developments, some of which, indeed, were projected before Lloyd George's government took office. Partial control, accompanying an inflationary financial policy, had led to intensified competition, steep rises in prices and profits, and ostentatious spending in the uncontrolled sections of the economy, with consequent irritation and unrest among workers which it was impolitic not to try to alleviate. Then, too, the shortage of essential supplies was becoming more acute, especially because of the increased losses of shipping while the German submarine campaign was at its most intense, just after the disappointing harvest of 1916. And there was also the cumulative influence of the piecemeal extension of the scope of the controls

---

[1] Hurwitz, *op. cit.*, pp. 258-9.

[2] *Ibid.*, pp. 176-7; Hancock and Gowing, *op. cit.*, p. 37; George, *op. cit.*, pp. 627-8, 642 and chaps. XLII and XLIV.

[3] Hancock and Gowing, *op. cit.*, pp. 36-40.

already established. As one set of restrictions or of allocations in a graded order of priority was imposed, measures had to be taken to deal with the situation of those whose business was consequently reduced or made more risky. As supplies of particular commodities had to be increased, the government itself had to provide some of the means of achieving the increase, because no one else could do so on a large enough scale or cheaply enough.

There are many examples of this spread of direct control simply through one thing leading to another. Thus, in 1917, shipping space was so scarce that practically all shipping movements were at the direction of the government and consequently cargo space was no longer available for many civilian needs. The raw material supplies of some industries, cotton and wool for instance, were cut and this in turn led to government intervention to deal with the effects on output and employment. So, in June 1917, to deal with one such situation the Cotton Control Board was established. This body tried to share the reduced raw material supply fairly by limiting the proportion of its machinery that each firm might run; but this, in turn, made workers redundant and a scheme of short-time working had to be applied and a method of financial compensation, through a levy on all cotton employers, worked out.[1]

In the contrasting case, such as that of food, where more, not less, had to be produced, a similar increase in the closeness of direction occurred. In the first year of war the government had not bothered to suggest even a voluntary effort to grow more food. By the end of 1916 it was turning to compulsion and set up a Food Production Department responsible to the President of the Board of Agriculture. Powers of direction were used to compel farmers to change their cropping and to bring about a large increase of the arable area; guaranteed prices and minimum wages were introduced to encourage willing acceptance of direction; and, where there was a lack of necessary supplies, the Food Production Department undertook the bulk buying and resale of such things as seeds, fertilizers and farm machinery. By such measures a 24 per cent increase in food production, in terms of calorific value, was achieved in one year.[2]

These are only illustrations of a widespread change in the organization of the British economy in the last two years of war. Before the

---

[1] Hurwitz, *op. cit.*, chap. XII.

[2] *Ibid.*, chap. XIII. A brief account by the responsible minister is given in Ernle, *Whippingham to Westminster*, chaps. XIII and XIV.

armistice the government was directly engaged in far more economic activities than ever before. It purchased abroad 85 per cent of all imported foodstuffs and was the sole buyer of many imported raw materials, including softwood, wool, hides, jute, indigo and Manila hemp, as well as of all the flax that was bought from Russia, spelter from Australia and sulphur from Italy. Besides operating about 250 munition factories it had taken temporary possession of the railways, coal-mines, flour mills and Irish distilleries.[1] Price control spread far and wide, and private dealings in many commodities were permitted only under licence; most of the chief home-produced foodstuffs, a wide range of raw materials, and such important manufactures and semi-manufactures as paper, glass, picric acid and iron and steel were subject to these latter restrictions.[2]

There were still gaps in the system of control, of which the most important concerned the supply of common consumer goods to private individuals and the use of labour. There was little success in applying price control to manufactured consumer goods, except for a few standardized types and qualities of footwear and clothing, and there was little rationing of the scarcest necessaries. Though steps were taken to equalize the distribution of food among different districts, there was no formal individual rationing scheme until 1918 when sugar, meat, butter, margarine, bacon, ham and lard were rationed, while there was local option in the rationing of tea.[3]

In some aspects of its dealings with labour, in contrast to everything else, the government actually lessened its attempts at direct control. By extending its power of military conscription and drawing up an elaborate schedule of reserved occupations, it obtained complete control over the division of the labour force between the services and industry, but control over the free choices of civilian workers was only loosely exercised. The attempt to exert negative control over labour mobility, through the use of leaving certificates, was abandoned in 1917 because of the hostility and strikes which it provoked, as was a later scheme for allowing employers to take on specified grades of worker only under licence. Strikes were met by concessions

[1] Morgan, *op. cit.*, pp. 47 and 49. Government possession of productive capacity often made little difference to the actual operation and management except for the financial terms. Thus government possession of the coal-mines was little more than a means of making very obvious the limitation on the profits of the owners, in order to overcome the hostility of the highly organized and restive miners. (Hurwitz, *op. cit.*, p. 179.)

[2] Morgan, *op. cit.*, pp. 49-51.

[3] *Ibid.*, pp. 51-2.

more often than by disciplinary measures to enforce broken agreements. For the attraction of workers to undermanned industries and districts reliance was placed on special calls for volunteers and on financial incentives which, though the government nominally had power to prescribe the wages for many classes of workers, were usually determined by bargaining for which the workers were in a strong position.[1] Earlier agreements about dilution of skill, the suspension of restrictive practices and the use of arbitration still operated, however, and helped to ease many of the labour difficulties. Despite all the gaps in control and much understandable human friction, half the employed males, together with a million women, had by the end of the war been brought into the armed forces, civil defence services and those heavy industries on which the military effort most depended.[2] But the price of this achievement, in concessions and delays, was considerable.

All in all, in spite of a few exceptions to the general trend, the British economy in the First World War showed a transition from a highly competitive condition, subject to the usual imperfections caused by immobility and by group organization, to one in which competition was narrowly circumscribed by government demands and decrees. Simultaneously, as the economic influence of the government expanded, its manner of exercise ceased to be almost entirely financial and finance became only an auxiliary to more direct controls. In the course of these transitions the economy became far more efficiently adapted to the waging of large-scale war, but, on balance, its permanent strength for meeting the needs of peacetime conditions was probably progressively reduced, though not all the changes worked in that direction.

In the first year of war Britain experienced loss of markets, a dislocation of international trade and finance, and a sharp rise in prices at home, without obtaining an adequate supply of munitions as compensation. Some of these things were unavoidable, but many were the consequence of inadequate administrative effort and feeble government finance. The rising cost of imports was the biggest single element in the general rise of prices and, though this was partly caused by an enforced change in sources of supply and by war risks, it was aggravated by the uncontrolled bidding up of rates for shipping. In the middle of the war, financial policy stiffened but its

[1] *Ibid.*, pp. 52-6.　　　[2] Hancock and Gowing, *op. cit.*, p. 28.

greater rigour scarcely matched the increased effort made to obtain adequate military supplies. Neither by financial policy nor by more direct measures was civilian demand curbed as military demand grew. The result was that, in many civilian activities, prices and profits rose fast, there was a scramble for scarce goods and blatant spending by some while great sacrifices were thrust on others, glaring inequalities which roused discontent. In the last eighteen months the combination of financial policy with greater direct control brought the worst of these evils almost to an end but did nothing to wipe out the effects of their earlier incidence. And even at this stage some new sources of inflation and inequality were active, notably the successful bid for higher wages by large sections of organized labour, which almost certainly was a major influence on the further rise of prices.[1] At the same time the loss of markets and of permanent international financial assets was proceeding faster and threatening greater difficulties for the future.

Though the war economy was a remarkable achievement which was an indispensable element in military victory, it was built up in a way that was both wasteful and provocative. It left Britain with an unfamiliar economic organization devoted to unfamiliar ends. Whatever merits parts of it might have for some more familiar purposes and whatever general guidance it might have to offer for the solution of newly emerging economic problems, they had not been plainly demonstrated. It is not surprising that the majority of a weary and sickened people was willing to be rid of it entirely as soon as possible

---

[1] *Cf.* Morgan, *op. cit.*, pp. 294 and 372.

CHAPTER TWELVE

The Economic Consequences of the War

THE war economy may have been only an interlude in British economic development, an aberration from normal economic organization, created *ad hoc* and dismantled in haste, but there was no possibility that its termination could make things as though it had never been. Nor was it only the economic aspects of the war that directly altered the economic future. Military destruction, political bargaining, moral and intellectual reactions to a harrowing new social experience—all had their effects on production and trade and on the resources that could be applied to them. Yet it is not easy to say just what were the economic consequences of the war. Comparison of economic conditions immediately before and after the war shows many important differences, but there is little doubt that some of them would have been much the same even if peace had been unbroken from 1914 to 1918. An estimate of the economic consequences of the war must take account of other powerful influences operating at the same time.

It is possible, however, to begin by considering a few things which obviously were directly brought about by the war itself. Permanent economic resources were destroyed in battle and others were disposed of for no other reason than to provide means of continuing the battle. Some current activities were distorted and some abandoned because they encroached on the war effort or because the circumstances of war had made it impossible to continue them as before. The effort to restore them and the impossibility of ever restoring some of them were a part of the price of war, though it was not always the war alone which prevented the undoing of changes which war had wrought.

The damage to British economic resources most clearly attributable to the war is to be found in the losses of manpower and capital. Some 745,000 men from the United Kingdom (i.e. about 9 per cent of all the men aged 20-45) were killed during the war and about 1,700,000 were wounded, of whom 1,200,000 received disablement pensions, though it is not known how many of these were per-manently incapacitated for work.[1] To these losses there should perhaps be added any reduction in the number of births, but the effects of the wartime reduction of the birth-rate were offset by a temporary rise immediately afterwards; and though in the next fifteen years there must have been some loss of potential births, because the excess of women over men in the younger adult age groups was increased as a result of war mortality, this appears to have been only a minor influence on demographic history. The long-term trend in the number of births shows no significant change at this point.[2] It is therefore best to take the numbers of killed and disabled as the quantitative indication of the effect of the war on manpower. These were heavy indeed. Almost exactly 10 per cent of all the deaths among the people of Britain in the decade 1911-21 were service casualties overseas.[3] Yet their *economic* influence may have been slight. The unusual conjunction of changes in birth- and death-rates from the late nineteenth century onwards resulted in a rapid replace-ment and increase of the numbers of adults, with a decreasing pro-portion of dependants to be supported by them.[4] Despite the casualties of the war Britain in the next twenty years could count on a considerably expanding labour force as one of its chief assets. In terms of quality there may be a different story. The killing of the most gifted and keenest has often been assumed to have been one of the chief adverse influences on subsequent political leadership; originality, talent and powers of leadership are not less necessary and valuable in economic affairs. Nor can one be sure that, for a year or two at least, grief and loneliness, widely spread among hundreds of thousands, were without any appreciable economic effect. Such things are among the unknowables of history, though not among its unrealities.

The physical loss of capital equipment was less severe for Britain than for some of the other belligerents because the country was free from invasion and the effects of naval and aerial bombardment were negligible. The largest loss was undoubtedly the sinking of over 7 million gross tons of shipping (about 40 per cent of the merchant fleet),[5] but much of this was replaced during the war and all of it very soon afterwards. The earning capacity of many of the new

---

[1] F. W. Hirst, *The Consequences of the War to Great Britain* (1934), pp. 297-9.
[2] *Report of the R.C. on Population* (1949), pp. 9-10.   [3] *Ibid.*, p. 10.
[4] *Ibid.*, pp. 11-13.   [5] Hancock and Gowing, *British War Economy*, p. 23.

ships was, it is true, less than that of the old, but this was not entirely a result of the war. Another source of capital loss was the neglect to make good all the depreciation of those assets of which the immediate wartime usefulness did not suffer thereby. It is impossible to suggest any accurate figure to indicate the amount of this and, in any case, it was probably offset by the creation, for war purposes, of new equipment which remained useful in peacetime. Altogether, in relation to the wealth of the country, the war did only slight damage to the physical stock of capital, though it doubtless hindered it from growing as it otherwise would have done.

The British loss of capital assets abroad was proportionately heavier. It is difficult, however, to be quantitatively precise about this loss also, because the nominal value of many capital transactions between governments during the war was very different from the realizable value of the securities created in the course of them. The British government lent abroad more than it borrowed,[1] but did not improve Britain's long-term creditor position by so doing. In fact, as far as the chief items (borrowings from the Americans and loans to European governments) were concerned, it adopted in 1922 the policy of not demanding from its debtors more than was needed to bridge the gap between its receipts from reparations and the amount it had to pay in respect of its war debts to the American government.[2] As a result of the settlements subsequently made Britain actually paid rather more to the United States on this account than it received in reparations and in interest on its own much larger wartime loans.[3] The effective change in the long-term creditor position was thus mainly the result of the sale of privately-owned investments. Earlier estimates of such sales put them as high as £850 million,[4] which is more than

---

[1] Many different figures are extant for the amount of wartime lending and borrowing. The whole position is complicated by such things as the deposit of gold as a partial offset to some borrowings, the addition of unpaid interest to the principal, and the continuation of loans for specified purposes after the armistice. The most reliable figures suggest that, to the end of 1919, the British government lent about £1,825 mn. to its allies and borrowed £1,340 mn. (Morgan, *op. cit.*, p. 342.) Discussions of the 'war-debt question' used different figures because they were not concerned with British loans to the rest of the Empire or British borrowings from countries other than U.S.A. and from private sources in the U.S.A. At the end of March 1919 the relevant figures for the major war debts were that Britain owed £841 mn. to the U.S. government and was owed £1,570 mn. by European countries. (*Ibid.*, pp. 317 and 320.)

[2] R. J. Stopford, 'Inter-Ally Debts' in A. J. Toynbee, *Survey of International Affairs 1926* (1928), pp. 110-11.

[3] *Ibid.*, p. 127.

[4] Royal Institute of International Affairs, *The Problem of International Investment*, p. 130.

20 per cent of the accumulated total of British capital abroad at the end of 1913, but this figure is almost certainly too large. It was more probably of the order of £550 million,[1] and, as a partial offset, new private investment abroad is estimated to have been about £250 million from 1914 to 1919 inclusive. Well over half of this new investment, however, was made in 1914; i.e. it was mainly the work of the last months of peace, whereas the sales of investments were almost entirely the result of the war.[2] Very roughly, one may conclude that the war caused a net sale of rather more than 10 per cent of Britain's long-term foreign assets. In addition many of the British assets in enemy countries and in Russia, which were some 4 or 5 per cent of the total British foreign investment, were lost by confiscation, and the earning capacity (and therefore the value) of some of the remaining assets was reduced.

The reduction of short-term capital assets and the increase of short-term borrowing abroad, which together amounted to a wartime loss of £250-£300 million, did not represent so completely irrevocable a change. It was in part a temporary reflexion of abnormal current trading conditions. Thus many of the short-term debits were simply the proceeds, not withdrawn from the London money market, of unusually large import surpluses from the British dominions.[3] A return of peacetime trading conditions could be expected to reverse, at least partially, this semi-automatic accumulation of debits and it is clear that in 1920 much of the wartime loss was, in fact, recovered. But the prewar creditor position was never fully restored, so there was some permanent change in the resources which Britain had available for the conduct of its international financial business.[4]

It was, indeed, only in the international field that the war appreciably reduced Britain's stock of economic resources and left it somewhat short of the means to carry on well-established lines of business in the way to which it was accustomed. It can, in fact, be argued that the smallness of capital losses at home, in comparison with that experienced in some other countries, was a positive handicap. In some European countries more plant was destroyed or annexed as a result of the war, which left a political and currency situation in which it was possible to replace the losses, at fairly low expense to the owners,

---

[1] Morgan, *op. cit.*, p. 331.   [2] *Ibid.*, pp. 264, 322-3 and 342.

[3] See tables of changes in value of imports and import surpluses from various countries in *ibid.*, pp. 307-9.

[4] *Ibid.*, pp. 343-4.

with something more up to date. This was particularly true of the Belgian steel industry (a great competitor of the British) and, to a less extent, of the steel and ancillary industries of France and Germany.[1] When, however, one turns to consider the changes in current activities induced by the war, and the state of world economic conditions at its end, the smallness of the change in economic resources looks less important, whether as a benefit or a handicap. The question that arises is whether the opportunities of using these resources had not permanently altered. The outstanding changes in British current economic activities during the war, apart from those associated with international long-term and short-term financial transactions, were in the nature and level of foreign trade and in the relative importance of different branches of production. Because of increasing concentration on the needs of war, as well as the loss or difficulty of access to many markets, much less of British production could be devoted to export, though it is impossible to show the extent of the change very precisely owing to the difficulty of measuring the amount of war production.[2] But the impairment of the export trade, while the needs of war were preventing an equivalent reduction in the flow of imports, shows plainly in the statistics. In 1913 the values of imports, re-exports and home-produced exports were respectively £769 million, £110 million and £525 million. In 1918, when prices had greatly increased, they were £1,316 million, £31 million and £501 million.[3] In terms of volume (measured in the prices of 1913) imports in 1918 are estimated to have been 27 per cent and exports (including re-exports) 63 per cent below the 1913 level.[4] This reduction, though abnormally large in the case of British exports, was in part the result of a general decline in the volume of world trade and there was hope that when the opportunity came to revive international dealings Britain's relatively sound industry and finance would ensure a full recovery of British foreign trade. For a few years after the war Britain did, in fact, obtain a slightly increased share of the diminished total of world trade. But during the war some of the most valuable foreign

[1] Burn, *The Economic History of Steel-making*, pp. 408-13.

[2] Schlote, *British Overseas Trade*, pp. 76 and 78, states that the ratio of exports to industrial production from 1914 to 1918 was only 74 per cent of its 1913 level and in 1918 was only 56 per cent of the 1913 level. But these figures should be treated with caution.

[3] *Ibid.*, pp. 123, 126 and 128. Munitions supplied to the forces overseas are not included in the trade figures.

[4] Calculated from *ibid.*, p. 130.

markets had been among those where supplies of British exports were most heavily reduced. The Far East, India, Canada and Latin America were all neglected in this way for long enough for new rivals to become entrenched. Since these were all areas that could conveniently be supplied from the United States or Japan, the two countries whose manufacturing production grew most during the war, the prospects of fully recovering all these partly abandoned markets were not bright.

Moreover, it was possible that changes in the distribution and use of British productive capacity had jeopardized future trading prospects. Some industries, like the textiles, for which sufficient raw materials and shipping space had not been available, had had to contract their output without reducing their capacity and were likely to run into financial (and therefore competitive) difficulty unless they could quickly regain the markets they had forgone. Others, like steel-making, shipbuilding and some branches of engineering, had enlarged their capacity in order to meet special war needs and could escape the burden of surplus capacity only if there were a general expansion in the postwar demand for their products. For some of them there were such high hopes (momentarily swollen by the immediate postwar boom) that this would be the case that still more plant was added just after the war.[1] The difficulties that ensued when most of these hopes were falsified must therefore be put down to mistaken judgment as much as to the war. Even the possible off-setting advantage, that the new capacity would be more efficient than the old, some of which might therefore be closed with more gain than loss, was not much achieved in practice. In the location, lay-out and finance of its new wartime plant the steel industry, for instance, made much less of a break with unsatisfactory earlier arrangements than it could have done.[2] Another weakness was that the coal industry, in the urgency of war, had used up so much of its remaining easily-worked deposits that it was almost bound to operate at higher cost subsequently, to the detriment of all other industries and of its own exports.[3]

The war thus left Britain with a legacy that was likely to make some activities rather more difficult even in a familiar and well-ordered world. But the world where a return to peace and prosperity was sought was one afflicted by economic and financial disorganization and by temporary impoverishment of some of its chief trading areas,

[1] Burn, *op. cit.*, pp. 385-92.   [2] *Ibid.*, chap. XIV, *passim*.   [3] *Ibid.*, p. 355

as well as one in which new centres of financial and industrial power had emerged to challenge the older leadership of Britain and Europe. The war interrupted the process of rapid productive expansion which was fundamental to the easy working of the pre-1914 international economy. The level of world manufacturing output in 1913 (a peak year) was not reached again until 1923 and it has been estimated that four and a half years' growth of world manufacturing output was lost. But Europe fared much worse than this. If prewar trends had continued, the European manufacturing output actually attained in 1929 would have been reached in 1921, so that, very approximately, Europe lost eight years' growth of output.[1] This relative retardation in the region with the largest international markets[2] was bound to upset world trading conditions. And, while Europe fared worse than average, other parts of the world must have fared better. Countries unable to obtain goods from the usual exporters sometimes sought to produce them at home. Some non-industrial countries engaged in the war also tried to increase their contribution to military supplies. Difficulty in obtaining the necessary plant hampered these efforts to industrialize, but there was some increase in the output of manufactures in countries which previously had relied on imports. The First World War was noted as a stimulus to industrialization in Canada[3] and in Latin America, especially Argentina and Brazil,[4] and several other predominantly agricultural countries increased their still tiny share in the world manufacturing output. Above all, the United States and Japan, less preoccupied by the war than the European belligerents, expanded their production while Europe fell behind. By 1920 Japanese industrial production was 75 per cent and American 20 per cent above the prewar level.[5] These two countries were thus in a position to make a much stronger bid for the available markets. The United States had, indeed, strengthened every side of its international economic position. Its predominance among the manufacturing nations had been reinforced and enabled it to become the most powerful of trading nations. Because it could earn

---

[1] League of Nations, *Industrialisation and Foreign Trade*, p. 140; Svennilson, *Growth and Stagnation in the European Economy*, p. 19.

[2] In 1909-13 European countries participated, as exporters or importers or both, in five-sixths of all international trade (Svennilson, *op. cit.*, p. 170.)

[3] W. T. Easterbrook and H. G. J. Aitken, *Canadian Economic History* (1956), pp. 519-21.

[4] G. Wythe, *Industry in Latin America* (1945), pp. 15, 82, 139 and 352.

[5] For changes in the output of different countries see League of Nations, *op. cit*, pp. 134-43.

the largest international surplus it also became the largest source of international capital, both long-term and short-term. Much of the war-effort in Europe had been financed out of the savings of the American people, but even if the dubious asset of the inter-governmental war debts is disregarded, the long-term capital position of the United States changed from a net debit of between £400 million and £600 million in 1914 to a net credit of about £1,200 million by 1922.[1] Thus Britain after the war re-entered a trading world in which its own financial hegemony, one of the great moulding influences on both its own and the world economy before 1914, was no longer unshared.

All this might not have mattered much if the war had left behind it conditions in which the restoration of trade expansion could easily be begun. Then there would have been new opportunities to offset the loss of old markets and the strengthening of competitors. There was a widespread belief that these conditions did exist and the development of a trade boom within four months of the armistice appeared to confirm it. Stocks of raw materials and consumer goods in most parts of Europe had been depleted and there was a rush to replenish them. But events soon showed the lack of any sound foundation for the boom.[2] Some of the countries with the greatest physical need of goods proved to have the least means of paying for them. In most of central and eastern Europe production and transport were disorganized, more by political and social upheavals than by physical destruction, and many countries, in addition to those of this region, could offer payment for imports only in currencies of uncertain and deteriorating value. Heavily unbalanced wartime budgets had depreciated some currencies to an extent that was fully revealed only when an attempt was made to trade freely with the rest of the world. Immediately after the war, purchasers, hungry for goods, were bidding up prices; organized workers cast aside enforced restraints and claimed their share of the expected prosperity by forcing up wages; and governments gave way to this pressure and met their own needs by creating more and more purchasing power. Inflation, more rapid than before the armistice, became general, but proceeded at very different rates in different countries. Great uncertainty was thereby imparted to business dealings. Credit was essential for the conduct of trade, the revival of production and the restoration

---

[1] Royal Institute of International Affairs, *op. cit.*, p. 130.

[2] For a clear contemporary exposition of the contrast between appearance and underlying reality in this boom see Brand, *War and National Finance*, pp. 197-218.

of currencies, but the granting of credit was very risky when no one knew what the value of a debt would be in six months' time. The governments which most needed foreign loans to tide them over currency and budgetary difficulties were those whose credit was worst. American and a small amount of other governmental lending, which continued until 1921, relieved some difficulties but was neither large enough nor well enough distributed to achieve fundamental improvement. The uncertainty increased, and so did the rewards as well as the risks of speculators. Governments had to choose between losing control over their currencies (and over the value of their revenue) and checking the insecure credit expansion which had kept up trade. Many of the immediate postwar shortages, especially of raw materials, were soon met by the movement of pent-up stocks from countries remote from the main centres of the war, and the low level of production in Europe prevented the continuance of an equivalent effective demand. About twelve months after its inception the boom began to break, leaving it plain for all to see that the war had left no ready-made conditions for the expansion of trade but widespread economic disorganization and financial chaos, which must be remedied before the restoration of a healthy international economy was possible.[1]

The difficulties were enhanced by some of the provisions of the peace settlement. Drastic frontier changes and the creation of new sovereign states in central and eastern Europe did much to add to the economic dislocation there. New frontiers brought many fiscal barriers within what had been the great free trade area of Austria-Hungary. Complementary industrial establishments were left on opposite sides of new boundaries; national railway systems and their rolling-stock were divided among successor states; lines which had provided direct routes within one state now crossed and re-crossed frontiers.[2]

Reparation demands helped to spread economic dislocation and uncertainty wider still. The political leaders of the victorious allies assured their peoples that the defeated central powers, and principally Germany, would be made to bear the cost of the damage they had done, and they prepared their terms accordingly with no consideration of what was either practicable or desirable economically. The

---

[1] For a succinct description and analysis of this postwar phase in Europe see W. A. Lewis, *Economic Survey 1919-1939* (1949), pp. 18-36.

[2] *Ibid.*, pp. 20-3.

armistice terms and the peace treaties contained only a few specific provisions about reparations in kind and in cash, but the Treaty of Versailles included clauses requiring the repayment of the full cost of various classes of vast expenditure and damage, the amount of which would be determined by May 1921. At the latter date this sum was announced as 132 milliard gold marks (a gold mark was approximately worth one English shilling) and a scheme for the payment of annual sums up to 3 milliard gold marks was introduced. There was never any chance that Germany could within a few years pay any significant proportion of all the sums that could come under the general headings in the reparation clauses of the peace settlement.[1] The uncertainty in reaching a final settlement destroyed the incentive of Germany to make economic reforms that would help to restore prosperity. The same uncertainty encouraged other governments to push their own budgetary problems aside until they saw what receipts they could expect from reparations. And when specific terms were laid down they inevitably introduced a complicated set of new international payments at a time when it was difficult enough to arrange all the payments that were needed for genuine commercial purposes.[2] Thus the politicians made the confusion worse confounded and ignored the realities of an economically disordered world which they might have striven to improve.[3]

In such a world, after so great a departure from the normal courses of economic life, the restoration of Britain's position could not be easy. It required a rational, intelligent appraisal of contemporary realities and a common effort to cope with them, not too much distracted by the fierce conflicts that could arise if strong rival groups pursued

---

[1] This was quite clear at the time to those economically informed and was brilliantly demonstrated in J. M. Keynes, *The Economic Consequences of the Peace* (1919). *Cf.* also Brand, *op. cit.*, p. 192: 'What Germany can pay per annum twenty years hence no man can say. What she can pay in the next five will be limited by the extent of her recovery and in any case cannot be large enough very seriously to alleviate the great financial problems which within that period the nations of Western Europe must have solved.'

[2] The reparation provisions and their administration at this time are described with a good deal of critical comment in A. McFadyean, *Reparation Reviewed* (1930), chaps. I-III. Fuller contemporary analysis of their economic effects, with detailed suggestions for remedy, is contained in J. M. Keynes, *A Revision of the Treaty* (1922).

[3] *Cf.* Keynes, *Economic Consequences*, p. 211: 'The Treaty includes no provision for the economic rehabilitation of Europe . . . nor does it promote in any way a compact of economic solidarity amongst the Allies themselves; no arrangement was reached at Paris . . . to adjust the system of the Old World and the New.'

opposite aims in which each whole-heartedly believed. The state of both industrial relations and national politics immediately before the war had evidently hampered the orderly adjustment of economic life to changing conditions,[1] and Britain's economic strength after it depended partly on political and social organization and attitudes.

In industrial affairs the war brought a fairly general enlargement and strengthening of organization, so that if different groups chose to fight each other they could fight harder and do more incidental damage to the nation. The high profits received by part of industry during the war, together with the influence of the postwar boom, encouraged the building up of larger concerns in some of the major industries. But probably more immediately significant was the over-haul and reconstruction of employers' organizations. The steel industry was not untypical. There, a new central association, the National Federation of Iron and Steel Manufacturers, was formed in 1918 to replace the old British Iron Trade Association, and dis-charged its functions more efficiently.[2] A sign of still greater change was the foundation in 1916 of the Federation of British Industries, the first really effective organization representing industrialists generally.[3] Two years later a separate body, the National Confedera-tion of Employers' Organizations, was established and took over its functions in relation to labour questions.[4] The ideas, purposes and comprehensiveness of the many different industrial associations varied a good deal. But in general they tended to increase the influence of industrial interests as political pressure-groups, to provide more control over competition and prices, and to promote greater unity of practice in dealing with labour.

Confronting the more highly organized employers was a stronger labour movement. The expanded wartime demand for labour and the necessity of negotiating with existing organizations in order to smooth the way for urgently needed changes in the use of labour had raised both the status and the membership of trade unions. In 1913 there were 4,189,000 trade unionists in the United Kingdom and in 1919 the total rose to 8,081,000. Successful growth, as in the case of

[1] *Cf.* pp. 258-9 above.

[2] Burn, *op. cit.*, pp. 375-6.

[3] There had previously been an Employers' Parliamentary Association. There is a brief personal account of the foundation and early work of the F.B.I. in C. Tenny-son, *Stars and Markets* (1957), pp. 119-20 and 141-59.

[4] *Ibid.*, p. 152. This body later changed its name to the British Employers' Confederation.

industrial companies, encouraged mergers which produced some unions of unprecedented size just after the war. And, to meet the wide opportunities and needs common to the whole movement, the Trades Union Congress was given a new constitution in 1921, with a new General Council, larger than the old Parliamentary Committee, and provided with more money and salaried assistance, to direct its day-to-day activities.[1]

The war had created new privileges and sectional interests which many of these various organizations might be expected to defend as long and as fiercely as they could. Many firms for several years enjoyed orders which kept them fully employed at very remunerative prices without the discomforts of competition. Others were severely hampered during the war and took the return of peace as a signal to throw off restraints and try to make up for lost time. The breaking of the postwar boom tempted both groups to safeguard themselves by keeping up prices if they could (they seldom could for long), resisting the demands of workers, and trying to cut wages. Organized workers, too, regarded the end of hostilities as an indication that privation was at an end and that all pressure must be exerted to ensure that the major share of the good things to come should accrue to themselves. Even in the later stages of the war such pressure had benefited many of them at the expense of the rest of the community. In the first three years of the war nearly all workers suffered a cut in their standards: the average money wages in a representative group of twelve occupations rose by 35 to 40 per cent while the cost of living index rose by 80 per cent, but in the next year the wages rose by 29 per cent against a rise of 13 per cent in the cost of living. From July 1918 to July 1919 wage increases much greater than rises in living costs continued to be obtained and real wages were back to their prewar level.[2] But some groups, especially women and unskilled men, had done better than this. In the middle of 1919, when the cost of living had doubled, or a fraction more, since mid-1914, the increase in the wages of engineering labourers had reached 152 per cent, that of building labourers 124 per cent and that of agricultural labourers 126 per cent.[3] These were new advantages to be consolidated, and at the same time those who had fared worse reacted against this position and against the difficulties of recent years by

[1] Roberts, *The Trades Union Congress 1868-1921*, pp. 351-5.

[2] Morgan, *op. cit.*, pp. 283-5 and 293-4.

[3] A. L. Bowley, *Some Economic Consequences of the Great War* (1930), pp. 146-7.

pressing many simultaneous demands—for wage increases, shorter hours, and the nationalization of some industries. It is hardly surprising that when the trials of war were followed, first by apparent prosperity and soaring prices, and then by declining trade, unemployment and wage cuts, the industrial scene should have been marked by strife and confusion. Strikes were numerous. Early in 1919 they were carried to the point of serious rioting in Glasgow. In the coal industry there was continuous labour unrest, year after year, countered by a mixture of concessions, delaying tactics and resistance. There was a national railway strike in the autumn of 1919 and there was repeated discussion of the possibility of a general strike. It might seem that the energies needed for economic revival were being squandered in conflicts as desperate as those of the immediate pre-war years, and all common purpose lost.

In fact, there were many signs that reason and common sense might predominate in industrial relations. Nothing came to lessen the bitterness in the coal industry, but few employers were as worried about their political and economic position as the coal-owners[1] and few workers as fierce in their accusations and as sweeping in their demands as the miners. The war had made consultation with trade unions a normal practice over a much wider range of matters than ever before and had made plain that much was to be gained by negotiation and the following of agreed constitutional procedures. A stronger trade union movement, allied to a larger and better organized political party, was willing enough, in all but a few circumstances, to stick to these methods. The Glasgow violence was mainly a flare-up of the wartime movement of shop stewards, than whom nobody was less loved by most trade union leaders. After the early months of 1919 there was less effort to encourage political change by industrial action. The miners failed to get the Trades Union Congress to back them by a general strike,[2] though there was later willingness to use this weapon to prevent the government giving military support to the Poles against the U.S.S.R.[3] The militancy of the miners, indeed, overstrained the loyalty of their allies on the railways and docks and virtually broke up the Triple Alliance.[4] The Russian Revolution

[1] The political danger was nationalization which was recommended by 7 of the 13 members of the R.C. on the Coal Industry. All seven did not sign the same report and the government refrained from acting on the recommendation, on the ground that the Commission had not produced a majority report. The economic difficulty was the coincidence of shrinking markets and rising costs, with wages as the only cost which it seemed possible to reduce.

[2] Roberts, *op. cit.*, pp. 319-25.   [3] *Ibid.*, pp. 339-44.   [4] *Ibid.*, p. 349.

roused many sympathies but few desires to seek the millennium by revolution at home. European doctrines of the conduct of class warfare by industrial action, which seemed to be gaining increasing influence before 1914, had waned since it had become clear that only a minority of those who had preached them were prepared to put them above national considerations. The war split the labour movement unevenly in all European countries and left as an ineffective minority the extreme proponents of industrial strife as the means to political power.[1] In Britain the establishment of a Communist Party in 1920 demonstrated the smallness and isolation of the extreme left rather than the emergence of more revolutionary thinking.

Organized labour was neither revolutionary nor reckless, though a few voices in its midst were both, and the majority of employers accepted the fact that they could not just dictate terms to their workers' representatives. The war and its aftermath had also brought some useful additions to the machinery for settling disagreements between them peacefully.[2] No one would choose the industrial scene after the First World War as an illustration of the reign of sweetness and light, or claim that the self-interest so fully displayed there was always enlightened. Much time and effort were wasted in the pursuit of illusory riches. But the crippling cleavages, the bitterness of spirit, the unrestrained irrationality, which had threatened before 1914, were less evident, except in the coalfields.

Much the same might be said of national politics. The postwar political scene was likely to raise many doubts in a detached onlooker.[3] The armistice was followed very quickly by a general election held in an artificially heightened atmosphere of mass-emotion in which the government gave an account of current conditions and future aims that was exceptionally unrealistic, even by the usual lax standards of electioneering. One of the two great prewar parties was irretrievably split on personal issues. A Liberal Prime Minister, whose capacity for manœuvre roused as much suspicion as his energetic ability to get things done excited admiration, held office on

[1] A. Sturmthal, *Unity and Diversity in European Labor* (1953), pp. 91-3 and 96-100 gives a useful short account of the splitting of the European labour movement by the war, and the postwar dominance of non-revolutionary elements, influenced above all by the British Labour Party.

[2] e.g. the joint industrial ('Whitley') councils set up for numerous industries and representing employers and trade unions in discussions of a wide range of matters affecting the industry; and the creation of a permanent court of arbitration, use of which, however, was rather rare.

[3] This phase of political history is summarized in C. L. Mowat, *Britain Between the Wars 1918-1940* (1955), pp. 2-21.

the sufferance of the Conservatives who dominated his government. The Labour Party had not only gained increased support but in 1918 had revised its constitution in such a way as to acquire a national organization of its own, with its own local branches and individual members;[1] and at the same time it pledged itself to the pursuit of socialist aims, which some of its opponents regarded as little different from criminal lunacy.

But even this last development did not really threaten undue dissipation of political energy in barren strife. The Labour Party was very cautious and patient in its approach to socialism—it would have lost many of its own supporters if it had been otherwise. The extension of collective services which it sought was a firmly established line of policy which the rest of the community at the moment would not extend as Labour wished but would not reverse; and wartime government had given both experience and responsibility to Labour politicians. There was not the material for irreconcilable hostility here, and the virulence of some of the prewar conflicts had diminished. The fantastic mutual accusations of Liberal and Conservative had been dissolved in a sharing of political responsibility. The sex war which had been injected into politics had ended in peace, and the appeal to the women's vote had become a factor to encourage more political concern with domestic security and well-being. The excessive belligerence of prewar politics had had ample military outlets in which to exhaust itself, and for the minority who were still not sated there was soon enough trouble in Ireland to cure them through surfeit. In home affairs, at least, there was sufficient mutual tolerance, sufficient readiness to attempt a dispassionate diagnosis of current problems, to offer hope of an orderly restoration of Britain's condition.

These, of course, were mainly negative advantages. Positive successes depended also on the level of ability that was applied to public affairs and on the kind of things to which most people thought it worth while to devote their efforts and resources. In both respects the war brought changes which were probably disadvantageous on the whole. The restrictions, personal distress and seeming futilities of the war produced a widespread reaction in social life, which showed itself in the more exclusive concern of large numbers of people with the affairs of their own private social circle and a greater determination to ensure immediate enjoyment. One manifestation of the

[1] G. D. H. Cole, *History of the Labour Party since 1914* (1948), pp. 39 *et seq.*

change was a lack of interest in politics among those who had been young in the war, and a consequent shortage of new talent in political life.[1] The immediate postwar behaviour of political leaders, which seemed to take little account of the efforts and deserts of those whose personal lives had been disrupted, doubtless contributed to this, and the economic upheavals of the same time, especially the rapid inflation, must likewise have strengthened tendencies towards changed economic habits, enhancing the temptation to let the future look after itself. In other ways, too, the postwar situation discouraged saving. Government expenditure had to remain high (by previous peacetime standards) because prewar social services had automatically grown a little and the national debt had been vastly increased at high rates of interest. So the people's private spendable income was kept down by taxation. And in spite of the creation of new rentier incomes and the profiteering of a minority, the general effect of the war was to lessen the inequality of incomes,[2] that is, to weaken the position of those who could be expected to make the largest private savings. In such circumstances it was not going to be easy to obtain savings for investment in the new activities needed to fit the British economy prosperously into a changed world. A rough estimate suggested that if the spending and saving habits of 1911 had persisted in 1924 (when real income per head was much the same), the British nation would have saved £675 million in the latter year, whereas in fact it saved only £475 million.[3]

It is not possible to add up all the many intangible changes in British society at the end of the war and say with any certainty whether on balance they made it harder or easier to wring safety and prosperity from the accumulated economic difficulties and opportunities. In the first eighteen months the influences were almost entirely adverse. There was too much wild optimism, too much easy assumption that all economic difficulties ended at the same moment as hostilities, too ready a belief that the only reason for being short of good things was backwardness in grabbing them. Economic recession doused many of the illusions of those months and gave a chance for the assertion of patient common sense and a surprising degree of common purpose and mutual tolerance—but always within the

---

[1] *Cf.* Mowat, *op. cit.*, p. 9.

[2] Bowley, *op. cit.*, p. 160, suggested that in 1924 the real income of the very rich, after taxation, was only half what it was in 1914, whereas the poorest of the working class had gained most.

[3] *Ibid.*, pp. 135-6.

limits imposed by lack of knowledge, the diversion of talent, and permanent changes in social habits and values.

In retrospect, however, it seems that, for a dozen years and more, even the most favourable conditions were prevented from bestowing their full advantage by one overriding influence: the importance which everyone attributed to the war, as a matter of course. The war was a social cataclysm, the like of which had never been known before, an event of such magnitude that it was plausible to attribute to its power all the changes observable after it. But the war was also a strictly temporary phenomenon, whose effects also should be temporary, especially if suitable steps were taken to speed up their removal. Seen in this way, the economic problem of the nineteen-twenties was to undo the damage wrought by the war, and in practice that came to the same thing as seeking happiness in the restoration of something very like the *status quo ante*. On some such lines it seems that the judgment of most informed and thinking men ran. And in so judging they were wrong. The most fundamental changes of the nineteen-twenties were not primarily the result of the war, and some of the greatest changes of which the war was one cause were irreversible. Had there been no war the United States would still have become the world's great creditor; industrialization would still have spread in new areas, to the destruction of some British export markets; substitutes for coal would still have grown in importance; the sources and costs of primary commodities would still have changed. Even many of the changes in British society would have come, too. Labour would still have become a stronger and more cohesive political force; women would still have gained the vote and wider social opportunities; there would still have been a larger scale of organization among firms and trade unions; doubtless, many tastes and consumer demands would have changed in just the same way.

The beginning of many changes that were attributed to the war was plainly to be read in the prewar figures of trade, production and national income and in the tensions within British society. Indeed, by 1914 it was already looking as though British adjustment to some of these developing changes was being left dangerously late. The war did two things. It accelerated many economic and social changes already in progress, carrying them near to completion earlier than otherwise would have happened, and thus marking a real division in the course of economic history. And it smashed the delicate framework of international economic and financial organization, which was the chief established instrument for guiding and easing adjustments to general economic changes. Thus, after the war, very large changes were necessary in the use of the world's economic resources, and Britain shared to an exceptional degree in the need for such changes. But they had to be attempted, if at all, in the midst of financial upheaval and without the assistance of a tried, comprehensive and efficient set of international economic institutions, such as had existed hitherto. That was the great economic evil directly wrought by the war. But it was enhanced by the war's indirect influence in diverting attention from the fundamental causes of many contemporary changes. By encouraging wrong diagnosis it led to many economic problems being mistakenly treated or left untreated for too long, and so its influence ran deep much later than it need have done. And it is there that the true tragic element in the economic consequences of the war is to be found.

PART THREE

1919-1939

In the case of our financial, as in the case of our political and social, institutions we may well have reached the stage when an era of conscious and deliberate management must succeed the era of undirected natural evolution. . . . The foundations of our financial system are being re-examined. Dogmas hitherto regarded as canonical are being questioned. The feeling is growing that our former easy-going ways will no longer ensure our prosperity in a crowded and increasingly competitive world. We are, indeed, at the parting of the ways and our future depends on whether we choose the right way.

MACMILLAN REPORT (1931)

CHAPTER THIRTEEN

The Opportunities and Difficulties of the Interwar World

SINCE Britain's whole livelihood was so closely bound up with international activities it is impossible to follow its economic history without examining the world conditions in which it was set. Imports contributed to the feeding of everyone in the country and entered directly into a large proportion of its products. If there were a permanent substantial drop in the vast income earned from exports and from services and loans to foreigners the British economy must suffer severely. The conditions of foreign business were thus of vital importance to the British people who, if they found them becoming increasingly adverse, must strive to alter both their own economic activities and the international environment. It has already been indicated that the highly successful late-Victorian accommodation between the British and world economies was becoming outdated by 1914, though without causing much immediate difficulty. The dislocations and the shifts of economic power caused or enhanced by the First World War have also been sketched. It remains to be considered a little more closely how these various conditions interacted with each other, which among them had the most prolonged and increasing effect, what parts of British business they concerned most closely, and what new and profitable economic opportunities they created for whoever could grasp them.

The influences that mattered most were those which caused lasting changes in the state of international markets, raising or lowering the total demand for imports, switching demand from one type of thing to another, creating extra sources of supply of some goods irrespective of the level of international demand for them, and so on. There were several distinctive influences of this kind in the 'twenties and 'thirties, and their combined effect was to modify profoundly the environment of international trade. Some of them had clearly existed earlier, but most of them had not developed far enough to be very powerful until after the First World War. Among them was a change in the rates of population growth in different parts of the world. On the whole, for most of the nineteenth century, population grew fastest in the regions which were most advanced economically or where additional resources could most readily be harnessed for productive use. By the second quarter of the twentieth century population increase was slowing down in many of the richest countries owing, it would seem, to a steadily extending use of birth-control among their peoples. At the same time, in many economically backward countries population was increasing faster, as contact with the West brought some improvement in hygiene and public services, which lowered mortality. Although the change was not so striking as it later became, when new life-saving drugs could bring down death-rates much more quickly, it was sufficient to have some economic significance. It is true that the European population was growing as fast as ever in the nineteen-twenties, but this was only because population growth had risen to a new peak of over 1·5 per cent per annum in Europe's poorest region, the east, whereas in the more industrialized north-west it had fallen from the peak of 1·1 per cent per annum (maintained between 1890 and 1910) to only just over 0·6 per cent per annum. In much of Asia and Africa the change in growth rates was very much less but was in the opposite direction.[1]

These demographic changes meant that the demand of industrialized countries for imported foodstuffs, which had been so important in the pre-1914 trading network, was unlikely to rise so rapidly as before, while in some of the poorest countries, whose international position depended on supplying that demand, the growth of the labour force available for the purpose was maintained or accelerated. The fact that much of the internationally traded primary produce was supplied by wealthy countries like the United States and the white British Dominions, which also experienced slower rates of population increase, was not a compensation, since they were able to offset slower growth in the labour force by great technical improvement in agriculture.[2] On the other hand, the way in which the slowing down of western population growth was coming about enhanced the effects on demand because it involved a steady increase in the proportion of

---

[1] A. M. Carr-Saunders, *World Population: past growth and present trends* (1936), pp. 21 and 42. In the late 'thirties there were few West European countries where natural increase was at more than half the rate prevailing at the beginning of the century, whereas in such countries as Ceylon, Japan and Chile the rate showed a modest increase.

[2] *Report of the Economics Committee* (*Papers of the R.C. on Population*, vol. III) (1950), p. 8.

active adults and a decrease in the proportion of children. In Germany, for instance, children under 15 were 34 per cent of the population in 1910 but only 26 per cent in 1925, and many other European countries showed a similar trend.[1] This meant that a smaller proportion of their income was likely to be spent on basic necessities, including the cheaper types of bulk foodstuffs, with a consequent still greater need for commercial adjustment in countries that relied on supplying such things.

This effect of a changing age-structure was, however, only one aspect of the more general effects of high living-standards. In highly industrialized countries and in highly capitalized agricultural countries the majority of the people had better living standards not only because they had fewer dependants to support, but also because rising productivity had increased their incomes. By the nineteen-twenties such countries had passed the point at which a bigger income meant, for most people, getting enough to eat and being soundly clad. When there was a further rise in the incomes of people who already had enough to eat they did not try to eat more; if anything, they were liable to eat rather less, since a rising living-standard is generally accompanied by a reduction of heavy manual labour. Instead they bought different types of food and a greater proportion of manufactured goods, especially the sort of goods which, at a modest cost, added to the comfort, convenience and amenity of everyday life.[2] Many of these goods in the interwar period were of new types and were quite different from the sort of things that had dominated prewar trade in manufactures. Moreover, there was another significant factor. As incomes rose, the proportion spent on material commodities declined and the proportion spent on services rose.[3] Since most, though not all, types of service are most conveniently supplied at home and are harder to import and export than merchandise, this trend made it unrealistic to rely on international trade keeping up with the growth of income. On the other hand, service activities

---

[1] League of Nations, *The Course and Phases of the World Economic Depression* (1931), p. 20. This book, written by B. Ohlin, is subsequently referred to as Ohlin, *op. cit.*

[2] *Ibid.*, pp. 21-5.

[3] e.g. in the U.S.A. expenditure on services (on a uniform definition) showed an almost unbroken rise from 26 per cent of total expenditure in 1869-78 to 38 per cent in 1929-38. (S. S. Kuznets, *National Product since 1869* (1946), p. 142.) The data available for the U.K. (Jefferys and Walters, *National Income and Expenditure of the U.K.*, pp. 20-1, 27 and 31-2), show little change over this period, but this is because they relate only to *personal* expenditure and exclude both the great increase in the consumption of services by public authorities and the effect of subsidies.

were coming to use both more elaborate types and greater quantities of physical equipment, and their growing relative importance clearly made it essential for producers and merchants to pay great attention to their needs.

The greatest effect of all these changes was on the nature and volume of demand, but there were others, equally potent, which had their first impact on supply. Increases in productive power, whether through the spread of industries to new areas or through the adoption of technical innovations, affected trade in this way. The stimulus given to the spread of industrialization by the First World War has already been noted,[1] but this was only part of a much larger trend. The most striking long-term development was that, as the world's manufacturing output grew, an increasing proportion of it was located in a few large countries outside western and central Europe, which had been the most industrialized region in the late nineteenth century. The share of the United States in the world's industrial production is estimated to have risen from 36 per cent in 1913 to 45 per cent in 1928 and though, because of depression and of industrialization elsewhere, this proportion was appreciably reduced in the 'thirties, it was offset by the rise of industry in the U.S.S.R. The Soviet Union's share in world industrial production, which was under 5 per cent in 1928 (rather less than the share of the old Russian Empire in 1913) was probably rather more than 10 per cent in 1938. Japan showed a similar trend, with 1 per cent of the total in 1913, 2·5 per cent in 1928 and 4 per cent in 1938.[2] While in the two former cases, especially that of the U.S.S.R., this great increase in industrial production found its outlets mainly in the home market, it did reduce the opportunities for some types of exports from other countries; and the surplus which an industrial giant like the United States had available for export, though only a small proportion of its total output, was, in absolute terms, enough to provide formidable competition in international markets.

Moreover, the conditions of international trade were complicated by economic changes in countries that had a much smaller share in the world's industrial production. Often these changes were

---

[1] P. 291 above.

[2] League of Nations, *Industrialisation and Foreign Trade*, p. 13; H. C. Hillman, 'Comparative strength of the Great Powers' in A. J. Toynbee and F. Ashton-Gwatkin (eds.), *The World in March 1939* (1952), pp. 429 and 439. These sources allot a higher share to the U.S.S.R. in 1938 but recent official revisions of the Russian statistics indicate that 10 per cent is probably nearer the mark.

internationally significant because they led to the local production of goods of kinds that had previously formed a large part of European and British exports. The outstanding example is the preponderance of textiles in Japanese industrialization. As late as 1929 half of all Japanese factory workers were engaged in producing textiles, which remained throughout the 'thirties the biggest group in Japanese manufactured exports.[1] But, in view of the key position which British textile exports to India and the Far East had in the pre-1914 network of world trade, there may seem still greater significance in what happened in some of the less industrialized countries. India and China both remained predominantly agricultural throughout the interwar period, but in both of them cotton manufacture was firmly established and growing. By the mid-twenties China had become a net exporter of cotton yarn, with India as its best market, and in the 'thirties it had only a small net import of cotton piece-goods.[2] In Europe there were several countries which had only a small share in the world's manufacturing output, simply because they were small in size, but which were becoming industrialized to such an extent as made a significant difference to international trade. Between the two world wars Finland, Sweden, Denmark and the Netherlands all increased their manufacturing output much more than the general average and, in proportion to their population, attained a level of industrial output comparable to that of Britain at the time of the First World War.[3] Moreover, some of this expanded output consisted of new types of goods, which thus came into competition with activities to which older industrial countries, like Britain, might have turned as world conditions became less favourable to the existing pattern of their trade.[4] Because of the continued preponderance of Europe in international trade the change in the character even of these relatively small, but relatively wealthy, countries, both as markets and as exporters, was by no means negligible.

Changes in the global distribution of manufacturing power and of particular large industries were partly dependent on technological innovations, which also enhanced their effects. The most influential

---

[1] Kate L. Mitchell, *Industrialization of the Western Pacific* (1942), pp. 19-20.

[2] G. E. Hubbard, *Eastern Industrialization and its Effect on the West* (2nd edn., 1938), pp. 194-5.

[3] Svennilson, *Growth and Stagnation in the European Economy*, pp. 204-8.

[4] *Ibid.*, pp. 180-5 and 293-9 for detailed statistics illustrating the difference between manufactured exports from Sweden and from older industrial countries.

of such innovations can be conveniently classified in two groups: those which tended to reduce employment in supplying certain important commodities, by increasing the efficiency of their production or of their industrial application, or by developing substitutes for them; and those which led to the production of new commodities that met widely-felt needs. The importance of agricultural innovations of the first kind has already been touched on, because of their tendency to reinforce the effect of demographic change in upsetting the balance of demand and supply in an important section of world trade. In many of the chief food-exporting areas the nineteen-twenties saw a great increase in the use of farm-tractors and more specialized machines, and the effects of mechanization were supplemented by advances in applied biology which developed, among other things, higher yielding strains of sugar-cane and new wheats of which some flourished in more arid districts, some matured in a shorter growing season, and some produced heavier crops in familiar conditions.[1]

Of the economizing innovations in industry the most generally influential were probably those concerned directly with the harnessing and application of energy. Many of them had been adopted earlier to a small extent and in a less efficient form, but they had their full influence only after the First World War. The improvement of the internal combustion engine, electric motors and hydro-electric plant, and the introduction of high voltage power transmission made manufacturing and transport undertakings less dependent on the burning of coal in their own steam-raising plant. Coal remained much the most important fuel but its consumption ceased to rise *pari passu* with the increase of manufacturing activity and by 1930 seemed to be beginning a permanent slight decline. Not only was it partially replaced by substitutes but great savings were effected in some of its most important uses. For example, the quantity of electric power obtained from a given quantity of coal doubled between 1920 and 1930 and was further increased in the next decade; the consumption of coal per ton of pig-iron in blast furnaces was reduced by nearly a quarter in Britain and a little less in the United States between 1920 and 1938; and there was also a reduction of a third in the coal consumption of steam locomotives between the wars.[2] International

[1] Ohlin, *op. cit.*, pp. 40-3 and 52.
[2] Svennilson, *op. cit.*, pp. 102-6; Leith, Furness and Lewis, *World Minerals and World Peace*, p. 20.

trade was particularly affected because newly industrializing areas, which lacked coal, were increasingly successful in keeping down their needs for it and because shipping turned very rapidly to the use of oil fuel; while the growing use and production of oil outside the chief producing and consuming country, the United States,[1] gave rise to a large trade in new directions. In addition, there were many indirect effects. Changes in the technique and economics of energy supply made it practicable to establish manufacturing industries in new regions. They were also among the pre-conditions of some of the changes in manufacturing equipment and techniques that led to the production of a wide variety of new and specialized commodities as well as to a transformation in the design, quality and cheapness of many more familiar goods.

Essentially, the technological situation was dependent on the gathering momentum of applied science in industry. The progress of mechanical engineering, chemistry and metallurgy, which was so marked from late Victorian times onwards, had established a far wider basis of both knowledge and equipment, on which to build specific improvements in almost every branch of production and distribution; and an awareness of this was making the organization of continuous industrial research more common. Consequently, though the general character and directions of technological advance were similar to those in the two preceding generations, their detailed results were often very different. For many years before 1914 nothing had had such a comprehensive influence as did the changes in the equipment for harnessing and applying energy after the First World War. Motor vehicles, vastly different in design and performance from those at the beginning of the century, became ubiquitous and encouraged social habits, business locations and forms of economic organization which took their ubiquity for granted. The cheaper and more widespread supply of electricity made it worth while to develop new types of industrial plant and of household appliances, which depended on its use. New types of industrial plant, in turn, made possible a still greater scope and variety in mechanized production. There was a great increase in the number of commodities of which

---

[1] Oil production in countries other than the U.S.A., most of which produced almost entirely for export, rose from 28 mn. tons in 1919 to 68 mn. tons in 1929 and 110 mn. tons in 1939. The U.S.A., which in these years produced 49 mn., 136 mn. and 168 mn. tons respectively, was also a net exporter throughout this period. (S. H. Longrigg, *Oil in the Middle East: its discovery and development* (1954), pp. 276-7.)

the manufacture could be broken down into a succession of processes, each capable of being done by machines with such uniform precision that the final product could be continuously assembled by machines; and there was a similar increase in the development of machines that would transfer work in progress from one stage to the exact position required for the next. It was particularly important that most types of machinery were among the commodities the production of which was affected in this way. Thus the cost of capital equipment was reduced relatively to that of labour, so that economic as well as technological factors encouraged the search for still more varied applications of machinery.[1]

The outstanding effects of these new achievements in technology were to make available a greatly increased number and variety of machines for use in both production and transport; to create a whole new range of fairly complex durable consumer goods, mechanical, electrical, electronic; and to enlarge the supply of simpler types of consumer goods by improving the materials of which they were made, or by more complete standardization and mechanization of their manufacture (as happened, for instance, in those sections of the clothing industries where handwork had hitherto still been general) or by easing their preservation and distribution through the development of new types of containers and methods of packing that could be completely mechanized. To some extent this new supply encouraged its own demand. The techniques which produced new machines also made it essential for any firm or any country that wished to maximize its industrial strength to buy much new machinery in order to do so. The increased productivity made possible by the new industrial plant could help to create the higher incomes out of which the more elaborate consumer goods could be bought. But there were many potential snags. The equipment required in order to make use of many of the new techniques involved very heavy initial cost, which was beyond the means of people in most countries. The goods which that equipment could produce must remain at luxury prices unless the initial cost could be spread over a huge market, which sometimes needed to be much bigger than some even highly

---

[1] For a fuller summary of the main aspects of technological progress and their economic impact see Svennilson, *op. cit.*, pp. 20-2. Many of the chief inventions of the twentieth century are discussed in Jewkes, Sawers and Stillerman, *The Sources of Invention, passim*, esp. chap. IV and the case histories in Part II. This work casts doubt (not very convincingly to my mind) on the view that technological progress was becoming more dependent on the organized application of science.

industrialized countries could provide within their own borders. Yet many of these goods were, in any case, beyond the means of nearly everyone in the poorer primary producing countries. Thus many of the characteristic commodities of the most advanced stage of industrialization could find a ready market only in the same few countries that had the knowledge and equipment which made it possible to make them.[1] They could not base their prospects on a spontaneous worldwide demand to the same extent as, say, British cotton goods had done when they were in the forefront of industrial advance in the mid-nineteenth century. If their outside markets were to spread, they would have to be strengthened by initial financial assistance and measures to raise permanently the incomes of the people who composed them.

This is a reminder that changes in productive ability, and even changes in the physical need of basic necessities, are not automatically transformed into changes in international trade. To turn increased productive ability into increased output, and increased output into increased sales, required investment and trading credits. For these things to be regularly supplied, on an ample scale at a moderate cost over an appreciable period, called for reasonable stability and security in international finance and for a large supply of funds which would be acceptable as liquid assets all over the world—called, in fact, for the same sort of conditions as had existed before 1914, though not necessarily for them to be established by the same means. Clearly, the chaotic international finance just after the First World War, when impoverished countries paid for essential needs simply by expanding and depreciating their currencies and thus made insecurity and uncertainty ever more serious,[2] was for the time being likely to upset international markets even more than the more fundamental economic changes that have just been described. Unless and until international finance was restored to order, the difficulties created by these changes were likely to grow without being detected, and the achievement of the potential advantages was even more likely to be frustrated.

[1] This tended to encourage the larger industrial countries to be more nearly self-sufficient in the newer types of manufacture and hence to make them more difficult markets for each other. Thus trade among the U.K., Germany and France was 19·9 per cent of all intra-European trade in 1913, but only 14·6 per cent in 1928 and, partly for quite separate reasons, only 8·9 per cent in 1938. (Svennilson, *op. cit.*, p. 197.)

[2] League of Nations, *International Currency Experience: Lessons of the Inter-War Period* (1944), pp. 218-19.

It becomes clear that, while international economic conditions after the First World War were bound to be permanently different from those before 1914, there were very varied possibilities of the form the differences might take. The substitution of unbalanced budgets, currency inflation, and wildly fluctuating exchange rates for stable national and international financial arrangements made a reduction of trade unavoidable. The more disorganized countries had only limited means to participate in international trade, and greatly increased risks and uncertainty discouraged the expenditure necessary to restore productive and earning power and to create and satisfy new markets. But, even when this disorganization was corrected, a return to prewar trends of expanding trade was dependent on deliberate changes in the kind of economic activities carried on in many different countries.[1] If no great effort was made to bring these changes about, then many unbalances in international supply and demand would exist, causing the saturation of some markets and unemployment in some major industries. Food exporting countries were likely to find themselves producing more than their best markets were willing to buy at a remunerative price. Such countries would fail, in consequence, to expand their incomes. Exporters of manufactures then faced a loss of some markets, partly because their customers could produce some of the goods for themselves and partly because those customers' incomes did not grow enough for them to buy large quantities of other types of manufactures. The natural consequence of this would be unemployment in countries exporting manufactures, which would keep down the demand for imported raw materials, which might have compensated for some of the changes in international food markets. It would also limit the growth of incomes and of the demand for manufactured goods in the industrialized exporting countries. Thus it would tend to make it difficult for the new manufacturing possibilities to be fully developed, except in countries that could maintain a large and prosperous home market for them without being much upset by the vagaries of international trade.

On the other hand, the advantages of a new pattern of specialization among different countries, which offered the probability of a general expansion of production, trade and incomes, were discernible. The outlines of this desirable system of specialization can be in-

[1] A discussion of the main types of changes needed and of the reasons why they were needed is contained in Svennilson, *op. cit.*, pp. 16-26.

dicated quite briefly. The older industrial countries needed to concentrate more on making the kind of goods in which the fewest
countries were anywhere near self-sufficient: machinery, transport
equipment, chemicals and durable household appliances were the
outstanding examples. Investment to expand the production of
these would stimulate the home market in such countries and raise
their demand for imports. At the same time, in order to sustain and
reward the investment, the existing export markets for goods of this
sort had to be developed. These export markets were in countries
that were beginning to industrialize and in countries that had high
average incomes without producing a full range of manufactured
goods, i.e. agricultural countries with a high output per man and
industrial countries of small size. The growth of these markets
depended on the further expansion (through intensive investment)
of one or two specialized branches of production in the countries
concerned, and in most cases some branch of manufacture was likely
to be the most suitable activity to expand. Finally, there was a need
to make primary producing countries into better markets by raising
their incomes. This need would be partly met by higher sales of
primary produce to industrial countries as a result of increased
economic activity there, but there were limits to what could be done
in this way and it was also necessary for primary producing countries
to raise their productivity in activities for which their home market
was expandable. This increased productivity might be sought either
in the improvement of agriculture for domestic consumption or in
the simpler types of manufacture, but, in either case, in most
countries it was likely to be partly dependent initially on some
foreign investment.

So the kind of economic world that had the best chance of prosperity
was one that would not ignore or resist the spread of industrialization
but would adapt itself to it and encourage it further, though not
indiscriminately. In such a world, very large countries with a firm
industrial basis, like the United States, would be expected to establish
almost the full range of manufactures, including the most complex.
Relatively wealthy countries of moderate size, like Britain or Germany, would concentrate particularly on the manufacture of high
quality goods, including many that require very advanced technique
and equipment. Countries of comparable wealth but smaller size,
such as Sweden or Canada, would devote most of their manufacturing effort to high quality goods requiring plant that was not too

costly to be remunerative in a fairly small market. And the simpler types of manufacture, such as many of the textiles, would spread more and more in the poorer countries, though few of these were as yet likely to become predominantly industrial.

In practice, the economic world that emerged between the wars conformed to neither the better nor the worse of the possible extremes, but it was nearer to the worse of them. Some progress in transforming production and specialization along the most promising lines was undoubtedly made, once the immediate postwar disorganization was brought under control. Two of the very large countries, the U.S.A. in the 'twenties and the U.S.S.R. in the 'thirties, did make great strides towards the establishment of a full range of manufactures and did take much advantage of the latest technical possibilities. There was a relative increase in the importance of more highly processed goods among the manufactures of the wealthier countries, and to that increase the development of a few specialized lines in some of the smaller countries made a significant contribution.[1] But this was not sufficient to give a sustained boost to the whole world economy. The industrial and commercial impetus of the U.S.A. was halted during the 'thirties and the industrial growth of the U.S.S.R. was based to a unique degree on internal resources, so that it had only minimal direct economic repercussions on the rest of the world. The expansion of the production and export of new classes of manufactures was rather slight in some of the chief industrial countries and, indeed, the greater proportion of such goods in their exports was the result less of an absolute increase in their amount than of an absolute decrease in the amount of other commodities.[2] Above all, there was too little change in the economies of the poorer primary producing areas. Their industrialization went far enough to upset some important European exports, but, neither by industrialization nor by changes in the type and efficiency of agriculture, was enough done to bring about any significant increase in the incomes of their inhabitants. The results that might have been expected duly followed: unsaleable surpluses or cut prices of some primary products and a slackening of demand for manufactured

---

[1] Svennilson, *op. cit.*, pp. 43, 48-9, 175-85 and 205-8.

[2] *Ibid.*, pp. 181 and 293-8. In 1929 only 4 per cent of British and German manufactured exports consisted of goods of which the value of world exports had risen by more than $2\frac{1}{2}$ times since 1913, whereas for the U.S.A. the corresponding figure was 29 per cent (W. A. Lewis, 'The Prospect before Us' in *The Manchester School*, XVI (1948), p. 149).

exports, with repercussions which retarded the expansion of international trade generally.[1] The demands of those countries which did carry their industrialization much further mitigated some of the worst effects but could not counter the general tendency towards stagnation in international trade. Many of these demands could be met out of home production or by interchange among a small number of appreciably industrialized countries. International economic conditions thus limited severely the growth of export opportunities generally and were most difficult of all for those countries that were heavily dependent on direct trade between highly industrialized areas and the poorer regions of primary production.

This account of international conditions implies very serious difficulties for British economic development, though the international influences were not in every respect adverse. Britain clearly had an interest in any set of measures necessary to promote the expansion of international trade, but in the interwar period some of these were of a kind that would create an unusual degree of disturbance in its activities at home. Those most readily perceived, however, seemed both familiar and, at first, manageable. Initially, the international problems appeared to be mainly the result of institutional weakness, for which the remedy was to rebuild a stable system of international finance, of which Britain should be the main architect and director. By example, by exhortation and negotiation, by special assistance to promote currency reform, and by a traditional judicious discharge of the functions of international banker and long-term investor, the British rôle was to ensure the re-establishment of such a system as quickly as possible and thereafter to keep it working always smoothly and safely. Britain did, in fact, play a leading part in the restoration of financial order in Europe and in the re-establishment of the international gold standard, and was rigorous in its efforts to restore its own international financial standing by a prompt reversal of the wartime and immediate postwar inflation.[2] But its ability to mould and support an international financial system was less than it had been. The interrelated activities of the international

---

[1] Much fuller argument on somewhat similar lines, with detailed illustration, is given in Lewis, *Economic Survey*, Part III, esp. chap. XIII.

[2] For a general summary of the international financial reforms of the 'twenties see H. V. Hodson, *Slump and Recovery 1929-1937* (1938), pp. 5-34. On Britain's leading rôle see Condliffe, *The Commerce of Nations*, pp. 443-4. The international gold standard was not restored in its pre-1914 form. The majority of European countries and nearly all other countries except the U.S.A. adopted the gold exchange standard. (*Ibid., op. cit.*, p. 508.)

markets for commodities, securities, gold and short-term finance of all kinds, which before 1914 had all been centred on London and regulated by the London money market, were now much more dispersed and subjected to the often conflicting pulls of different national centres of finance and trade. Britain by itself had not the means to reintegrate them. Its savings and its current international surplus had both diminished so that less was available, as a direct result of British economic activity, to be invested abroad or to be used as a fund of international liquid assets. A rival centre of international finance had grown up in New York, where a bigger current surplus was regularly earned, without there being either the machinery or the incentive to use it in the same way as London had been accustomed to use its surplus in the past.

In addition, the demands made on an international banking centre by foreign countries were liable at any time to be greater and less controllable than before. There were many reasons for this, but among the most important were the changes in the purposes for which foreign balances were kept in international centres. Before 1914 such balances had resulted mainly from ordinary day-to-day commercial transactions and were kept for ordinary commercial purposes. Now a substantial part of them was kept as part of the reserve for the currencies of most countries,[1] instead of gold, and had no regular commercial purpose to tie it to one centre. Thus the amount of foreign funds in a great international centre was liable to fluctuate wildly, and, since many movements of such funds from one place to another were made either for safety or for the manipulation of the credit base at home, the variation of interest rates in the international centre, in the pre-1914 manner, could not in all circumstances give much control over them. Britain could not, in fact, be sure of meeting all the demands that would be made on an international banking centre unless it could build up a bigger current international surplus and could count on some agreement among the principal trading countries to follow complementary financial policies.[2]

Thus the institutional aspect of international economic change really presented Britain with a dilemma rather than a favourable

---

[1] Between 1924 and 1930 foreign exchange was never less than 35 per cent of the total gold and exchange reserves of the 23 European countries on the gold exchange standard. (League of Nations, *International Currency Experience*, p. 35.)

[2] For descriptions of the changed conditions and organization of international finance see Ohlin, *op. cit.*, pp. 25-37 and Condliffe, *op. cit.*, pp. 504-25.

opportunity to use its traditional financial skills and organization for its own and the general benefit. Britain had an exceptional interest in the renewed expansion of world trade. World trade would be very hard to expand except within a framework of institutions which maintained international financial stability. Only Britain already possessed the experience and the specialized market organizations which could provide the controlling nucleus of such a system. But Britain had not sufficient funds of its own to work the system safely and smoothly in all probable conditions and it had no means of acquiring them, for several years at the very least, except through the unsafe expedient of short-term borrowing. What was needed was some international arrangement to supplement the supply of long- and short-term international capital and to agree on policies for its use, either through the existing organization of the London, New York and subsidiary money markets or through new institutions specially created for the purpose. To secure agreement of this kind and put it into operation was perhaps impossible—few bankers and statesmen were convinced of its necessity—and would certainly take years, while financial upheavals, hampering world trade, would continue for lack of it. In the absence of international agreement, if Britain did not take the lead in trying to operate an international financial system no other country would do so, stability would not be achieved and trade would suffer. If Britain, with diminished foreign earning power, attempted to carry the increased commitments of chief international banker it was putting its economic resources under strain and exposing itself to risks that might well cause late Victorian city men to turn in their graves.

The less obvious but even more fundamental choices which international conditions posed to Britain were those which concerned the character of its chief internal economic activities. There were few industrial countries which conformed so little to the pattern of international specialization which was becoming the optimum. Of the three biggest prewar industries, two—coal and cotton—were everywhere specially vulnerable to changes in techniques and the effects of spreading industrialization, and in Britain all the more so because of the exceptional degree to which they produced for foreign markets. In 1907, 89 per cent of the cotton piece-goods made in Britain were exported and just over 80 per cent (by value) of the total production of cotton yarn and piece-goods was sold abroad.[1] Of the record

[1] A. E. Kahn, *Great Britain in the World Economy* (1946), p. 93

British coal output in 1913 one quarter (by weight) and just over one-third (by value) was exported.[1] These commodities provided a dangerously high proportion of all British exports. In the years 1911-13 textiles were 39 per cent and coal 9 per cent of total exports (excluding re-exports)[2] and nearly two-thirds of the exports of manufactures just before the First World War belonged to commodity groups which had a declining share of world trade in the interwar period.[3] Moreover, the distribution of British export markets made future selling prospects still more gloomy. To a much greater extent than the other European industrial countries, Britain sold its manufactured exports in distant markets,[4] often in poor and under-developed countries. The outstanding importance of the Indian market in the British trading system is very familiar, but the dependence on markets of a similar kind was even greater. In the late nineteenth and early twentieth centuries the proportion of British exports which went to agricultural countries gradually increased and between 1909 and 1913 it averaged 70 per cent.[5] Such countries were, on the whole, likely to find it specially easy to discover other sources of supply to replace some of their imported British textiles and specially difficult to achieve the new forms of investment and bigger incomes which might make them into good markets for other kinds of foreign manufactures.

Not everything was unpromising, of course. Machinery and transport equipment had the best selling prospects of all types of goods and Britain was not unfitted to supply them in quantity, since engineering had become its biggest manufacturing industry. But, hitherto, engineering had been only moderately concerned with the export trade: for 1911-13 machinery formed 7·5 per cent of total exports of home-produced goods, and railway rolling-stock and motor vehicles a further 2 per cent.[6] In any case, the specific types of equipment that were most in demand were constantly changing and success in expanding sales therefore called for repeated modernization and redesign in engineering firms. Even so, however, the strength of the engineering industry was probably Britain's best

---

[1] Kahn, *op. cit.*, p. 85.

[2] Calculated from Schlote, *British Overseas Trade*, pp. 71, 73 and 74.

[3] Svennilson, *op. cit.*, p. 181.

[4] In 1913 almost half of the European goods sold in other continents came from Britain although British exports were only 26 per cent of all European exports. (*Ibid.*, pp. 171-2.)

[5] Schlote, *op. cit.*, p. 82.   [6] Calculated from *ibid.*, pp. 71 and 74.

hope for the future. Some of the other industries which could meet growing needs of the world generally—chemicals, for instance— were still fairly small in Britain and heavily overshadowed by foreign rivals, though the needs of war had given a fillip to the British chemical industry, which was a useful preliminary to the search for new peacetime economic opportunities.[1]

All this suggests strongly that Britain had reached a point at which the maintenance of a high level of prosperity depended on exceptionally drastic shifts in the use of productive resources and greater ingenuity in the development of new types of finished products. Some of what had been, for a century or more, the country's chief industries could not escape contraction and it was desirable for some of their resources to be transferred as quickly as possible to other activities. New industries were needed and those old ones, like engineering, which could profitably be expanded, needed to turn out a greater variety of products, including entirely new ones. To bring about such changes was not easy. Many of them were so contrary to the experience of the last three or four generations that they were bound to be opposed by a stubborn barrier of deep-rooted ideas. The age-structure of the population was changing in such a way that the distribution of new entrants to employment could no longer make so great a difference to the total distribution of labour among occupations; the rise and fall of different industries involved much difficult variation in the employment of mature workers. And the difficulty of keeping resources of all kinds in reasonably full use while the balance of the economy was changing was probably enhanced because, on the whole, the industries which it was advantageous to expand needed a bigger ratio of capital to labour than those which must contract.

Nor were changes in production sufficient by themselves. For both old and new products it was unlikely that all the foreign countries that had been Britain's best customers in the past could continue to be so; it was necessary to seek bigger sales in fresh markets. There was, moreover, a need for some change in the general relationship of foreign trade to the British economy as a whole. In manufacture the trend was towards the production of more highly processed goods, in the cost of which the value of the incorporated materials

[1] Svennilson, *op. cit.*, pp. 162-5. In 1913 the U.K. produced 11 per cent of the world's output of chemicals, but its production was less than half Germany's and less than one-third of that of the U.S.A.

represented a declining share. Imports of both raw materials and food were likely to grow less in proportion to the growth in the output of manufactures than they had done previously. It was therefore to be expected in a healthy economy that, while British foreign trade would increase absolutely, there would be declines in the ratio of imports to total consumption and in that of exports to total production. This might not happen, however, if there were a large substitution of imported for home-produced raw materials, or if a large proportion of the demand for new types of manufactured goods were supplied by foreign instead of home producers. But the only large practicable change of the first kind was an increased reliance on oil as a source of energy, and it is improbable that there was any economic advantage in the extreme specialization which changes of the second kind would imply. A high proportion of the more complex manufactured goods depended on the use of similar classes of equipment and a common body of advanced technical knowledge, and a country that produced a few of them could just as advantageously produce many unless its home market were too small to sustain the heavy overhead costs involved. On balance, then, a foreign trade rising absolutely but decreasing relatively to industrial production could be regarded as a desirable objective after the First World War.

It is instructive to compare the needs for economic adaptation in the nineteen-twenties with those that arose forty or fifty years earlier, when there were comparably great, but different, changes in techniques and in the state of the world economy. It was necessary in late Victorian Britain to make plenty of changes in the methods of production and the kind of goods manufactured, changes which lowered the profits of many firms, squeezed some out of existence and contributed to a widespread belief that there was economic depression. But there were many other ways of economic advance. There were large new and readily accessible markets for familiar types of manufactures; and the full strain of adaptation did not have to be borne by manufacturing industry, because of the relative ease and cheapness with which Britain could expand the supply of coal, the raw material for which world demand grew most, and because it was practicable to increase earnings from international services very considerably. Perhaps most important of all, any greater difficulties in economic development at home could be offset by participation in complementary activities in places abroad where conditions of development were easier for the time being. And Britain was able to provide the organization and funds for an international financial system which made it just as easy for any country to receive the fruits of its foreign as of its home enterprises.

After the First World War hardly any of these favourable conditions remained. There were no new markets for old types of manufactures. Coal could no longer come to the rescue because it was less sought after by foreign customers and, in any case, to keep its output at the 1913 level was impossible without a steady rise in costs. There was still a brisk and potentially growing market for the services in which Britain excelled (though it was disturbed by financial insecurity), but there was greater international competition to provide some of those which were most profitable. The combination of favourable political and social conditions with access to a new abundance of natural resources, which had made foreign investment a superior alternative to many not unprofitable types of home investment, had passed away. Heavy international investment was as necessary as ever to the maintenance of prosperous and growing world trade and there were plenty of projects abroad from which the investor could ultimately expect a large direct, as well as indirect, return. But the majority of the most permanently advantageous of such projects were likely to need more capital, a greater concentration of technical and managerial skill, and more patience than before. Even had it not been difficult for Britain to set aside as much as before for foreign investment, it would have been impossible to initiate so many and such widespread enterprises. Moreover, the changed conditions of foreign investment made it more rare for its attractions to appear better than those of home investment projects, and even the most promising schemes had their risks increased by the weaknesses of the international financial system. For Britain to make the best of what the times made possible was, for all these reasons, much more difficult than it had been.

It has to be remembered, however, that a reliable set of international financial institutions was not achieved at all and only partial progress was made towards the optimum international specialization of economic functions. The world in which Britain had to make its way was not one that was very close to what its immediate potentialities suggested it should be. But this did not essentially alter the nature of the changes that were necessary for economic health in Britain. The decline in the demand for some of Britain's chief products and exports was not avoided, though it may have been just a little slower than it would have been in a more vigorous world economy. And a shift towards the production of a much bigger proportion of highly processed goods and their sale in the wealthier markets remained easily the most effective remedy, though its advantage may have been slightly reduced. What the discrepancy between the potential and the actual world economy did for Britain was to lessen or postpone the penalties for failure in economic adaptation. One result of the discrepancy was to prolong the unbalance between the demand for and the supply of many kinds of food and raw materials and to bring their prices very low. If Britain did not make the drastic economic adjustments that were indicated, nothing could save her from having many productive resources (including human beings) unemployed; but her consumption might still grow steadily because her expenditure on necessities was being reduced independently of her own efforts. Such a situation looked like a mitigation of current difficulties, but it is doubtful whether it was not, in the long run, a misfortune. With a recent war to blame as the temporary cause of all immediate ills, and cheap imports to blunt their sharp edge for most people, it was harder to see the necessity of drastic economic changes and there was less incentive to attempt them. But the fundamental changes in technical knowledge and in the international distribution of population, wealth and productive ability persisted. There was no going back to late Victorian conditions, and the sooner the British economy was adjusted to a new world the better for both Britain and the world.

CHAPTER FOURTEEN

The Chief Economic Activities

FROM the eighteen-seventies to the First World War certain
trends of change in the distribution of economic activities
showed themselves so persistently that they seemed to belong
almost to the permanent order of things. While economic growth, as
indicated by the size of the national product, was very large, agricultural production was more or less stagnant, so that agriculture
steadily declined to a relatively minor place in the economy. Within
that general stagnation two contrary tendencies were concealed: an
absolute decline in arable and an expansion of livestock output.
Industrial production was growing roughly at the same rate as the
economy in general (perhaps just a little less) but this achievement
owed much to the exceptional and prolonged expansion of coal-
mining. Manufacture, relatively to other activities, was barely holding
its own and building, though following a very irregular course,
appeared by the twentieth century to be definitely falling behind.
But transport, distribution and various commercial and financial
services were becoming relatively more important. Simultaneously,
relations with the outside world were changing. Though external
merchandise trade grew more slowly than before, this was partly
offset by the increase in 'invisible' trade, especially that associated
with a large export of capital, and both production and consumption
at home became more than ever dependent on foreign trade. In short,
the late Victorian and Edwardian economy was one in which primary
and secondary production were of gradually declining relative
importance and services of gradually increasing importance, and in
which a growing involvement in an international economy took place
and was dependent on a large supply of international capital and
services.

The discussion of the world economic environment in the interwar
years suggests that the same trends could hardly continue unmodified
in this period as part of the permanent order of things. Small changes
in them could hardly be avoided; larger changes deserved to be

sought and welcomed, as a condition of maximum prosperity. In particular, it seemed doubtful whether continually increasing dependence on foreign trade was any longer either worth while or possible; and doubtful whether even the maintenance of the existing degree of dependence would not have to rest more on dealings in commodities. In that case there was a presumption that it would be advantageous to change the trend of industrial production and, especially, to build up manufacture to a relatively more important place in the economy.

Attempts to estimate the magnitude and, sometimes, even the direction, of the changes in economic trends are still handicapped for this period, as for earlier ones, by a shortage of appropriate statistics, though some improvements had been made. In the interwar period there was still no satisfactory information about the functional distribution of capital, though estimates of gross capital formation in the different sectors of the economy have been made for the years from 1924 onwards. But there was fuller material on the use of labour. The decennial census maintained the practice, begun in 1911, of making a full classification of the population by industry as well as by occupation, but the categories were not consistent from one census to the next and the lack of a full census between 1931 and 1951 left a large gap.[1] The great extension of unemployment insurance, however, provided a new and much more continuous supply of information not only about the numbers belonging to most industries but about the numbers actually in employment in them at any specified time. For mining, manufacture and building there was also more indication of the growth of output, both in total and in detail, because censuses of production were more frequent—they were taken in 1924, 1930 and 1935—and, in some respects, rather fuller. For other economic activities continuous, direct records of output were no more common than before, though there were rather more statistical data of the kind which give some indirect indications of it and which may sometimes provide a basis for its reasonably approximate estimation. In foreign trade, information about dealings in merchandise had long been fairly adequate. In the interwar years there was a bigger flow of official statistics about the invisible items

---

[1] The census figures for England and Wales in 1921 and 1931 are analysed in D. C. Marsh, *The Changing Social Structure of England and Wales 1871-1951* (1958), p. 105. The comparable figures for Great Britain are given under slightly different headings in Clark, *The Conditions of Economic Progress* (2nd edn.), p. 408, which adds figures from other sources for 1938 and 1939.

in the balance of payments but, though this was useful, it is doubtful whether these figures were much more reliable than the unofficial estimates that have been made for earlier years. It is clearly impossible to give a complete and reliable quantitative account of the development and changing structure of the British economy between the wars. But, though there are so many deficiencies in the data, it is possible to obtain a not too inexact picture of many of the principal features.

Changes in the relative importance and absolute size of different economic activities may be measured in at least three ways, none of them satisfactory for all purposes, but each usefully supplementing the others and providing a check upon them. One may look at the numbers and proportions of people employed in each occupation or industry; or one may try to discover and compare the changes in the value of the net output of each activity; or one may look for changes in the volume or physical output of the chief activities—the actual quantity of goods made or sold or, in the case of transport, the weight of goods moved and the distance over which they are carried. The first of these is the one in which fairly accurate measurement is easiest and is also the one which is least affected by imprecision in the concepts involved, but its usefulness is, of course, limited by differences in the proportion of capital to labour employed in different activities. Nevertheless, the distribution of the labour force still retained great economic significance in the interwar period. This is fortunate for the historian, because it is the only indicator about which the data are full enough to permit comparisons which cover the whole economy. Information about the value of the net output of activities other than the production of material goods was too scanty and unreliable to be of help, and there are many important activities of which the output is not measurable in physical terms.

For a picture of the broad changes in the various groups of economic activities one must, then, rely on the figures of the numbers of workers, preferably the numbers actually employed rather than those claiming a particular occupation as their own. An attempt to show the distribution of labour actually employed,[1] with allowance for short time as well as total unemployment, is made in Table XI.

[1] It should be noted that these percentages are based on the numbers of *employees*, i.e. no account is taken of employers and the self-employed. Industries in which the latter were relatively numerous thus employed rather higher proportions of the *total working population* than those indicated here. 'Agriculture and forestry', 'distributive trades', and 'professional services' were probably the groups most affected.

TABLE XI

Percentage Distribution of Numbers of Employees by Main Industrial Groups in the U.K.*

Selected years 1921-38

Industrial Group	1921	1925	1929	1933	1937	1938
Agriculture and forestry	6·6	5·8	5·3	5·0	4·0	3·8
Fishing	0·3	0·3	0·3	0·3	0·2	0·2
Mining and quarrying	6·2	6·6	5·5	4·3	4·4	4·2
Manufacturing	33·7	35·8	35·7	33·3	35·2	34·6
Building and contracting	5·3	5·2	5·5	5·4	6·1	6·2
Gas, electricity and water	1·2	1·2	1·3	1·5	1·5	1·5
Transport and communication	9·1	8·7	8·5	8·2	8·0	8·0
Distributive trades	10·6	10·7	12·0	13·6	12·9	12·9
Insurance, banking and finance	2·1	2·3	2·3	2·5	2·4	2·5
National government service:						
Civilian employees	1·5	1·0	0·9	1·0	1·1	1·2
Armed forces	3·2	2·2	1·9	2·0	2·0	2·3
Local government service	2·5	2·6	2·7	3·0	2·9	3·0
Professional services	4·8	4·7	4·7	5·1	4·9	5·0
Miscellaneous services	12·9	12·8	13·3	14·8	14·4	14·6
TOTAL	100·0	100·0	100·0	100·0	100·0	100·0

Source: Agatha L. Chapman and Rose Knight, *Wages and Salaries in the United Kingdom 1920-1938* (1953), p. 20.

*Southern Ireland excluded throughout.

Manufacturing is so much larger than any of the other groups in this table that it is desirable to consider it in a little more detail. When this is done some important changes, concealed in the general figures, become evident. Among them are the opposite tendencies in

two of the chief classes of manufactures. From 1922 to 1929 inclusive, textiles always employed a little over 20 per cent of the
manufacturing workers, but 1933 was the only year in which this
proportion was ever reached again and by 1938 it had fallen to 15·1
per cent. As this figure dropped, that for the wide assortment of
industries engaged in engineering, shipbuilding and the manufacture
of electrical goods rose. Soon after the First World War their
proportion of the manufacturing workers fell because of the contraction of shipbuilding. From 1922 to 1930 it was very steady at about
15 per cent, but, after a temporary drop in the depression, it climbed
from a minimum of 12·9 per cent in 1933 to 18·2 per cent in 1938. The
production of vehicles which, though closely associated with these
industries, was classified separately, expanded more steadily. It
accounted for 5·8 per cent of all employment in manufacturing in
1921, 7·6 per cent in 1929, and 9·2 per cent in 1938. The other chief
groups of manufactures showed less change. The largest of them were
clothing (10·8 per cent in 1921 and 9·8 per cent in 1938) and food,
drink and tobacco (10·7 per cent in 1921 and 11·1 per cent in 1938).[1]
The size of the labour force in some of the largest individual industries illustrates the shifts within the industrial sector of the
economy still more clearly. The number of insured workers in July
1939, expressed as a percentage of the number in July 1923, was only
67·5 in the cotton industry, 67·6 in shipbuilding and ship repairing,
69·5 in coal mining and 82·6 in the woollen and worsted industry.
For all industries and services (excluding agriculture) it was 126·4.
Figures for large industries which, by contrast, showed great expansion included 259·4 for the manufacture of electrical cable and
apparatus, 242·2 for the manufacture of motor vehicles, cycles
and aircraft, 205·5 for electrical engineering, 174·6 for building and
contracting and 172·1 for miscellaneous metal industries.[2]

For the production of goods, this information can be supplemented
by figures of the value of net output which, however, are much less
continuous. These figures suggest that industry expanded its output
nearly enough to keep pace with the growth of national income, but
that agriculture failed to do so until the late nineteen-thirties.

---

[1] Chapman and Knight, *Wages and Salaries in the U.K., 1920-38*, p. 20.

[2] G. C. Allen, *British Industries and their Organization* (3rd ed., 1951), pp. 30-1.
The industries mentioned are those which had over 120,000 insured workers in
July 1939 and had expanded or contracted most. 'Miscellaneous metal industries'
were concerned mainly with the production of finished hardware goods, as distinct
from engineering goods or metal semi-products.

Estimates of the net annual agricultural output of the United Kingdom, at current prices, averaged £157 million for 1924-29 and £140 million for 1930-34, figures which amount respectively to 3·8 and 3·6 per cent of the national income. The same investigator put the annual net output for 1935-39 at £159 million, which was only 3·4 per cent of the national income,[1] but more recent enquiries suggest that for these latter years the estimate is too low. A later calculation of *gross* output for 1936-38 is £63·5 million higher than that from which the net figure of £159 million for 1935-39 is derived.[2] The signs are that, by this time, agricultural output had begun to expand considerably. In one other respect the figures are a little misleading. Agriculture appeared to provide a much smaller proportion of the national income than just before the First World War, but the difference was mainly a statistical change caused by the removal of Southern Ireland, which was predominantly agricultural, from the United Kingdom.

Figures of the net output of industry (i.e. manufacturing, mining and building) were collected in the censuses of production and show that, in complete contrast to the prewar situation, it was mining which held back its growth. The value of the net output of mines and quarries, at current prices, fell by 40 per cent between 1924 and 1935, while that of industry as a whole rose by just under 2 per cent. Manufacture, on the other hand, began to expand a little faster than most other activities. The value of its net output was 26·9 per cent of national income in 1924, 26·3 per cent in 1930 and 27·3 per cent in 1935. The corresponding proportions contributed by industry as a whole were 38·7 per cent, 37·2 per cent and 37·4 per cent respectively and were very similar to those found in 1907.[3]

As with the statistics of employment, further sub-division reveals greater changes. For agriculture it was impossible to distinguish all the different purposes to which equipment and purchased supplies were put, and consequently only the gross output figures for all the major products have been estimated. These suggest that the increase

---

[1] Ojala, *Agriculture and Economic Progress*, p. 66, and Jefferys and Walters, *National Income and Expenditure of the U.K.*, p. 9. Mr Ojala's own figures for agriculture's contribution to the national income are based on higher estimates of total national income and are 0·2 per cent lower than those given here.

[2] C. Clark, *The Conditions of Economic Progress* (3rd edn., 1957), p. 648.

[3] Calculated from Jefferys and Walters, *op. cit.*, p. 9, and G. L. Schwartz and E. C. Rhodes, *Output, Employment and Wages in the United Kingdom, 1924, 1930, 1935* (1938), pp. 2, 3 and 22. The latter memorandum summarizes and compares the main statistics of the three interwar censuses of production.

of livestock relatively to crop output, which had gone on for so long, was carried no further. The output of cereals fell very heavily from the greatly expanded wartime level until by the 'thirties it was much below that of the early years of the century. The only crops of which the output increased appreciably were sugar-beet, scarcely produced at all before the First World War but worth £5,790,000 a year in 1935-39, and vegetables (including glasshouse tomatoes). These, however, were sufficient to maintain the relative importance of crop output, for vegetables could no longer be regarded as minor crops; the output of them, which was estimated at a yearly average of £20,760,000 for 1935-39 was then nearly four times that of wheat, a state of affairs which would have dumbfounded mid-Victorian farmers. The main changes in livestock output were a steady decline in the proportion contributed by meat, except for pigmeat, and an appreciable rise, especially after 1930, in that contributed by eggs and poultry.[1]

For industry the changes can be stated in terms of net output. The rise and fall of different industries, suggested by figures of employment, is confirmed by the lists on page 332, in which the chief industries are ranked in order of the value of their net output. These lists include all industries with a net output of more than £30,000,000, i.e. roughly 2 per cent of total net industrial output.[2]

The figures of net output also draw attention to other significant changes that resulted from the specially rapid growth of particular industries which, while not among the country's major activities, were by no means negligible. Industries whose history between 1924 and 1935 fitted this description were concerned in most cases with the production of metal goods, transport equipment or building supplies. They included some of the lighter sections of the iron and steel industries, in particular the hardware, hollow-ware, metallic furniture and sheet metal group and the chain, nail, screw and miscellaneous forgings group, and also the non-ferrous metals industries (other than copper and brass), a group which included lead, tin and aluminium.

---

[1] Ojala, *op. cit.*, p. 208. For a more detailed account of these changes and the conditions underlying them see Viscount Astor and B. S. Rowntree, *British Agriculture* (1938), esp. chap. III.

[2] Schwartz and Rhodes, *op. cit.*, pp. 6-22. The figures in brackets are the value of net output in £ mn., omitting excise duties. 'Iron and steel' covers the blast furnace, smelting and rolling, and foundry sections of the iron and steel industries. Some gas and electricity is included in the output of local authorities. For this reason the figures are not exactly comparable with those for 1907, given on p. 77. Other differences from those figures arise from the division of 'engineering' into mechanical and electrical, and from the separation of newspaper and other printing.

	1924		*1930*		*1935*

<table>
<tr><td>1. Coal-mining (210)</td><td>1. Coal-mining (139)</td><td>1. Coal-mining (121)</td></tr>
<tr><td>2. Mechanical engineering (87)</td><td>2. Building and contracting (94)</td><td>2. Mechanical engineering (96)</td></tr>
<tr><td>3. Cotton (84)</td><td>3. Mechanical engineering (93)</td><td>3. Building and contracting (87)</td></tr>
<tr><td>4. Building and contracting (81)</td><td>4. Iron and steel (57)</td><td>4. Motor and cycle (61)</td></tr>
<tr><td>5. Iron and steel (54)</td><td>5. Motor and cycle (54)</td><td>5. Iron and steel (60)</td></tr>
<tr><td>6. Woollen and worsted (53)</td><td>6. Clothing and millinery (49)</td><td>6. Electrical engineering (56)</td></tr>
<tr><td>7. Brewing and malting (46)</td><td>7. Brewing and malting (46)</td><td>7. Electricity (50)</td></tr>
<tr><td>8. Motor and cycle (45)</td><td>8. Electrical engineering (45)</td><td>8. Clothing and millinery (49)</td></tr>
<tr><td>9. Clothing and millinery (45)</td><td>9. Cotton (42)</td><td>9. Woollen and worsted (43)</td></tr>
<tr><td>10. Railway companies (44)</td><td>10. Electricity (40)</td><td>10. Brewing and malting (43)</td></tr>
<tr><td>11. Other printing and bookbinding (38)</td><td>11. Railway companies (40)</td><td>11. Cotton (40)</td></tr>
<tr><td>12. Electrical engineering (33)</td><td>12. Woollen and worsted (38)</td><td>12. Gas (39)</td></tr>
<tr><td>13. Newspaper printing and publication (32)</td><td>13. Other printing and bookbinding (37)</td><td>13. Newspaper printing and publication (38)</td></tr>
<tr><td>14. Local authorities (32)</td><td>14. Local authorities (37)</td><td>14. Other printing and bookbinding (37)</td></tr>
<tr><td></td><td>15. Newspaper printing and publication (37)</td><td>15. Railway companies (36)</td></tr>
<tr><td></td><td>16. Gas (35)</td><td>16. Chemicals,dyestuffs, drugs (36)</td></tr>
<tr><td></td><td>17. Tobacco (31)</td><td>17. Bread and biscuits (36)</td></tr>
<tr><td></td><td>18. Bread and biscuits (31)</td><td>18. Local authorities (33)</td></tr>
</table>

Other industries with comparable growth included brick and fireclay production, the manufacture of building materials, glassmaking, the paint, colour and varnish industry, and aircraft production. The inclusion of the latter is especially remarkable when it is remembered that nearly all aircraft firms found these years very difficult and that the chief fillip to the growth of the industry did not come until the beginning of rearmament in 1935.[1] Two notable expanding industries which did not fit into the same categories as the rest were wholesale bottling and the manufacture of preserved foods. They seem, however, to reflect the same trend as showed itself in the

---

[1] On the position of the aircraft industry before and after 1935 see M. M. Postan, *British War Production* (1952), pp. 5 and 18-19, and W. Hornby, *Factories and Plant* (1958), pp. 18-20 and 195-203.

widely diffused growth of a miscellany of small consumer-goods industries, which ranged from bacon-curing and sausage manufacture to cardboard box-making and the manufacture of printers' ink, gum and wax, with the cutlery and the metal smallwares industries thrown in for good measure.[1]

Finally, in order to attempt a just appraisal of the industrial changes, it is advisable to look also at the data on physical output, which make clear that some of the apparent limitations of growth were merely the reflexion of a falling price-level that affected different products in very different degrees, and which also permit comparisons over a longer period than separates the production censuses of 1924 and 1935. Measures of industrial production as a whole are only approximately reliable, and their exact levels for particular years are often disputable. One index of manufacturing production, which stood at 101·6 for 1913, averaged 82·6 in 1920-24 and 100 in 1925-29. In 1932 it was down to 93·0 but thereafter rose steadily to a peak of 146·9 in 1937 before falling back to 135·1 in 1938.[2] The inclusion of mining would reduce the growth of this index a little but the inclusion of building as well would more than offset this.

Figures for individual commodities show that some, though not all, of what had been the principal industries contracted less or expanded more than appears from the value of their output. Thus the value of coal until the end of 1924 was inflated by various wartime and postwar influences (notably the French occupation of the Ruhr mines in 1923 and 1924) which thereafter were removed. Coal certainly was a declining industry, but the decline was gradual. Physical output fell only from 267 million tons to 222 million tons between 1924 and 1935, and the 227 million tons mined in the rather depressed year, 1938, were still nearly four-fifths of the record output of 1913.[3] The picture of the iron and steel industry is less changed, however, except that it is possible to show the rapidity of expansion after 1935 and to confirm the reality of the legacy of expansion which the First World War had left. In 1920 steel output exceeded 9 million tons, which was well above the highest prewar level, but this figure was reached again in only two of the next fourteen years. After 1934 there was a change and output rose to 13·2 million tons in 1939, after a temporary setback in 1938.[4]

[1] Schwartz and Rhodes, *op. cit.*, pp. 6-22.
[2] Svennilson, *Growth and Stagnation in the European Economy*, p. 304.
[3] Allen, *op. cit.*, p. 59.   [4] *Ibid.*, p. 119.

On the other hand, some of the industries that were rising to major importance in the interwar years achieved great reductions in prices, which conceal much of the true magnitude of their expansion. Three outstanding examples are the electricity, cement and motor industries. Between 1929 and 1938 the consumption of electricity per unit of industrial production doubled, though it remained lower than in most other countries of western and central Europe.[1] Outside industry and transport, however, the consumption rose in the same period from 58 to 187 kilowatt-hours per head, a much higher level than for any other country which lacked large hydro-electric resources.[2] Altogether, the amount of electricity generated rose from 4,275 million kwh. in 1920 to 26,409 million in 1939.[3] Output of cement, the growth of which reflects both the increasing importance of the building and construction industry and the adoption of new techniques, doubled in the nineteen-twenties and underwent a much larger absolute expansion in the 'thirties, though the rate of growth slowed down a little; in 1938 the output was 7·7 million tons.[4] The number of motor vehicles produced grew far faster than the value of the industry's output. The total was 95,000 in 1923, 212,000 in 1928, 286,000 in 1933 and 445,000 in 1938, with a maximum of 508,000 in 1937. During the 'thirties Britain, which previously had often been matched or surpassed by France, became much the largest European producer of motor vehicles.[5]

Such figures as these refute any suggestion that British industry as a whole had become unadaptable and shied away from novelty. Yet, when one looks back over the various types of evidence of which samples have just been presented, many reservations about the speed and extent of the adaptation seem justified. Relatively to other economic activities, the production of material goods changed little in the interwar years, though there were signs that it might be becoming a little more important by the mid-thirties. It is disputable whether the smallness of the change in this respect mattered much, but less disputable that great changes were needed in the type of commodities to be made, if the full benefits of productive ability were to be obtained. It is easy to overlook the changes that were already in existence in the early nineteen-twenties. The expansion of the steel and

---

[1] Svennilson, *op. cit.*, 117.   [2] *Ibid.*, p. 118.

[3] E.C.A. Mission to the U.K., *Economic Development in the U.K. 1850-1950*, p. 52.

[4] Central Statistical Office, *Annual Abstract of Statistics 1938-50* (1952), p. 179, and Svennilson, *op. cit.*, p. 282.

[5] Svennilson, *op. cit.*, p. 149.

chemical industries and of some types of engineering was a significant modification of the immediate prewar economy. Current conditions in the world encouraged much greater modification, however, of which only a little was forthcoming in the nineteen-twenties. The rapid rise of the motor industry and the marked improvement of its products year by year was the most striking example, but, on the other hand, some of the largest established staple industries of the past, such as cotton, coal and shipbuilding, clung to their position, unable to achieve much, if any, expansion, waiting for something to turn up; and not a great deal that was new appeared and demonstrated alternative lines of development. From 1933 there were bigger changes in the type of things produced. At this time British industry was clearly coming to concern itself much more with producing the capital-goods essential to a world using an ever more varied machine technology and the costly and elaborate durable goods, or the cheap and simple time-saving things, which more and more attract spending in the communities with the highest living standards. The growing importance not only of motor vehicles but also of such things as machine tools, vacuum cleaners and preserved foods all fitted into this pattern.

What seems probable, however, is that, in the 'thirties, though many promising and profitable types of production were begun, a large proportion of them were not carried nearly as far as they might have been, or as far as they were in competing countries. Some of the signs of these limitations showed themselves most clearly in the details of imports and exports, but there were also many indications of them in the level of production and the almost complete absence of some products for which there was a good demand. For instance, the British machine-tool industry manufactured little of the specialized equipment needed by the rapidly growing motor and light engineering industries and though, particularly under the stimulus of rearmament orders, the weight of machine tools produced was rather more than doubled between 1935 and 1939 it was impossible to fill in many of the gaps in the range of equipment manufactured. Here, of course, the deficiency arose from the neglect of opportunities before 1935.[1] Examples of limitations where a long-accumulated backlog was not a relevant factor may be found in the output of some of the more elaborate types of household equipment. The contrast between

[1] Hornby, *op. cit.*, pp. 323-7. In 1935 Britain was more dependent on foreign types of machine tools than in 1913.

1930, when retained imports of vacuum cleaners totalled 140,130 and home production only 37,550, and.1935, when retained imports were down to 13,150 and home production up to 409,345,[1] showed what could be achieved in this field. But indications that the number of electric cookers produced was stagnant or declining after 1935,[2] trade estimates of an annual output of only 85,000 electric water-heaters in the late 'thirties,[3] and the low level of exports of comparable goods support the suggestion that some promising beginnings remained only beginnings.

The data about the growth of other economic activities are in many ways less satisfactory than those about the growth of industry. There are no good direct estimates of the proportion of the national income which accrued to transport, trade, and financial and other services. If they are considered together, as a residual item to be deducted from the total national income, it is probable that they obtained a rather larger share than before the First World War, though the change cannot have been very marked.[4] But there must have been rather greater changes in some specific activities. For instance, greater financial activity is indicated by the growth of bank clearings per head from an annual average of £344 in 1911-13 to £866 in 1936-38.[5] Then, too, figures of employment suggest an appreciable rise in the importance of the distributive trades and a fall in that of transport. These figures, however, are not in all respects an accurate reflexion of what was happening. The larger numbers in the distributive trades may merely have been needed to keep up the standard of service in an activity in which productivity grew a good deal more slowly than in many others, though the information available is too slight for this to be asserted confidently.[6] The employment figures for transport, on the other hand, have to be interpreted in the light of the rapid rise in the output of motor vehicles. Much more passenger transport than before was provided by consumers who drove their own vehicles, while in public road transport services, both passenger and goods, a much bigger output per man was possible in a given time with motor vehicles than with the horse-drawn vehicles which they largely superseded in the interwar years. Because

---

[1] P.E.P., *Report on the Market for Household Appliances* (1945), p. 211.

[2] *Ibid.*, p. 68.   [3] *Ibid.*, p. 156.   [4] *Cf.* Clark, *op. cit.* (2nd edn.), p. 443.

[5] Calculated from E.C.A. Mission, *op. cit.*, pp. 70-2.

[6] *Cf.* Clark, *op. cit.*, pp. 314-17 and 336-42 for a summary and discussion of some of the few available figures.

of this it may well be that transport was really one of the most markedly expanding economic activities of the time.

Although the information about the value of the output of the various tertiary activities is so poor, there are more precise indications of the magnitude of the growth of some of them and a good deal of descriptive evidence to show the changes underlying the growth. As far as transport is concerned there is not the least doubt that the decisive factor of change was the great increase in the use of motor vehicles. The railways, which had previously been the dominant force in transport except over very short distances, had come to the end of their rapid expansion. It is unlikely that they were experiencing any absolute decline, except in their profits, though several changes in the form of the official railway statistics make it difficult to be sure. New additions to the railway system were negligible and though some search for economy was made through the closing of branch lines, chiefly in the nineteen-thirties, it was not carried far. The length of railway routes in operation in Britain in 1939 was roughly 100 miles less than in 1913.[1] The number of passengers carried rose to a new maximum in 1920 but thereafter fell below the prewar level and remained there, despite a recovery after 1932; the annual average number of passengers carried in the years 1935-39 was 1,249 million.[2] The decline, however, was mainly in short-distance traffic, and in terms of passenger-miles there was an increase of 3 per cent in railway passenger travel between 1923 and 1938, even though 1923 had the highest total number of passengers for any year after 1920. The increase in passenger mileage was probably still greater in comparison with the years just before the First World War, but there are only guesses to support this.[3] The quantity of freight carried was reduced much more, particularly as a result of the fall in the output of coal, which was much the biggest item in railway goods traffic. The tonnage of freight carried in 1913 was never reached again and after 1929 it fell much lower than before, the average in the later 'thirties being under four-fifths of the tonnage carried in 1913.[4] In terms of ton-miles, however, there may have been a slight increase, though it cannot have amounted to much.[5]

[1] E.C.A. Mission, *op. cit.*, pp. 37-8. There were rather more lines where passenger services ceased to operate, though goods traffic continued.
[2] Calculated from *ibid.*, p. 39. The statistics exclude the London underground railways.
[3] Svennilson, *op. cit.*, p. 144.   [4] Calculated from E.C.A. Mission, *op. cit.*, pp. 37-9.
[5] Svennilson, *op. cit.*, p. 144.

That the railways had kept up their traffic as well as this was partly due to gains they had made from some of their competitors. The wartime difficulties of coastal shipping had caused much of its traffic to be transferred to the railways and a good deal of this was never recovered. The official figures show a reduction of 15 per cent between 1913 and 1924 in coastwise shipping, but this reduction would undoubtedly be larger if the British foreign-trading vessels going empty coastwise could be eliminated from the statistics.[1] There was no real revival. Even though coastal shipping had earlier come to concentrate more of its activities on fewer and larger ports, the poor state of many of the secondary ports remained a serious handicap,[2] and the stagnant condition of the coal trade lessened the opportunities of employment for coastal vessels. It is true that by the late 'thirties the tonnage of shipping arriving and departing coastwise was, if allowance is made for the changed classification of movements between Britain and Ireland, rather higher than in 1913. But the proportion carrying cargo (well under half) was much lower than in 1913[3] and suggests that the figures were greatly distorted by the inclusion of vessels belonging to the foreign trade. Some decline in genuine coastwise trade seems overwhelmingly probable.

The decline of the canals was still more evident. Nearly all the prewar canals continued to operate, but the poor profits that many of them had been receiving for a long time discouraged proper maintenance and led to a deterioration of service in many parts of the system. Changes in the proportions of different classes of goods to be transported also worked to the disadvantage of the canals. The annual amount of goods carried by canal, even in the years of brisker trade, was usually between 14 and 16 million tons and cannot have been more than about 40 per cent of the quantity carried in the years just before the First World War.[4]

The introduction of regular air services was of no great importance in internal transport. In the late 'thirties, on air services within the United Kingdom, the annual traffic amounted to some 10 million revenue passenger-miles and about a million ton-miles of cargo movement.[5] Such figures are negligible in comparison with those for either road or rail.

[1] Macrosty, 'Statistics of British Shipping' in *J.R. Stat. Socy.*, LXXXIX, 496-7.
[2] *Final Report of the R.C. on Transport (P.P.* 1930-31, XVII), pp. 137-8.
[3] Central Statistical Office, *Annual Abstract of Statistics 1937-47* (1948), p. 200.
[4] *Final Report of the R.C. on Transport*, pp. 116-17.
[5] *Stat. Abstract 1937-47*, p. 201.

But the growth of road traffic was very rapid. The number of vehicles rose every year by tens of thousands. The total number registered in the United Kingdom was 498,000 in 1922, 1,524,000 in 1930, and 2,422,000 in 1938, out of which the number of passenger cars was 353,000 in 1922, 1,127,000 in 1930 and 1,846,000 in 1938, the remainder being goods vehicles and buses.[1] In the nineteen-twenties much was also done to assist the more effective use of this vast increase in equipment. Most of the schemes for new main roads drawn up during the First World War were carried out and a new programme for the modernization of trunk roads was begun in 1924, though within the great cities, especially London, far too few street improvements for the relief of congestion were undertaken.[2] In the nineteen-thirties the further extension of the road system ceased to be at all commensurate with the growth of vehicular traffic, though many subsidiary improvements were made.[3] On the whole, however, this threatened difficulties for the future rather than created them for the present. Congestion in towns remained as a cause of serious inconvenience and loss but, outside the towns, the roads of 1930 were mostly capable of accommodating much more traffic without serious strain. Though there was obvious unwisdom in allowing the margin of spare road capacity to dwindle rapidly, not much of the penalty for this had to be paid before 1939.

In these conditions a great increase in the use of road transport was all the easier. No one can accurately measure its extent. Much of the use of private cars for pleasure was a virtually new part of social life and of economic consumption, unknown in quantity. The much greater spread of urban areas, the wider separation of homes and workplaces, the increasing dependence of outlying towns and villages on the services of a regional centre, all contributed to more frequent movement, especially of passengers, in which private motoring had some share but public bus and tramway services almost certainly a greater one. By 1933 the annual number of passenger journeys by bus and tram had risen to 9,450 million. On trams alone it was 4,032 million, which was nearly one-quarter higher than in 1913, and the majority of the bus journeys must have been a net addition to

---

[1] Svennilson, *op. cit.*, p. 278.

[2] W. Rees Jeffreys, *The King's Highway* (1949), pp. 229-31; *Final Report of the R.C. on Transport*, pp. 50-4 and 60-1.

[3] From 1929 to 1939 the mileage of public roads in Britain increased only from 179,095 to 180,527, that of first- and second-class highways (including 'trunk' roads) from 41,275 to 45,179.

traffic.[1] The same tendencies also made necessary some increase in the local movement of goods and thus helped to expand a demand which had always been met principally by road transport and was coming to be served almost exclusively by it. In the long-distance carriage of goods, road transport did not attain so dominant a position, partly because the railways still had many competitive advantages and partly because from 1930 government policy deliberately tried, by means of restrictive licensing, to limit the increase in road haulage services which were directly competitive with the railways. Nevertheless, it has been estimated that by 1936 the roads and the railways carried about equal quantities of goods other than coal. Since, however, very little coal was carried by road, except for local delivery, the share of road transport in the total tonnage of goods carried was probably only about one-quarter.[2] This growth of goods traffic on the roads was much more than enough to offset any possible decline in rail traffic and some of it, like most of the road passenger transport, was a new addition to the output of transport service. With the railways approximately maintaining their prewar level of traffic, the impression is confirmed that the use of transport was among the most rapidly expanding economic activities of the interwar period.

The same was true of communications. By 1929 the number of items carried by letter-post was 6,400 million and was already nearly 1,000 million more than in 1914. By 1939 it had risen to 8,150 million, and the 185 million parcels delivered that year were about one-third more than in the years just before the First World War. The telegraph system continued to run at a loss and to be much less used than at the beginning of the century, but the telephone made great progress. In the quarter century preceding 1939 the number of telephones increased fourfold to nearly $3\frac{1}{4}$ million; the number of exchanges doubled and more than half of them were operated automatically; a wider public was reached by the erection of nearly 50,000 public call-boxes; and the total annual number of calls rose to 2,237 million. At the same time the exploitation of radio had brought a new form of communication which contributed to entertainment and education as well as the rapid diffusion of information and which, in the course of the 'thirties, came to serve almost the entire

---

[1] Broster, *An Economic Study of the Growth of Travel in Great Britain 1903-33*, tables IV and VI.

[2] G. J. Walker, *Road and Rail* (1942), p. 16.

public. By 1939 almost 9 million people held wireless licences.[1]

All these data about transport and communication suggest that it was in more frequent personal travel and exchange of information rather than in a greatly expanded exchange of goods that the principal change was to be found. What we know about internal trade confirms this. Immediately after the First World War retail trade appears to have undergone a rapid expansion which soon slowed down, whereas in the 'thirties its growth was slower than that of most other economic activities, though sales were still somewhat larger in relation to national income than they were before the First World War. If the estimated value of total retail sales is re-calculated at constant prices there was an increase of 24·3 per cent from 1915 (or from 1910, when the volume of sales was the same) to 1920; but from 1920 to 1938 the increase was no more than 27·9 per cent. After 1935 there was, indeed, no perceptible increase at all.[2]

This does not mean that consumers had only a trivial share in the rise of manufacturing output and of incomes in the 'thirties, though it is true that their share was increasing more slowly than that of public authorities.[3] It means rather that most people did not wish to buy much more of the basic necessities and chose to consume more of other things, both services and durable goods, which are not sold in retail shops—things as diverse as houses, motor vehicles, electricity, permanent waves and visits to the cinema. Even among the goods sold over the counter similar trends are evident. Thus, before the First World War sales of food were generally about 58 per cent of all retail sales, but the proportion fell steadily to less than 47 per cent in the later 'thirties. On the other hand there were much more than average increases in the sales of chocolate and sugar confectionery, tobacco goods, chemists' goods, radio and electrical goods, and furniture and furnishings.[4] Even in major trades which roughly maintained their relative position there was declining emphasis on the simple basic items. This was notably so in the clothing trades where there was a shift away from the sale of piece-goods for making up and towards the sale of ready-made shirts, blouses, dresses and

---

[1] H. Robinson, *Britain's Post Office* (1953), chaps. XVIII and XIX; and *Stat. Abstracts*.

[2] Estimates of retail sales are given in Jefferys, *Retail Trading in Britain 1850-1950*, p. 45. The price index used in re-calculating these at constant prices is that for consumer goods and services, with 1912-13 as base period, given in Jefferys and Walters, *op. cit.*, pp. 39-40.

[3] Jefferys and Walters, *op. cit.*, p. 16.

[4] Jefferys, *op. cit.*, pp. 45 and 453.

underclothes.[1] In all these ways Britain's internal trade reflected general economic and social changes, of which there were similar signs in the history of transport and of industry. There was a diminishing concern with sheer quantity of only slightly processed material and more concern with the greater variety of goods that could be made from that material, with the application of more elaborate techniques, and with the provision of greater service. All these things went together. Indeed, the growth of the labour force in the distributive trades is, in part,[2] a testimony to the increase of service—wider delivery areas, more variety of goods in stock (calling for more book-keeping), greater shopping amenities; and only the shift in incomes and tastes, which reduced the dominance of the very cheap, could have made this economically possible. The expansion in the value of retail sales may have been comparatively slow. It is likely that the contribution made to that total value by the distributive trades themselves grew faster than the cost of producing the goods that were sold in this way.

While it is not impossible that the same contrast in the relative shares of producers and distributors may also have affected foreign trade, there were fewer signs in this field that either group was, in general, in a very satisfactory position. There were, in both imports and exports, changes in the type of goods which increased the need for special knowledge and service from merchants. Many of the commodities were more complex, more expensive, less obviously capable of being graded, less indispensable; and therefore more likely to call both for the arts of salesmanship and for special treatment in such matters as cataloguing, packing and delivery. But for most people concerned with the export, if not the import, trade the dominating fact of business life was the failure of markets to grow as they had done before the First World War.

Though exports soon climbed far above the low level to which they had fallen by 1918, they never (in real terms) returned to the pre-1914 level until 1950. Throughout the nineteen-twenties, it is true, the value of exports was higher than before the First World War, but this was only a reflexion of the great increase in prices, which was already in process of reversal. In the 'thirties the value of exports fell

---

[1] Jefferys, *op. cit.*, pp. 294-5.
[2] In part also it was no doubt due to a decline in the over-working of shop assistants.

below that of 1913. If the values are re-calculated in terms of the prices of 1925-29, then even in the years of greatest revival in Britain's foreign trade, 1927 to 1929 inclusive, the average volume of exports was no more than 84 per cent of that achieved in 1913. In the black years from 1931 to 1933 this figure fell to 55 per cent and recovered only to 67 per cent in the period from 1936 to 1938.[1] Even these figures do not quite reveal the full extent of the decline, because the change in the area of the United Kingdom had the effect of slightly enlarging the export figures from 1923 onwards.[2]

Of all the changes in Britain's interwar economy this decline in exports is the most immediately striking and calls for explanation. To some extent it was the counterpart of a general stagnation in international trade, especially in the nineteen-thirties, but British exports fared worse than those of most countries. In 1913 they had amounted to 13·11 per cent of the world total, but this proportion fell to 11·10 per cent in 1927, 9·92 per cent in 1932, and 9·87 per cent in 1937.[3] Immediately, a large part of the British export decline can be traced to the loss of markets for two or three commodities of exceptional importance and the failure to develop substantial replacements for them. In the 'thirties less than 60 per cent of the British output of cotton piece-goods was exported whereas in 1907 not quite 90 per cent of a far larger output had gone abroad; and the value of exports of cotton yarn and piece-goods from 1933 to 1935 was less than one-third of what it had been in 1924.[4] The quantity of coal exported fell from 61·7 million tons in 1924 to 35·9 million tons in 1938, an amount which was not quite half as much as in 1913.[5] Yet even as late as 1933 textiles still accounted for 27 per cent of the value of all British exports (excluding re-exports) and coal for 12 per cent.[6] Thereafter these proportions declined, but there were few commodities other than motor vehicles and their components which achieved a substantial increase of exports, though chemicals showed a slight advance.[7] While some exports were made of new types of

---

[1] Calculated from Svennilson, *op. cit.*, p. 314.

[2] British sales to the Irish Free State, which came into the U.K. export figures from 1923, exceeded Irish sales to countries other than the U.K., which simultaneously went out of the figures.

[3] Kahn, *Great Britain in the World Economy*, p. 132.

[4] *Ibid.*, p. 93. [5] *Ibid.*, p. 85.

[6] Calculated from Schlote, *British Overseas Trade*, pp. 71, 73 and 74.

[7] *Cf.* the charts in Svennilson ,*op. cit.* ,p. 184.

M

goods introduced in the nineteen-thirties, it was evident (especially in the markets for machinery) that Britain was lagging behind the U.S.A. and Germany in the sale of those classes of manufactures for which there was a growing world demand.[1] It is probable, indeed, that Britain imported more of such goods than she exported, although many of them were manufactures calling for advanced techniques of production which Britain was well suited to employ.

Associated with the decline of exports, and with the preponderant influence which dwindling sales of textiles had upon it, was a change in the destination of exports, especially in the 'thirties. The growing competition in the textile market showed itself most markedly in the diminishing importance of the Indian and other Asiatic markets. It also had some influence on the slight fall in the proportion of British exports that went to South America, where the general increase in the competitive power of the United States had also to be reckoned with. To offset these changes there was a relative increase in the share taken by the Australasian markets, to which some 10 per cent of total exports were going for most of the interwar period, though the proportion was rising somewhat in the last few years. In the 'thirties, too, there was an increase in the value of African markets, particularly in the tropical British colonies. By the late 'thirties exports to Africa and Asia were roughly equal, each taking about one-sixth of the total. This was partly because there was in tropical Africa a good demand for some of the simpler manufactures which were still a substantial part of British exports, and was partly the result of a deliberate reliance on politically sheltered markets. In fact, the political shift in the direction of exports was as prominent as the geographical. Between 1909 and 1913, 35·4 per cent of Britain's home-produced exports went to the Empire, and between 1919 and 1926 the proportion had risen only to 38·4 per cent. But in the years 1935-39 the countries of the Empire were buying almost half of Britain's exports.[2]

The chief 'invisible' exports, the rapid growth of which in the late nineteenth century had been an invaluable compensation for the slower expansion of merchandise exports, could not in this later period exert a fully comparable influence, though they remained substantial. Foreign investment was resumed after the First World

---

[1] Allen, *op. cit.*, pp. 129-30; Lewis, 'The Prospect Before Us' in *The Manchester School*, XVI, 147-9.

[2] Schlote, *op. cit.*, pp. 89, 160 and 161.

War, though not on so large a scale as just before it. The new additions to foreign investment from 1919 to 1925 inclusive have been estimated at £607 million and were probably a little more than sufficient to wipe out the wartime losses.[1] By the end of 1927 the accumulated total was put at the new peak of £4,290 million, and yielded an estimated annual income of £299 million, but from 1929 the upward trend was reversed. Much of the most recent investment, which had gone increasingly into government and municipal loans, especially in the British dominions, had been only modestly remunerative; and the decline of international trade discouraged further foreign investment and led to a fall in the value and yield of existing foreign assets. Estimates of the position in the nineteen-thirties differ appreciably. The most widely used figures suggest that at the end of 1938 British foreign investments were worth £3,700 million (which is rather less than in 1913) and that the income from them was then about £185 million, after having fallen as low as £150 million in 1933.[2]

The earnings of shipping, the second largest item in the 'invisible' exports, were almost as difficult to maintain. The stagnation of international trade prevented the emergence of many new opportunities of profitable ocean carrying and, for a variety of reasons, British shipowners could secure only a smaller proportion of the available carrying trade than before. Though wartime losses of ships were soon replaced, some of the new ships built in emergency conditions were less satisfactory for the profitable performance of their work than the earlier ones. Other vessels were rendered prematurely redundant by technical innovations and by changes in the commonest types of bulk cargo on offer. Above all, a combination of national aspirations with special wartime needs and opportunities led many other countries greatly to increase the size of their merchant fleets, often with the aid of subsidies. So, although the merchant navy of the United Kingdom kept up its size (and slightly increased it) during the nineteen-twenties, it formed a diminishing proportion of the world's supply of shipping. And the general increase in the world's supply caused intense competition which had the result of driving down many rates to unprofitable levels. After 1931 there was a change of policy. In six years the chief shipowning countries scrapped five million tons of superfluous ships, and the United Kingdom's

---

[1] Morgan, *British Financial Policy 1914-1925*, p. 340.
[2] E.C.A. Mission to the U.K., *op. cit.*, pp. 110-13. The estimates given here are those of Lord Kindersley. They are unlikely to be too high, but may be too low.

346 An Economic History of England: 1870-1939

merchant fleet was reduced by about two and a half million tons. Thereafter most of the shipping business returned to a very modestly profitable level, as the available supply was no longer, in general, very far beyond needs. It was estimated that in 1937 there was 30 per cent more |ocean carrying to be done in the world than in 1914 and a 40 per cent greater tonnage of shipping with which to do it.[1]

A few more detailed figures readily illustrate the change in the economic position of the United Kingdom's merchant shipping. The total gross registered tonnage of steam and motor vessels, which was down to 17,160,000 in 1919, surpassed the prewar level of 19,145,000 in 1925, rose to a maximum of 20,332,000 in 1930, declined to 17,298,000 in 1935 and stood at 18,046,000 in 1939.[2] But the United Kingdom's share of the world total is estimated to have fallen from 44·2 per cent in 1915 to 32·1 per cent in 1925 and 28·2 per cent in 1935.[3] This declining proportion was accompanied by a decline in the share of carrying trade obtained, especially outside the British Empire. Whereas the ships of the British Empire, the great majority of which belonged to the United Kingdom, continued almost to monopolize the carrying trade within the Empire, their share in the trade between the Empire and the rest of the world is estimated to have fallen from 61 per cent in 1912 to 52·5 per cent in 1931 and 47·2 per cent in 1936. Their share in the trade between non-British countries fell even more sharply, from 22 per cent in 1912 to 13 per cent in 1931 and 12 per cent in 1936. Nevertheless, British shipping still had a major place in the world's commerce, and the ships of the British Empire are estimated to have had 39·5 per cent of the world's seaborne carrying trade in 1931 and 1936, which is to be compared with 47·5 per cent in 1912.[4]

As might be expected, the earnings of United Kingdom shipping fluctuated a great deal according to the state of international trade and the extent of the surplus of shipping available in the world. Throughout the nineteen-twenties, mainly because of higher prices,

[1] R. H. Thornton, British Shipping (1939), pp. 95-104.

[2] E.C.A. Mission to the U.K. op. cit., pp. 44-5.

[3] M. G. Kendall, 'United Kingdom Merchant Shipping Statistics' in J.R. Stat. Socy., CXI (1948), 136. Professor Kendall used slightly different figures of U.K. tonnage but the differences are insignificant in the present context.

[4] H. Leak, 'The Carrying Trade of British Shipping' in J.R. Stat. Socy., CII (1939), 252. N.B. These figures refer to the ships of the whole British Empire and not only those of the U.K. They are therefore not strictly comparable with those given earlier.

the net shipping income[1] was above the probable immediate prewar level of about £100 million, and reached £140 million in 1924 and 1927. But it fell as low as £65 million in 1933 before recovering to £130 million in 1937 and £100 million in 1938.[2] Thus there was no general expansion in United Kingdom shipping earnings during the interwar period. The best that can be said is that they did not decline to the same degree as merchandise exports and may, on the whole, have been just about maintained near the prewar level. Nor did any compensation come from external air services, which were still too few to have much commercial significance. In 1938 they carried only 72,000 passengers and 2·1 million short tons of freight, other than mail.[3]

The other 'invisible' exports had always been so much smaller than those already discussed that, whatever happened to them, they were unlikely to have a large direct effect on the national financial position. In fact, most of the signs suggest a downward trend in the majority of them. There must, for instance, have been less profit to be derived from London's services as an international financial centre. Some of the business of short-term finance, lost during the First World War, was never recovered,[4] and the widespread restrictions on multilateral trade in the 'thirties reduced it still further. The business of raising long-term loans for foreigners fell even more sharply. New issues in London for countries other than the United Kingdom, which had averaged £177 million in 1910-13, shrank to an annual average of £120 million in 1926-30 and £30 million in 1934-38.[5] On this latter sum the amount of profit to be earned in foreign exchange must have been, from a national standpoint, negligible. It would not be surprising, however, if the earnings from other distributive services abroad, in connexion with both exports and imports, were fairly well maintained, though there may have been an

---

[1] 'Net shipping income' means the receipts of British ships *less* their expenditure abroad *plus* the expenditure of foreign ships in British ports. It is not a direct measure of the foreign exchange earnings of shipping, since much of the income consisted of payments in sterling for the shipping of imports into the U.K. In fact, the income from carrying British imports probably formed an increasing proportion of the total shipping income and was a major influence operating against its decline. For a discussion of the various ways of calculating shipping earnings, with special reference to the detailed figures available for 1936, see Kendall, *loc. cit.*, pp. 143-4.

[2] Kahn, *op. cit.*, p. 126.   [3] *Stat. Abstract 1938-50*, p. 248.

[4] *Cf.* p. 288 above.

[5] Kahn, *op. cit.*, p. 139. The figures appear to exclude re-funding and conversion issues, on which there was also some profit to be made.

offset to this from greater expenditure by the British on similar services performed by foreign firms. The official figures, which for this period were based on very limited information, may be too pessimistic in their estimate of the amount earned in such ways. On the basis of these figures, the annual average income from 'invisible' items, other than shipping earnings and dividends and interest on long-term investment, averaged £77 million in 1924-28, £54 million in 1929-33 and £42 million in 1934-38.[1] Even though the figures must have an appreciable margin of error, the trend seems clear. Moreover, though similar official figures were not prepared before the First World War, it is probable that, in the last few years before 1914, earnings from the same items were rather higher than even the best of these figures, although the price level then was lower than in the 'twenties.

Since exports as a whole, including 'invisible' items as well as merchandise, tended to decline during the interwar period, it might have been expected that imports also would have been difficult to maintain at their former level. But this proved not to be the case. The volume of imports grew quickly after the bottom of the postwar slump had been reached in 1921. In 1924 it surpassed the level attained in 1913, and in 1929 the volume of imports was almost 20 per cent greater than in 1913. In the early 'thirties it remained rather lower but from 1936 onward it was even higher than in 1929.[2] This happened despite two influences working in the opposite direction. One of these was that the changed basis of the trade statistics, which resulted from the removal of the Irish Free State from the United Kingdom, made the import figures rather lower than they otherwise would have been. The other was that fewer of the imports were re-exported: whereas just before the First World War re-exports were usually 14 or 15 per cent of total imports, the proportion gradually fell in the 'twenties and was below 10 per cent from 1929 onwards.[3]

In many ways the growth of imports after the First World War appeared to be a resumption of tendencies that had been prominent in the last quarter of the nineteenth century. Once again there was a steady increase in the proportion of manufactured goods in total imports, iron and steel, machinery and electrical goods providing a large part of the increase. Once again, too, there was a marked rise in

---

[1] Kahn, *op. cit.*, p. 126.   [2] *Ibid.*, p. 180, and Schlote, *op. cit.*, p. 130.
[3] Calculated from Schlote, *op. cit.*, pp. 133 and 138-9.

the imports of the more expensive types of foodstuffs. Meat and dairy products formed 45·3 per cent of the expanded total of food imports by 1927-29 and 46·7 per cent in 1932-33.[1] In 1932, tariff policy imposed a check on the rise in imports of manufactures, but as industry revived later in the decade, manufactures regained their relative share in imports. The position in most years was that 45 to 50 per cent of imports consisted of foodstuffs, around 30 per cent were raw materials and the rest were manufactures.[2]

There are two main reasons why the growth of imports was possible in a time of difficulty for exports. One is that the prices of most of the foodstuffs and raw materials, which made up the greater part of the imports, fell much more than the prices of British exports. This was already apparent just after the First World War; and in the world-wide depression after 1929, when surpluses of primary products flooded the markets, the divergence went further. An index of Britain's net barter terms of trade, taking the 1913 ratio as 100, averaged 130·1 from 1919 to 1923, 124·1 from 1924 to 1932 and 138·0 from 1933 to 1937.[3] Throughout the 'thirties, expenditure on imports remained well below the level of 1929 (for four years it was even below the level of 1913) although the quantity obtained became greater. The second reason was that a bigger proportion of Britain's total earnings abroad was used to pay for imports of merchandise. Before the First World War the surplus on Britain's other current international transactions had been much greater than the deficit on merchandise trade, and a large part of it had gone to finance new long-term investments abroad. With the decline in the making of new foreign investments in the 'twenties and, much more markedly, in the 'thirties, it was possible to let the surplus fall while maintaining or increasing certain foreign payments despite a reduction in income from abroad. Some of these inroads into the surplus probably helped to finance such things as small increases in expenditure on foreign travel and the payment of dividends and interest on foreign investments in Britain which, though still small, had undoubtedly grown. But for the most part they helped to pay the bigger import bill.[4]

[1] *Ibid.*, pp. 55, 65 and 67.

[2] The proportions vary with the way in which different commodities are classified. For instance, the U.K. official figures put the imports of manufactures rather higher because they classify refined oils as manufactures, not raw materials.

[3] Kahn, *op. cit.*, p. 144.

[4] Hirschman, *National Power and the Structure of Foreign Trade*, p. 143, shows that the import surplus increased from 12·2 per cent of total merchandise trade in 1913 to 21·6 per cent in 1925-29 and 26·9 per cent in 1933-37.

Even so, it appeared by the 'thirties that imports were outrunning exports to a dangerous extent. The prewar surplus had been derived from transactions with a limited and contracting part of the world, especially with India,[1] and when trading difficulties were encountered there the surplus became harder to achieve. During the 'twenties little was done to alter this, but from 1932 the difficulties were so much more acute that it became an objective of commercial policy to switch purchases to some extent away from those areas with which the British balance of trade was heavily adverse. Thus, for instance, the adverse balance with the U.S.A., which averaged £554 million in 1925-29 and was still as high as £320 million in 1931, averaged £207 million in 1932-33. Though it increased again as trade revived it remained well below the level of the 'twenties and averaged £326 million in 1936-38.[2] There was also a sharp reduction in imports from Western Europe. On the other hand imports were bought increasingly from those areas, chiefly in the tropical parts of the British Empire, with which there had been an export surplus, and from those areas, particularly some of the white British Dominions, such as Australia, which were heavily indebted to the United Kingdom. On the whole, it does not appear that these shifts did much good to the British balance of payments. The reduction of imports from some areas was offset by a similar loss of export trade to them; the switch of imports was carried so far that, in trade with those tropical regions in which Britain had long been able to rely on earning a surplus, a deficit appeared; and the whole series of changes added to the difficulties of maintaining multilateral trade and payments, in which Britain still had a clear interest.[3] The result was discouraging. According to the official figures Britain first had an adverse balance of payments on current account in 1931, when the deficit was £104 million. Things were not so bad again, but only in 1935 was a surplus recorded and it amounted to no more than £32 million.[4] These figures are not very reliable. The recorded deficits were small and may amount to less than the margin of error that should be allowed in the figures. It would, therefore, not be safe to say that Britain, besides ceasing to assist the growth of international trade by foreign investment, had actually begun to live on its capital. But it had not fully

---

[1] *Cf.* p. 161 above.   [2] Calculated from E.C.A. Mission, *op. cit.*, pp. 128-9.
[3] For a more detailed analysis of changes in the trade balances of the chief regions of world trade see League of Nations, *The Network of World Trade*, pp. 89-92.
[4] Kahn, *op. cit.*, p. 126.

adjusted its trade to world economic conditions. Though imports provided a slightly lower proportion of the total supply of goods than they had done before the First World War, the change was less than in most other countries. So Britain's imports, which in value were 15·24 per cent of the total for all countries in 1913, amounted to 15·92 per cent in 1927 and 17·03 per cent in 1937;[1] and this increase was taking place while the British share of total exports was diminishing. This is an indication of greater insecurity in Britain's foreign trading position.

To look back over the economic activities of the interwar years is to see evidence of many large changes, generally in the direction that economic and technical developments in the world as a whole made advantageous. Though Britain did not succeed in giving the production of material goods a greater place in its economy, it came to rely less on the exploitation of wasting natural assets, such as large coal deposits, and was able to depend a little more on manufactures, where continuing and accumulating skill and knowledge had the opportunity to earn an increasing reward. Among the manufacturing industries, too, it turned more and more to some of those in which skill and ingenuity counted for most and which turned out products increasingly wanted in the wealthier communities. And in developing these activities a vast number of technical improvements was successfully sought out and applied in practice: the production of new alloys, the introduction of ball-bearings in machine construction, the great improvement of welding, and the modification of many chemicals to give them new, specialized properties were but a few of a whole series of related innovations, particularly important in an economy where electricity, the motor vehicle and more complex machine-tools were counting for much more than before.[2] All these were signs of desirable adaptability within the sphere of production, though, as has been seen, reservations can be made about the speed and extent of some of the changes; and it might be contended that they were not as fully matched as they could have been by improvements in agricultural production.

In external affairs, this period saw the end of that long-sustained trend in the direction of ever-greater dependence on international

[1] *Ibid.*, p. 132.
[2] *Cf.* R. S. Sayers, 'The Springs of Technical Progress in Britain, 1919-39' in *Econ. Journ.*, LX (1950), 275-7.

dealings which had so great an influence on economic history before 1914. This, too, as long as it involved no absolute contraction of foreign trade, might be accounted a change in accordance with the general needs of the times. But, in fact, the absolute decline of British exports and of total earnings abroad was a much more striking change than the small decline in the proportion of goods which was obtained by import. The British economy remained heavily involved in international dealings, as it was bound to do, and it had become more vulnerable in them. This was in part a sign of the general confusion in the world economy, on the persistence of which British actions and omissions were no more than contributory influences among many others. But it was also a sign that the changes in economic activity had not been drastic enough to ensure that Britain could go on indefinitely paying its way in the world. However many of them had clearly been begun in the right direction, more were still needed for the continued maintenance of economic security and prosperity.

CHAPTER FIFTEEN

Economic Organization

MANY changes in the way in which business was run, in the institutions on which it depended, and in the arrangements through which it made its impact on the public were becoming obvious at the opening of the twentieth century. They were changes which suggested that economic activities generally were becoming more elaborately organized, less individualistic, more impersonal, more concentrated within large and powerful bodies under unified control. The rapid adoption of corporate form, the amalgamation of firms, the more frequent appeal to the impersonal investor, the enlargement of establishments in many branches of business, the increase in the number and scope of representative bodies among both employers and workpeople were all signs of what was happening. But before 1914 they had not wrought a complete transformation in economic organization. There was at that time still plenty of scope for the small firm and the individual; most types of business were highly competitive; and most of the decisions which had the greatest effect on the relations of businesses with employees or customers were local and limited in their application. To some extent the incompleteness of the change was an illustration of the familiar time-lag in the making of social adjustments to new conditions. But it was partly due also to the continuance, in some fields, of conditions which offered no fatal obstacle to small-scale localized activities and informal, often improvisatory, industrial relations.

In most respects the events and conditions of the 'twenties and 'thirties favoured a much greater extension of the new trend in organization. Machinery was applied to nearly all those few industrial processes which had hitherto defeated it, and much machinery became more elaborate and costly, thus encouraging larger establishments. Some large industries, such as cotton weaving, in which there had been a highly competitive structure of many fairly small units, declined. On the other hand, the chief expanding industries, like automobile production and electrical engineering, depended on the use of costly equipment and advanced technical knowledge, which was often (though not invariably) most remunerative in large factories. Difficulties in maintaining trade suggested the need for structural changes in industry and led to efforts to escape from the full rigours of competition. Greater homogeneity in tastes among large sections of the public all over the country created a mass market in many more commodities and offered great opportunities to large undertakings which could cater for it. A similarly increased homogeneity in aspirations and a more widely diffused awareness of common interests, strengthened by the rise of a popular press that was national not local, created a demand for industrial agreements with a much more extensive application and therefore helped to promote larger negotiating bodies.

The most convenient subject with which to begin an examination of the organizational changes that took place in this setting is probably the individual firm. One most obvious change was the continued increase in the adoption of corporate form, which even in 1914 could reasonably be regarded as typical. The total of 62,762 limited liability companies which existed in that year had grown to 95,055 by the end of 1925 and to 162,470 by the end of 1939,[1] a rate of increase far greater than that in the volume of business. This, however, represents to only a small extent the introduction of incorporation into important activities where it had previously been unfamiliar. It was probably only in retail trade, where a large number of multiple shop firms became public companies,[2] that a substantial change of this sort occurred. The great increase in the number of companies consisted entirely of private companies—the number of public companies was slightly less at the end of 1939 than in 1914—and probably indicates no fundamental change of scale or structure. It may be attributed principally to the greater convenience and financial advantage that corporate form had for many one-man or family businesses or small partnerships as taxation became heavier and tax law more complicated. Such businesses swelled the statistics of companies and perhaps made the small firm appear more important and tenacious than it was: the average paid-up capital per company actually fell a little between 1914 and 1939. But they had only a minor part in the economic activity of the country. The public companies in 1939 were only just over one-twelfth of the total

[1] Board of Trade Committee on Industry and Trade (Balfour Committee), *Factors in Industrial and Commercial Efficiency* (1927), p. 125; *Stat. Abstract 1937-47*, p. 242.

[2] Jefferys, *Retail Trading in Britain 1850-1950*, p. 69.

number but they had more than two-thirds of the paid-up capital and probably a much greater share of the capital reserves.

There were, in fact, many signs that a gradually increasing proportion of British business was being concentrated in the larger firms. This was very obvious in one or two activities in which the total number of participating firms had been reduced by amalgamations to a mere handful. The series of large amalgamations in banking, for instance, during and just after the First World War, had completed a protracted movement which left five great joint-stock banks in a predominant position.[1] In railway transport, where most of the constituent firms had always been large, the government resisted strong pressure to put the whole business into the hands of a single vast nationalized undertaking. But, by the Railways Act of 1921, it compelled all existing railway companies (with a few tiny exceptions) to come within a scheme of reorganization into four large groups, with effect from 1 January 1923.[2] Some increase in concentration, however, was taking place in a much wider range of activities. There are various ways of measuring concentration, but all would support this conclusion. One study of the companies quoted on the stock exchange in selected years from 1885 onwards indicates a continuous, though not very rapid, increase of concentration in the economy as a whole until 1939.[3] Studies confined to industry illustrate clearly and in great detail what was happening there. By 1935, 55 per cent of the labour force, 57 per cent of the gross output and 58 per cent of the net output of industry came from business units with 500 or more employees each.[4] Several industries showed a very high degree of concentration, as indicated by the share of their three

---

[1] See p. 167 above.

[2] The Railways Act is summarized in C. E. R. Sherrington, *A Hundred Years of Inland Transport* (1934), pp. 311-17. Some of the prescribed amalgamations were completed voluntarily before the statutory date. (*Ibid.*, p. 319.)

The apparent strengthening of organization may have been reduced by the financial arrangements arising from the period of government operation. If allowance is made for deficiencies of maintenance and the fall in the value of money, the railways probably had fewer financial resources in proportion to their capital needs than they had had in 1914, despite compensation payments by the government which, at first sight, seemed large.

[3] P. E. Hart and S. J. Prais, 'The Analysis of Business Concentration: a statistical approach' in *J.R. Stat. Socy.*, Series A (General), CXIX (1956), 154-5. In this study the measure of concentration is the relative dispersion of the sizes of firms (as indicated by the market value of their securities.) The trend towards greater concentration showed a reversal after 1939 and concentration in 1950 was less than in 1924, though greater than in 1907.

[4] H. Leak and A. Maizels, 'The Structure of British Industry' in *J.R. Stat. Socy.*, CVIII (1945), 146. A 'unit' in this study is a single firm or aggregate of firms owned or controlled by a single company.

biggest units in the total labour force or output. Of the 249 trades or sub-divisions of trades distinguished in the census of production, there were 33 in which the three biggest units produced over 70 per cent of the total output. Eight of these were in the chemical and allied group, six in the engineering, shipbuilding and vehicles group, and five in the food, drink and tobacco group.[1] It was in the chemical and engineering groups of industries that concentration had, in fact, gone farthest. In both of them more than 40 per cent of the workers in the group were employed by only three units.[2] On the other hand, there were still several important industries in which the very large undertaking had made little headway. The three largest units employed only 2 per cent of the workers in building and contracting, 3 per cent in the timber (saw-milling, etc.) industry, and 4 per cent in cotton weaving.[3]

In retail trade, however, where the small business had been exceptionally strong, its relative decline, which had begun slowly in the late nineteenth century, became somewhat more pronounced. Of the three types of large-scale retail business, the co-operative stores increased their estimated share of total retail sales from 7·5 per cent to 10·75 per cent between 1910 and 1939, while the corresponding change for department stores was from 2·25 per cent to 5 per cent and for multiple shops from 6·75 per cent to 18·75 per cent.[4] The large-scale retailer continued to gain a bigger share in all the trades (except the meat trade) in which he had established himself before the First World War, and in a few of them attained a preponderant position. By 1939 the large-scale retailers were estimated to be making 61 per cent of all the sales of footwear, 47 per cent of those of women's clothing and 47 per cent of those of grocery and provisions.[5] In addition, the multiple shops invaded several trades where previously they had been almost unknown. For instance, at the end of the First World War the sudden appearance of United Dairies Ltd. and Mac Fisheries Ltd. had a great effect on the milk and fish trades, and during the next twenty years multiple shop trading made marked advances in the bakery trade, the sale of furniture and furnishings, the electrical and radio trades, and the jewellery trade.[6] Another type of large retail undertaking which developed rapidly was the variety chain store, which put on display a wide range of goods with clearly-marked low prices, and invited the customer to walk round, without

---

[1] Leak and Maizels, *loc. cit.*, p. 160.   [2] *Ibid.*, p. 157.   [3] *Ibid.*, p. 155.
[4] Jefferys, *op. cit.*, p. 73.   [5] *Ibid.*, pp. 74-6.   [6] *Ibid.*, pp. 66-7.

pressure to buy, and, for whatever took his fancy, to pay cash and carry it away. Some shops of this sort existed in the eighteen-nineties and the best-known firm in the business, F. W. Woolworth and Company, opened its first British store in 1909. But in 1920 there were only about 300 such shops, doing less than 3 per cent of the total multiple shop trade. By 1939 their number had grown to 1,200, the average size of shop had increased, especially since 1930, and variety chain stores were responsible for about 20 per cent of the total trade of multiple shops.[1]

Though the increasing importance of large-scale organization was to be found in so many diverse parts of the economy, it was not universally attributable to any one sequence of events. The most obvious common factor was amalgamation among firms engaged in the same line of business. This development, which had been decisive in determining the structure of banking and railway transport, also had considerable effect on retail trade. Almost every substantial grocery or meat-trading multiple firm of the pre-1914 period was involved in amalgamation during the interwar years, and of the twelve largest multiple firms in 1939 (each with more than 500 branches) all except W. H. Smith and Son and Boots Pure Drug Company had achieved much of their expansion through amalgamation.[2] There were also many mergers among department stores and by 1938 some 200 of them (about 40 per cent of the total) were controlled by only four firms. In this case, however, though the mergers brought financial integration, they did not usually involve centralization of direction.[3]

In industry the picture is less clear. The pure horizontal amalgamation of directly competing firms, though by no means unknown, was not very common in the interwar years, while there were numerous examples of the internal growth of two or three particularly efficient firms carrying them to a dominant position in one industry. Courtaulds in rayon manufacture, the Dunlop Rubber Company in the manufacture of tyres, and Morris Motors in the automobile industry are notable examples of firms that grew mainly in this way in the interwar years in industries with a high degree of concentration.[4]

---

[1] *Ibid.*, pp. 69-70.   [2] *Ibid.*, p. 64.   [3] *Ibid.*, p. 60.

[4] W. A. Lewis, *Monopoly in British Industry* (1945), p. 3. Examples of a high degree of concentration resulting from the internal growth of a handful of firms could, of course, be cited in non-manufacturing activities as well, e.g. oil distribution and meat importing. (B. Fitzgerald, *Industrial Combination in England* (2nd edn., 1927), p. 2.)

In a growing number of industries even a firm with only one factory had to be quite large if it was to adopt the most profitable methods. By 1930, to take only two instances, 60 per cent of the output of electrical goods and 54 per cent of the output of steel smelting and rolling mills came from establishments employing over 1,000 workers each. Where such conditions prevailed and the markets expanded, it was only to be expected that a firm which had successfully run one large establishment would be well placed to capture more of the market by starting another. And, in fact, this process of internal expansion appears to have been the greatest single influence on the increase of business concentration, which would have been much greater but for the continual entry of new firms, the average size of which was considerably less than that of the firms already in being.[1] But, even if amalgamation was not the major direct influence, it carried the trend towards greater concentration somewhat farther than would otherwise have been the case,[2] and it is also probable that amalgamation at one stage of a firm's existence often facilitated its internal growth later on.

Moreover, this by no means exhausted the significance of amalgamation for the structure of business. Together with a frequent tendency shown in the choice of new lines of internal expansion, amalgamation did much to bring about two widespread changes: greater integration of successive processes under one management, and a financial interest for one firm in a greater variety of products. At the end of the First World War, when there were accumulated profits available for investment and some doubts about the security of supplies as well as of outlets for the increased production, there was a series of vertical integrations centred on the steel industry—steel firms buying ore-mines and collieries, shipbuilders buying steelworks, steel and armament firms taking over businesses in various sections of the engineering industry.[3] Yet even here the biggest amalgamation, which led in the later stages of the war, to the creation of the United Steel Company, was primarily a horizontal combination with some admixture of diversification—a fusion of a rather miscellaneous set of firms in Sheffield, Cumberland and Lincolnshire, which had some products in common as well as their own individual lines.[4] And over the next twenty years the relatively few new combinations which took place, mostly as a result of pressure from the banks in times of

[1] Hart and Prais, *loc. cit.*, pp. 166-7.   [2] *Ibid.*, p. 169.
[3] Burn, *The Economic History of Steel-Making*, pp. 373-4.   [4] *Ibid.*, pp. 371-2.

financial difficulty, were of this mixed kind—mergers of firms which were in part competitive, in part complementary, and in part not rationally matched at all.[1]

Much the same seems true of other industries in which combination was particularly prominent. In the soap industry Lever Brothers acquired several competing firms in 1919 and 1920, including the soap-making subsidiaries of Brunner, Mond, the strongest firm in the chemical industry, which thereafter kept out of the soap industry. Lever Brothers then controlled 60 per cent of the British soap production. But the rest of their numerous amalgamations in these and the next few years were of a different kind. The acquisition of the Southern Whaling and Sealing Company and of the Niger Company provided for the supply of essential raw materials, but the latter brought with it an assortment of other interests remote from the main business. Other acquisitions had little apparent commercial *rationale* at all. Lord Leverhulme's social and philanthropic enthusiasm for the Hebridean island of Lewis and Harris led him in 1919 to acquire a chain of retail fish shops which would be a secure outlet for its produce and by 1921 he had built up this chain, under the name of Mac Fisheries, to 360 shops. In the pursuit of the same policy he also acquired, *inter alia*, the Aberdeen Steam Trawling Company and the Helford Oysterage, and bought the sausage-manufacturing business of T. Wall and Son mainly, it would seem, because no fish shop is complete without sausages to sell. And, in turn, since sausage-making is a seasonal industry, underemployed in summer, this firm took him into the ice-cream business to compensate for the summer slackness. All these businesses, which were originally Leverhulme's personal acquisitions, were soon unloaded on to the firm of Lever Brothers Ltd., which thus became a most incongruously diversified body.[2]

The chemical industries, too, witnessed a merging of very diverse elements, even though the juxtapositions were less startling than in the soap industry. Down to the end of the First World War there had been several large horizontal combinations. The alkali industry had come to be dominated by the two firms of United Alkali and Brunner, Mond, the latter of which absorbed several of its chief competitors during the war. Under pressure of wartime needs, and with government support, the British Dyestuffs Corporation was

[1] *Ibid.*, pp. 438-43 and 451-2.
[2] Wilson, *The History of Unilever*, I, 246-62 and 274-5.

created from firms producing three-quarters of the output of dye-stuffs, and amalgamation was pressed among the explosives manu-facturers until in 1918 a new Company, Nobel Industries, was formed with an almost complete monopoly of the industry. But when, in 1926, all these four great firms were amalgamated into Imperial Chemical Industries Ltd., the largest of all British companies, this was in the main a fusion of non-competing elements, though to some extent they were customers for each other's products, and their programmes of research and development drew on a common stock of knowledge.[1] The undertaking that emerged from this operation was in the 'thirties manufacturing not only such expected products as heavy chemicals, fertilizers and explosives, but also such varied things as non-ferrous metals, zip-fasteners, paints, insulators and leather-cloth.[2]

In one other way these particular combines are specially note-worthy: the extent to which they made a firm into an international organization. One of the explicit motives for the formation of Imperial Chemical Industries was the wish to deal with large foreign combines on equal terms, and the firm, which inherited numerous international interests from its constituents, especially Nobel Industries, soon developed others. Besides setting up subsidiaries of its own in Australia and New Zealand, it controlled African Ex-plosives and Industries Ltd., in association with the great South African firm of De Beers Consolidated Mines; it established interests in Argentina and Canada jointly with the American firm of Dupont de Nemours; and it had various associations and agreements with the chief German chemical firm, I. G. Farbenindustrie.[3] In the soap and edible fats industries both Lever Brothers and their chief Dutch and Central European rivals had wide-ranging international interests. When they all came together in 1929 in the huge Anglo-Dutch firm of Unilever, the undertaking which emerged was in control of over 500 companies engaged in all stages of the business from the raising of oil-bearing crops to the retailing of groceries, with locations scattered over most parts of the world.[4] Even in the rayon industry, which was almost untouched by amalgamation at home, there were many international combinations. Courtaulds had already established an American company before the First World War and in the inter-war years they set up others in Canada and France. They also secured

---

[1] Fitzgerald, *op. cit.*, chaps. VII-IX.

[2] A. Plummer, *International Combines in Modern Industry* (2nd edn., 1938), p. 58.

[3] *Ibid.*, pp. 57-9, and 147.   [4] Wilson, *op. cit.*, I, xvii-xix and II, 301-7.

associates in Japan, Argentina and Switzerland, and had close links with the chief German manufacturer, with whom they jointly controlled the biggest Italian producer.[1] Nevertheless, though these events were symptomatic of the way things were going they can hardly be regarded as typical. A high degree of international control over an industry was less uncommon in 1939 than it had been but was still the exception, not the rule.

Of more general significance at this stage was the emergence of new problems of industrial administration which showed themselves in the most extreme form in the biggest and most varied combines but, in varying degrees of acuteness, affected a host of other businesses also. When new and heterogeneous products had to be turned out from a selection of materials, of which some were common to many products and some specific to only one and some obtainable within the firm and some only from outside, and when the products were divided among markets that differed greatly in location, size and stability, then the internal co-ordination of the firm's activities and the long-term planning of its stock-holding, level of output and deliveries gained a supreme importance that they had not had before. And the more the business was dependent on the use of large quantities of very costly machinery for continuous flow production, the more necessary to success and the trickier these tasks became. The functions of industrial administration were profoundly changed at the top,[2] and this was bound to alter both the duties of executive managers at a lower level and the kind of knowledge and ability needed in them. In turn, since the carrying out of more detailed plans involved greater precision and closer timing at every stage of the work, it was desirable to have new arrangements to delimit each individual task and to ensure the proper briefing and willing co-operation of each worker. In this way the institutional character of many business firms underwent a more fundamental change than was often realized, the extent of the change probably being the more hidden because of the slow progress made in formalizing and publicizing the techniques of the developing subject of management.[3]

The biggest firms, of course, could not fail to be acutely, and sometimes uncomfortably, aware of it. In the early 'twenties, for instance,

---

[1] Plummer, *op. cit.*, pp. 35-8; Allen, *British Industries and their Organization*, pp. 252-5.

[2] *Cf.* Urwick and Brech, *The Making of Scientific Management*, II, 15.

[3] On the slow progress of management studies see *ibid.*, II, 126-9, 140-5 and 225-34.

Lever Brothers Ltd. was seriously weakened financially by its miscellaneous acquisitions, partly because some of them were unprofitable when taken over, but partly also because it took several years to work out administrative arrangements which could co-ordinate them with other sections of the firm's activities and enable them to make economic use of its central administration.[1] In a different but equally pressing form somewhat similar problems presented themselves in the 'thirties in integrating the various elements in the new structure of Unilever.[2] And there were comparable tasks in Imperial Chemical Industries, where there had to be several years of experiment in dividing up the administration of diverse elements of the business in such a way as to assist the most efficient operation of each division without weakening the co-ordination of the whole.[3] Most firms did not need to be so radical in their approach to administration as these. But so many undertook new functions, even if it were no more than running their own sales department to do what had formerly been left to specialist wholesalers[4]—and it was often much more—that they were bound to find themselves running their business in a rather different way from what they had been used to do.

Small firms, which continued to exist in large numbers though their share of the nation's business was declining, were not subject to most of these pressures of internal reorganization. But it would be misleading to suggest that they were not seriously involved in the more general changes in the structure of business. It was not only individual firms but also whole industries and trades which experienced a modification of their internal relationships, and this had repercussions on the activities and competitive position of small as well as large firms. Small shopkeepers, for instance, were very much affected by the spread of the practice of resale price maintenance, which by 1938 applied to goods to which about 30 per cent of consumers' expediture was devoted, as compared with 3 per cent in 1900. When resale price maintenance was supported by a strong organization of producers and distributors, most shopkeepers could not stand out against it, even had they wished to do so. Consequently their

---

[1] Wilson, *op. cit.*, I, Part IV, *passim.*   [2] *Ibid.*, II, 309-16.

[3] Plummer, *op. cit.*, pp. 59-60.

[4] It was estimated that in 1938 53 per cent (by value) of all consumer goods passed directly from the producer or importer to the retailer. There can be no doubt that this was a much higher proportion than before 1914 and that the transfer of functions from retailers and wholesalers to producers was very widespread. (Jefferys, *op. cit.*, pp. 47-9.) For more detailed study of the position in 1938 see J. B. Jefferys, *The Distribution of Consumer Goods* (1950), chap. I.

functions and policies were bound to change. For a wide range of articles they were spared the effort of deciding what to charge and competition in price was abolished, so that more attention had to be given to competition in service and location. At the same time the assurance of a fixed and ample profit margin on more and more commodities tempted many shopkeepers to stock a wider range of goods beyond the traditional limits of their own trade.[1]

Behind such developments there was a great increase of association among firms which had been, and for some purposes still were, direct competitors. Before 1914 the number of retail associations was small and the number which had the essential co-operation of producers for the enforcement of resale price maintenance was smaller still. An association of producers (which, in defiance of literal meaning, has usually been termed a 'trade association') was common in many industries, but usually served only a limited selection of purposes. Some associations were concerned only with the exchange of information or with negotiations with local authorities and government departments on behalf of their members; many were primarily concerned with labour questions; only a few, it would seem, were regularly concerned with the determination of prices.[2]

Various influences altered this situation. During the First World War the large degree of control which the government came to exercise over economic activity was easier to apply where the details could be settled with some body representing those most immediately affected. There was positive government encouragement for the formation of more of such institutions, and circumstances helped to determine their functions more precisely. The result was that industry became more completely covered by associations and that for the most part, though there were important exceptions, employers' organizations for dealing with labour were kept distinct from other trade associations. This state of affairs remained permanently.[3] Thus there were more associations among competing firms and they were in a better position to give their attention to matters immediately concerning their supplies and their markets. Moreover, when (as was not uncommon) the number of competing firms was reduced or one firm became more dominant through sheer increase of size, it

[1] Jefferys, *Retail Trading in Britain*, pp. 53-5. For the origins and characteristics of resale price maintenance see pp. 131-2 above.

[2] See pp. 100-1 and 295 above.

[3] A. Flanders and H. A. Clegg (eds.), *The System of Industrial Relations in Great Britain: its History, Law and Institutions* (1954), p. 213. *Cf.* p. 295 above.

was probably all the easier to secure agreement on positive measures of regulation. Several other factors pushed trade associations into greater activity in this way. One was that some industries found it increasingly difficult to sell their products, especially in the early 'thirties, and became desperate for some device that would ensure an adequate profit. A second was that changes in technique and scale in many industries made overhead costs a larger proportion of total costs and thus, in conditions of acute competition, made price-cutting both easier and, in the long-run, more unprofitable to all producers. More manufacturing industries, in fact, were subject to conditions analogous to those that had led to the formation of shipping conferences in the late nineteenth century.[1] A third, partly linked to the other two, was that far more producers were concerning themselves directly with the terms on which their goods were sold to the ultimate consumer.

The outcome was a considerable increase (which probably accelerated in the 'thirties) in the proportion of goods of which the price and output were fixed by agreement among producers or distributors or both. The number of retail trade associations grew perhaps even more than that of similar bodies in industry, and close relations between the two were common. In some cases both producers and distributors were members of the same association, in others their separate organizations were represented on some further body which dealt with matters of mutual concern.[2] Many wholesalers and retailers, nevertheless, remained unorganized, but, if they were dealing in manufactured goods, it was quite common for their terms of resale and their stocking of competing products to be strictly prescribed by an association of producers and enforced by such means as the threat of a withdrawal of supplies or the payment of a deferred rebate. In many industries by the 'thirties the relevant trade association had a price-fixing committee, while in others the secretary of the association prepared price lists. Not all of these imposed restrictions on retailers and wholesalers, but they did their best to ensure that their members never undercut each other and that the list prices would cover every member's costs, and in some cases the price lists were reinforced by the allocation of output quotas to each member.[3]

---

[1] *Cf.* p. 155 above.

[2] H. Levy, *Retail Trade Associations* (1942), esp. chap. 5.

[3] A. F. Lucas, *Industria Reconstruction and the Control of Competition* (1937), chap. IX.

This was the commonest way in which the structure of whole trades and industries was modified, but in special cases more drastic reorganization was attempted, usually with the approval, or even at the instigation, of the government. Governmental willingness to see competition reduced, in an effort to secure greater efficiency and economies of scale, was evident after the First World War, especially in relation to public utilities. Besides the reorganization of the railways, there was the creation of the Electricity Commissioners to exercise supervision over the electricity supply industry; and from 1926 the same policy was greatly extended when the Central Electricity Board was given the task of concentrating electricity generation at selected stations (privately operated), which would supply a complete national grid.[1] But it was in an attempt to lessen the difficulties of the large, depressed industries that the most striking changes of the 'thirties were made. Iron and steel, shipbuilding, coal and cotton were all affected.

Iron and steel became the most completely self-regulated British industry after reorganization had begun as part of an understanding with the government in return for tariff protection, which was granted in 1932. The machinery of control and price lists for many products were arranged in consultation with the Import Duties Advisory Committee established by the government, and the appointment of the independent chairman of the British Iron and Steel Federation, the industry's new supreme controlling body, also had to have government approval. At a lower level there were 27 different producers' associations within the industry by 1937, each fixing prices, and sometimes allocating output quotas, for a different group of products. Most prices were fixed high enough to enable high-cost producers to carry on, but from 1937 uneconomic plants in some sections of the industry began to be subsidized from the proceeds of a levy on steel output, on the understanding that they would be closed down as soon as new productive capacity was created. By 1939 this kind of price scheme operated throughout the heavy section of the industry.[2]

The coal and cotton industries both received government backing in reorganization. From 1930 a government-created Coal Mines

[1] For a brief summary of changes in the arrangements for electricity supply and its supervision see Ministry of Transport, *Report of the Committee on Electricity Distribution* (1936).

[2] Lucas, *op. cit.*, chap. V; Allen, *op. cit.*, pp. 111-13; Burn, *op. cit.*, pp. 452-3 and 471-83; W. Ashworth, *Contracts and Finance* (1953), p. 163.

Reorganization Commission was in operation, with powers for the compulsory amalgamation of mines and the supervision of prices; and from 1936 there was a nation-wide coal cartel, set up as a result of government pressure. Total output was fixed by a central committee of colliery owners; each of seventeen districts was given a quota; and in each district there was a committee to fix prices, to fix a quota for every mine, and to operate or supervise a central selling scheme for all the mines in the district.[1] In cotton-spinning the reorganization was much less comprehensive, but there were price-fixing schemes for a few products and some voluntary co-operation in closing down surplus capacity; and from 1936 a Spindles Board appointed by the Board of Trade was financed by a levy on the industry for the purpose of purchasing and destroying redundant spindles.[2] Somewhat similar co-operation was shown in the shipbuilding industry, though there the initial capital for the purchase and closure of surplus capacity came from the Bankers' Industrial Development Company, which had been formed by the Bank of England for just such purposes. Soon, however, the industry began to finance the scheme by means of a levy on all ships built, and the co-operation thus established led to much closer control over prices and tenders.[3]

All of these schemes embodied a certain amount of rather confused improvisation. None of them was as complete in practice as it appeared on paper: even in the iron and steel industry some firms remained outside the associations which dealt with the type of products they made,[4] and in all the schemes there were numerous omissions and delays in what was attempted. All of them could be regarded as exceptional, though they were exceptions that covered a substantial part of British industry. But their existence and their relations with the government were symptomatic of a change in ideas about the virtue of competition and the ideal form of economic organization. If more evidence is needed to demonstrate this, it can be seen, from 1932 onwards, in the introduction (with statutory authority) of schemes for the regulation of prices and output in some sections of agriculture, which had been the most individualistic and least organized of all the chief economic activities. It is true that there was suspicion and hostility from many farmers and that not more

[1] Lucas, *op. cit.*, chap. IV; Allen, *op. cit.*, pp. 73-7. The type of selling arrangement adopted in 1936 varied from one district to another.

[2] Allen, *op. cit.*, pp. 212-14.   [3] *Ibid.*, pp. 152-4; Lucas, *op. cit.*, pp. 126-35.

[4] Lewis, *op. cit.*, p. 11.

than about one-third of the output of agriculture was brought within the scope of organized marketing schemes.[1] But even this measure of change would have been unthinkable before 1914. As in some of the old staple industries, stagnant trade and foreign competition undermined some old ideas and practices, and the defensive ideas and organizations which succeeded them spread their influence to industries and trades that were never touched by depression. An environment was thus created that was favourable to the multiplication of associations among business firms. Instead of such organizations being regarded as conspiracies against the public (as once they would have been) there was a vague but growing belief that, in contemporary conditions, they might be essential instruments for the preservation of trade and employment. Here, perhaps, is the most pervasive reason why other influences encouraging closer association received a response which, in quite a short time, modified so much more of business life than might have been expected.

This increase of association and of scale and complexity of organization could hardly have been maintained if there had not also been considerable changes in other institutions. Relations with both the labour and capital markets were bound to be altered. On the whole, the formal machinery of both these markets must have come to serve directly a bigger part of the business world. As far as capital was concerned, the old nineteenth-century sources had become less adequate. The accumulation of personal savings for direct investment in one's own business, which down to 1914 had been very important for the foundation and expansion of manufacturing or trading enterprises, while not an obsolescent method of finance, was now likely to leave bigger gaps than before. The tendency for the scale of firms to increase and, in particular, the importance of large scale in some of the newer, expanding manufacturing industries were bound to have an effect. It was still possible, even in some industries which contained very large firms, to set up new businesses so much below the average in size that it was within the means of a small group of people to raise their capital privately. But if the business then took root and prospered it was becoming more likely that it would have to seek outside finance, sooner or later. For one thing, technical factors often required that, once existing productive capacity was being worked to

---

[1] Marketing schemes were introduced for hops in 1932, pigs, bacon and milk in 1933, and potatoes in 1934. For a fuller discussion see Lucas, *op. cit.*, chap. X.

its absolute maximum, any further expansion would have to be in bigger jumps than before, and this might create a need for a lot of extra capital in a short time. For another thing, the heavier incidence of death duties made it more difficult to preserve financial continuity. The death of one large shareholder in a private business could easily mean the withdrawal of so large a proportion of its capital that the surviving shareholders would be unable to continue the business on their own resources.

Thus business at home had more occasion to seek capital from the general public through the stock exchange. The need for this was probably modified gradually by the increasing prevalence of big firms because, in times of good trade, these could follow policies which would build up large reserves from which they could finance much of their future expansion. But it is doubtful whether, before the late 'thirties, there was sufficient co-incidence of increased scale and expanded trade for this to be more than a minor factor; and even then it sometimes happened that expanding trade imposed the heaviest need for extra capital on firms that had not the largest reserves.[1] Over the interwar period as a whole, the need of home business to raise much more capital by formalized, impersonal means is unquestionable.

The machinery of the London stock exchange and new issue market was, of course, very highly developed but it had hitherto served the needs of home industry to only a fairly small extent, partly because it was abundantly occupied in dealing with foreign loans, partly because (except for the biggest firms) it provided an expensive means of raising capital, and partly because most of the industrial capital could be obtained elsewhere. The changed needs of home business after the First World War coincided with a changed situation in the City of London, brought about mainly by a loss of foreign financial business. For 1910-13 the annual average of new issues in London for investment overseas (outside the British Empire) was £100,570,000; for 1926-30 it was down to £49,457,000, and for 1934-38 it was only £4,047,000.[2] Though new issues to the Empire, which between 1910 and 1913 accounted for just over one-third of the capital raised in London, were fairly well maintained until 1930,

---

[1] For a specific illustration from the aircraft industry see Ashworth, *op. cit.*, pp. 199-200. Between 1935 and 1939 thirteen aircraft firms increased their fixed assets and their holdings in associated companies by £6·9 mn. Towards this they were able to supply £2·0 mn. from their accumulated reserves.

[2] Kahn, *Great Britain in the World Economy*, p. 139.

these also declined heavily after that. Thus there was a large gap, which the needs of British business might help to fill.

There were a few snags, however. One was the appearance of other large new borrowers, of which the most important were British municipalities.[1] Another was the difficulty of making any but very large issues, except at prohibitive expense. A third was the effect of changes in the distribution of incomes and in saving habits, which meant that the fairly wealthy minority, that had been the chief source of personal investible funds, was no longer able to invest quite so much through the stock exchange.

None of these created insuperable difficulties for home business. There were bigger sums on the new issue market than municipalities could absorb, and the estimated annual average of new issues for home production and trade rose from £19·1 million in 1910-13 to £89·0 million in 1927-30 and, despite the subsequent depression, was still as high as £66·6 million in 1933-35.[2] Moreover, the collapse of oversea financial business after 1930 compelled the institutions of the new issue market to change their practices in order to attract alternative custom, and consequently they became more useful to the firm of moderate size. The minimum amount of capital which it was practicable to raise in one issue was reduced and there was an increased number of small issues.[3] There were also various changes which probably brought the savings of a bigger section of the public to the stock exchange. The most important was the growth of insurance business. The large insurance companies came to be among the biggest investors in the market and they put an increasing proportion of their funds into industrial securities, especially from 1932 onwards, when the government's cheap money policy reduced the income they could obtain from government securities. By 1936 they had invested funds of over £1,500 million, of which between one-quarter and one-third were in railway companies and industrial and commercial enterprise.[4] An increase also took place in the number of other institutions which served as intermediaries between the saving public and the industrial borrower and which may have attracted some new and smaller investors by helping them to spread their risks. The commonest of these institutions were investment trusts, which raised capital from the public and derived their income from

[1] A. T. K. Grant, *A Study of the Capital Market in Post-War Britain* (1937), p. 171.
[2] *Ibid.*, p. 172.   [3] *Ibid.*, p. 182.   [4] *Ibid.*, pp. 189-90.

investment in a variety of other companies. Between 1925 and 1929, 82 investment trust companies were formed, and from 1932 they were supplemented by the establishment and growth of unit trusts,[1] though it was another quarter of a century before the latter began to make rapid progress.

In these various ways the organization of the capital market was fairly well adapted to meet the needs of British trade and industry for long-term capital. This was the field in which change was most necessary, and if the available capital did not find its way to the most productive destinations the blame could not be attributed to out-dated institutions; it belonged rather to the way in which the institutions were used and to the public policies which affected the market.

Less change was needed in the institutions dealing with other classes of capital. There were well-established arrangements by which short-term capital was obtainable from the banks and by credit from suppliers. The main changes in the working of the short-term market were associated with government rather than business finance. It is possible, however, that there was a slight influence from an increased ability of the larger firms to provide circulating capital from their own resources, with less recourse to loans from the banks. There were also greater changes in the short-term financing of foreign trade. Rather less of this business was to be had, in any case, and a smaller proportion of it was financed by means of bills of exchange, other forms of direct transfer of credit being increasingly used; and at the same time the joint-stock banks greatly increased their direct participation in foreign dealings. Many of the old merchant bankers had therefore to change both their techniques and the balance of their interests, some of them, for instance, turning more to new issue and underwriting business at home.

One other change worthy of note arose from the need of a small section of home business for a new type of medium-term capital. Increasing attempts were made to stimulate the sale of some types of durable consumer goods, such as furniture and furnishings and

---

[1] Grant, *op. cit.*, pp. 172 and 192. An investment trust is a company like any other, which may have a geared capital structure and may accumulate reserves from un-distributed profits, and the shares in which are quoted on the stock exchange in the normal way. A unit trust is not usually quoted on the stock exchange. Its managers sell units (which are all of equal value) and are always prepared to repurchase them at the current price, which is determined by the quoted value of all the securities in which the funds of the trust are invested, and is calculated in accordance with a formula approved by the Board of Trade. A unit trust does not accumulate reserves but normally distributes to unit-holders all its income minus a charge for the management of the trust.

household electrical appliances, by the offer of hire-purchase arrangements. The manufacturers and retailers usually had not the means to finance these schemes entirely by themselves, the joint-stock banks kept out of them, and, since the rate of interest charged to purchasers was high, there was an incentive for the formation of specialist firms which would raise capital specifically for this purpose. The 'thirties saw the establishment of a small number of financial intermediaries of this new type, which came eventually to be described as 'industrial bankers'. Their significance, however, lay mainly in the future, since hire-purchase still applied to only a very small, though growing, proportion of retail trade.[1]

To complete the account of the main changes in the way in which economic life was organized, it is necessary to look at the institutions of the labour market, and to consider to what extent workpeople united for their own purposes, where their strongest associations were to be found, and what policies they conceived and could effectively apply. The First World War had greatly strengthened the trade union movement, giving it a large increase in membership, a much bigger say in matters affecting its members, power to negotiate on a national rather than a local scale, and the assurance that goes with control of a scarce commodity.[2] These wartime changes had important permanent effects on the organization of labour and the conduct of industrial relations. But some of the changes were not lasting, and consequently there were many subsequent variations in the use to which the new organizational framework was put.

The most significant reversal of wartime developments was in the number of trade unionists and their distribution among different industries and occupations. The total membership of trade unions reached a maximum of 8,346,000 in 1920 but declined rapidly in the ensuing trade depression to 5,429,000 in 1923. Thereafter, though trade recovered somewhat for a time, the decline continued, more slowly but steadily, until in 1933 a minimum of 4,392,000 was reached. Then the tide turned and membership increased quickly after 1935 to a total of 6,298,000 in 1939. It is also noticeable that the membership of unions which were affiliated to the T.U.C. fell rather more irregularly but, on the whole, slightly faster than that of

[1] Hire-purchase was not an invention of the interwar period. Examples of it can be traced at least as far back as mid-Victorian times. But its extent was negligible before the First World War.

[2] *Cf.* p. 295 above.

the others, and that from 1935 this trend also was reversed: between that year and 1939 the proportion of trade unionists whose unions were affiliated to the T.U.C. rose from 74·3 to 77·6 per cent but was still below the 82·1 per cent at which it stood in 1919.[1]

For this protracted decline and belated recovery several reasons may be suggested: the drift of workers away from wartime jobs to which they had come temporarily; the decline of some industries in which unionism had been very strong; slowness in organizing workers in some of the expanding industries; the persistence of much unemployment in some areas. Some of them are similar to the influences which altered the industrial distribution of trade unionists. Between 1910 and 1914 the dominance of the skilled craftsmen had already been reduced by the rapid growth of unions of the unskilled, and this development was continued in the First World War. This shift in the location of strength within the trade union movement was not subsequently reversed (indeed, the continued decline of the miners was one of the outstanding features of the next twenty years), but it was modified by postwar developments. This was partly because technical changes brought some skilled workers within the field of the general unions which originally had catered almost entirely for the unskilled, and partly because the greatest expansion of union membership in the interwar years was among clerical and similar workers, though this was not fully reflected in the unions affiliated to the T.U.C.[2]

Another important feature, strengthened during the First World War but becoming still more prominent afterwards, was the predominant position of a few large unions. Between 1917 and 1924 there was a spate of amalgamations, in the course of which there emerged such large unions as the British Iron, Steel and Kindred Trades Association, the Union of Post Office Workers, the Amalgamated Engineering Union, the Civil Service Clerical Association, the Transport and General Workers' Union and the National Union of General and Municipal Workers.[3] By 1937 half the total trade union membership was to be found in only twelve unions, with an average membership of 238,000.[4] There were also some provisions

[1] B. C. Roberts, *Trade Union Government and Administration in Great Britain* (1956), pp. 474-7.
[2] *Ibid.*, p. 479.
[3] *Ibid.*, p. 10. For a detailed account of one of these large amalgamations see H. A. Clegg, *General Union: a Study of the National Union of General and Municipal Workers* (1954).
[4] Roberts, *op. cit.*, p. 489.

for common action among groups larger than any single union, but where they involved workers in quite separate industries their strength can easily be overstressed. Regular arrangements for a united policy, such as the miners, railwaymen and transport workers had established in 1914, broke down when first severely tested in 1921 and were not renewed, though in 1925 plans were being prepared for a new Industrial Alliance.[1] The most significant new development was the enhanced authority of the General Council of the T.U.C., which was able, in some circumstances, to intervene in industrial disputes and to carry out negotiations on behalf of the trade union movement generally or a group of unions, particularly when the government was involved. But in practice there seems to have been no clear agreement among the leaders of individual unions as to how much sovereignty they allowed the General Council in such matters. This ambiguity was clearly illustrated by the relations between the T.U.C. and the miners' leaders in the general strike of 1926.[2]

To the high degree of association within the labour movement the organization of employers was a fairly close counterpart. As has been seen, regular association of employers spread to more industries during and after the First World War, and organizations for the conduct of industrial relations were often separated from those for other purposes. These employers' associations were usually larger than the trade associations. A single employers' organization generally covered a whole industry, often on a federal basis.[3] It is also probable that employers' associations had a more complete membership than trade unions: in 1932 the National Confederation of Employers' Organizations claimed to represent the employers of 7,000,000 workpeople, and this figure was probably fairly steady until the Second World War.[4] In one respect, however, association was less close than among the trade unions. Although there were two large central bodies representing employers, the Federation of British Industries and the National Confederation of Employers' Organizations, neither had as extensive an authority as the T.U.C. The first of them was mainly confined to manufacturing industry and did not concern itself with labour questions. The second had a

---

[1] J. Symons, *The General Strike* (1957), pp. 8 and 28-9. The project was overtaken by the general strike and consequently was never completed.

[2] *Ibid.*, pp. 43 and 45-6 for examples.

[3] Flanders and Clegg, *op. cit.*, pp. 216-17.   [4] *Ibid.*, p. 199.

broader membership but never participated in negotiations or disputes; it confined itself to presenting employers' views to the government and international bodies and to providing a common meeting ground where members of the constituent associations might discuss and co-ordinate their policies.[1]

In spite of these limitations, the scale and closeness of organization in the labour market were such as to make possible either widespread conflict or agreements with a very extensive application. This increase of scale was the most important change since 1914. The urgent needs of war had caused a fairly general replacement of local by national negotiations, and most employers and trade union leaders found this preferable. Indeed, the help which many employers obtained from national agreements in a time of labour shortage did much to make them more friendly to the permanent maintenance of collective bargaining, and this was also extended by the setting up of Joint Industrial Councils in many industries.[2] The unrest of the three years after the armistice did some damage both to the new machinery of industrial negotiation and to the goodwill needed for its effective use.[3] But, though many Joint Industrial Councils broke up under the strain, about fifty of them survived and the general trend towards collective bargaining on a national basis was fairly well maintained.

There was, however, one great exception, which threatened to disrupt the whole machinery. In the coal industry the owners, many of them in economic difficulty, were determined to reduce the power of the unions and, as a step towards this, to get back from national to local agreements; they were also concerned to reduce labour costs and to resist any 'outside' suggestions for reorganization that might make their industry more remunerative. The miners, led with much spirit and little subtlety, stubbornly resisted all change as far as they could, despite the economic difficulties afflicting the industry; having been given much about which to be unreasonable, they went on to be unreasonable also in those matters where reason could have been to their own advantage. Nevertheless, when the situation was aggravated by deflation and the rapid fall of coal prices after the restoration of output in the Ruhr mines in 1924, the miners' case roused much sympathy. Faced in 1925 by the coal-owners' insistence on severe wage reductions, the abolition of the minimum wage and the lengthening of the working day, they were able to get the T.U.C. to

---

[1] Flanders and Clegg, *op. cit.*, p. 232.   [2] *Ibid.*, pp. 276-8.
[3] *Cf.* pp. 297-8 above.

back their resistance by a policy of sympathetic strikes, in which the Transport and General Workers' Union and the Associated Society of Locomotive Engineers and Firemen agreed to take part. This threat was averted when the government agreed temporarily to subsidize the coal industry to the extent needed to avoid changes in wages and hours, while a Royal Commission enquired into the state of the industry.[1] But this was only postponing the conflict, as the government recognized in the many preparations it made for the maintenance of essential activities in the event of widespread strikes. The Royal Commission, among its other recommendations, felt bound to propose reductions in wages, although these were less drastic than those the owners had demanded; the miners refused to agree to any reduction; and the owners gave notice of a lock-out from 30 April 1926, the day on which the government's temporary subsidy was due to expire.

The sequel was the nine-day national strike, which came to be known as the 'General Strike', though the adjective rather exaggerates the reality. From midnight on 3 May the workers in transport, printing, iron and steel, the metal industries, electricity and gas supply, and most of the building trades were called out on strike by the T.U.C., in support of the miners. The response to the strike call was enthusiastic and almost complete, and the normal activities of the community were gravely disrupted, though large numbers of volunteers were able to maintain a minimum of such indispensable services as the distribution of food supplies. Despite the strong support which they received, the T.U.C. leaders were uneasy about their course of action. Though it was not meant to be a revolutionary movement, the general strike was bound to be an act of coercion by a minority against the rest of the community and the lawfully constituted government. It did not make sense unless its leaders were prepared to take over governmental responsibilities in defiance of constitutional processes. Only a handful of people wanted that. After some inconclusive negotiations the leaders resolved their dilemma by calling off the general strike, without having secured anything for the miners or even clearly safeguarded the position of the other workers who had been supporting them. Many of these did, in fact, remain on strike for several more days and thereby generally ensured that they would go back on no worse terms than those in force before the strike. The miners continued on strike

[1] Symons, *op. cit.*, pp. 8-16.

N

alone until, late in the year, their resistance collapsed piecemeal, and they had to accept complete defeat.[1]

This divisive episode might easily have altered the whole course of industrial relations and ruined the machinery through which they were conducted. In the coal industry that is more or less what happened; national agreements came to an end, and for the future there were only district negotiations, with the miners in a weakened position and an embittered frame of mind. But in the rest of industry and trade the general strike made surprisingly little lasting difference. Its duration was short; such violence as accompanied it was slight and localized; its leaders were moderate men; and the government refrained from exerting its full strength against it—little use was made of troops, for instance. When it was over there were in the early days some dismissals and demotions of strikers, some attacks by employers on established agreements, but these never became very widespread. Both King George V and the Prime Minister, Baldwin, publicly exerted their influence to encourage moderation. The chief formal changes resulted from the Trade Disputes and Trade Unions Act of 1927, which made sympathetic strikes illegal, debarred trade unions from requiring any member to contribute to their political fund unless he contracted in writing to do so, prevented established civil servants who were not already members of unions affiliated to the T.U.C. from becoming so, and defined intimidation as a legal offence. This measure, which has often been described as 'savage', hit the finances of the Labour Party (the number of trade unionists paying the political levy was over one-third less in 1928 than 1926) and provided a symbolic focus of opposition.[2] But in all other respects its practical effects were very mild, and trade unionism continued much as before, though with a greater care for cautious, empirical methods. In the eighteen months after the general strike, trade union membership fell more sharply than at other times, but even this appears in perspective as no more than a minor fluctuation in the middle of a sustained trend.

In these circumstances the tendency for questions of wages and working conditions to be settled more and more on a national basis, through negotiations between large organizations, was continued.

---

[1] The best short account of the general strike is in Mowat, *Britain between the Wars*, pp. 290-337. A useful recent study at rather greater length is Symons, *op. cit.*, though some of its comments may seem unfair.

[2] Its repeal in 1946 was one of the earliest measures of the first Labour government with a clear majority.

Though many trade unions were weakened by the depletion of their funds in 1926 and by the existence of unemployment in the industries with which they were concerned, the employers outside the coal industry made no attack on either their existence or their rights in collective bargaining.[1] If the economic weakness of many trade unions was one reason for the pacific course of industrial relations from 1927 to 1939, it was not the only one. Something was also attributable to the maintenance and improvement of the negotiating machinery and the willingness of both employers and workers to use it fairly. There were, of course, exceptions in cases of special difficulty, particularly in declining industries which suffered increasingly from foreign competition. In the cotton industry, for instance, collective bargaining was being gradually eroded after 1929, and even when agreements were reached in the old way many firms outside the employers' organizations maintained worse terms of employment. But this disintegration was checked from 1934 when the agreements negotiated voluntarily for the industry were given statutory force,[2] and the government's increasing willingness to intervene in this way in a number of industries strengthened the representative negotiating bodies and helped to make national agreements still more usual. Thus, despite the difficulties of the intervening years, highly centralized, comprehensive arrangements for the regulation of industrial relations were more numerous and more representative in 1939 than in the early 'twenties. The interwar years saw further developments on these lines in activities, such as railway transport and the building trades, where they were not new; and they also saw the successful introduction and maintenance of collective bargaining, through Joint Industrial Councils, in public utility services, transport (other than the railways, which already had their own machinery, and road haulage, which remained poorly organized), flour-milling, brick-making, cement-making and the chemical industries.[3]

This does not mean that everything was given over to the big battalions. There were still millions of workers, including the great majority of those outside industry and transport, whose wages and conditions of employment were not determined in this way. Some had simply to accept or reject what they were offered, or stand out

[1] Flanders and Clegg, *op. cit.*, p. 214.   [2] *Ibid.*, pp. 280-1.

[3] *Ibid.*, pp. 279 and 282. Comparable arrangements in several other industries were just coming into regular use in the late 'thirties; and collective bargaining in some of the basic industries had been thoroughly established in the nineteenth century.

individually for what they could get from an employer; some were members of organizations which could negotiate agreements covering one district or a single establishment; some belonged to organizations which could press a common point of view but had no recognized place in negotiations; some belonged to no organization but had statutory protection, for example from trade board legislation. Even in those industries where national organizations of employers and workers made agreements on behalf of everybody concerned, there was plenty of detail that could be dealt with only in each district or each individual establishment. For example, the emergence of shop stewards in the closing years of the nineteenth century was a spontaneous result of the transfer of some trade union negotiations to national officials. There was a need for someone who was familiar at first hand with the way in which a specific group of people in a particular establishment was affected by the application of general agreements or by the methods of management and who could raise, in an explicit way, any difficulties that were encountered. Though there was often friction between union officials and shop stewards, more and more of the latter were found necessary, and trade unions had to try to fit them into their organizations, with defined responsibilities.[1] Likewise, the successful use of national associations and national agreements, far from relieving firms of a certain individual responsibility, often depended on greater care and new developments in their own management, and particularly on specialized provision for personnel management and the conduct of labour relations within the plant. The smaller constituent elements in the world of industry and labour had not lost their identity and functions in a vast new macrocosm; they had simply come to occupy a different but essential place in close relation to it.

All this is, in an important way, illustrative of the nature of the change that had come over economic organization generally. The need to perform new functions, or to perform old functions in new ways, was not confined to very large firms or to associations which in some way limited competition, but was very widespread. Even though the environment had been changed in ways beyond their individual control, the success and survival of most organizations usually depended to a great extent on their own adaptability and enterprise

[1] For details of the way in which different unions dealt with this question see *Roberts, op. cit.*, pp. 58-79.

within that changed environment. Nevertheless, the lack of individual control over conditions which were designed to distort the free working of the market could be very important. The adaptability and enterprise needed for survival could be greatly reduced, or an impassable limit set to the rewards of success, irrespective of the efforts of those responsible for the individual organization, and it is worth asking how far the changes of the time may have had such an effect.

Whether it is the commodity or the capital or the labour market that is under consideration, the first impression is that over the greater part a high degree of competition still prevailed. Most observers of industry in the nineteen-twenties concluded that amalgamation and the growth of large firms had not gone so far as to inhibit the working of competition, though they were aware that this was a possible future prospect. In the manufacturing and extractive industries it was estimated that in the early 'twenties not more than one-fifth of the total (as measured by the number of people employed), and possibly much less, was directly affected by combinations.[1] A later estimate suggests that by 1939, in manufacturing industry alone, the non-competitive sector (which was largely confined to the iron and steel, non-ferrous metals, engineering and chemical industries) had grown to 29 per cent of the total.[2] The competitive character of the capital market had long been established. The readier availability of new issue facilities to more and smaller borrowers, and a tendency to have shares of smaller denomination, would appear to have enhanced it. In the labour market of Great Britain there were in 1939 probably some 12 million persons in employment who were neither trade union members nor the employees of any member of an employer's association; these people far outnumbered the organized workers. Facts such as these are a necessary corrective to any impression that Britain in the nineteen-thirties was overrun by oligopolists who settled down to the enjoyment of organized torpor.

On the other hand, restrictions on competition had some effect over a wider area than appears at first sight. The strongholds of oligopoly included in the 'thirties large sections of the country's basic industries which, as customers and suppliers, could send out diminishing ripples of influence over much of the rest of the economy. Even where no formal restrictive institution existed there was sometimes an increasing regulation of competition as a result of

[1] Balfour Committee, *op. cit.*, p. 9.　　[2] Lewis, *op. cit.*, p. 19.

government policy; this was particularly true in the labour market. And technical factors sometimes worked against those institutional arrangements that made for maximum competition. Thus, the growing number of new projects that required heavy investment at an early stage, or elaborate facilities for development, tended to bring the small pioneering producer within the influence of the dominant established firm and partially offset the effect of extended services from the stock market to the small firm. It would also be unwise to overlook the influence of example which the practices and standards of large, associated bodies exerted on others of a different constitution, though this cannot be measured.

Since the days before the First World War there had been a substantial change in the structure of the business world and the way it was run; and the growing influence of large institutions and attempts to limit (but certainly not to remove entirely) the workings of competition had a key place in the change. To a great extent these were the result of the combined influence of many different developments, especially in technique, and not the deliberate creation of conscious policy. So far as the latter influence was responsible for them it was guided primarily by the search for more convenient ways of running things and for protection against immediate economic difficulties. That valuable successes were achieved in both respects is evident in the easier adjustment of labour relations in many industries and in the removal of destructive price-cutting that was denying the opportunity for the rehabilitation of some industries with heavy overhead costs. But these were not the only things required of any system of economic organization: adaptability, the pursuit of greater efficiency, and the creation of new goods were called for. Competition did not always meet these requirements. In the steel industry in the nineteen-twenties, for instance, the firms with several plants neglected to establish adequate specialization among them, while those that had the constituents of an integrated chain of production failed, on the whole, to make the most of it; and both were unable to put pressure on their competitors by producing at appreciably lower cost.[1]

Where such things happened they encouraged the argument that a larger, closer and less competitive organization might have positive advantages in the promotion of greater efficiency. There is no certainty that this argument was empirically vindicated in the nineteen-thirties. Where competition disappeared or was greatly reduced,

[1] Burn, *op. cit.*, pp. 372-3 and 441.

those responsible were not generally prone to force prices very high or to keep customers short of supplies, but it was often doubtful whether some of them were not using their high-cost associates as a comfortable cushion instead of exploiting their own abilities to the full. Even the steel industry, which had a formal commitment to the government to rationalize itself, was slow and compromising in its introduction of schemes to raise efficiency.[1] Whether the examples of the pursuit of progress at no more than an easy jog-trot outweighed the large improvements in products, techniques and management, achieved by some firms in industries little troubled by competition, it is impossible to say. Both existed at the same time, just as the traditional virtues attributed to competition could still be found alongside their negation in that large sector of the economy unaffected by close association. It is certain, however, that the continuous adaptability of the whole economy was becoming more dependent on the maintenance of an enterprising spirit where the old extremes of competition no longer survived to foster it. Large associations—of firms, of employers, of workpeople—had shown too much utility for them to be discarded. Firms which remained small tended to have a limited life, whereas firms which attained a large size tended to achieve permanence.[2] By the nineteen-thirties these had become inescapable and dominating facts of economic organization. They made it clear that, for the organization to be turned to good account, these things were necessary above all: enterprising skill in the conception of policy and the executive management of large institutions; and such a framework of law and of governmental policy as would prevent these large institutions from pulling against each other or against the public, and would give ample opportunities for the continuous emergence of new enterprise and new men to direct it.

[1] *Ibid.*, pp. 483-92 and 507-8.   [2] Hart and Prais, *loc. cit.*, p. 166.

CHAPTER SIXTEEN

Public Policy and its Effects

QUESTIONS about the proper limits and content of public policy in economic matters were bound to present themselves in an acute form after the First World War. Influential opinion hitherto had, in general, been moving gradually towards the acceptance of a greater degree of public economic enterprise and regulation, but it had scarcely been prepared for what had come to pass by 1918. There was abundant material for argument about which of the innumerable public activities then in operation were indispensable or generally beneficial, which were inescapable commitments that must be honoured even though they were both controversial and expanding, and which could be treated as temporary expedients to be discarded as soon as possible.

Because the tightness of wartime control went so far beyond anything imagined in 1914 it was to be expected that there would be a strong reaction against it. But the marked increase in the scope and cost of public economic policy between 1890 and 1914, as well as the sheer weight of the changes found both necessary and feasible during the war, made it likely that the economic influence and activities of public authorities would nevertheless remain greater than they had previously been in peacetime. One factor making for such a result was the natural growth of new services begun in the early years of the century. Old age pensions and compulsory insurance against sickness and unemployment were examples of innovations that had been adopted in response to sustained political pressure and in recognition of the changed circumstances of contemporary economic and social life. But all had been introduced on so small a scale that, unless they proved complete failures, it was difficult to make out a rational case for leaving them within their original narrow limits; and conditions from 1920 drew attention to the urgent need to extend them. Morale-boosting promises about future reconstruction, which were made by members of the government during and immediately after the war, also foreshadowed new items of public expenditure, since they could not be altogether ignored. In particular, they made it inevitable that the provision of houses (a costly item of expenditure) should be undertaken by public authorities to a much greater extent than ever before.

In addition, however strong a reaction there might be against wartime restrictions, the war economy left a legacy which could not be completely jettisoned overnight. Public enterprise had been greatly extended in manufacturing and trading, and the ramifications of government economic control had spread wider still. By 1918 at least two-thirds of all the gainfully employed workers were in activities directly subject to some form of governmental control.[1] Even if all these measures were undone, the position of the government in the economy would still not be the same as before. The finance of the war had greatly increased the national debt and on that account alone, apart from anything else, government expenditure for an indefinite period ahead was likely to be much higher than before, the more so as most of the wartime borrowing was at high rates of interest. Moreover, the magnitude of the borrowing and, in particular, the large amount of floating debt, had put the government in a new and dominating position in the money market; and the financial methods used had seriously depreciated the currency. As a result the setting of all economic life had been subjected to distortions and uncertainties that could be removed only by acts of public policy.[2] The situation was further complicated by the chaotic conditions of international finance and trade immediately after the war. It was impossible just to stand aside and say that the field was clear for bankers and traders to resume their proper rôle. There were too many problems with which individual firms were powerless to deal and which could be settled only by agreements between governments.[3]

One other element in the background ought to be noted. This was the stirring of change that showed itself in the economic doctrines which the different political parties accepted. On the whole, despite the fierce verbal battles between Conservatives and Liberals and the wide divergences between them in some fields, the fifty years preceding the First World War showed remarkable continuity in economic and social policy, irrespective of party politics. Neither party was formally pledged to much increase in governmental intervention but both contributed steadily to it while in office. The

---

[1] R. H. Tawney, 'The Abolition of Economic Controls, 1918-1921' in *Econ. Hist. Rev.*, XIII (1943), 3.
[2] See Chap. Eleven above.   [3] See pp. 292-3 and 313 above.

most that can be said is that, as long as Gladstone was active, his dislike of all increases in public expenditure helped to make the Liberal contribution less than the Conservative, and that in the early twentieth century the position was reversed. But a break in the continuity of policy and the reappearance of an old form of intervention were foreshadowed by the tentative Conservative commitment to some degree of tariff protection from the time of the 1906 election onward. This change of programme had proved unpopular enough for it to be pushed into the background, but it had not been abandoned. Immediately after the war the Conservatives were politically stronger than they had been at any time since 1906 and were confronted by an international economic situation so disturbed that some kind of protective intervention might have a strong appeal. The Liberals, still firmly attached to free trade, were weakened by internal divisions that contained the seeds of future disintegration. The rising Labour Party, while not committed to protection, was not likely to find lasting difficulty in fitting it into its general plans, and in other respects was prepared to use the power and authority of the state in economic and social matters much more extensively than the two older parties. Thus the balance of political forces seemed to be making for increased intervention in the economy, in the long run, if not immediately.

In the confused conditions of the early postwar years not all the long-run influences were likely to have much scope. The determination of policy was much affected by such things as dislike of current restraints, nostalgia for the familiar ways of the most recent time of peace and the need to tackle a number of urgent problems in rapid succession without much time to consider how the remedy prescribed for one would react on the next. The general approach to economic questions was to accept and try to make the best of such additional items of public expenditure and activity as were absolutely inescapable and otherwise to make 'back to 1914' the constant aim to be achieved as quickly as possible.

Two things in particular reflected this determination to restore prewar conditions. One was the hasty termination of the public enterprises and controls which had been an integral part of the war economy. Many of these had been introduced for a specified period only and were therefore bound to lapse unless some positive reason was found for their renewal.[1] But no general survey of the merits

[1] Tawney, *loc. cit.*, p. 12.

and defects of different controls was made. Business interests, the press and the Treasury all told the government that controls must be abolished to enable industrialists and traders to revive business; and the government was conscious that it must not impede business expansion, without which it would be impossible to employ the demobilized men and displaced munition workers.[1] Most of the control organizations operated by the Board of Trade and the War Office were abolished in the course of 1919, long before the trading disturbances inseparable from the transition to peace had been removed. A few special organizations, such as the Ministries of Food and Munitions, the Coal Control and the Railway Executive, remained until 1921, but the last of all the wartime controls, that on the sale of alcoholic liquor, ended in August of that year. Very little survived as a permanent inheritance: a Mines Department within the Board of Trade, a remodelled organization for the railways, a few changes in the liquor licensing laws; little else.[2] So rapid and so complete was the abandonment of the wartime measures that the power of government policy to influence the course of industry and trade in the first three years of peace, when it was most erratic and most susceptible to external disturbances, was much reduced.

The other outstanding decision was in the field of finance. The government in 1918 accepted the recommendations of the Cunliffe *Committee on Currency and Foreign Exchanges after the War* that the gold standard should be restored as soon as possible at the prewar parity and that the size of the note issue not covered by gold should be brought under control and progressively reduced. Such a decision implied many corollaries, of which the most general was a return to a semi-automatic regulation of currency and credit, with the Bank of England rather than the government as the chief source of control and guidance, and the foreign exchange position rather than the movement of prices and activity at home as the indicator of what the Bank's actions should be.

The full implementation of the decision was clearly not possible at once. Indeed, in a formal sense, the government went further away from the gold standard. In March 1919 the government ceased to use its dollars to hold the sterling-dollar exchange rate stable and, in order to guard against the effects of any consequential fall in the rate,

[1] *Ibid.*, pp. 13 and 19.
[2] *Ibid.*, pp. 7-8; A. C. Pigou, *Aspects of British Economic History 1918-1925* (1947), pp. 115-26.

it prohibited the export of gold.[1] But various steps were soon taken towards limiting the financial licence which the government had exercised and restoring the position of the Bank of England in the money market. From the end of 1919 a limit was set to the fiduciary issue of currency notes by making the actual maximum issue in each year the legal maximum for the next year. This proved to be one step which in 1920 induced others on traditional lines to curb the expansion of credit.[2] To restore the old relation of the government and the Bank in the regulation of credit also required a change in the structure of the National Debt, because of the effect which the floating debt had on the money market. By the end of 1918 the volume of outstanding Treasury bills had risen to over £1,000 million and was so enormously greater than the volume of all other short-term securities that the rate at which Treasury bills were offered made ineffective all other influences on the short-term rate of interest. Since, however, the needs of the government were so large it was sometimes difficult to renew all this mass of short-term credit just when required, and then the government had to increase its borrowing on Ways and Means from the Bank of England. This operation meant that the market received additional liquid resources even if the Bank wished to tighten credit; in effect, the volume of the government's short-term needs prevented the Bank from regulating the money market. Control was gradually restored to the Bank between 1920 and 1922 by two methods. One was the adoption of very high interest rates (in April 1920 the Bank rate went up to 7 per cent and the tap rate for Treasury bills to 6½ per cent) which reduced the need for recourse to borrowing on Ways and Means. The other was the rapid reduction in the volume of the floating debt from the end of 1921. The latter was made possible mainly by a greater use of other securities, such as Treasury Bonds and Savings Certificates, and to some extent by a fall in day-to-day needs as the level of government expenditure fell.[3]

To return to the old system in external finance was more difficult.

[1] Pigou, *op. cit.*, p. 145. Previously, though Britain was effectively off the gold standard, the export of gold was not illegal; it was impracticable because a shipment of gold could not be insured against war risks.

[2] Morgan, *British Financial Policy*, pp. 220-1. Bank of England notes, the fiduciary issue of which was still limited by the 1844 Act, could serve as backing for the Treasury's issue of currency notes. Owing to the continued high demand for the latter in 1920 it was necessary to use more Bank of England notes in this way, with a consequent reduction in the Bank's reserve.

[3] *Ibid.*, pp. 141-50 and 375-8; Committee on National Debt and Taxation, *Report (P.P.* 1927, XI), pp. 37-42.

Even if the international gold standard could be restored, the conditions in which it must operate had changed greatly and the financial resources which Britain could deploy in its service had diminished without prospect of their early replenishment.[1] For Britain to return to gold at the old parity was harder still, because the maintenance of adequate international reserves was temporarily hampered by the competitive advantage obtained in the export trade by countries the external values of whose currencies had depreciated unduly in relation to their purchasing power at home. It became yet more difficult as a result of the postwar inflation, in the course of which the purchasing power of the pound fell a good deal faster than that of the dollar. In order to bring back the exchange rate to par it was necessary to lower the British price level relatively to the American as a means of decreasing Britain's international expenditure relatively to its earnings. Since the American price level began to fall rapidly in 1920, the reductions needed in British prices were formidable indeed. To bring them about a drastic restriction of credit was applied, mainly by means of high interest rates, despite the adverse repercussions this must have on business activity and employment. This restrictive policy continued even in the depths of the slump in 1921 and 1922, when every other consideration would have suggested the opposite measures. Such was the prestige of the gold standard, however, that hardly anyone of authority or influence questioned the rightness of the policy.[2] It certainly did most of what was asked of it. By the end of 1922 there was not much difference between American and British prices, but sterling remained somewhat below par. Gradually and unevenly over the next two years, as trade improved and, eventually, speculators began to buy sterling in anticipation of the restoration of the gold standard, the exchange (after slipping back) again approached par. In May 1925 the pound returned to the gold standard at the prewar parity.[3]

---

[1] Morgan, *op. cit.*, pp. 359-60. *Cf.* pp. 318-19 above.

[2] One of the few notable exceptions was J. M. Keynes who, in his *Tract on Monetary Reform* (1923), expounded a comprehensive alternative scheme for a managed currency with a stable internal price level as its first objective. For the generally hostile reception of this scheme see R. F. Harrod, *The Life of John Maynard Keynes* (1951), pp. 339-45.

[3] Pigou, *op. cit.*, pp. 148-51; Morgan, *op. cit.*, pp. 210-15 and 360-7. Whether British prices had been completely brought back into line with American prices is a matter of some controversy. Keynes maintained that the restoration of the prewar parity meant a 10 per cent over-valuation of sterling but most price figures would indicate that he was exaggerating. The real trouble was that, even with the same relative prices, British ability to sell abroad had declined.

Thus by 1925 and to a considerable extent as early as 1922, in the supreme regulating field of finance, the government had deliberately reduced its activity and restored the power of a private institution. But it would be misleading to conclude that the scope and influence of governmental financial policy were no greater than before 1914. Co-operation between the Bank of England and the Treasury, in the settlement both of broad lines of policy and of many matters of detail, had to be greater than ever. Despite the reduction of the floating debt and the partial revival of the commercial bill market, Treasury bills remained much the most abundant securities in the short-term money market. While they were particularly useful to the Bank in enabling it to extend its open-market operations and thereby to strengthen its control of the market, their volume and the method of issuing them gave the Treasury scope for manœuvre, which needed to be co-ordinated with the Bank's actions. The introduction and operation of the gold standard depended partly on international agreement and some mutual international financial assistance, which had to have the authority of governments, even if most of it was delegated to their central banks.[1] That the leading protagonist should have been the Governor of the Bank of England was doubtless due to the exceptional personality of Montagu Norman, who was appointed in 1920 and, instead of occupying the office only for the customary two years, retained it until 1944.[2] There is no doubt that his views were a most powerful influence on the shaping of government policy, but in his many activities at international conferences he was furthering government and not only Bank of England policy.

Moreover, the Bank's ability to make the gold standard an effective instrument was, to some extent, dependent on other aspects of government policy. The expenditure of the government was large enough for fiscal policy to have a significant effect on the level of incomes and therefore on the level of prices and the state of the money market, thus reinforcing or hampering the activities of the Bank. In the years when the return to the gold standard was being prepared, the large surpluses of government revenue over expenditure did much to strengthen the deflationary effect of high interest rates, though they

[1] The restoration of gold as an international currency standard was proclaimed as the main aim of policy by international conferences at Brussels in 1920 and Genoa in 1922.

[2] For a detailed account of his career and influence see H. Clay, *Lord Norman* (1957).

appear to have been achieved mainly by accident, as a result of faulty estimating, rather than by deliberate policy.[1] From 1925 to 1929 fiscal policy had the opposite effect. It was soon evident that, at the restored gold parity, Britain could not currently earn a big enough international surplus to enable it to carry on its financial business securely; there was a need for a further lowering of prices. But while the Bank of England sought to attract more foreign money by means of high interest rates, which incidentally helped to restrain demand and keep down prices, fiscal policy was slightly inflationary. Repeatedly the budget was balanced (on paper) only with the aid of windfall items which were book-keeping entries rather than true revenue. And the Unemployment Insurance Fund, a new and substantial addition to the government's extra-budgetary accounts, was allowed to run into a deficit,[2] doubtless for the sake of political and social quietude. In all this there were signs that the government was not just leaving finance to the bankers for them to manage in accordance with narrowly financial criteria, though it was not presenting more than occasional, uncoordinated fragments of an alternative approach.

Other aspects of public policy in the nineteen-twenties give a clearer impression of a somewhat enlarged rôle in economic affairs. Most striking was the permanent increase in the proportion of the national income which was spent by public authorities. From 1920 public expenditure (i.e. the current expenditure of the central government, the insurance funds and local authorities, and the gross expenditure on current account of public trading services) settled down at just over 30 per cent of the national income, instead of the 15 or 16 per cent which had prevailed until 1914.[3] Initially, the biggest increase was in the service of the national debt, an item which in the early 'twenties was fourteen times as much as in 1913[4] and could not quickly be reduced. Indeed, the anxiety to cut down the floating debt and put more of the debt on a longer-term basis meant that the cost of debt service actually increased a little and, as prices fell, the real burden of it became heavier. By 1925-26, 46 per cent of the central government's budget expenditure went on debt service, which came to 7 or 8 per cent of the national income.[5] This, of

---

[1] Morgan, *op. cit.*, pp. 95-106.
[2] Hicks, *British Public Finances 1880-1952*, p. 186.   [3] *Ibid.*, pp. 11-12.
[4] Ursula K. Hicks, *The Finance of British Government 1920-1936* (1938), p. 380.
[5] Morgan, *op. cit.*, p. 98; Hicks, *British Public Finances*, p. 177.

course, did not involve any appreciable claim by the government on the productive resources of the nation but was only a large transfer of income from one section of the community to another—to some extent even a transfer from one pocket to another of the same individuals. It did, however, make taxation a good deal more burdensome and thus stimulated a demand for the reduction of other items of government expenditure. This search for economy reached almost panic proportions in the slump of 1921 when, in accordance with the familiar belief that the government must set the example of retrenchment in the face of hard times, a committee under Sir Eric Geddes (a former Minister of Transport) was set up to recommend specific reductions in the government's estimates. The committee proposed cuts so large and so fatuously indiscriminate that they startled even the government that had asked for them—they ranged from the abolition of the Ministry of Transport and drastic reductions in the size of the armed forces to the refusal of school entry to children under 6 and lower salaries for teachers and policemen. Fortunately the proposals were never carried out in full, though they were a factor in the rapid reduction of central government expenditure in the early 'twenties, which restricted the development of some government activities.[1]

Nevertheless, there were important examples of expanded public activities, especially in the social services. Schemes of compulsory insurance were extended: after the passage of the Unemployment Insurance Act of 1920 over 11 million people were insured against unemployment—five times as many as in 1914. In 1921 the period for which benefit could be drawn was lengthened and small allowances were introduced for the dependants of unemployed persons; inevitably, with the prevalence of a higher level of unemployment, expenditure on the insurance schemes rose considerably. Pensions also absorbed much more expenditure because of provision for war casualties; and in 1925 the tentative beginning of 1908 was greatly extended when a government scheme of contributory pensions (10s. per week after reaching the age of 65) was introduced for insured workers. And despite the demands of these recent services, some of those established earlier were able to expand, though not so much as they might have done but for the Geddes cuts. In 1923, for instance, 2·2 per cent of the national income was devoted to public education, as compared with 1·1 per cent in 1910; the postwar years

[1] Hirst, *The Consequences of the War to Great Britain*, pp. 168-89.

saw the first really strong effort to build up a public system of secondary education.[1] Housing also became a much larger element of public policy. Various schemes of financial assistance by the central government to both private builders and local authorities followed each other from 1919 onwards and local authorities began to provide a high proportion of the new houses: over 40 per cent in 1928, when the local authority output exceeded 100,000 houses.[2]

This increased activity in house-building had a special economic significance because, unlike most of the other items of growing public expenditure, it involved large demands on productive resources and because it increased the share of public authorities in total national investment. There were one or two other developments which had a similar effect, notably the further expansion of local authority trading services. The outstanding changes in this field were the entry of more municipalities into the business of electricity supply, the increase in the scale of some of the earlier public electricity undertakings, and the rapid growth of municipal bus services. In 1920, 48 local authorities operated 649 buses and carried 74 million passengers; in the financial year 1929-30, 100 local authorities operated 4,737 buses and carried 823 million passengers. Despite these innovations, however, the growth of expenditure on public trading services as a whole was gradual rather than spectacular and was much slower than that on the social services.[3] Other public expenditure with a predominantly economic, rather than social, purpose was on a smaller scale and made fewer calls on productive resources. Although numerous new commitments were accepted, the common feature of most of them was the use of public funds in fairly small amounts to assist private activities in specified and very limited ways or to relieve them of particular burdens. Grants to assist industries to establish co-operative research associations,[4]

[1] Hicks, *op. cit.*, pp. 30-44; Mowat, *Britain Between the Wars*, pp. 45-6, 127-9 and 206-9. For changes in social insurance, numbers insured and rates of benefit and contribution see *Social Insurance and Allied Services: a report by Sir William Beveridge* (P.P. 1942-43, VI), pp. 211-17.

[2] For details of the various subsidy schemes and of the number of houses built see Marian Bowley, *Housing and the State 1919-1944* (1945), pp. 16-23, 36-42, 48 and 271; see also Hicks, *op. cit.*, pp. 46-9.

[3] For annual figures of the expenditure of local authority trading services and of the other major items of economic expenditure, i.e. the cost of road maintenance and of the post office, see Hicks, *The Finance of British Government*, p. 381.

[4] For details of these see Balfour Committee, *Factors in Industrial and Commercial Efficiency*, pp. 308-13 and 333-4.

the Trade Facilities scheme operating between 1921 and 1927, under which the Treasury could guarantee loans raised privately for approved purposes by business undertakings, and a new system of export credit guarantees, operated by the Board of Trade from 1921, were on a small scale and cost little.[1] After 1920, when the war economy had been dismantled, there were very few direct government subsidies to business, though there were small regular payments to assist sugar beet production and civil aviation. The biggest item was, in effect, an increase in the incomes of producers generally, through the de-rating provisions applied in 1929. Agricultural land and farm buildings (which previously had been relieved of half their rates) ceased to pay rates at all, and industrial property and the railways were relieved of three-quarters of their liability for rates, subject to the condition that the saving to the railways must be passed on to the iron and coal industries in the form of lower freight charges. The loss of revenue to local authorities was made good by a new block grant from the central government.[2]

Thus, although the new level at which public expenditure settled down in the nineteen-twenties appeared to many to be alarmingly high, public authorities encroached very little on the accepted fields of private enterprise and increased only slightly their importance as investors. Most of the increased expenditure consisted of transfer payments from one section of the community to another. The expansion of the rôle of public policy came from a greater interference with the level of private incomes and the conditions on which they could be obtained. As Neville Chamberlain, then Minister of Health and the chief architect of new social legislation, put it in 1925, 'Our policy is to use the great resources of the state, not for the distribution of an indiscriminate largesse, but to help those who have the will and desire to raise themselves to higher and better things'.[3] To compensate for accidental inequalities and disabilities, and to supplement and regulate, rather than to replace, existing private activities was the essence of such a policy. It was, however, a very incomplete, piecemeal policy, somewhat arbitrary and inconsistent in its choice of those who were to be helped by the resources of the state.

[1] The various measures of financial assistance to industry and trade are set out in ibid., pp. 384-97.

[2] Hicks, British Public Finances, pp. 57-8 and 123.

[3] Quoted in Mowat, op. cit. p. 338.

In one respect the incompleteness of regulation was a most un-welcome frustration to which many politicians submitted reluctantly. A large section of the Conservative Party wanted a protective tariff (generally with the addition of a system of imperial preference) and believed it was the only cure for the difficulties of trade. But only a few steps were taken towards it. The McKenna duties of 1915[1] were retained after the war, although the main reason for their imposition—a shortage of shipping space—had disappeared, and from 1919 an element of imperial preference was incorporated in them. They were supplemented by the Safeguarding of Industries Act, passed in 1921. This measure imposed duties of 33⅓ per cent *ad valorem* on the products of a few 'key industries' alleged to be vital for national security. Optical glass and instruments, radio valves, hosiery latch needles, various fine chemicals, and compounds of thorium, cerium and other rare earth metals were among the things affected. These duties were originally imposed for five years but were subsequently renewed. The same act also permitted the imposition of similar duties as protection against imports which had been cheapened by currency depreciation or were being dumped at prices below cost of production, and which were damaging employment in British industry. Very little action was taken under these provisions, but in 1923 the Conservatives fought an election on the proposal to introduce general tariff protection, which the Labour as well as the Liberal Party decided to oppose. The electorate rejected protection and before the next election, in 1924, the Conservatives, who then returned to office, undertook not to introduce a general tariff. Consequently, there were few changes in commercial policy. The McKenna duties, which the Labour government of 1924 had repealed, were restored in 1925 and were subsequently extended to cover commercial motor vehicles and tyres. A few additions were made to the list of products subject to 'safeguarding' duties, and in 1925, as an isolated innovation, duties were imposed on silk and rayon and goods made from these materials.[2] Not until 1930, when another Labour government was in office and trade was shrinking, was pressure for a general tariff strongly renewed.

The other main element in commercial policy was an attempt to foster international agreement for the reduction of trade barriers. This was a necessary supplement to the restoration of the international gold standard if the hoped-for return of the liberal

[1] See pp. 270-1 above. [2] Balfour Committee, *op. cit.*, pp. 398-415 and 435-52.

pre-1914 trading system was to be achieved, though it was clearly difficult to reconcile with attempts to secure tariff protection for Britain. There was, however, no thought of giving Britain any more drastic protection than had been common to nearly all other countries before 1914, whereas the movement to reduce international barriers was aimed at the more numerous and more stringent duties and prohibitions that had grown up since then. In any case, when outside opinion seemed most favourable to more liberal policies, in the later 'twenties, the British drift towards protection was held in check. But hardly anything was accomplished. The World Economic Conference which met in Geneva in 1927 passed unanimous resolutions in favour of greater liberty of trade, which it distinguished from 'free trade'; lesser conferences discussed particular measures for liberalizing some sections of trade; and early in 1930 a British proposal for a customs truce came up for international discussion. But existing barriers to international trade were little changed, though the previous upward trend of customs duties was halted, and by 1930 trade was contracting so fast that every country began to think of shoring up its commercial defences and all hopes of more liberal policies disappeared.[1]

The tentative and frustrated character of British commercial policy in the nineteen-twenties was not altogether unrepresentative of public policy more generally, which often seemed to be oscillating between the opposite horns of a dilemma and to be handicapped by too limited views of both what was necessary and what was possible. There was a recognition that the number of things which were specially conducive to the well-being of society, yet difficult for individuals to accomplish, was larger than used to be believed, and there was a willingness to use public authority to fill the gap; but the limits were fairly strict. There was a realization that economic affairs were so disturbed that they needed some sort of positive action to improve them; but it was at odds with the belief that the best sort of management was that which would restore an economic system as nearly self-regulating as possible. There was an awareness that the conditions in which such a system would have to work were new, yet there was reluctance to release it from rules and customs which were adapted to different conditions and had therefore proved helpful in the past. When familiar remedies for difficulties could not be applied there was a disposition to wait for conditions to change rather

[1] League of Nations, *Ten Years of World Co-operation* (1930), pp. 196-205.

than try unfamiliar measures, and to justify this on the ground that if there had been any merit in the unfamiliar measures it would have been demonstrated long ago.

In the expansion of social policy there was some vigour and consistency, though the diversion of so much revenue to debt service (which had effects directly opposed to those of much of the social legislation) restricted the financial resources available for social measures. But in economic, and especially financial, policy the inconsistencies and the defensive approach were evident. They showed in the shortage of direct measures to encourage new activities in trade and industry; perhaps most clearly in the strong and, in most cases, unreasoning hostility to proposals of public works schemes for the creation of employment, such as Lloyd George brought into political prominence in 1929.[1] They showed, too, in the credit policies which were pursued. There were curious anomalies in the operation of the gold standard. For instance, although gold coins were never restored as the circulating medium at home, when the Treasury note issue was merged in that of the Bank of England in 1928 the Bank was still restricted to a fiduciary issue (£260 million) well below the maximum note issue needed by trade and had to keep gold against the remainder of the note issue. Thus, although the Bank's international obligations were larger (and subject to sharper fluctuations) than before, the greater part of its gold reserve was often not available for international purposes; yet it was serving no real domestic function.[2] Still more striking was the failure of the gold standard to recover the semi-automatic character which had been one of its most welcome characteristics. Though the safety of Britain's international financial position was still the primary guide to credit policy, the difficulties of trade, industry and employment at home were so serious that the Bank could not ignore the repercussions of its measures on them, even if the government had not been always ready to remind it. In 1927, for instance, Norman was telling the Governor of the Bank of France that, though other considerations might indicate that bank rate should be raised, 'he thinks seriously that he could not do it at present without provoking a riot'.[3] And in

---

[1] Harrod, *op. cit.*, pp. 395-6. Not all the hostility was unreasoning. Sir Richard Hopkins presented a very cogent defence of the Treasury's opposition. (*Ibid.*, pp. 420-3.)

[2] *Ibid.*, p. 394; Committee on Finance and Industry (Macmillan Committee), *Report* (P.P. 1930-31, XIII), pp. 28-9 and 137-43.

[3] Clay, *op. cit.*, pp. 230-1.

1928 and 1929 the Bank was finding it desirable to insulate the supply of credit at home as far as possible from the effects of variations in the level of the exchange reserves. In order to do this it met any strain on the exchange, as far as it could, by selling dollar securities (deliberately accumulated in spells when financial conditions were easy) instead of parting with gold, and it immediately used the proceeds of the sales to buy sterling securities, so that no money was taken off the market.[1] But even so, credit policy appeared to fall between two stools. Interest rates had to remain fairly high to ease the strain on the exchange and the best that could be done for the supply of credit at home was to keep it fairly stable, though the lagging revival of industry and trade and the loss involved in the unemployment of productive resources made plain the need for credit expansion.[2] Something of the international advantages of the gold standard was sacrificed without the difficulties at home being thereby resolved.[3]

This is not to say that all the economic policy of the nineteen-twenties was confused and ineffective. At home, a large part of the people was enabled to have much greater economic security than before, at small cost to itself, and substantial new public contributions were made to well-being. Abroad, whatever the inconsistencies of financial policy, the re-establishment of an orderly institutional framework for trade and finance (even though it was a precarious one) was a most important achievement, in which Britain had an outstanding share. But such things did not directly build up economic activity nor did they do nearly as much to release creative enterprise as had been hoped. Indeed, the manner in which some of them were achieved, especially the financial restrictions they involved, had the opposite effect. Yet the pressures to try to achieve more by economic policy were not strong. Britain remained well on the right side of solvency. The economic difficulties of the time did not hit a

---

[1] Clay, *op. cit.*, p. 255. *Cf.* also W. A. Brown, jr., *The International Gold Standard Reinterpreted 1914-1934* (1940), p. 684: 'The whole course of Bank of England credit policy was designed to prevent domestic currency movements and international gold flows from influencing directly the balances of banks at the Bank of England.'

[2] *Macmillan Report*, pp. 99-102 (esp. paras. 229-30).

[3] For an elaborate account of the management of the restored gold standard in Britain see Brown, *op. cit.*, chap. 19, esp. pp. 672-730. The controlling circumstances are summarized thus: 'Great Britain's position as a gold standard country had to be maintained by unorthodox methods pending a reduction in her costs and a redistribution of her productive powers. These methods involved the artificial creation of a stable credit base.' (*Ibid.*, p. 706.)

substantial proportion of people hard enough for the failure to disperse them to become politically dangerous. And few of the influential or the expert had anything better to suggest. Their attitude was generally that, with minor exceptions, British policy was doing as well as it could in the adverse conditions that were the aftermath of a great war.

After 1930 public policy was bound to be somewhat different because the pressures for a change became much greater. In 1929 most of the world fell into the worst economic depression ever experienced, which for more than three years continued to deepen. Although Britain was not so hard hit as many other countries, the deterioration in its trade and employment was serious enough for it to be politically inexpedient not to take new steps in search of a remedy. In addition, one eventual consequence of the worldwide depression was to bring about a crisis in Britain's international financial position in 1931, when in two months from mid-July there was an external drain of over £200 million from the London money market.[1] Since the safety of the international financial position was the main objective of financial policy, no more convincing evidence of the inadequacy of previous policy could have been forthcoming, and drastic new measures were unavoidable. Moreover, this was happening at a time when positive proposals for action were being pressed on the government not only in Parliament and the press, where tariffs and imperial preference were the familiar panaceas most advocated, but also by bodies from which the government was deliberately seeking advice.

The most noteworthy of these bodies were the Committee on Finance and Industry (with Lord Macmillan, a well-known lawyer, as chairman), which had been appointed by the Treasury in 1929, and the Committee on National Expenditure, under the chairmanship of Sir George May, a former secretary of the Prudential Assurance Company. The latter was set up early in 1931 as a sequel to a Liberal motion in the House of Commons, calling for an independent review of government expenditure. Both committees reported in the summer of 1931. Of the two reports that of the Macmillan Committee, much influenced by the then unorthodox economic views of Keynes, one of its members, was the more searching, intelligent and lasting in its influence. But that of the May Committee, which was less technical, had far more immediate impact.[2] Nevertheless, there were several

[1] Hodson, *Slump and Recovery*, p. 79.   [2] Clay, *op. cit.*, p. 389.

immediately significant features of the Macmillan report. In the first place, by making very clear the difficulties of the British trading position in the 'twenties and the failure of financial policy to overcome them, it may have strengthened the doubts of some foreign financiers about the safety of holding sterling. In the second place, it proposed new objectives and methods of policy. It insisted that the maintenance of the maximum output and employment at home must be one of the objectives of credit policy, along with international considerations.[1] It emphasized, too, that Britain must have a managed, not an automatic, monetary system, though it accepted continued adherence to the gold standard.[2] And six of its fourteen members made additional proposals for an expansion of domestic credit, a programme of public works and, as a means of improving the balance of payments, the adoption of a revenue tariff.[3]

The May report was written from a very different standpoint. Though less sweeping and indiscriminate than the Geddes reports of 1921 and 1922, it had much in common with them. It asserted that political and financial conditions were always biased in favour of expenditure, and indicated that the outcome was a situation in which the government was living beyond its means and was faced immediately and for an indefinite time ahead by the prospect of a large budget deficit. The remedy was retrenchment and a balanced budget.[4] Detailed proposals were made for an immediate saving of £96 million in government expenditure. Two-thirds of this were to be at the expense of the Unemployment Insurance Fund, through an increase of contributions and a reduction of benefits, and most of the rest was to come from reductions on education (including a 20 per cent cut in teachers' salaries) and on road construction and maintenance.[5] There were also more general proposals designed to limit public commitments in the years ahead, since (as the report emphasized in heavy type) 'some further action is needed if retrenchment is not soon to give way once more to expansion'.[6] The report presented an

[1] *Macmillan Report*, pp. 119 and 132.

[2] *Ibid.*, pp. 108-10 and 118-20. The trade union members, Ernest Bevin and Sir R. Allen, suggested that it might become impossible to remain on the gold standard. (*Ibid.*, p. 240.)

[3] *Ibid.*, pp. 190-210. The signatories to these additional proposals included such influential figures as Bevin, Keynes and McKenna, though Bevin, in a reservation, treated a tariff as, at best, the lesser evil in an unpleasant choice.

[4] Committee on National Expenditure (May Committee), *Report* (P.P. 1930-31, XVI), chap. I.

[5] *Ibid.*, pp. 215-18.   [6] *Ibid.*, p. 222.

overdrawn picture of the existing financial position; its diagnosis of the causes underlying it was inaccurate; and many of its proposals (including the biggest of them) were not only harsh but were likely to make the economic situation worse, not better. But it was believed and was regarded, even by influential members of the Labour government, as a guide to salvation; and little attention was paid to the minority report presented by the trade union members of the committee, who maintained, with much justification, that deflation had done far more than public extravagance to bring things to their present pass.[1] Foreigners assumed from the report that Britain was on the edge of financial disaster, and its publication therefore helped to prolong the drain of sterling, which had begun primarily because of the need of foreign governments and money markets to call in their liquid assets to meet urgent claims upon them. The public, at home and abroad, was persuaded of the 'unsoundness' of the Labour government; and that government, faced by a loss of confidence and suggestions for economies which some of its members believed were indispensable and some believed were a betrayal of its principles, became divided and ineffectual and resigned office three weeks after the publication of the report.[2]

Subsequent policy was the work of the 'National', overwhelmingly Conservative, government, which soon obtained such a huge parliamentary majority that it could be little influenced by opposition. The changes in policy were very much determined by the conditions and ideas prevalent in 1931, though they were also affected by the proposals popular with many Conservatives in the previous decade but not then politically expedient. In general, policy conformed to the orthodox restraint which characterized the May report, but circumstances led to some limited innovations which were gradually developed rather more in the expansionist spirit of the Macmillan Committee. In September 1931 the new government introduced most of the cuts suggested by the May report, though many of them were not applied in full, and thereby produced a balanced budget. Thus the growth of the social and economic services of government was checked. But this was not a permanent result. Trade and public revenue improved and other savings in public expenditure were achieved, and these gains were applied in 1934 and 1935 to the

---

[1] *Ibid.*, pp. 227-8 and 270.
[2] For a succinct narrative of the events of these weeks see Mowat, *op. cit.*, pp. 381-93.

restoration of the cuts imposed in 1931. Social and economic expenditure continued gradually to increase and the economies enforced in the early 'thirties appear as no more than a brief interruption in the long-term trend.

The departures from orthodoxy were associated with the sudden abandonment of the gold standard in September 1931. This was an almost unavoidable act, since Britain, though quite solvent as an international banker, did not have the abnormally high liquid reserves that were needed in 1931 and was unable to continue borrowing them as, to a limited extent, it had been doing in the summer of that year.[1] But though the act was caused by temporary conditions, it had important lasting results. The most obvious immediate consequence was that the value of sterling depreciated and thus helped exports by lowering their prices. But this was of no permanent significance, since other currencies were depreciating, and any relative advantage to Britain was wiped out by the devaluation of the dollar in 1933-4.[2] The outstanding permanent changes were that, in future, exchange stability must depend on techniques of deliberate monetary management, that it was practicable to separate the movements of the domestic and international reserves much more completely from each other, and that (when the speculative drain on sterling had ceased) it was no longer necessary to defend the level of the reserves by high interest rates.

The regulation of the state of the exchange depended a good deal on the co-ordination of policies among different countries, especially those of the sterling *bloc*, which comprised practically the whole of the British Commonwealth and a few countries outside. In the course of the 'thirties the international earnings of all these were, in effect, pooled in London and therefore strengthened the capacity of any member to tide over temporary fluctuations. Regulation also depended on new institutions, notably the Exchange Equalisation Fund, which the Treasury established in 1932 with assets consisting mainly of £150 million in Treasury bills and small amounts of foreign currency and gold; its supply of Treasury bills was augmented in 1933 and 1937. The purpose of the Fund was to operate in the gold and foreign exchange markets in order to offset speculative dealings in sterling and the effects of international capital movements which did not arise from ordinary commercial dealings. Within the limits imposed by the amount of its assets it could keep the exchange value of

[1] Hodson, *op. cit.*, pp. 71-9.   [2] *Ibid.*, pp. 214-28.

sterling very close to any selected level, with only limited repercussions on the reserves of the Bank of England and it could conduct its operations with much less publicity than the Bank.[1] In practice, it kept the exchange very steady down to 1939 and, by absorbing an increasing influx of foreign money, probably prevented an appreciation of sterling which would have hampered exports.

This achievement also owed something to the maintenance of the cheap money policy, adopted in 1932, partly to discourage the heavy inflow of foreign money, which was then becoming evident, and partly as a means of lowering government expenditure without causing unrest, as well as incidentally stimulating employment.[2] As long as there was a crisis of confidence in sterling, high interest rates were maintained to try to overcome it. But by June 1932 confidence had been completely restored and the borrowings of the previous year had been repaid. Bank rate, which had first been lowered in February, was brought down to 2 per cent and was kept unchanged until the outbreak of war in 1939.

Several important consequences flowed from this decision. It became possible to lower the interest paid on a large part of the national debt. The cost of debt service, which had been £355 million in 1929 was down to £224 million in 1935,[3] and thus the expansion of social and economic services could be resumed without any increase in the burden of taxation. In the private sphere, there was a lowering of costs in those activities, such as housing, in which capital charges were a substantial element in total costs; and investment in many types of business was made to look more attractive by comparison with the low yield on government securities. Finally, the cessation of changes in Bank rate necessitated the adoption of new methods of credit regulation. Even in the 'twenties, Bank rate changes were probably less influential than the Bank's operations in the open market, and the latter continued to be important. But the outstanding change in the 'thirties was the passing of the main controlling power from the Bank to the Treasury, through the manipulation of the public debt. While this was possible because the Treasury was learning to exploit the dominant position in the money market which it had had since the First World War, the transition was made all the

---

[1] See the two articles on 'The British Exchange Equalisation Fund' by F. W Paish in *Economica*, New Series, II (1935), 61-9 and III (1936), 79-81.

[2] E. Nevin, *The Mechanism of Cheap Money. A study of British monetary policy 1931-1939* (1955), pp. 57-8.

[3] Hicks, *The Finance of British Government*, p. 380.

easier by a further great reduction in the supply of commercial bills in the market as a result of the shrinking of international trade and the limitation of multilateral payments. The government had a complete range of investments, from the shortest to the longest term, to offer to the market. It could supply them in the amounts which the market was willing to absorb at very low rates of interest. If it had more on issue than this, it could hold the excess off the market to a more convenient time by using the temporarily unemployed balances of government departments and the Exchange Equalisation Fund to take up the excess. If there was still difficulty in getting the market to lend enough (which there seldom was to any serious degree, because of the shortage of alternative investments) it could be made more liquid without any immediate risk of adverse repercussions on the exchange position. In these ways it proved possible to keep the rate of interest on Treasury bills well below 1 per cent from 1933 onwards.[1] Except in 1932 and at times when it was preparing to convert substantial amounts of long-term stock to lower rates, the Treasury confined its manipulations to short-term securities and did not seek directly to control long-term rates.[2] But the influence of the very low short-term rates was bound to affect all classes of securities to a considerable, though varying, extent. Long-term rates did, in fact, slowly rise after 1935, without interference by the Treasury, but despite this the period from 1932 onward remained a time of cheap money for the whole economy.

The cheap money policy was the only large new stimulus to economic activity at home which the government provided directly. Though more was beginning to be understood about the way in which budget deficits could be used to assist recovery and about the repercussions of public works on the rest of the economy, and though several other countries were applying this knowledge to new experiments in public policy,[3] the British government preferred to stick to the older orthodoxy, and thereby helped to restore confidence within the private business community. Any influence from the timing of public works and deficit finance was small and accidental. At the bottom of the depression, in 1932, there was a small budget deficit as

---

[1] For summary accounts of the experience gained in maintaining cheap money and of some of the techniques used, see R. S. Sayers, *Financial Policy 1939-1945* (1956), pp. 146-52 and Hicks, *British Public Finances*, pp. 186-91.

[2] Sayers, *op. cit.*, p. 150.

[3] For comparative information on this point see Lewis, *Economic Survey 1919-39*, part II.

a result of inaccurate estimating, and some of the capital schemes already begun by local authorities did not peter out until recovery had begun. From 1935 the government's rearmament schemes were also assisting industrial expansion.[1] But, in general, the government relied on the renewal of confidence among private businessmen for the growth of new enterprise.

More comprehensive efforts were made to provide industry with better market prospects by substituting protection for free trade. An emergency tariff on non-essential imports was imposed in the autumn of 1931, and in 1932 the Import Duties Act established the framework of a permanent system. It imposed a general 10 per cent tariff on imports except for some foodstuffs and raw materials, and set up an Import Duties Advisory Committee (with Sir George May as chairman) which was empowered, without further legislation, to impose a tariff of not more than $33\frac{1}{3}$ per cent in favour of any industry that applied for it, provided the committee was satisfied that this would be in the 'national interest'. In fact, by 1935 the committee had recommended tariffs covering nearly all industry. Since, however, food and raw materials formed a large proportion of British imports, the position was that about a quarter of the total still came in duty-free and another quarter paid not more than 20 per cent duty.[2]

An attempt was also made to use the protective system as a bargaining counter to secure concessions which would promote trade in particular channels. The largest arrangement of this kind was that providing for imperial preference. A series of agreements was negotiated among the self-governing countries of the Commonwealth at Ottawa in 1932, but instead of introducing mutual tariff concessions, as Britain had hoped, they generally provided discrimination by increasing the duties on non-Empire goods.[3] The principle of imperial preference was also applied to the colonial empire, except for Aden and Gibraltar, which were engaged almost entirely in transit trade, and most of the mandated territories, where discrimination of this kind was forbidden by the mandates. There were also various bilateral trade treaties with countries outside the Empire, with provisions intended to bring British exports and imports to and

---

[1] The government's fixed capital investment in rearmament rose from £4·8 mn. in the financial year 1936-37 to £28·9 mn. in 1938-39. (Ashworth, *Contracts and Finance*, p. 252.)

[2] F. C. Benham, *Great Britain Under Protection* (1941), pp. 25-45.

[3] *Ibid.*, pp. 90-109; Hodson, *op. cit.*, pp. 165-70.

from them more nearly into balance.[1] Many of these agreements prescribed import quotas for particular commodities, but though this was a common device in international trade at the time, the tariff in Britain was supplemented to only a small extent by quantitative import controls. The chief commodities affected were certain food-stuffs, such as potatoes, bacon, meat and sea-fish, the home market for which it was desired to reserve for home producers to as full an extent as they could supply.[2]

There is no sign that these protective devices improved British foreign trade as a whole at this time. What was gained by the promo-tion of trade in some channels appears to have been lost in the more intense competition resulting in the remainder.[3] But the existence of protection encouraged the government in some of its more limited, piecemeal efforts to promote the reorganization and increased efficiency of particular industries. The most perceptive comment of the May Committee had been that the difficulties of trade were not of a temporary kind, as had been assumed, and it had declared that their cure could be found only 'in a resolute grappling with the fundamental problems of each industry, in a frank recognition of world changes that are irreversible and in a re-alignment of our economic life to meet them'.[4] While industry was left to carry out the major part of this task for itself, the government joined in at many points with a mixture of coercion and small-scale financial assistance. Some public money was forthcoming as loans for specific capital undertakings, such as railway electrification schemes or the building of two huge ships for the North Atlantic passenger service, and some as direct subsidies. Most of the latter went to agriculture, which in 1938 was receiving £14,000,000 a year to encourage the production of cattle, milk and sugar-beet and to cheapen the price of fertilizers.[5] There were, however, small subsidies for some other activities. The sums involved were too small to make much difference to the budget, but large enough to mark a clear change of principle. Where govern-ment help was given by loan, subsidy or tariff protection, it could be made conditional on changes within the activities concerned. In this way systems of organized marketing and price regulation for various agricultural products were made less unpalatable to in-dividualistic producers and some measure of reorganization was

---

[1] Benham, *op. cit.*, pp. 128-48; League of Nations, *Trade Relations Between Free-Market and Controlled Economies* (1943), pp. 46-9.
[2] Benham, *op. cit.*, pp. 52-3 and 60-9.   [3] *Cf.* p. 350 above.
[4] *May Report*, p. 13.   [5] Hicks, *op. cit.*, p. 58.

demanded of such basic industries as coal, steel, cotton and shipping, without always being achieved as fully as was needed.[1] In a few cases the government-sponsored reorganization even went so far as to involve public ownership and operation. In 1933 all public passenger transport services in Greater London (except those of the main line railways) were taken over by a public board which was given a monopoly. In 1938 all coal royalties were compulsorily purchased by the government, which thus obtained ownership of all unmined coal. And in 1939 legislation was passed for the compulsory merging of the private airlines receiving subsidies into a new public body, British Overseas Airways Corporation, which began its formal existence in 1940.[2]

Another type of intervention was intended to improve not particular industries but the general economic condition of particular districts in which there was heavy concentration of declining industries.[3] In 1934 four areas were designated 'Special Areas' and £2,000,000 was granted for their assistance. Three years later a similar sum was added to permit concessions of rent, rates and taxes to firms which would settle in the areas, and this made it possible to establish trading estates with new factory premises.[4] But the scale of expenditure and activity was too small for the local level of employment to be greatly raised.

As a whole, home economic policy (apart from finance) was characterized in the nineteen-thirties by a multiplicity of measures which were small in scale and uncoordinated. In social provision (in the fields of education, health, insurance and pensions) there was steady expansion towards a comprehensive service, on which an annual amount of £10 per head was being spent by 1939. But economic policy proper was much more opportunist and less coherent. A problem tackled (often half-heartedly) in one industry was left untouched in another, and, apart from support for the lessening of competition, no common principles could be distinguished. There was a miscellany of expedients which led to some economic improvement but which were insufficient to bring about the restoration of Britain's competitive economic power in the world.

---

[1] See also pp. 365-6 above.   [2] Mowat, *op. cit.*, pp. 448-51.

[3] For accounts of the economic state of these districts see Ministry of Labour, *Reports of Investigations into the Industrial Conditions in certain Depressed Areas* (*P.P.* 1933-34, XIII).

[4] The Special Areas Trading Estates are described in Royal Commission on the Distribution of the Industrial Population, *Report* (*P.P.* 1939-40, IV), pp. 285-8.

Nevertheless, the changes in public policy were of great importance in the history of the interwar years. They reveal shifts in the location of economic power and influence, in the methods by which it was exercised, and in the objects which it secured. Because they undertook so many more tasks and spent so much more of the national income than before, public authorities greatly strengthened their economic position *vis-à-vis* private institutions and individuals, and came to have more influence on the general movement of the economy. And, among the public authorities, economic influence became more concentrated in the central government. Not only did it take over some of the controlling functions of such a half private, half public institution as the Bank of England, but it completely reversed the late Victorian and Edwardian trend towards ever more varied municipal activity. The public services that grew fastest were mostly those fairly recently established and operated by the central government, whereas some of those operated by local authorities, particularly those coming under the Poor Law, were reduced or were absorbed in some other centrally administered service. For most of the interwar period the local authorities were responsible for only about 35 per cent of public expenditure, whereas in the first decade of the century they had spent more than the central government;[1] and even of this reduced share much less was financed from local sources after 1929. Exchequer grants thereafter regularly met over 35 per cent of the cost of rate fund services.[2] Only in one respect did the local authorities retain and perhaps even enhance their importance in the public sector of the economy. Because of their trading services and their new activity in house-building, they undertook most of the public capital formation and by 1938 were probably responsible for about a quarter of the total national capital formation.[3]

Although economic power was more concentrated in the central government, it could not be said that it was consequently applied to narrower purposes or with less regard for the interests of the many. On the contrary, there was more conscious effort than before to make the government an instrument for mobilizing the financial

---

[1] Hicks, *op. cit.*, p. 108.   [2] *Ibid.*, p. 119.

[3] The amount of capital formation cannot be precisely determined. A figure of £206 mn. for gross capital formation by local authorities in 1938 is given in *ibid.*, pp. 20 and 65, where it is compared with £34 mn. by the central government and £530 mn. by private sources. But these figures are dubious. That for the central government is undoubtedly too low, the combined total of the three items is higher than that estimated by other writers, and an alternative figure of £151 mn. (compiled on a different basis) is given for local authorities in *ibid.*, p. 117.

resources of the nation and applying them to the needs of all, with less regard for individual capacity to pay. This was brought about by changes in both the objects of expenditure and the methods of raising revenue.

On the one hand there was the continued rise in the proportion of public outlay which was devoted to the social services,[1] the consumption of which was widely diffused over most of the nation and was lowest among the rich. On the other hand there was the raising of an increasing proportion of the public revenue by means of taxes on income and capital and a decreasing proportion by taxes on outlay, despite the large number of customs and excise duties imposed after 1931. Between 1913 and 1923 the proportion contributed by income and capital taxes rose from 35 per cent to 49 per cent and remained thereafter in the region of 44 per cent or rather more, and the standard rate of income tax, which before the First World War never exceeded 1s. 3d., was afterwards never less than 4s.[2] Moreover, outlay taxes fell a little less on articles of mass consumption and income tax became more progressive. The only group of outlay taxes with a rapidly growing yield was that concerned with motor vehicles and hydrocarbon oils, which produced £10 million in 1920 and £80 million in 1936.[3] The variety of income tax reliefs had gradually increased in the First World War—the income limit for entitlement to child allowance was twice raised and in 1917 allowances were introduced for a wife and for dependent relatives—and in 1920 the method of assessment was drastically altered. The old abatements were abolished and replaced by a personal allowance higher than the biggest of them. The separate rates of tax on earned and unearned income were done away with and an earned income allowance was introduced and was deducted from total income before the calculation of assessable income. The rate of tax payable was made to depend on the amount of income after the deduction of all reliefs and allowances, instead of on the total income as before. The reliefs were granted to all individuals, whatever the size of their income, but to reduce the benefit to the richer people, the exemption

---

[1] The proportion was well under 20 per cent in 1920 but always over one-third after 1929. (Hicks, *Finance of British Government*, p. 380.) The rise in the nine-teen-twenties was made possible by a fall in defence expenditure; that in the nine-teen-thirties by a fall in the cost of debt service.

[2] Hicks, *British Public Finances*, p. 75. These proportions exclude social in-surance contributions, which in the nineteen-thirties were around £90 mn. a year, when total public outlay was of the order of £1,300 mn.

[3] Hicks, *Finance of British Government*, p. 384.

o

limit for super-tax was lowered to £2,000 and the rates of super-tax were increased.[1] The general effect of these changes was that married persons with families paid less up to some fairly high level of income (£8,000 if they had three children), that single persons (whose liability was nil if they earned under £150) paid less if their incomes were between £150 and £350 or between £2,500 and £5,000, and that the rest paid more.[2] Income tax, which was such an important contribution to revenue, was very much a minority tax. In 1938, when 20 million people were employed, there were less than 4 million income-tax payers, of whom under 1 million were weekly wage-carners.[3]

These features of revenue and expenditure showed that the power of the government and the wealth of the nation were being deliberately applied, as never before, to the social benefit of the weekly wage-earners. Despite the recent growth of social services, this largest section of the population was still a net contributor to public revenue in 1913. But it has been estimated that, in the form of direct transfer payments or of social services the cost of which was borne by other people, it was a net recipient of about £80 million in the financial year 1925-26 and £100 million or rather more in 1935-36.[4]

Even in 1938 the rôle of the government in economic and social affairs remained more that of a regulator than an entrepreneur, though the balance had changed a good deal since 1921. But here was evidence of the adaptation of public finance clearly and persistently to new political and social objectives. The adaptation to strictly economic objectives was much less clear and successful, at first because the place of government in the achievement of economic advance was under-estimated, and later because the relation between means and ends in some fundamental sections of public economic policy was very imperfectly understood. The government had long been exerting a greater economic influence than it realized and in the nineteen-thirties it was made aware that its political security

---

[1] Committee on National Debt and Taxation, *Appendices to the Report* (1927), pp. 32-6.

[2] *Ibid.*, pp. 126-7.

[3] Hicks, *British Public Finances*, p. 77. The number of incomes on which tax was paid was rather higher than the number of income-tax payers, as some husbands were also paying tax on the incomes of their wives, who were included in the total of persons employed.

[4] Hicks, *Finance of British Government*, pp. 58-9. There are other estimates which are appreciably higher than this.

depended in part on the acceptance of greater responsibility for the national economy. Its response was to be seen in the many new measures that were introduced, its ignorance in its inability to adapt to the new purposes which it had taken up much of the influence it had always possessed, as well as in the unresolved conflicts between some of the new measures themselves. The result was a policy that mingled elements of revival and of frustration, and in so doing served as both the mirror and the shaper of the times.

CHAPTER SEVENTEEN

The Course and Outcome of Economic Change

YEAR by year accounts of the course of British business activity in the interwar period present, at first sight, a discouraging story. As before, there were irregular alternations of expansion and contraction, but whereas the recessions were sharp and deep, the spells of expansion were prone to interruption and halted far below their potential peaks. There were three major cycles during the period. The great burst of activity which began very soon after the armistice of 1918, when customers were restoring their depleted stocks, reached its height in 1920 and was followed by an equally rapid plunge into depression, which went exceptionally deep. Recovery began some time in 1922 and did not reach its maximum until 1929, but was repeatedly checked. Industrial activity declined in the early months of 1925 and the general strike and protracted coal strike of 1926 brought another reversal, followed by a brief stimulus to make up some of the arrears in 1927. Late in 1929 activity turned down again and the depression rapidly grew worse; never, in all probability, had there been a wider fluctuation within so short a time. The bottom of the depression was touched at the beginning of 1933 and a fairly steady upward movement followed until 1937. The recession which began later that year was rather sharp but not comparable in severity with those of 1920 and 1929 and it was halted in 1939 by the needs of war.[1]

In most respects British experience conformed to a general pattern affecting all countries that were appreciably involved in international trade and finance. Naturally there were differences in the timing of some of the turning points and in the extent of the minor fluctuations within the major cycles, especially in the earlier years, when currency and budgetary conditions varied greatly from one country to another. But the sequence of major cycles, with maxima in 1920, 1929 and 1937-38, was practically worldwide.[2] A much more significant

---

[1] Cf. the index of industrial activity in Beveridge, *Full Employment in a Free Society*, p. 313.

[2] Cf. Ohlin, *The Course and Phases of the World Economic Depression*, chap. III.

discrepancy in the British experience was in the intensity of the movements, as shown particularly in the level of unemployment. In the years just after the First World War the only statistics of unemployment were still those relating to trade union members. In 1920 the average percentage of trade union members unemployed fell to 2·5, which was as low as in almost any peacetime boom year of the recent past. But in 1922 it rose to 17·2, which was much higher than in any year since records were first kept. The occupational distribution of trade union members slightly exaggerated the comparison in that year but could not make it wholly misleading. From 1921 unemployment figures became available for the whole insured population of the United Kingdom and provided a striking comment on the incompleteness of revival. Only in 1927 did the annual average unemployment figure again fall below 10 per cent.[1] Even in a peak year of activity, such as 1929, it was 10·4 per cent and in the ensuing depression it exceeded 20 per cent in both 1931 and 1932. The best achievement of the 'thirties was a level of 10·8 per cent in 1937.[2] It appeared that the rate of unemployment in boom years in the interwar period was such as in the late nineteenth and early twentieth centuries had been known only in the blackest years of depression. Though experience varied, hardly any other country had so bad a record of unemployment as Britain during the revival of the 'twenties,[3] and the peculiarity of the British record is shown further by the way that trade and industrial production lagged behind the growth achieved elsewhere. After 1929, however, the position changed. Unemployment rates as bad as or worse than the British became common, and production in most industrial countries (except the U.S.S.R. and Japan) fell more during the depression and revived more slowly thereafter than it did in the United Kingdom.

Even deep depressions might not be too serious if they were superimposed on a sharply rising long-term trend. But, in general, this was not the case in the 'twenties and 'thirties. The volume of world trade grew only a little between 1914 and 1939,[4] and Britain's declining share showed itself in a downward trend of exports. The trend

---

[1] The trade union rate was only 9·1 per cent in 1924 but the rate among the insured population was 10·3 per cent. On the other hand in 1922 the rate among the insured (14·3 per cent) was below the trade union rate.

[2] Beveridge, *op. cit.*, p. 47.   [3] Ohlin, *op. cit.*, pp. 68-9.

[4] The average volume of world trade was 11·4 per cent higher in 1936-38 than in 1911-13, but the volume of world trade in manufactured goods was 3·6 per cent *lower* in the later period than the earlier. (Calculated from League of Nations, *Industrialisation and Foreign Trade*, p. 157.)

of manufacturing output in the world as a whole was, it is true, just as sharply upward as before 1914, but the prolongation of this trend beyond 1929 was mainly due to the rapid industrialization of the U.S.S.R., which had little effect on the markets of the rest of the world. Britain shared in the slower rate of industrial expansion that was common among the older industrial countries. Over the long period its achievement was not seriously inferior to that among the rest of these, but it was a little less than experience had made customary.

In important ways, then, the economic history of the interwar years suggests a slowing down in the rate of progress established earlier and a partial failure to cope with the problems involved in keeping the economic system adequately employed. Since these features, though very prominent in British experience, were also found in much of the world beside, it is obvious that they are not explicable solely in terms of British conditions and actions. The depressions of the time were international in origin as well as incidence and their exceptional severity was directly linked with the weakening of the influences sustaining a long-term trend of economic expansion, most of which were also of an international character. A comprehensive explanation of them would go far beyond the confines of a work on British economic history. But some of the factors which remained most influential year after year, making depressions worse and hampering recovery, were things in which Britain was specially interested. The most decisive shortcoming of the time was probably the failure to go far in carrying out that extensive change in international productive specialization which was called for by new demographic and technical conditions and by the effects of higher incomes on the state of consumers' demand.[1] Particularly important was the fact that many of the poorer primary producing countries were not becoming more efficient producers and better markets, a change hard to achieve without a continued outflow of capital such as had come in the recent past from Britain but was no longer strongly maintained anywhere.[2] Another most important and pervasive influence was the weakness of the institutions and organization of the international financial system, which led to its partial breakdown in 1931 without adequate replacement in the following years. This was something of which British governments and the Bank of England had been

[1] See the discussion of the conditions calling for such changes, pp. 305-13 above.
[2] See pp. 315-17 above.

vividly aware and which in the 'twenties they had striven hard to mend. Their lack of success resulted partly from errors of judgment in the formulation of policy, but still more from the unwillingness of all the chief interested countries (including Britain) to devise genuinely international institutions with functions which no one country could any longer perform unaided. Over other powerful sources of difficulty Britain had less influence. She had, for instance, little to do with the unfortunate distribution of American foreign investments or with the fantastic speculative pursuit of capital gains on the American stock markets, the collapse of which in 1929 did more than anything else to precipitate the depression[1] and to spread it rapidly by way of America's foreign debtors.[2]

But the individual peculiarities of British experience call for explanation in terms of Britain's own economic situation. The immediate source of her relatively poor showing before 1930 is very obvious. It was mainly the exceptional decline of the old staple industries, in nearly every case as a result of a heavy fall in exports, and the failure to develop much new industry to replace them. Cotton, coal, iron and steel, shipbuilding and some other branches of the heavy engineering industries accounted for practically all the increase in British unemployment throughout the interwar period. Their continued predominance down to 1930 was reflected in the slow growth of industrial production. Afterwards the greater emphasis on a variety of newer industries contributed to a much bigger increase in output, but as the productivity of labour was also rising appreciably this made quite a limited contribution towards the removal of unemployment; it only prevented it from being much worse than in the previous decade. Much of the decline in the older industries was an unavoidable result of general changes in world economic conditions and was the more severe because of the preponderance of poor agricultural countries among Britain's export markets. But the question arises: why was the adjustment to these conditions so belated and incomplete?

Several suggestions can be made in answer. There was the encouragement which the events of 1919 and 1920 gave to those who could not recognize that conditions had permanently changed.

---

[1] For a recent account of this episode, stressing its decisive influence, see J. K. Galbraith, *The Great Crash, 1929* (1955).

[2] For short accounts and analyses of the international economic problems of the period see Lewis, *Economic Survey 1919-1939*, Parts I and III, and W. Ashworth, *A Short History of the International Economy 1850-1950* (1952), chaps. VII and VIII.

One glorious year persuaded many people that the old industries were only beginning their best days and they responded by expanding the productive capacity of such industries as cotton and steel. It took years of hard experience to convince them that subsequent losses were the result of something more than a passing phase of ill luck. Then, too, there was the difficulty of obtaining the investment necessary to alter the pattern of industry. Part of the declining cotton industry was able to prop itself up with new capital because, years before, it had been financed by part-paid shares on which additional calls were now made. But new projects with better commercial prospects were often variously handicapped. The facilities of the new issue market were only gradually adapted to their needs. Interest rates were high, partly because of a heavy demand for loans in many countries, partly because of financial uncertainty, partly because of the difficulties inherent in Britain's chosen monetary policy. In particular, the moderately high returns obtainable on short-term securities may have discouraged long-term investment on promising but unproved productive schemes. Not until 1932 was there an appreciable reduction of these handicaps, and even then others of a different kind remained. The burden of surplus capacity which hampered the reorganization of the older industries was reduced, but the cutting out of unnecessary and inefficient establishments was not ruthless enough;[1] and the deliberate lessening of competition helped, in some parts of the economy though not in all, to prolong the obsolescent and leave less room for new enterprise.

Perhaps just as important as any of these factors were the experiences which made it possible to doubt whether much more economic adjustment was needed and which certainly diminished the sense of urgency. There is an element of paradox in the economic history of the interwar years. While the story of declining exports and heavy unemployment is undeniable, it is also possible to claim this period as one of rapid economic progress, with the great majority of people sharing in the advances. The total net national income at factor cost (i.e. excluding the outlay taxes in the prices of goods and services sold) has been estimated for 1939 at £5,234 million. If this figure and the corresponding amounts for earlier years are recalculated at constant prices (those of 1912-13) it appears that there had

[1] Much of the difficulty caused to the coal and cotton industries in the late nineteen-fifties by the survival of uneconomic capacity can be traced back to the failure to carry very far the schemes of reorganization applied to these industries in the nineteen-thirties.

been an increase of just over 40 per cent since 1914 (or since 1920, when real national income was much the same).[1] Average real income per head in the decade 1930-39 was 17·7 per cent higher than for the previous decade. For 1925-34 the increase above the preceding decade was 14·5 per cent.[2] There are many difficulties in the precise measurement of national income, especially for a period that saw great changes in the price level, which no one price index can represent with complete accuracy. But there is no reason to doubt the general order of magnitude of these figures. They are not quite so favourable as those of late Victorian times, but they indicate that the slow progress at the beginning of the twentieth century was again being surpassed.

There is no difficulty in reconciling this state of affairs with the weaknesses which showed in some aspects of the economy. Many of the conditions which, in the late nineteenth century, had begun to assist a more rapid growth of income still continued. The conditions of foreign investment, which had been so helpful then, were no longer very favourable, but, for the time being, this was offset by a great improvement in the terms of trade. Since imports formed so large a part of British consumption, the fact that they became relatively cheaper than exports in the 'twenties, and cheaper still in the 'thirties, was very important for the growth of income. Besides the large direct addition to the supply of goods, there was an indirect stimulus to home-produced income, as cheap raw materials probably helped the industrial revival of the 'thirties. Other important contributions came from the application of improvements in technology and organization, which were many and widespread and, after 1930, were prominent in the older as well as the newer industries. Suggestions are sometimes made that Britain at this time was lagging behind its foreign rivals in the discovery of new techniques. Even if this were wholly true (and it is apt to be exaggerated) the adoption of technical advances which originated abroad would nevertheless increase the efficiency of production at home. In fact, in the 'thirties the margin by which labour-productivity in Britain lagged behind that in Germany and the U.S.A. appears to have been reduced. In 1936 and 1937 the average productivity of labour in British manufacturing industry has been estimated as 20 per cent higher than in

[1] Calculated from Jefferys and Walters, *National Income and Expenditure of the U.K.*, pp. 9 and 40.
[2] *Ibid.*, p. 14.

1929.[1] Some further increase in output per head could also be attributed to the continued gradual rise in the proportion of people engaged in tertiary industries, i.e. such things as transport, distribution, the public services, the professions and entertainment. Productivity is generally higher in these (considered as a whole) than in manufacture or primary production, though this is not true of every separate tertiary industry.

All these factors together could be expected to produce a substantial rise in national income. On the other hand, heavier unemployment must tend to have the opposite effect. There are, however, some considerations which suggest that the strictly economic (as distinct from the social and moral) effects of the high unemployment figures may easily be over-estimated. The non-insured section of the population was much less subject to unemployment than the insured, to whom alone the official statistics referred. It may well be that the rate of unemployment for the entire working population was 2 per cent or more below the rate for the insured, with the margin tending gradually to widen. Another statistical difficulty arises when comparisons are attempted with earlier periods. The trade union figures of unemployment, which have to be used for lack of anything better before 1921, are much less comprehensive than those derived from the operation of unemployment insurance. The average recorded unemployment rate among the insured was 14·4 per cent for the period 1921-38; that among trade unionists was 4·8 per cent for the period 1883-1914. But Lord Beveridge, after a detailed examination of the differences in the coverage of the two series, concluded that, for a true comparison, the figure for the earlier period should probably be raised to 6 per cent, though he suggested that his emendation was subject to an appreciable margin of error in either direction.[2] Thus, although there was considerable loss from the less full employment of the available labour, the change was not quite as great as appears at first sight. And if comparison is made with periods further back in the nineteenth century, when casual labour and

---

[1] L. Rostas, 'Industrial Production, Productivity and Distribution in Britain, Germany and the United States' in *Econ. Journ.*, LIII (1943), 48-9.

[2] Beveridge, *op. cit.*, pp. 328-37. It appears to me that Lord Beveridge's figure of 6 per cent is more likely to be too low than too high. While his assessment of the T.U. figures is probably excellent for the immediate pre-1914 years, it does not seem to allow for the probability that earlier they understated the true position more drastically, because the non-unionists then included a lower proportion of people in secure jobs and a higher proportion of casual workers, existing in a state of chronic under-employment.

under-employment were widespread, it is probable that the proportionate loss of man-hours from involuntary causes, high as it was in
the interwar years, was lower than in, say, mid-Victorian times,
when notable economic progress was nevertheless achieved.[1] This,
of course, merely shows that a substantial rise of national income was
quite compatible with a high level of unemployment. It does not
contradict the plain fact that unemployment prevented the nation
from deriving the full benefit from the other factors favourable to a
rapid growth of income.

A consideration of the amount of employment rather than of unemployment brings to light another helpful influence. Not only did
the labour force grow in absolute numbers as the population increased but the number of people actually in employment increased
more rapidly than the total population. Changes in birth- and death-
rates were altering the age structure of the population. In 1911 the
persons aged 15 to 64 inclusive were 63·9 per cent of the people of
Great Britain; in 1939 the proportion had reached 69·7 per cent.[2]
This meant that the ratio of producers to dependants could be
appreciably increased and, if the maximum increase was not sought,
the quality of part of the labour force could be improved by the
provision of education and training for longer periods. Both these
things happened. After the First World War the people who would
not ordinarily have sought paid employment, but who had been
called on to meet wartime needs, gradually withdrew from the
labour force (i.e. all the persons available for paid work, whether
actually in employment or not) and this had contracted to normal size
by 1921. According to the census of that year, the labour force in
Great Britain was then 19·36 million and it is estimated that an
average of 17·62 million were at work during the year. Estimates for
1938 put the labour force at 21·86 million and the average number in
work at 20·07 million.[3] Put another way, these figures indicate that
between 1921 and 1938 the labour force increased from 45·3 per
cent to 47·3 per cent of the population, and the number of persons
in work from 41·2 per cent to 43·4 per cent.[4] Thus, despite the heavy

---

[1] See pp. 22-3 above.   [2] R.C. on Population, *Report*, p. 88.
[3] Clark, *The Conditions of Economic Progress* (3rd edn.), pp. 137-8.
[4] 1921 is used as the basis of comparison because there is fuller information
about it than about neighbouring years. But it was a very bad year and if 1920 were
used the comparison would be less favourable to 1938. But the trend over the whole
period would not be greatly altered, and in any case 1921 and 1938 occupy similar
positions in relation to the business cycle.

unemployment, jobs were found for a growing proportion of the people, and the bigger labour force consisted to a rather greater extent than before of adult men.[1]

The paradox that heavier unemployment should be accompanied by more rapidly rising national income can in these ways be resolved. But the national income is a generalized abstraction; the unemployed were individual people; and the questions remain, what form did the benefits of a bigger national income take and to whom did they accrue? The spending of a higher national income might result in more guns and less butter, more for the government and no more for private institutions and persons, more for investment and no increase in current consumption, or more for a few and no more for the many. In fact, none of these things occurred to any significant extent. From 1935 the government's expenditure on goods and services rose much more sharply than any other part of the national expenditure,[2] and this was directly associated with the increased contribution which armaments made to the national product. But this was not typical of the interwar years as a whole. Most of the increased income went to provide consumers with a bigger supply of goods and services. Their share in the total national expenditure increased, and until 1935 the flow of goods and services to consumers in the private sector of the economy grew faster than the national income.[3] There were also some significant changes in the expenditure on different types of goods. The proportion that went on food fell from 33·9 per cent in 1920-29 to 30·3 per cent in 1930-39, while the proportion devoted to tobacco, which was always under 2 per cent before the First World War, was 2·9 per cent in 1920-29 and 3·8 per cent in 1930-39. Durable consumer goods absorbed a persistently rising share of the expenditure. The 5·1 per cent devoted to them in 1910-14 was raised to 7·0 per cent in 1920-24 and reached 8·2 per cent in 1935-39.[4]

Such changes in the pattern of consumption suggest the likelihood

[1] Besides the reduction in the proportion of juveniles employed, owing to the increased average time at school, it is probable that the proportion of women seeking paid employment declined a little in the 'thirties. This cannot be stated certainly because the Ministry of Labour statistics had (until 1948) omissions of a kind which caused them slightly but persistently to understate the proportion of women in the labour force.

[2] Jefferys and Walters, *op. cit.*, p. 9.

[3] *Ibid.*, p. 15. Some of the increase in the value of the flow of goods was due to increased indirect taxation, which is excluded from the calculation of national income. But this does not greatly alter the position.

[4] *Ibid.*, pp. 20-1.

of a widespread increase in the material standard of living and there is other information to support the view that the benefits of a higher national income were widely, if unevenly, diffused. Though the national income continued to be very unequally distributed, the earlier tendency for less to be concentrated in the hands of the very rich was maintained. An estimate for 1935 suggested that, before the payment of taxes, the richest 12 per cent received 42 per cent of the national income,[1] and this may be compared with the 50 per cent that the same proportion of people were believed to have had in 1908.[2] Study of the distribution of property confirms the probability of a change in this direction. In the absence of severe measures of confiscation, a lessening in the inequality of the distribution of property would not be expected unless there were a greater reduction in the inequality of incomes. There is no doubt that, though the ownership of any substantial amount of property was still confined to a small minority, the distribution was widening. Estates of £5,000 or more formed two-thirds of all private property in both 1911-13 and 1936, but, while only 0·8 or 0·9 per cent of the persons aged 25 or over owned this amount of property at the former time, the proportion had risen to 1·7 or 1·8 per cent in 1936. Even in 1936 only a quarter of the persons aged 25 and over possessed property worth as much as £100, but the proportion had doubled since 1911-13,[3] while prices had risen by only about one-half.

What sections of the mass of the working population shared directly in the diminution of inequality, and to what extent, is hard to state with both precision and certainty, since average figures of wages are the resultant of so many constituents which are often changing in opposite ways. The reward of labour was an appreciably higher proportion of the national income just after the First World War than it was just before, but the proportion rose little further, if at all, before 1939. One estimate, for the United Kingdom's non-agricultural income, puts the share of labour at 59·5 per cent in 1911, 70·3 per cent in 1924 and 72·2 per cent in 1938.[4] The beginning of

[1] A. M. Carr-Saunders and D. C. Jones, *A Survey of the Social Structure of England and Wales* (2nd edn., 1937), p. 98.

[2] See p. 248 above. Changes in taxation made the contrast sharper.

[3] H. Campion, *Public and Private Property in Great Britain* (1939), p. 109.

[4] Clark, *op. cit.*, p. 619. These proportions include an estimate for the elements of labour-reward in the incomes of self-employed persons. Other estimates of the wage and salary bill of the U.K. are given in Chapman and Knight, *Wages and Salaries in the United Kingdom 1920-1938*, p. 22. These include agriculture but exclude the self-employed and bear much the same relation to national income in 1920 as in 1938.

this change seems to have been closely connected with the dis-proportionate increases obtained by manual workers, especially the unskilled, in the three years after 1917.[1] After 1920 conditions altered. Studies of the average movement of real wages suggest that, though they rose absolutely, their rise was slower than that of the real national income. By 1935 they were one-third higher than in 1914,[2] and so were the average incomes of the population as a whole. This meant that the advance of wages relatively to other incomes between 1914 and 1920 had been practically cancelled out by changes since then, and mainly since 1923. The chief reasons why the reward of labour nevertheless maintained its increased proportionate share of the national income were that a rising proportion of the population was included in the labour force and that more workers were moving out of wage-earning into salaried occupations, where rates of pay were generally higher.[3]

Most money wages tended downwards from 1920 to 1934 or 1935 and increases in average real wages came immediately from reductions in the cost of living. Those workers who could maintain fairly regular employment and were subjected only to moderate pressure on money rates of wages found themselves in rather favourable conditions. The others fared less well. Thus between 1924 and 1933, when retail prices fell by about 20 per cent, the average money earnings per man-year in manufacturing industries fell by only about 4 per cent, but, in some of the industries most hit by competition and loss of markets, heavier wage cuts took away much of the gain from a lower cost of living. Money earnings per man-year fell by about 20 per cent in textile finishing and by over 10 per cent in the cotton, woollen and worsted, and coal-mining industries, whereas they rose sub-stantially in the tobacco industry and by smaller amounts in such industries as mechanical engineering, the manufacture of vehicles and paper-making.[4] And since, in some of the harder-hit industries, few workers had anywhere near a full year's employment, the differ-ences widened. The average rate of unemployment among male workers from 1927 to 1936 was 23·4 per cent in textile finishing, 22·1 per cent in the cotton industry, 16·9 per cent in the woollen

---

[1] See p. 296 above.   [2] Bowley, *Wages and Income since 1860*, p. 30.

[3] Salaried workers (including hairdressers and shop assistants) were 22 per cent of all employees in 1924 and 25·5 per cent in 1938. (Chapman and Knight, *op. cit.*, p. 19.)

[4] *Ibid.*, pp. 68 and 105-6.

and worsted industry and 24·6 per cent in coal-mining, but only 12·0 per cent in the manufacture of vehicles, 7·8 per cent in paper-making and 5·8 per cent in the tobacco industry. But not all the industries in which real wages improved most had the further advantage of relatively low unemployment rates. Unemployment among men was rather higher in general engineering than in the woollen and worsted industry; and in shipbuilding, where the money earnings of those in full employment also tended slightly upwards, unemployment among men averaged 40·8 per cent from 1927 to 1936.[1]

These contrasts were evidently giving rise to new elements of economic inequality which had little relation to skill, training or social class. Some other changes either brought advantages which were more evenly shared among the majority of workers or else gave a little extra advance to those who had been poorest. The most significant change of the former kind (though it may have seemed a mockery to those who went for years without a job) was an increase of leisure. During the boom of 1919-20 workers succeeded in obtaining not only large increases in weekly wage-rates but also a shortening of the working week by about five hours, i.e. roughly 10 per cent, and this gain proved permanent. In practically all occupations normal working hours were fixed at from 44 to 48 per week (most commonly 48), spread over five and a half days.[2] Except for an increase in the length of coal-miners' shifts, there was little further change until after the Second World War. But in the late 'thirties another important contribution was made to the increase of leisure with no off-setting loss of pay. This was the rapid extension of paid annual holidays, which had previously been a privilege mainly confined to the salaried, and not universal among them. The Ministry of Labour estimated that in March 1925 a million and a half manual workers received paid holidays under the provision of collective agreements and that in April 1937 the number was not more than another quarter of a million higher, though the addition of those entitled under other arrangements to a paid holiday brought the later total to 4 million.[3] The subject then came under official enquiry, and even while this was in progress agreements for holidays with pay were multiplying. By April 1938, out of the 18½ million workers earning under £250 a year, 7¾ million were entitled to a paid annual holiday. In that year

[1] Beveridge, *op. cit.*, pp. 316-19.   [2] Bowley, *op. cit.*, pp. 18 and 26.
[3] J. A. R. Pimlott, *The Englishman's Holiday* (1947), pp. 214-15.

legislation was passed which enabled the responsible authorities to grant paid holidays in agriculture and the trade-board industries and which strengthened the hand of the Ministry of Labour in encouraging the inclusion of provisions for paid holidays in collective agreements. The number of manual workers entitled to holidays with pay reached 9 million by November 1938 and 11 million by June 1939. Most of them were granted one working week plus recognized public holidays, but in the public utility and government services many received a fortnight's holiday.[1]

Changes which specially helped the poorer included a narrowing of the differences between the wage-rates paid for labour of different grades of skill. The large relative gain made by the unskilled during and just after the First World War was partly lost through flat rate reductions in the next few years.[2] But it was not wholly wiped out and the higher relative position of unskilled wages remained fairly steady from the mid-twenties. So, to take one example, in 1936 when the money rates of bricklayers in London were 53 per cent higher than in 1914, those of builders' labourers were 65 per cent higher.[3] Another feature, which was probably symptomatic of similar changes, was a lessening of the difference between the average level of salaries and that of wages. While this was doubtless due in part to a relative increase in the numbers of the least skilled salaried workers, such as shop assistants, hairdressers and junior clerks, the trend is much the same if shop assistants and hairdressers are classed as wage-earners instead of salaried employees.[4] It therefore seems likely that salaried occupations suffered some reduction of their differential advantage. A different type of influence on the inequality of incomes was that attributable to public social expenditure and the incidence of the taxation which paid for it. There can be no doubt that this decreased the spending power of the rich much more than it had done before and augmented that of the wage-earning population and of those unable, for any reason, to work.[5]

Such changes as these did something to reduce the number of people living in extreme poverty, but were still quite insufficient to bring the abolition of poverty within sight. Between 1928 and 1939 independent surveys of incomes and living conditions were made in

---

[1] Pimlott, *op. cit.*, pp. 217-21.

[2] Bowley, *Some Economic Consequences of the Great War*, p. 151.

[3] Bowley, *Wages and Income since 1860*, p. 15.

[4] Chapman and Knight, *op. cit.*, pp. 13-14 and 23.   [5] *Cf.*, p. 408 above.

several large towns,[1] and they suggested similar conclusions: that things were a good deal better than they had been a generation back and that a very slight further redistribution of income would suffice to bring everyone well above subsistence level, but that, as it was, a substantial minority of families could still not afford the minimum means of healthy existence.[2] Particularly illuminating were the surveys of London and York, which permitted direct comparisons with the results of similar surveys carried out at the end of the nineteenth century. In 1929 it was found that, if use was made of the same 'poverty line' as Charles Booth had applied, the proportion of London's population living in poverty was less than one-third of what it had been at the time of his survey, but, of course, the sight of new amenities gained by those a little better off brought higher notions of what was a tolerable minimum.[3] How much difference such changes in conventional standards could make was illustrated when Rowntree repeated in 1936 the survey of York he had made in 1899. By adopting in the second survey a definition of poverty based on what he called 'minimum human needs' (which were much more than minimum needs for physical subsistence) he found a higher rate of poverty than before, while showing that if he had retained the same standard the proportion of the population living in poverty would have been only about two-fifths what it was in 1899.

Differences of this kind indicate how impossible it is to give any absolute measurement of poverty, but they also suggest how narrow for many families was the margin between tolerable comfort and a struggle for existence. Because of this a slight change in economic activity could temporarily make a lot of difference to the degree of comfort and, in particular, fluctuations in employment could reinforce or almost cancel out the influence of the other factors tending to diminish economic inequality. In Southampton in 1931, 21 per cent of working-class households were found to be below a defined 'poverty line' which attempted to indicate subsistence needs, though some of

---

[1] Among the most useful are London School of Economics, *The New Survey of London Life and Labour* (1930-35); D. C. Jones (ed.), *The Social Survey of Merseyside* (1934) which devotes most of vol. I to questions of income and poverty; P. Ford, *Work and Wealth in a Modern Port: an Economic Survey of Southampton* (1934); H. Tout, *The Standard of Living in Bristol* (1938); and B. S. Rowntree, *Poverty and Progress* (1941).

[2] For brief comment on the general conclusions from these surveys see *Beveridge Report on Social Insurance*, pp. 7 and 165-6.

[3] London School of Economics, *op. cit.*, IX, 39. For fuller details see also *ibid.*, III, 5, 78-96 and 123-52.

these may have been slightly over-estimated. At the unemployment rate of 1928 the proportion would have been reduced to 13 per cent.[1] Unemployment was not the only source of poverty—large families, low wages in a few occupations and old age all had a significant influence on it—but it affected it more than anything else did; for instance, there was unemployment in two-thirds of the families below the 'poverty line' in Southampton. The other factors that had made for severe poverty at the bottom of society had all been much diminished. There were so many things making for general economic improvement among the wage-earners that, had unemployment not become much greater than before, security for nearly all from absolute want must have been brought near enough to look attainable. Even among the unemployed there had been enough improvement to ensure that the margin by which those in poverty fell short of the minimum standards applied by social investigators was usually fairly narrow. Old age rather than unemployment was the main source of the deepest poverty of all and many, perhaps most, unemployed families in the 'thirties had rather more purchasing power than those of unskilled labourers in Edwardian times.[2] But, even with this modifying influence, unemployment added to the numbers in poverty so many who otherwise would have escaped from it that it hid the new possibility that the poor need not always be with us.

So the answer to the question about the distribution of the benefits of a rapidly rising national income proves to be complex. Except for a tiny minority of the very rich, for whom life nevertheless remained more than comfortable, all sections of the community gained some material benefit, though many individuals met misfortunes which brought them nothing but loss. Apart from this, security of employment appears to have been the most decisive influence. For many middle-class people, in professional, executive or senior clerical positions, and for most grades of worker in the expanding industries which served a sheltered home market, economic improvement must have been large. So it must have been also for those who were able, by luck or parental effort or the widening of educational opportunity, to move from different origins into positions of that kind. For most of the rest even the material improvement must have been much

---

[1] Ford, *op. cit.*, pp. 114-18.

[2] This might not be true for most of the unmarried. It was the allowances for dependants, which were incorporated in unemployment insurance and unemployment assistance benefits but were almost unknown in the wage system, that tipped the balance.

slighter and its reality obscured by some of the social conditions in which it took place.

The odd mixture of expansion and decay prompts other questions. Were economic conditions fundamentally so adverse that the elements of prosperity could be only temporary gains at the expense of proper provision for the future? Or were the advances so much the result of new efforts and new adjustments to a changing world and developing knowledge that they gave promise of soon overcoming the elements of adversity?

The fact that consumption was growing faster than the national product might suggest an affirmative answer to the first question, but it need not necessarily do so. The offset to an increase in the proportion of the national income devoted to consumption was a decrease in the proportion invested abroad, and there were many reasons for thinking that heavy foreign investment could no longer *directly* help the British economy (through high dividend yields and the development of the cheapest sources of essential imports) so much as it had done in the past. Two sources of weakness did emerge, however. First, the change went too far. Not all the direct and immediate advantages of foreign investment had disappeared, but in the 'thirties Britain's net lending abroad may have become negative. Second, for the restoration of healthy conditions of international trade, which affected most people's prosperity, there was a need for just as much investment as before in undeveloped parts of the world, though its full direct yield might be slower to appear. It could have come only if a wider variety of countries had been willing to invest abroad, with Britain as one important investor but no longer dominant over all the rest. In fact, as British lending shrank no other source adequately replaced it.

British investment at home changed much less in relation to national income. It is fairly certain that an increasing part of gross investment had to be devoted to making good depreciation instead of adding to the accumulated wealth.[1] Nevertheless, net capital formation at home has been estimated at 6·6 per cent of national income in 1924-28, 4·6 per cent in 1929-33 and 7·7 per cent in 1934-38.[2]

[1] In 1938, 53·5 per cent of gross investment was absorbed by depreciation. (Calculated from P. Redfern, 'Net Investment in Fixed Assets in the United Kingdom, 1938-1953' in *J.R. Stat. Socy.*, series A, CXVIII (1955), 153.)

[2] Jefferys and Walters, *op. cit.*, p. 19. These figures, unlike those of Mr Redfern, make allowance for changes in stocks, and for that reason are less reliable. *Cf.* the figures for 1870-1913 given in table X above.

Experience elsewhere, and in Britain a little earlier, suggests that these proportions were generally a little lower than might be desired but, except in the depression of 1929-33, might be adequate for a fairly high rate of economic expansion; and the tendency towards the end of the period was very much in the right direction. Gross investment in fixed capital was higher in 1936-38 than at any time since the First World War.[1] What causes more doubt is the type of investment that was undertaken. In 1938, 30 per cent of gross fixed capital formation went on housing and the proportion was generally rather higher in the preceding ten years. And, since much the greater part of the expenditure was devoted to building new houses, the share of housing in net fixed capital formation in 1938 was as much as 46 per cent. Improved housing was a most desirable service and the first twenty years of the century had left many arrears to be overtaken, but it was a form of investment that could contribute only gradually to an increase of productive power. If it was to absorb so much of the total investment, then there was a need for the total itself to be higher. Other activities were kept short. In particular, fixed investment in transport and communications declined and in 1938 the net amount was only £21 million, as compared with £127 million in housing. Translated into descriptive terms, this meant the virtual cessation of new highway construction, slow progress in railway electrification and the survival of obsolete railway depots and rolling-stock, especially for freight service. Gross capital formation in manufacture and distribution showed a notable expansion after 1934, but even so the net investment in 1938 was no more than £85 million.[2] This fits in with the picture of a welcome introduction of new industries in the 'thirties, not carried far enough to have a decisive influence on unemployment and foreign trade.

To concentrate attention on the domestic aspects of the economy is to receive an impression of a nation first clinging for too long to bygone ways and then, in the 'thirties, introducing new methods and new activities, more in keeping with current technical possibilities and economic demands, without going as far and as fast in the new direction as it might have done. Because this was a turning away from frustration and towards opportunity, it seemed, despite its limitations, to offer a hopeful prospect of relief from a time of

[1] Redfern, *loc. cit.*, p. 153.

[2] All these figures are from the tables in *ibid.*, pp. 153-4, which give estimates of gross investment from 1924 and of both gross and net investment from 1938.

bewildering difficulty. But the hope needed to be much damped down. Despite all the new beginnings, unemployment after the depression was heavier than before it, exports were lower, and it was not practicable to attempt a cure by gradually carrying further the kind of domestic changes already begun. Britain's economic difficulties could not be overcome without a change in international conditions, since its international financial position, though stable enough for the time being, had shifted on to rather precarious foundations. Keeping money cheap, which was the main contribution of public policy to domestic economic expansion, was safe and practicable only so long as there was no danger of a serious loss of international financial reserves. The reserves were secure after 1932 for the threefold reason that unemployment at home kept down the demand for imports, that world trade was so disorganized as to make many imports exceptionally cheap, and that in a disorganized world it was as safe and rewarding for foreigners to keep funds in London as anywhere, despite the small profit to be obtained. If domestic economic expansion had gone a great deal further, with a large reduction in unemployment, the demand for imports would have risen, the balance of payments would have become seriously adverse and the value of sterling more difficult to maintain, London would have looked a less safe financial centre, and general economic crisis would have loomed. No doubt a partial corrective would have come from the export of some of the extra production, but, however attractive the goods, it could have been only very partial as long as the conditions of world trade and finance remained as confused as they were in the 'thirties. But hardly anything was being done to lessen this confusion.

It is this neglect that makes it difficult to maintain that in the 'thirties either Britain or the world in general had learned from past mistakes and was moving towards a solution of its economic problems, even though it had not yet reached it. The restoration of order and security in international economic affairs was recognized as a prime necessity after the First World War and great efforts were made to achieve it. Unfortunately, the methods chosen were backward-looking and did not prove workable for long. But the reaction in the 'thirties was to abandon the objective rather than to improve the means of achieving it. Unless there were some organized institutional arrangements that would keep the general level of exchange rates predictable for long periods without imposing wholesale restrictions on the international transfer of currency, there was no hope of achieving the large flow of investment and the new patterns of trade, which were essential for the creation of markets adequate to the world's productive capacity. Without such markets there was no chance for a country such as Britain (and, for that matter, most others) to come anywhere near to full employment. To rejoice in freedom from the 'tyranny' of the gold standard, as was common in the 'thirties, was therefore short-sighted. The new monetary techniques and credit policies which Britain developed at that time helped to create a more favourable environment for enterprise at home and were a valuable supplement to an international standard. But they were not a substitute for it, and the absence of such a standard killed more opportunities of new enterprise and employment than did the presence of even so ramshackle a one as that set up in the 'twenties.

Britain's capacity to make the most of the immense opportunities which were present throughout the interwar period depended, economically, on two sets of changes above all else: the redeployment of many of its productive resources in new activities and the achievement of a steady expansion of world trade. The first was not wholly practicable without the prior fulfilment of the second, and the second was only to a very limited extent within the control of the British people and their government. In fact, the second requirement was not fulfilled and, though some progress was made towards meeting the first, it was impossible at the end of the period to grasp any greater proportion of the opportunities than at the beginning. Yet, as Lord Beveridge put it, 'across this waste period of destruction and dislocation, the permanent forces making for material progress— technical advance and the capacity of human society to adjust itself to new conditions—continued to operate'.[1] The opportunities were so many that a lively and intelligent people, with an abundant inheritance of capital, institutions, experience and training, could not fail to obtain substantial gains even when so many potentialities were left unrealized.

But to say no more than this would be to leave a false impression. Unsolved economic problems could do far greater damage than just retard the growth of income and wealth a little. They could destroy the unity and resilience of society, thereby weakening its continued ability to overcome the challenges it must encounter, whether they

[1] *Beveridge Report*, p. 166.

were economic or political or military or moral. The economic failures showed themselves most prominently in the form of unemployment, which, economically, might be no more than a minor source of loss, but, socially, was a never-lifting blight that overshadowed the economic improvements more darkly than all the other negligences and ignorances of the time. It was especially damaging because it was so heavily concentrated in industries that were highly localized. The unemployment rate year after year remained more than twice as high in north-west as in south-east England, and for Wales as a whole, which was most severely affected of all, for five consecutive years from 1931 to 1935 the rate never fell below 30 per cent. In the different towns and districts within these large areas there were still wider individual variations.[1] In a town where a third or a half or even more of the workers were unemployed there was for many of them no other prospect than a wait of months or years before they could find another job. In June 1937 (very near the peak of the business cycle) almost a quarter of the unemployed had been without a job for at least a year. There were in Britain 300,000 of these unfortunates, and more than five in every six of them came from Wales, Scotland or the north of England.[2] It was a disastrous social situation, more pervasive than mere figures might suggest, since far more than these 300,000 either experienced lengthy spells of unemployment at some time, or had reason to live in fear of them.

Men who went without work month after month were bound to suffer a corrosion of skill and were placed in conditions likely to produce either revolt or apathy. Insurance and relief payments were probably enough to turn the sharp edge of a rebellious spirit, but to have bred apathy where before there had been energy was an inglorious achievement for an expanding economy. And, in addition, the terms on which assistance was given to those who had been unemployed so long as to have exhausted their claims to benefit under the insurance scheme often produced a sense of humiliation. The amount paid was dependent on a household means test, which could make an unemployed father a burden on any of his children who had a job and lived with him. To the divisions between man and man were added those between district and district. The local concentration of unemployment made industrial Britain almost into two cruelly contrasted countries. Even to casual outward observation the contrast

---

[1] Beveridge, *Full Employment in a Free Society*, pp. 61 and 324-7.
[2] *Ibid.*, pp. 65-9.

became all the more blatant because so many of the towns where unemployment was rife had long ago, even in the days of their prosperity, been given ashes for beauty and now lacked any relief to the physical signs of their decay. As time went on the contrast became greater still because those who brought new enterprise in the 'thirties took it where the money was, so that the signs of revival were concentrated too, as distant as possible from the centres of decline.[1]

Of course, economic change had also wrought much that was more favourable in the outlook and condition of society. For millions of people there were new homes, more comfortable living arrangements, longer and healthier life and more varied experience. There was less waste of talent through inadequate educational opportunity, rather more people could find a new and better position in society, and more of the young had been equipped to exercise responsibility with common sense and enjoyment. A host of people had reason to think that they had gained something worth preserving and would have the chance to gain more, and their spirit and ability had been sufficiently nourished to make them tenacious of their inheritance.

Yet more was needed. Britain's position in the world was becoming more precarious in the later 'thirties. Even in the narrowest economic terms, however secure it seemed for the moment, there was need of a great upheaval and effort to bring it on to safer foundations. But it was becoming evident that the economic and every other aspect of the immediate future would be determined by war. Nothing could be afforded that seriously lessened either the purpose or the skill of the whole nation in first resisting military onslaught and then retaining sufficient determination and energy to set about material and economic and social rebuilding above the wreckage there must be. The elements of disunity, unfairness, apathy and waste, which inseparably accompanied the economic advances of the 'twenties and, still more, the 'thirties carried the threat of such a loss. Fortunately, they were not yet so deep and protracted as to be irreparable. There was, with the help of public policy, some deliberate diminution of social inequality, which may have taken a little of the sting out of some feelings of injustice. Of those who had been through the worst

[1] From 1932 to 1935 the excess of factories opened over factories closed in Gt. Britain as a whole was 311, but for Greater London alone it was 378. For N.E. and N.W. England and Scotland the number *closed* exceeded the number opened by 182. (See table I in the Board of Trade's *Survey of Industrial Development* for each year.) The Special Areas policy subsequently did a very little to redress the balance but revival continued, to be centred in England other than the N.E. and N.W. (*Cf.* British Association, *Britain in Recovery* (1938), pp. 108-10.)

of unemployment many could feel that the most evil days were behind them. And at the very end there was a gradual realization that knowledge had been acquired which showed how unemployment could be controlled and kept low. Though many were still unconvinced of this, there was at last a hope that policies which, with the best of intentions, had only made things worse would come to an end; and there was a challenge to the creeping apathy induced by the suspicion that unemployment was an inevitable ill which could be relieved but not cured.

It was none too soon. Despite all the hopeful new enterprise and expanding industry, the nineteen-thirties brought burdens and cleavages which no society could indefinitely bear with safety. But a margin of time was given. British society inherited enough of knowledge and productive wealth and tested tradition to put a brake on any disintegration. Contemporary effort, though confused in both aim and achievement, was enough to suggest that the future need not be wholly bleak for anyone. And the threat from the world outside of domination by something incomparably worse than was ever known at home was a force to make men forget their differences and hardships. In 1939 it was not too late for the British people to turn again to their reserves of unity, purpose and skill and find them a little concealed and a little damaged, but not too hard to repair; and, having found them, to direct them more steadfastly than before towards survival in war and, in peace, prosperity for all.

Index